Black Sea

İkiztepe

İnandık　Ferzant/Büget　Yeşilırmak

Kazankaya
Alaca Hüyük　Maşat

el
lan　Boğazköy-Hattuša

Alişar Hüyük

Halys　Kültepe
Kayseri

Acemhüyük

Firaktin

Korucutepe
Tepecik
Arslantepe　Norşuntepe
Malatya

Tigris

Euphrates

Porsuk

Seyhan

Ceyhan

Tarsus
Mersin

0KM

THE BRONZE AGE

University Museum Monograph 73

GORDION EXCAVATIONS FINAL REPORTS III

E.L. Kohler, Editor

THE BRONZE AGE

Ann C. Gunter

Published by

THE UNIVERSITY MUSEUM
of Archaeology and Anthropology
University of Pennsylvania
Philadelphia
1991

Design, editing, production
Publications Department
The University Museum

Printing
Science Press
Ephrata, Pennsylvania

*Publication of this volume was made possible in part by a generous grant from the
National Endowment for the Humanities and The Gordion Publications Fund in
Memory of Rodney S. Young.*

Library of Congress Cataloging-in-Publication Data
(Revised for vol. 3)

The Gordion excavations.

(University Museum monograph / University Museum,
University of Pennsylvania ; 43, 73)
Includes Index.
Bibliography: v. 1, p. xxxvi-xxxvii.
Contents: v. 1. Three great early tumuli / Rodney S.
Young -- v. 3. The Bronze Age / Ann Gunter.
1. Gordion (Turkey) 2. Excavations (Archaeology) --
Turkey--Gordion. I. Series. II. University museum
monograph ; 43, etc.
DS156.G6G67   1981   939'.26   81-13373
ISBN 0-934718-39-3 (set)
ISBN 0-934718-95-4 (v. 3)

Printed on acid free paper.

Ann C. Gunter is curator of ancient Near Eastern art at the Freer Gallery of Art and the Arthur M. Sackler Gallery, Smithsonian Institution, and holds a faculty appointment in the Department of Near Eastern Studies, The Johns Hopkins University. She received an A.B. degree from Bryn Mawr College in 1973 and a Ph.D. from Columbia University in 1980. Prior to her arrival at the Smithsonian Institution in 1987, she held teaching appointments at the University of California at Berkeley, the University of Minnesota, and Emory University.

Since 1974 she has participated in excavations and studied archaeological collections in Turkey at the sites of Gordion, Sardis, Boğazköy, Labraunda, Erbaba, and Gritille Hüyük. From 1976 to 1979 she held a Fulbright-Hays Grant for dissertation research in Turkey, and from 1978 to 1979 served as Director of the American Research Institute in Turkey office in Ankara. She is currently completing a study of the marble sculpture from the site of Labraunda, in southwestern Turkey, for publication by the Swedish Research Institute in Istanbul.

Contents

Plans

Figures

Plates

Minor Abbreviations

D.	Diameter	inv.	inventoried
Est.	Estimated	L.	Length
GPH.	Greatest Preserved Height	Max.	Maximum
GPL.	Greatest Preserved Length	PL.	Preserved Length
GPW.	Greatest Preserved Width	Th.	Thickness
GTh.	Greatest Thickness	TB	Terrace Building
H.	Height	W.	Width

Bibliographical Abbreviations

AJA	*American Journal of Archaeology.*
Alaca 1936	Koşay, H.Z., *Ausgrabungen von Alaca Höyük, Vorbericht...1936.* TTKY V 2a. Ankara: TTK, 1944.
Alaca 1937-1939	Koşay, H.Z., *Les fouilles d'Alaca Höyük. Rapport préliminaire 1937-1939.* TTKY V 5. Ankara: TTK, 1951.
AnatSt	*Anatolian Studies.*
AthMitt	*Mitteilungen des Deutschen Archäologischen Instituts, Athenische Abteilung.*
Belleten	*Belleten Türk Tarih Kurumu.*
Beycesultan I	Mellaart, J. and S. Lloyd, *Beycesultan* I, *The Chalcolithic and Early Bronze Age Levels.* Occasional Publications 6. London: British Institute of Archaeology at Ankara, 1962.
Beycesultan II	Mellaart, J. and S. Lloyd, *Beycesultan* II, *Middle Bronze Age Architecture and Pottery.* Occasional Publications 8. London: British Institute of Archaeology at Ankara, 1965.
BibO	*Bibliotheca Orientalis.*
Boğazköy IV	Bittel, K. *et al., Boğazköy* IV, *Funde aus den Grabungen 1967 und 1968.* Berlin: Gebr. Mann, 1969.
Boğazköy VI	Bittel, K. *et al., Boğazköy* VI, *Funde aus den Grabungen bis 1979.* Berlin: Gebr. Mann, 1984.
BSA	*Annual of the British School at Athens.*
CAH	*The Cambridge Ancient History,* rev. ed. Cambridge: University Press.
Etiyokuşu	Kansu, S.A., *Les fouilles d'Etiyokuşu.* TTKY V 3. Ankara: TTK, 1940.
Expedition	*Expedition: The University Museum Magazine of Archaeology and Anthropology.*
Festschrift Bittel	R.M. Boehmer and H. Hauptmann, eds., *Beiträge zur Altertumskunde Kleinasiens, Festschrift für Kurt Bittel.* Mainz: P. von Zabern, 1983.
Frühe Keramik	Orthmann, W., *Frühe Keramik von Boğazköy.* WVDOG 74. Berlin: Gebr. Mann, 1963.
Gefässmarken	Seidl, U., *Gefässmarken von Boğazköy.* WVDOG 88. Berlin: Gebr. Mann, 1972.

Geography	Garstang, J. and O.R. Gurney, *Geography of the Hittite Empire*. London: British Institute of Archaeology at Ankara, 1959.
Gordion	Körte, G. and A., *Gordion, Ergebnisse der Ausgrabung im Jahre 1900*. Jahrbuch des Kaiserlich Deutschen Archäologischen Instituts, Ergänzungsheft V. Berlin: Reimer, 1904.
Gordion Special Studies I	Roller, L.E., *Gordion Special Studies* I. *The Nonverbal Graffiti, Dipinti, and Stamps*. University Museum Monograph 63. Philadelphia: The University Museum, 1987.
Heth. Keramik	Fischer, F., *Die hethitischen Keramik von Boğazköy*. WVDOG 75. Berlin: Gebr. Mann, 1963.
Hitt. Cem.	Mellink, M.J., *A Hittite Cemetery at Gordion*. Philadelphia: The University Museum, 1956.
Ilıca	Orthmann, W., *Das Graberfeld bei Ilıca*. Wiesbaden: F. Steiner, 1967.
ILN	*Illustrated London News*.
IstMitt	*Istanbuler Mitteilungen*.
Jahresbericht Frankfurt	*Jahresbericht des Instituts für Vorgeschichte der Universität Frankfurt a.M.*
JIES	*Journal of Indo-European Studies*.
JNES	*Journal of Near Eastern Studies*.
Karahöyük-Konya Damga	Alp, S., *Konya cıvarında Karahöyük Kazılarında bulunan silindir ve damga mühürleri*. TTKY V 31. Ankara: TTK, 1972.
Keramik aus Inneranatolien	Orthmann, W., *Die Keramik der Frühen Bronzezeit aus Inneranatolien*. Istanbuler Forschungen 24. Berlin: Gebr. Mann, 1963.
Kleinfunde	Boehmer, R.M., *Die Kleinfunde von Boğazköy*. WVDOG 87. Berlin: Gebr. Mann, 1972.
Kleinfunde Unterstadt	Boehmer, R.M., *Die Kleinfunde aus der Unterstadt von Boğazköy*. Berlin: Gebr. Mann, 1979.
Korucutepe 3	Van Loon, M.N., ed., *Korucutepe*. Final Report on the Excavations of the Universities of Chicago, California (Los Angeles) and Amsterdam in the Keban Reservoir, Eastern Anatolia 1968-1970. Vol. 3. Amsterdam: North Holland, 1980.
Kültepe-Kaniş II	Özgüç, T., *Kültepe-Kaniş* II, *New Researches at the Trading Center of the Ancient Near East*. TTKY V 41. Ankara: TTK, 1986.
Maşat I	Özgüç, T., *Excavations at Maşat Höyük and Investigations in Its Vicinity*. TTKY V 38. Ankara: TTK, 1978.
Maşat II	Özgüç, T., *Maşat Höyük* II, *A Hittite Center Northeast of Boğazköy*. TTKY V 38a. Ankara: TTK, 1982.
MIO	*Mitteilungen des Instituts für Orientforschung*.
Nordwesthang-Büyükkale	Schirmer, W., *Die Bebauung am unteren Büyükkale-Nordwesthang in Boğazköy*. WVDOG 81. Berlin: Gebr. Mann, 1969.

OIP 28   Von der Osten, H.H., *The Alishar Hüyük, Seasons of 1930-32*, Part I. Oriental Institute Publications 28. Chicago: University of Chicago Press, 1937.

OIP 29   Von der Osten, H.H., *The Alishar Hüyük, Seasons of 1930-32*, Part II. Oriental Institute Publications 29. Chicago: University of Chicago Press, 1937.

Osmankayası   Bittel, K. *et al.*, *Die hethitischen Grabfunde von Osmankayası*. WVDOG 71. Berlin: Gebr. Mann, 1958.

Porsuk I   Dupré, S., *Porsuk* I, *La céramique de l'âge du bronze et de l'âge du fer*. Paris: Editions Recherches sur les civilisations, 1983.

SIMA   *Studies in Mediterranean Archaeology.*

TAD   *Türk Arkeoloji Dergisi.*

Tarsus II   Goldman, H., *Excavations at Gözlü Küle, Tarsus* II, *From the Neolithic through the Bronze Age*. Princeton: Princeton University Press, 1956.

Troy I   Blegen, C.W. *et al.*, *Troy* I, *General Introduction. The First and Second Settlements*. Princeton: Princeton University Press, 1950.

Troy II   Blegen, C.W. *et al.*, *Troy* II, *The Third, Fourth and Fifth Settlements*. Princeton: Princeton University Press, 1951.

TTAED   *Türk Tarih Arkeologya ve Etnoğrafya Dergisi.*

TTKY   Türk Tarih Kurumu Yayınları (Turkish Historical Society Publications), Ankara.

UMB   *University Museum Bulletin.*

WVDOG   *Wissenschaftliche Veröffentlichungen der Deutschen Orient-Gesellschaft.*

Yanarlar   Emre, K., *Yanarlar, A Hittite Cemetery near Afyon*. TTKY VI 22. Ankara: TTK, 1978.

Young Symposium   DeVries, K., ed., *From Athens to Gordion, The Papers of a Memorial Symposium for Rodney S. Young*. Philadelphia: The University Museum, 1980.

Editor's Foreword

With Volume III The University Museum is publishing the first of several pottery publications which will appear among the Final Reports upon its excavations of 1950 to 1973 at Gordion, Turkey.

The volume in hand discusses the characteristics and development of the various Bronze Age pottery fabrics, shapes, and modes of decoration as represented in examples from the deep soundings at Gordion, dating from the Early Bronze Age to the coming of the Phrygians. The stratified deposits of Bronze Age pottery retrieved at Gordion are centrally located under the greatly expanded citadel of the Phrygians. The strata in which Bronze Age and Iron Age wares overlap, the Hittite pottery coexisting with Phrygian wares, will be treated both here and in the early Phrygian pottery volume. Detailed plans and sections for the Bronze Age architecture with which the pottery was associated are discussed in the Appendix prepared by Machteld J. Mellink. It is to be noted here that the former, directional, building names of pre-Kimmerian Phrygian megara applied in the preliminary reports have been standardized into a simpler numerical series.

Eight Hittite burials from the 1962 excavations are added here to bring up to date the reporting on the Hittite cemetery on the Northeast Ridge, the initial excavations of which, in 1950-1952, were published by Mellink in *A Hittite Cemetery at Gordion* (1956).

During the years of excavation and study of the materials published here, many Directors General of the Department of Antiquities and Museums of Turkey gave their time and thought to the Gordion project. The government representatives sent by them to Gordion during the years when the excavation was concentrating on the Bronze Age strata were: Raci Temizer (1950-1952), Lütfi Tuğrul and Necati Dolunay (1961), Osman Aksoy (1962), and Çetin Anlağan (1965); and during the years of Dr. Gunter's study sessions: I. Cem Karasu and Edip Özgür (1978), Filiz Yılmaz (1979), Nihal Koloğlu (1979, 1980), Meral Gözübüyük (1981), Ayfer Aker (1982), Fuat Özçatal (1983), and Nihal Kalaycioğlu (1985). To all these our deep gratitude is owed for their unfailing, competent, and friendly support. To Bay Raci Temizer and Bay Osman Aksoy, Directors Emeriti of the Museum of Anatolian Civilizations, Ankara, we express special thanks for their ever-gracious hospitality to Gordion authors studying under their auspices.

Partial financial support for the preparation of this volume for press was given in grant #RO-20790-84 from the National Endowment for the Humanities. This was supplemented by the Gordion Publications Fund in Memory of Rodney S. Young, a source within The University Museum constantly being replenished by generous donations from individual friends of Gordion.

The production and design were coordinated by the Publications Department of The University Museum.

Ellen L. Kohler
Philadelphia, 1986

Preface

Gordion, located approximately 100 km. southwest of Ankara in west central Turkey, has long been identified as the capital of the Phrygian Empire, which flourished in the early first millennium B.C. Excavations conducted by the University of Pennsylvania between 1950 and 1973 have uncovered monumental architecture, burial mounds and accompanying finds from this impressive period of Gordion's history. Its Bronze Age ancestry is less well known. In addition to excavation of the Hittite Cemetery from 1951 to 1953 and in 1962, soundings were made below Phrygian levels on the City Mound in 1950, 1961, and 1965. These investigations were intended to probe the prehistory of the mound and to shed light on the early history of the Phrygians and the circumstances of their arrival in central Anatolia, as well as on their relationship to the Hittite Empire. The soundings revealed a stratification beginning in the late third millennium B.C., long centuries of settlement before the Phrygian era. While more extensive exploration of these levels remains a desideratum for future fieldwork, the information already recovered merits detailed publication, providing at once a glimpse of pre-Phrygian Gordion and an important sequence of late third and second millennium occupation in west central Anatolia.

In preparing this material for publication I have studied the excavated finds now housed at the site and in the Museum of Anatolian Civilizations in Ankara. All pottery recovered from the pertinent soundings was kept and labeled by the excavators, and remains available for consultation in the excavation depot. Catalogued artifacts of Bronze Age date, from the soundings, burials or miscellaneous contexts on the City Mound, are on display in the Gordion Museum or stored in its depot. Descriptions and photographs made when finds were inventoried have supplied the sources for a few objects that could not be located for reexamination. All other documentation has been obtained from the records maintained by the Gordion Archives at The University Museum, University of Pennsylvania.

Acknowledgments

In preparing this volume I have had the benefit of information, support, and encouragement from individuals and institutions whose contributions deserve recognition and a formal acknowledgment of my appreciation. Research in the Museum of Anatolian Civilizations in Ankara, and in the Gordion Museum and excavations storerooms was carried out in 1979, 1981, 1982, and 1985 with the kind permission of the Turkish Department of Antiquities. Dr. Nuşin Asgari, then director of the Istanbul Archaeological Museum, kindly allowed me to examine Gordion material from the Körte excavations. Professor Tahsin Özgüç, director of the Kültepe excavations, and Dr. Peter Neve, director of the Boğazköy excavations, generously granted permission to examine pottery from these sites. Dr. David H. French, director of the British Institute of Archaeology at Ankara, discussed some of the Gordion material with me and kindly allowed me to examine samples from the Institute survey collections. Research in Turkey was made possible in 1981 by a grant from the American Research Institute in Turkey, in 1982 by a Grant-in-Aid from the American Council of Learned Societies, and in 1985 by a University of Minnesota Faculty Travel Grant.

The Gordion Publications staff has extended every courtesy and assistance during my visits to consult archives and discuss production of this volume. Ellen L. Kohler, series editor, Karen Brown Vellucci and Anita Liebman answered endless requests for information and help, and designed the book and illustrations. Professor Robert H. Dyson, Jr., Director of The University Museum, read and commented constructively on successive drafts of the manuscript. His suggestions and encouragement have been invaluable. I am also grateful to Julie Perlmutter and Elizabeth Simpson for advice regarding the illustrations and for the many improvements that have resulted from their expert judgment.

Other Gordion excavators and authors have supplied indispensible information and support. G. Kenneth Sams helped to launch my study of the pottery in 1979, and I remain deeply indebted to him for much practical assistance with ceramic analysis in general and that of the Gordion pottery in particular. Keith DeVries, director of the Gordion study seasons, kindly made arrangements for my work in Gordion and Ankara and for assistance with drawing and photographing. My warmest thanks are to Machteld J. Mellink, who suggested that I undertake the study of Bronze Age Gordion, and has generously made available her unrivaled knowledge of Gordion and Bronze Age Anatolia. Her good judgment and good will have made the project possible in every other way.

Ann C. Gunter
Atlanta, 1986

I

The Excavations

A Bronze Age settlement at Gordion has been documented since 1900, when A. Körte recovered handmade pottery and stone artifacts from the City Mound and recognized their prehistoric affinities.[1] The investigations begun in 1950 by The University Museum of the University of Pennsylvania included three soundings beneath the Phrygian levels on the City Mound; the results were briefly described in preliminary reports.[2] Burials encountered during the excavation of Phrygian tumuli on the ridge to the northeast of the City Mound furnished additional Bronze Age remains. Most extensive of these was a cemetery dominated by pithos burials, the Hittite Cemetery, excavated from 1951 to 1953.[3] In 1951 an individual Early Bronze Age burial was recovered beneath Phrygian Tumulus F. During excavations to the north and east of the Hittite Cemetery in 1962, additional Hittite burials came to light. A brief description of the pertinent soundings on the City Mound and a full discussion of the 1962 burials are presented here. M. J. Mellink has kindly contributed a schematic section through the three deep soundings (see Plans 11 and 12) and a commentary on the stratigraphy (see Appendix, pp. 107-108).

The Site

Gordion lies in the river plain of the Sakarya, the classical Sangarius, at an altitude of 688 m. above sea level. The principal habitation area on the site is a low, flat mound whose topography has furnished the name of the adjacent modern village of Yassıhüyük, "Flat Mound" (Pl. 1A; Plan 1).[4] This area, here referred to as the City Mound, measures approximately 250 by 400 m., rising 24 m. above the surrounding plain. To the southeast lies the "Small Mound," Küçük Hüyük, separated from the City Mound by an ancient bed of the Sakarya. To the northeast and southeast are low ridges with a few outcroppings of bedrock whose natural formations are partly echoed in the tumuli constructed on top of some of them. Here lay the cemeteries of Gordion's inhabitants throughout antiquity.

Bronze Age Levels and Building Remains

Architectural remains and stratified deposits of pre-Phrygian occupation have been sampled in three deep soundings on the City Mound (Plans 11 and 12): (1) North Central Trench (NCT), which was dug through the rear of the cella of Phrygian Megaron 12 (formerly designated the Northwest Building); (2) Trench PN-3/3A, which was located in front of the anta of Megaron 12; and (3) below Megaron 10 (formerly referred to as the North Building). The location of these two Phrygian megara is shown in Plan 2.

---

1. *Gordion*, 151-152 (A. Körte); 196, figs. 193-194 (G. Körte); also A. Körte, *AthMitt* 22 (1897) 24. The rock crystal disk (*Gordion*, 174, no. 3), now in the Istanbul Museum, is probably of Archaic date. Compare F. Brein, *AnatSt* 32 (1982) 89-92 for similar objects.

2. Below, notes 5, 7, and 8.

3. M. J. Mellink, *Hitt. Cem.*, esp. 1-17.

4. A. Körte, *Gordion*, 28-35, for local topography.

DEEP SOUNDING UNDER MEGARON 12

In 1950 a 20 x 14-m. test trench (NCT) was opened in the north central area of the City Mound.[5] During the 1951 season, at the level of Phrygian Megaron 12 (Plans 2, 11, and 12), a smaller sounding (3 x 10 m.) was continued beneath the cella and carried to the water table, a depth of some 15 m. from the surface of the mound and 4 m. below datum zero.[6] Of the six major levels distinguished in NCT, the upper levels—I through IIIB—represented occupation of the Hellenistic through Phrygian periods. The lower three levels—IV through VI—were reached in the deep sounding below the cella. Level IVA-B produced principally Late Bronze Age pottery together with Phrygian wares and a few sherds of handmade pottery. Level VA-C yielded Middle and Late Bronze Age pottery. The lowest level reached, Level VI, contained handmade, red-slipped pottery of Early Bronze Age date.

Level IVA contained a narrow wall (maximum preserved width 0.20 m.) running north-south for a preserved length of 3 m.; the top of the wall was at 4.25-4.15 and the bottom at 3.80-3.70 m. It seemed to represent the wall of a house with a return to the east at the southern end of the north-south wall. In the northwest corner of the trench was a hearth with mudbrick rim and gravel center; it lay at 4.20 m. To the east of the north-south wall, in the interior of the house, was found a large gray porous grinding stone; it sat on an intact thin white floor of the house at 3.70 m. Level IVA produced a majority of red and buff pottery together with gray and black wares similar in type to examples encountered in the upper levels. Level IVB consisted of a layer of burned debris, including mudbrick, and unburned fill on a plaster floor at 2.30.

Below 2.30 m., two levels of fill containing grit and ashes, labeled VA and VB, yielded pottery (red and buff wares) and a few nonceramic finds (three flint blades in VB). Coherent architectural remains occurred only in Level VC. At 0.05 m., the top of a wall appeared (Pl. 1B). Further excavation revealed a floor of pink-buff crushed stone to the south of the wall. The wall continued down into Level VI, with the bottom of the wall at -1.50 m. for a maximum preserved height of 1.60 m. It was constructed of large limestone blocks and mudbricks (0.18 x 0.40 m.). The pottery of Level VC was generally of the same wares and shapes as that of Levels VA and VB, although showing more similarity to Hittite styles. The ceramic evidence from Level VI showed unmixed Early Bronze Age material.

TRENCH PN-3/3A

In 1961 a trench measuring 6 x 15 m. called "PN-3" was opened to the northwest of the North Central Trench which contained Megaron 12. A total of eight layers was recognized in PN-3, Levels 1 through 6 representing Hellenistic through Phrygian occupation. Below the Phrygian paving (designated as Level 6) were two levels, 7 and 8, which yielded principally handmade pottery of Early Bronze type (Plan 3).[7]

The upper Early Bronze level, 7 (Plan 3), consisted of a burned clay and pebble floor covered with charcoal ash and a layer of clay. Sloping down from 4.98-4.51 m., running south-north, was preserved one course of a wall (Wall I) which was traced for ca. 6 m.; it measured up to 1 m. thick and consisted of large conglomerate blocks and thin limestone slabs (Pl. 2B). The joints between stones, approximately 0.10 m. wide, were filled with mud mortar and small stones. The wall appeared to have served as a low stone foundation for a mudbrick superstructure. In the burned material to the east of the wall were solid pieces of charcoal, up to 0.07 by 0.18 m. long, suggesting that wooden beams had also been used in the construction. Stone paving slabs which, like the wall, were set into a layer of clay some 0.25 m. thick were also found in this area. On the Level 7 floor to the east of Wall I was preserved a hearth of burned stones; nearby were two large fragments of grinding stones. From undisturbed areas of Level 7 came intact or restorable vessels of Early Bronze date (**17**, **22-24**, **25**, **26**, **28**, **51**, **52**) as well as numerous fragments. The Level 7 deposit east of the wall at 4.65 m. appeared to contain no later material. At the east end of the trench the deposit had been disturbed by Phrygian construction. The fill from this disturbed area of the trench produced mixed pottery lots, including a minority of Phrygian, and a few Middle and Late Bronze sherds in addition to the Early Bronze examples.

Within the PN-3 trench a smaller test pit was excavated from the Level 7 floor; at 4.11 m. a hard-packed floor, designated Level 8, was encountered. On it were a small hearth constructed of field stones, and a burned area. A rubbish pit, cut into Level 8 at the east end of the trench, contained charcoal, ash, and sherds primarily of Early Bronze date but with an admixture of later material in the upper part. The test pit was excavated to a depth of 3.75 m., but no further building remains were encountered. Excavations in this area continued in 1965, when an extension, 3 x 5 m., was

---

5. The North Central Trench was excavated by Machteld J. Mellink. The Bronze Age levels are described in Gordion Notebooks 5 (1950) 150-162 and 10 (1950, 1951) 16-30, 50-62, 64-74. The preliminary report on this sounding was published by R. S. Young, *Archaeology* 3 (1950) 197-198.

6. Point zero refers to the Gordion 1950 datum, as shown in Plan 1. See also absolute level zero in Plans 11 and 12.

7. PN-3 was excavated by Aubrey Trik in 1961; see Gordion Notebook 98, pp. 31-57. In 1965 M. J. Mellink opened PN-3A as an extension and then continued excavating PN-3 and PN-3A together. See Gordion Notebook 98, pp. 58-107. Preliminary publication: R. S. Young, *AJA* 66 (1962) 168.

opened against the northwest front of Megaron 12. This trench, called PN-3A, expanded PN-3 to the southeast (Pl. 3; see note 7). Starting at the level of the upper Phrygian pebble pavement associated with Megaron 12, Levels 1, 2, and 3 consisted of pebble and flagstone pavings of Phrygian date; under Level 3 lay a stratum of Phrygian debris mixed with Bronze Age material (Level 4), and immediately below this lay a stratum of mudbrick debris with burnt soil containing only Early Bronze Age artifacts (Level 5). Level 5 was disturbed by several shallow pits, measuring between 0.70 and 3 m. in diameter (Plan 3A, Pl. 2A). Three of these—Pits A, B, and C—contained Phrygian pottery and had evidently been dug for storage purposes before the pebble pavement covered them. The remaining pits—D, E, F, and G—contained Early Bronze sherds. To the north, in the area of the original PN-3 trench, two larger pits were also now cleaned, H and I, which contained Early Bronze pottery in addition to associated occupation debris and fill. Pit I, the earlier of the two, measured ca. 3 m. in diameter. It was overlapped slightly by Pit H, ca. 1.80 m. in diameter, which had a separate northeast curb made of stone and mudbrick.

Two Early Bronze Age levels were distinguished in PN-3A. The upper level, I, corresponds to Level 7 as defined in Trench PN-3. Wall I was left in place, and the adjacent area to the east and west was excavated to reveal a series of earlier building levels, designated IIa-c, containing floors and structures (Plan 3).

At the south lay a complex, Building II, the northwest corner of which was exposed (Plan 3A, Pl. 2B). This east-west wall (Wall II) preserved a doorway 0.90 m. in width, furnished with a pivot stone. On the exterior to the west of the doorway was an annex, ca. 0.70 by 1.25 m. The door in Wall II led into a corridor bordered by a parallel mudbrick wall (Wall P) ca. 1.50 m. to the south. The corridor was filled with mudbrick tumble containing sherds and a few nonceramic artifacts. Wall II continued to the southeast under Megaron 12.

Also in 1965, further excavation west of Wall I revealed a series of floors and mudbrick constructions separated by fill, representing two sublevels associated with Building II (Plan 3B, C; Pl. 2B). The lowest revealed a two-room complex, the earliest floor of which, at a depth of 3.60-3.70 m., may be associated with the stone foundation level of Wall II. A mudbrick partition wall was traced for about 1.45 m. in an east-west direction; it formed a north and a south room, both of which yielded evidence of domestic habitation in the form of burnt floors, occupation debris, and fea-

tures. The fill of the north room contained several fragmentary vessels (6-8) and a whetstone (11). On its floor was also a "fire-dog" of lightly baked mudbrick (H. 0.125, W. 0.115, Th. 0.115 m.). In the south room was a semicircular curb of fine light clay, 0.05 m. high, underneath which were ashes and burnt material from earlier hearths.

DEEP SOUNDING UNDER MEGARON 10

In 1965 a sounding which began below the anteroom of the Phrygian Megaron 10 and probed deepest along the back wall of the main room, provided the principal evidence at Gordion for a habitation sequence of second-millennium Bronze Age date. The area initially measured ca. 7 by 15 m., gradually decreasing in extent as a series of ledges were left to allow access to the excavation (Pl. 4A). The sounding revealed superimposed earth floors with a few architectural remains, extending to the water table at ca. 8 m. below the uppermost Phrygian floor in the anteroom (see stratification in Plan 11A).[8]

The uppermost layer to 3.18 m. corresponded to floor levels inside the main room of Megaron 10.[9] It and the subsequent Layers 2 and 3 contained Phrygian pottery mixed with Late Bronze Age pottery, the latter increasing to some 50% in Layer 3. Layer 4 (under floor 4) yielded Late Bronze Age pottery with a few examples of handmade pottery and Phrygian wares. This level inaugurated a series of superimposed floors of hard-packed earth containing some burned habitation and mudbrick debris and much fragmentary pottery. Features or architectural remains were scanty and very poorly preserved. On Floor 5 was part of a hearth or oven. In Layer 8 were two pits, A and B, dug from Floor 8 (Plan 12). These measured approximately 2 m. in diameter and 0.65 m. in depth and contained sherds as well as nonceramic implements. Floor 8 also produced a wall built of small stones with a mudbrick superstructure. In Floor 9 (Plan 4, Pl. 4B) a paving of small flat stones (cobbles) was preserved, probably the bed for a floor of clay or earth. It measured 4 m. from north to south and ca. 3 m. across.

In Layer 12 were two pits, A and B, containing darker earth than the floor through which they were cut. These measured 0.35 and 0.20 m. deep, and included animal bones and burned mudbricks in addition to sherds. Layer 13 also yielded a pit containing burned habitation debris, sherds and animal bones, lined with mudbrick blocks ranging in size from 0.48 x 0.30 x 0.10 m. to 0.32 x 0.25 x 0.10 m. Layer 14 con-

8. Excavated by R. S. Young in 1965; see Gordion Notebook 117, pp. 54-120. Preliminary publication: R. S. Young, *AJA* 70 (1966) 276-278.

9. Since Young began with a cleaned floor (the latest floor in Megaron 10), in this stratification "Layer" 1 lies below "Floor" 1, etc., throughout.

tained a circular clay basin, 0.32 m. in diameter and 0.16 m. deep, with walls 0.05-0.08 m. thick; it rested on Floor 15 (Plan 5). The basin appeared to be a storage container, although it contained only a fragmentary bowl (**177**). Below the section of Layer 14 not sealed by a floor level was a deposit labeled 14B, consisting of fill with broken mudbricks, stones, animal bones, and earth with many cinders.

In Layer 15 (Plan 5) was a northwest-southeast wall of small stones and mudbrick, 0.38 m. thick, plastered with mud. Traces of a hearth or fireplace southwest of

the wall suggested that this represented the interior space, east of the wall the exterior. Below this, but still associated with Layer 15, a burned mudbrick wall running northeast-southwest was preserved to some 0.25 m. in height. At this level the trench began to fill with water, restricting continued digging to the northwest side of the wall. On Floor 17 were a hearth and perhaps also the bed for a wall. In Layer 18 (Plan 5) were a fragment of stone walling and a piece of burned mudbrick wall at -3.80 and -3.97 m., respectively. There the water table was reached, halting further investigation.

Burials

Bronze Age burials were recovered from Gordion in the area also used for the cemeteries of the first millennium, the high ground to the northeast of the City Mound. The City Mound itself has yielded no certain evidence for use as a Bronze Age cemetery. Skull fragments were found below a floor of Level 8 in trench PN-3, but no intentional burial was evident.

CIST GRAVE UNDER TUMULUS F

In 1951 a tumulus containing a Phrygian cremation burial was opened some 120 m. north of the Hittite Cemetery main trench; it also covered an Early Bronze Age stone cist grave preserved in semicircular form *ca.* 1 m. west of the center of the tumulus (Plan 6, Pl. 5A). This earlier grave, oriented approximately north-south, consisted of six stones ranging in size from 0.72 x 0.46 m. to 0.43 x 0.44 m., set on edge to enclose an oval area 1.22 m. north-south x 0.95 m. east-west (Plan 7). At -0.48 m. below ancient ground level lay a poorly preserved skeleton in contracted position, on its left side, head south and facing west; the hands were drawn up in front of the mouth. A plain inhumation of first-millennium date, part of the Phrygian common cemetery, extended into the cist grave on its northwest side, disturbing this area of the stone enclosure and the lower extremities of the skeleton. The excavator assumed the cist grave skeleton to be that of an adolescent male.[10]

Inventory:
ca. 0.20 m. west of skull:
   1 Bowl
   2 Jar

beneath right shoulder blade:
   3 Copper or bronze hook-shaped object
   4 Flint blade

Burials in cist graves were also found in the Hittite Cemetery under Tumuli H and I. Pottery and metal objects associated with them, as grave gifts or in overlying fill, assigned them to the early second millennium B.C.[11]

The only other burial certainly of third-millennium date was an inhumation from the Hittite Cemetery, H 28. It contained a handmade vessel of typologically early, Early Bronze Age manufacture.[12]

The pottery from the early burials is discussed below in chapter II.

HITTITE CEMETERY: THE MUSEUM SITE

From 1951 to 1953 a cemetery of inhumations, cist graves and pithos burials of early to mid-second-millennium date was excavated under Tumuli H and I. Burials uncovered in the main cemetery trench and in trial trenches opened to the north, east, and southeast indicated that the cemetery occupied an area approximately 100 m. east-west by 60 m. north-south (Plan 8). In 1962 an area located within the limits of the trial trenches was selected as a possible site for the Gordion Museum and consequently excavated (Plan 8). The "Museum Site," an area measuring 16 x 25 m., yielded an additional eight pithos burials of second-millennium type (Plan 9, Pl. 5B). These lay at a depth of 0.30-0.80 m. from the surface, set diagonally to the slope, in a compact, light-colored stratum termed

---

10. Tumulus F was excavated by E. Robert Gallagher in 1951. See Gordion Notebook 16, pp. 6, 12-16 for reference to the Bronze Age burial under the tumulus. Cf. also *ILN*, Jan 3, 1953, p. 21, fig. 6.

11. M. J. Mellink, *Hitt. Cem.*, 4-5 (H 3; H 31, double burial; H 40).

12. *Ibid.*, 3, 5, 6 (H 28).

hardpan, or in the gravel and sand layer above it.[13] As in the area excavated from 1951 to 1953, the second-millennium burials were much disturbed by Phrygian and Roman graves as well as by constructions of the Phrygian period. In all examples the second-millennium skeletal remains were poorly preserved. The burials correspond closely to those excavated from 1951 to 1953 in the forms of pithoi, preferred southeast-northwest orientation, contracted skeletal position, and number and type of accompanying gifts. They increase the size of the early to mid-second-millennium necropolis at Gordion to some 55 excavated burials of which 42 are in pithoi.

Six of the eight Museum Site burials contained a few grave gifts, including ceramic bowls and metal or bone artifacts, in addition to the burial pithoi themselves. The burials found in 1962 are grouped here by pithos types following those recognized during previous excavation of the Hittite Cemetery, and continue in numerical sequence those published in 1956.

The pottery from these burials is catalogued in chapter III (pp. 81-82).

RIBBED PITHOI

H 49 to H 52

H 49 Section R, southeastern part (see Plans 9 and 10, Pl. 6A). Ribbed pithos set obliquely in layer of gravel and sand. Orientation SE-NW. Mouth covered by a stone slab and several mudbricks, fixed in place by mud sealing.

L. of pithos with capstone: 1.28 m.; mudbrick cover: 1.05 m. x 1 m.

Skeleton, adult female, very fragmentary; in contracted position on right side?[14]

Inventory:
 497 Pithos
to left and right of upper rib cage:
 501 copper/bronze toggle pin
 502 copper/bronze toggle pin
 Several pieces of much disintegrated wood

H 50 Section N, northeast corner (see Plan 9, Pl. 6B, C). Ribbed pithos set in hardpan. Orientation SE-NW. Cover of mudbrick blocks and capstone, rim sealed further by thin layer of mud.

L. of cover and pithos together 1.25 m.; cover: 1.10 m. x 0.35-0.40 x 0.25 m.

Skeleton poorly preserved, probably adult; in contracted position on left side.[15]

Inventory:
 498 Pithos
at bottom of pithos:
 495 Bowl
 496 Bowl
scattered within pithos:
 504 26 knuckle bones, 19 beneath area where skull rested

H 51 Section N, southwest corner (see Plan 9, Pl. 7A, B). Ribbed pithos set in hardpan and gravel mixed with sand. Orientation SE-NW. Cover of capstone and mudbrick blocks sealed with mud; in addition, upper layer of stones placed above rim and cover (0.90 x 0.40 m.); grave marker?

L. of pithos, capstone and mudbrick cover: 1.60 m.; L. of pithos and capstone: 1.08 m.; mudbrick cover 1.25 x 0.56 m.

Fragmentary skeleton, apparently in contracted position.[16]

Inventory:
 below burial:
 3 fragments of copper/bronze wire

H 52 Section Q, northwest corner (see Plan 9, Pl. 8A, B). Ribbed pithos set in hardpan and mixture of earth and sand. Orientation SE-NW. Stone and mudbrick cover preserved.

L. of pithos and cover: 1.50 m.; mudbrick cover 0.20 x 0.55-0.90 m.; stone cover 0.90 m. in total length.

Skeleton fragmentary.[17]

Inventory:
 recovered near mudbrick cover:
 494 Bowl

PITHOI OF COOKING-POT TYPE

H 53 to H 55

H 53 Section Q, east side, just below surface soil (see Plan 9). Pithos of large cooking pot type, upper side badly damaged, embedded in hardpan. Orientation SE-NW.

L. pithos 0.96; D. 1.35 m.

Fragmentary skeleton; no burial gifts.[18]

H 54 Section O (see Plan 9, Pl. 9A). Large cooking-pot pithos, upper part broken, set in gravel *ca.* 1.50 m. below surface. Orientation SE-NW.

Fragmentary skeleton apparently in contracted position, head facing NE.[19]

---

13. G. Roger Edwards and Diantha Haviland excavated the "Museum Site" in 1962.

14. D. Haviland, Gordion Notebook 103, pp. 182-187 (MS 20).

15. *Idem,* Gordion Notebook 104, pp. 76-81 (MS 36).

---

16. *Ibid.,* 81-88 (MS 48).

17. *Ibid.,* 88-94 (MS 53).

18. D. Haviland, Gordion Notebook 103, pp. 168-172 (MS 9).

19. G. R. Edwards, Gordion Notebook 102, p. 53 (MS 44).

Inventory:
    503 Six knuckle bones

H 55   Section T, southwest corner (Plan 9, Pl. 9B). Pithos of large cooking-pot type in layer of gravel mixed with sand. Orientation SE-NW. Covered with mudbrick blocks and mud sealing; no stone cover preserved.
    L. of pithos and cover: 1.10 m. Skeleton very fragmentary, apparently in contracted position on left side.
    Fragments of charred wood at bottom of pithos.[20]

Inventory:
    506 Pithos

at bottom of pithos after removal of skeleton:
    505 Silver ring fragments

PITHOS FORM UNSPECIFIED

H 56

H 56   Section S (see Plan 9). Pithos of coarse red ware laid in gravel depression; mudbrick cover still partly *in situ* (W. 1.15 m.), with fallen block in front of vessel mouth. Orientation SE-NW. Burial much disturbed in antiquity; fragments of burial pithos and bone found in this vicinity.[21]

Miscellaneous Contexts

In addition to the excavated sources discussed above, Bronze Age artifacts have been recovered from Phrygian and Hellenistic contexts on the City Mound at Gordion. Most of these are second-millennium ceramic finds—pottery, figurines, and implements—retrieved from the Clay Deposit laid over the ruins of the Early Phrygian city as a leveling device for subsequent construction. This fill, varying from 2.50 to 4 m. in depth, contained numerous sherds of second-millennium type, both red- or brown-slipped and burnished wares and the coarser buff and orange plain wares.[22] One area, below the South Cellar in Trench CC3A, produced several finds of apparently similar Late Bronze Age date, relatively well preserved and in close proximity (**515, 516, 531**). Middle and Late Bronze Age sherds were also present in the Clay Deposit below Level V of Küçük Hüyük, the small mound southeast of the City Mound (Plan 1).

The source of the Hittite sherd-filled clays is uncertain. Much material from this context appears waterrolled, smoothed and worn, suggesting that an area of the second-millennium settlement cut through by the Sakarya river was selected for this purpose.

Summary

Investigation of Bronze Age remains at Gordion took place principally during the campaigns of 1950, 1961, 1962, and 1965, in two areas of the site. On the City Mound, soundings in the North Central Trench and Trench PN-3/3A revealed Early Bronze levels, the latter area containing fragmentary mudbrick and stone architecture, with evidence for a final burning. In the North Central Trench the Early Bronze level, VI, lay below several layers of second-millennium accumulation (Level VC-A). In PN-3/3A two successive layers containing Early Bronze Age pottery lay directly beneath levels of the Phrygian period. This area may well represent the top of the main Early Bronze mound or citadel, which saw no further construction until the Phrygian era. The Early Bronze habitation in the North Central Trench and below Megaron 10 is on a lower terrace.

In the North Central Trench in the sounding under the Phrygian Megaron 12 and in a deep sounding under the Phrygian Megaron 10 were stratified deposits representing second-millennium habitation. Architectural remains were scanty. The North Central Trench deposit consisted of levels of fill: VB, VA and IVB, with a layer of burned debris separating IVB from VA. The deposit under Megaron 10 consisted of superimposed floor levels, occasionally with associated interior features such as stretches of stone or mudbrick walls (Layer 15), pebble paving (Floor 9) or hearths (Floor 5). The lack of major architectural remains underneath the interior space of the Phrygian buildings suggests that struc-

---

20. D. Haviland, Gordion Notebook 104, pp. 70-75 (MS 54).
21. *Ibid.*, 3-6 (MS 26).

22. R. S. Young, *AJA* 60 (1956) 264.

tures of closely similar plan lay beneath them. In both soundings, levels containing Late Bronze Age pottery were succeeded without observable break by deposits of the Early Phrygian period.

On the ridge northeast of the City Mound, in an area occupied by part of the first-millennium necropolis, were burial grounds of the pre-Phrygian inhabitants. A cist grave under Tumulus F and a plain inhumation in the common cemetery under Tumuli H and I were the earliest burials excavated, dated to the Early Bronze Age by associated pottery. A few sherds of handmade red-slipped pottery were also recovered from the general area of the Hittite Cemetery and from the mantle earth of Tumulus E. They suggest that additional Early Bronze burials were placed in this area, but no concentration of such graves has come to light. The Northeast Ridge area under Tumuli H and I also yielded a cemetery of early to mid-second millennium date, dominated by pithos burials but also including cist-graves and simple inhumations. The cemetery consisted of at least 55 burials, in an area covering some 600 sq. m.

Early Bronze Age Pottery

Early Bronze Age pottery was recovered from Level VI in the sounding below Megaron 12 and from Levels 10-7 in the PN-3 sounding of 1961 and 1965. In addition, miscellaneous contexts on the City Mound and a cist grave below Phrygian Tumulus F produced a few specimens assignable to this period on the basis of comparisons with stratified material from Gordion or from other excavated sites in central and western Anatolia.

Analysis of the Material

Early Bronze Age contexts at Gordion have yielded a corpus of pottery consisting of some 50 restored or intact vessels, and 1,300 sherds. As described in chapter I, most of this material was retrieved from levels disturbed by subsequent building activity or pits, so that few lots were entirely free of later ceramic admixture. In contrast to the second-millennium levels, however, the Early Bronze deposits contained a high proportion of well-preserved specimens, intact or restorable, providing detailed information on the shapes represented in this period.

The catalogue includes all well-preserved pots, and diagnostic sherds—rims, handles, or decorated fragments—selected to document shapes or ornament not illustrated among the intact or restored examples. Descriptions of fabrics, shapes, and the assemblage from each level of the soundings are based on an examination of all preserved specimens. Sherds too fragmentary to catalogue have occasionally provided information on the presence or relative quantity of certain shapes or forms of decoration; these are generally noted in the descriptions of material from each sounding as "not catalogued."

Examples located or recorded in 1985 could not be incorporated into the catalogue sequence. These have been grouped as "Supplementary Entries," given a number beginning with **S**, and listed separately at the end of the catalogue in chapter III (pp. 85-91). The information they contribute to the assemblage from each level is included in the description of each level in the two deep soundings.

Parallels with examples from other sites in central and western Anatolia are cited as appropriate at the end of individual catalogue entries. They are limited to very precise similarities in shape, surface finish, and ornament, drawing primarily on published material from excavated contexts. The relationship of the Gordion corpus to broader ceramic categories or phases of development in Early Bronze Age central Anatolia is outlined in the following descriptions of fabrics, shapes, and decoration.

Description of the Pottery

FABRICS

HANDMADE RED-SLIPPED

The principal fabric recovered from the Early Bronze levels is a handmade red-slipped burnished pottery. The clay is fired buff, orange, or light red in color (Munsell 7.5YR 7/4, 5YR 6/6, 2.5YR 6/6); it is often micaceous and usually well fired. Examples are classified here as fine, medium, or coarse, with medium by far the most numerous. Fine examples are of clean clay, with few or no visible inclusions; any sand or gritty particles are less than 2 mm. in size. Medium wares occur in the same clay but are consistently gritty in temper, with inclusions between 2 and 5 mm. A few specimens are classified as coarse, containing numerous gritty particles and inclusions larger than 5 mm. Vegetal temper is present in some examples, together with the usual gritty or sandy inclusions. Both fine and medium wares are covered with a fired slip ranging in color from orange to red to brown (Munsell 2.5YR 5/6, 7.5YR 5/6, 10R 6/8). Most vessels are slipped on both interior and exterior surfaces, and exhibit signs of stroke-burnishing; many preserve a highly lustrous finish. Nearly all examples are handmade, but a few appear to be wheelmade, or wheelformed and finished by hand.

The fabric was used for a variety of shapes, principally pitchers, bowls, dippers, and jars; there are examples of other shapes, such as vessel stands and pithoi. Surface ornament is a frequent feature. Incised decoration is found on teapots, bowls, and jars. Impressed ornament occurs on a similar range of shapes, sometimes together with incision. Plastic decoration, in the form of crescent-shaped or miniature lugs, is used on bowls. Relief ornament and cut-out decoration are also documented for this fabric. Horizontal or torsional fluting occurs on bowls and jars. Handles of pitchers and dippers are sometimes given a knobbed or twisted surface. General and specific correlations are with the "Copper Age" pottery of central and west central Anatolia, dating to Early Bronze II and III, and with Polatlı's "local ware."[1]

PAINTED POTTERY

This category is basically identical in clay, variation in temper, and firing, with the red-slipped fabric, distinguished only by its surface treatment. Pottery with painted decoration appears rarely and apparently in very few shapes: cups, small bowls, and jars, all handmade. Two types are distinguished. The first has red patterns (Munsell 10R 4/8, 2.5YR 6/6) painted on the cream- or buff-slipped (Munsell 7.5YR 6/4-7/4) interior surface of cups or small bowls with solid, lustrous red-slipped exteriors (33, 52, 63, 65, 97, 99). Patterns consist of single stripes from the rim converging at the center of the vessel, and triangles or chevrons formed by multiple stripes. This red-painted group as a whole belongs to the west central Anatolian version of the red-cross bowl.[2] The second painted style consists of brown (Munsell 2.5YR 5/3) painted patterns on a tan-slipped (Munsell 7.5YR 6/6, 5YR 6/6) surface, both with matt finish. The only documented shape for this

second style is a globular jar with vertical handles (56). Painted designs are geometric, represented here by multiple chevrons and a net pattern (56, 64). Closest parallels are with examples from nearby Polatlı, but the style is related also to the "Intermediate Ware" of central Anatolian sites.[3]

SHAPES

As noted above, the Early Bronze Age deposits yielded a relatively high proportion of well-preserved examples, contributing to knowledge of vessel forms and ornament represented in this period. Principal categories are described below and related briefly to the ceramic repertory of pertinent sites in central and west central Anatolia. Specific parallels from excavated contexts are given in individual catalogue entries. The order of shapes presented here follows the sequence of the catalogue.

BOWLS

Bowls are open hemispherical vessels greater than 0.10 m. in diameter, distinguished by variations in profile and by the presence, form, and location of handles or surface ornament. Bowls with a single vertical handle are designated as dippers and grouped separately. Together these categories form the dominant vessel type in all Early Bronze levels, not only at Gordion but also elsewhere in central and western Anatolia.

Handleless bowls are common (1, 14-32, 84-86), although some may have had handles not preserved on the fragmentary examples. Bowls with lug handles form a distinct subgroup, encompassing examples with miniature lugs of decorative intent (34-37) and with more substantial versions which probably served to fasten lids (38, 87), and one with pierced lug handles (5). Bowls with horizontal handles are uncommon and only of large size (39-41). Bases document a variety of contemporaneous forms: flat (1, 23, 30, 87), indented (5, 17, 25, 28), and gently rounded (22).

Incised ornament is found on several specimens (29, 31, 32). A few examples have red-striped painted interiors (33, 97, 99), overlapping with cups preserving similar decoration (52, 63). These represent the west central Anatolian version of the red-cross bowl, known also from Early Bronze contexts at Polatlı, Ahlatlıbel, and Asarcık Hüyük.[4]

1. M.J. Mellink in R.W. Ehrich, ed.,*Chronologies in Old World Archaeology* (Chicago 1965), 112-114, with further references; *AnatSt* 1 (1951) 44-45, 54-58 for "local ware."

2. References cited under 33, 97. Also *AnatSt* 1 (1951) 46; J. Mellaart, *CAH* I:2 (Cambridge 1971), ch. XXIV (a), 692, 699.

3. A. Öktü, *Die Intermediate Keramik in Kleinasien* (Berlin 1973), 98-100, for the Gordion and Polatlı examples. Also discussed below, pp. 13-14 with n. 18.

4. References cited above, n. 2.

PANS

Pans are large shallow vessels of rectangular or oval shape, made by hand. Three fragments from Gordion document the type in PN-3 Level 7 (**43**, **44**) and Megaron 12 Level VI (**95**). Vessels of this shape occur at a number of sites in central Anatolia, as the parallels cited in the catalogue indicate. They are known by a variety of designations, including "trays" and "baking platters." As they are sometimes blackened on one or both surfaces, they most likely served as baking trays or pans. An example found in an oven in Early Bronze Beycesultan, Level XIII, strongly supports this interpretation.[5]

Pans are a long-lived vessel type, occurring in Early Bronze I contexts or earlier at Beycesultan and in the Troad (Kumtepe Ia-Ib).[6] In central Anatolia they are found in Early Bronze II and III levels at many sites, as the parallels cited below demonstrate. At Boğazköy a fragment of a related vessel type in Nordwesthang-Büyükkale, Levels 8c-8d, suggests continued production in the Middle Bronze Age.[7]

DIPPERS

This term designates a distinctive group of bowls with a single vertical handle attached at or just below the rim. Dippers are a characteristic vessel shape in Early Bronze II and III contexts in central Anatolia. Early Bronze levels at Gordion have produced a number of well-preserved examples, furnishing evidence for a range of subtle variations within the type. The bowl form ranges from deep (**8**, **47**) to relatively shallow hemispherical versions (**45**); rim diameters vary from *ca.* 0.14-0.21 m. Bases are gently rounded to flat (**6**, **7**, **89**, **90**) or flat with a slight indentation (**46**, **88**). Handles show the most variation. They can rise above the rim (**6**, **7**, **47**, **88-91**) or be set entirely below the rim (**45**, **46**, **48**); sometimes they have fluted ornament (**48-50**) or angular form (**89**, **90**). Handle sections vary from oval to concave (**45**, **88**), and may be ribbed vertically (**6**, **46**, **49**) or arrised.

JARS

As employed in this catalogue, jars refer to closed vessels of a wide range of shapes and dimensions. Only a few fragmentary examples illustrate this category in Early Bronze levels. A globular vessel with two vertical handles (**56**) is painted in a style resembling "Intermediate Ware." **57** is a coarse hole-mouth container. The small fluted jar (**55**) may be restored as a spouted vessel by analogy with an example from nearby Polatlı. A sherd with a horizontal handle (**75**) may also belong to a large jar. A fine brown-slipped handle (**54**) is probably from a large two-handled jar or a storage pitcher. From the cist grave below Tumulus F is a bottlelike vessel (**2**).

PITCHERS

Pitchers are vessels with spouts, opposite which is a handle. They form another characteristic pottery shape in Early Bronze Age Anatolia. Several well-preserved examples from Early Bronze Age contexts at Gordion document a wide range of sizes and variations in form. Intact specimens include a large storage pitcher (**59**) and two small vessels suitable for table use (**58**, **94**). Spouts are upturned (**58**, **59**, **61**), beaked (**94**), or tubular (**60**, probably from a teapot with basket handle). A small fluted vessel (**55**) resembles an example from Polatlı preserving a tubular spout, and may belong to the pitcher category. A handmade vessel neck with ribbed handle (**S63**), from Megaron 10 Layer 4, is almost certainly from a pitcher of Early Bronze Age manufacture.

The fragmentary handles (**76-78**) probably also belong to pitchers. Red-slipped pitchers with similar knobbed or twisted handle ornament occur at Demirci Hüyük, Polatlı Phase II, Beycesultan Level VIa, and at Boğazköy Büyükkale Level Vc.[8] An example in metal was also a surface find at Polatlı.[9] A fine brown-slipped handle (**54**) probably belongs to a large two-handled jar or a storage pitcher.

VESSEL STANDS AND LIDS

Gordion has yielded only one Early Bronze Age example of each of these categories: a fragmentary stand from PN-3 Level 9 (**9**) and an intact vessel lid from Megaron 12 Level VI (**96**). The stand (**9**) can be associated with examples from the Ankara and Çorum areas of central Anatolia, although no exact parallels are known. The lid (**96**) belongs to a type with fairly broad distribution in central, west central, and southwest Anatolia. It is too large for any of the vessels with which it was placed in pithos **92**; most likely it covered a large cooking pot.

5. *Beycesultan* I, 90, Level XIIIC.

6. *Beycesultan* I, 90, occurring in Levels XXXI-XXV; also example from Level XIIIC mentioned above, n. 5. Kumtepe: J. Sperling, *Hesperia* 45 (1976) 322; fig. 10 and pl. 72, nos. 136-138; fig.16, no. 315; fig. 18, no. 534. Troy: *Troy* I, 56, no. 224; 75, shape D 23 (references to examples in Early Helladic Greece); 240, fig. 407:II-363; *Troy* II, 33, 136, 248 (Levels III-V).

7. *Frühe Keramik*, 37, no. 257, pl. 37, if not an extrusive specimen from an earlier level.

8. *Demirci-Hüyük*, pl. 7:12; *AnatSt* 1 (1951) 41, fig. 9b:10; *Beycesultan* I, 243, fig. P.67:16; 245, fig. P.68:4; *Boğazköy* VI, 23, fig. 5 (also illustrated in K. Bittel, *Die Hethiter* [Munich 1976], 79, fig. 53).

9. *AnatSt* 1 (1951) 61, fig. 14:14.

VESSELS WITH PLASTIC, INCISED, OR IMPRESSED DECORATION

Plastic or incised ornament is a characteristic feature of Early Bronze Age pottery at Gordion, represented on a variety of vessel shapes. Knobbed or twisted ornament occurs on handles of dippers (48, 50) and of larger vessels, probably pitchers (76-78). Related to this surface modeling are the angular handles of dippers (89, 90) and a pitcher (94). The vessel stand, 9, has plastic cabling along its base and upper edge. Horizontal fluted treatment of vessel surfaces appears on a bowl (28) and a jar (55). Ribbed handles are a feature of dippers (6, 46, 49) and pitchers (S63). Plastic crescents (71, 72) or miniature lugs (34-37) are often placed on the upper wall of small bowls. Other examples of surface modeling, such as that on sherd 70, are on vessels of unknown form.

Incised or impressed ornament is also well documented. Rows of incision decorate rims of bowls (31, 32) and a small vessel of uncertain shape (66, jar or teapot?). Multiple chevron patterns occur on several sherds, probably cups or jars but possibly representing other vessel types (65, 67, 68, 100). A large coarse vessel fragment, probably a pithos, preserves finger-impressed ornament below the rim (93).

Similar treatment of vessel surfaces and of functional parts, such as handles, is typical of Early Bronze II and III assemblages in central, west central, and southwestern Anatolia.[10]

Early Bronze Age Soundings

TRENCH PN-3

Four levels, 10-7, were distinguished below the Phrygian deposit in this sounding. They were associated with building remains, and represent successive floors and occupation fill.

Level 10 (5)

A single item, a red-slipped bowl (5), has been catalogued from this level. No other sherds can be securely assigned to this level.

Level 9 (6-11)

About 90 sherds were saved from Level 9. They consist almost exclusively of handmade red-slipped pottery, in both fine and coarse varieties, among which were recognizable a dipper (8) and a vessel stand (9). Some of the vessels appear to be wheelformed and finished by hand, like the dippers 6 and 7. Fragments of a coarse ware vessel (10, handle), bowls, a pan, and a lug handle (fragments, not catalogued) were represented. Also from Level 9 is a well-preserved whetstone (11).

Level 8 (12 and 13)

This level was disturbed, its contents generally mixed with Level 9 or Level 7; in addition, several wheelmade samples indicated further contamination. Most of the approximately 100 available sherds are selected diagnostic specimens from both Levels 9 and 8. They consist principally of handmade red-slipped fragments, including bowls, dipper handles, and lugs, shapes represented by better-preserved specimens from Level 7. A cup (12) and a whetstone fragment (13) have been included in the catalogue.

Level 7 (14-83)

Investigations in 1961 and 1965 in the uppermost Early Bronze level in PN-3 yielded some 1,100 intact or restorable vessels and sherds. The initial probes in 1961 produced ceramic material mostly from disturbed deposits, several containing second-millennium and Phrygian sherds. The fill between Phrygian Level 6B and the clay layer above the floor of Level 7 also yielded some mixed lots, in which the Early Bronze material was clearly distinguishable from that of later date. Several well-preserved vessels were found on top of the Level 7 floor and in the burned material above it (17, 23, 46, 58, 59), in addition to a copper or bronze pin (82). The 1965 investigations in the trench also produced Early Bronze pottery, occasionally mixed with second- or first-millennium sherds in Phrygian pits and in the fill above Level 7. Much of the pottery was retrieved from the area disturbed by Pits H and I; it has been grouped here with examples from Level 7. Since Pits H and I, both of Early Bronze Age date, extended to a depth of 2 m. from their upper surfaces, their contents may include pottery from Level 7 and earlier levels. The recorded context of each artifact accompanies the catalogue description.

Pottery of Level 7 is dominated by orange and buff gritty fabrics with orange- and red-slipped surfaces.

---

10. Specific parallels are cited for individual catalogue entries. Similar "Copper Age" pottery is found in Early Bronze III Tarsus (*Tarsus* II, 134-135).

Favored shapes are handleless bowls (**14-32**), bowls with miniature lugs or lug handles (**34-38**), dippers (**45-50**), and pitchers (**58-61**). Surface ornament is common, occurring in the form of horizontal or torsional fluting (**28, 55**), plastic crescents (**71-73**), and incised or impressed decoration (**29, 31, 32, 65-69**). Fluted or knobbed adornment is frequent, especially on handles of dippers and pitchers (**48-50, 76-78**). Painted decoration in red and cream is found on bowl or cup interiors (**33, 52, 63**). The samples of painted decoration in brown-on-cream patterns (**56, 64**) are closely related to the Early Bronze III "Intermediate Ware" of central Anatolia, as noted above. A few wheelformed specimens also occur, in addition to one wheelmade beaker of tan ware (**53**).

MEGARON 12, LEVEL VI   (**84-96**)

The lowest level reached in the initial deep sounding, Megaron 12 Level VI, produced some 50 sherds, and 7 intact or restorable vessels. Although a small corpus, the Level VI material contained no later admixture and thus appears to represent an undisturbed deposit. A group of vessels found together inside a pithos (**92**) consisted of a bowl (**87**), dippers (**88-90**), a pitcher (**94**), and a lid (**96**), apparently deposited at the same time. The pithos also contained three pumice stones (ST 170) and a fragmentary flint flake (ST 59).

Level VI pottery consists exclusively of tan and orange grit-tempered fabrics with orange- and red-slipped surfaces; all vessels are handmade. Some sherds are poorly fired at the core or fired black throughout. Shapes include bowls (**84-87**), dippers with handles attached to or rising above the rim (**88-91**), a beaked pitcher (**94**), a pan (**95**), and a lid with band handle (**96**). Finger-impressed ornament is found on a coarse pithos rim (**93**). Knobbed or angular ornament occurs on handles of dippers (**89, 90**) and a pitcher (**94**).

MEGARON 10   (**97** and **98**)

The sounding under Megaron 10 produced no defined levels containing Early Bronze pottery; the earliest deposit here appears to date to the Middle Bronze Age and is described in full in chapter III. A few isolated specimens of Early Bronze pottery, however, occurred in the lowest levels, Layers 18-15 (**97, 98**). They demonstrate that Early Bronze occupation levels, at present inaccessible below the water table, lie underneath the second-millennium levels exposed here.

MISCELLANEOUS CONTEXTS   (**99-101**)

In addition to the Early Bronze material from stratified deposits, a few examples were retrieved from Phrygian or Hellenistic contexts on the City Mound (**99-101**). They can probably be ascribed to the Early Bronze Age through comparison with well-stratified finds from Gordion and other central Anatolian sites.

Internal Correlations and Chronology

A relative chronology of Early Bronze Age remains at Gordion, including burials and habitation strata, will help to establish the periods represented in the two areas of the site. As noted in the descriptions of excavated remains, some mixing of the deposits in PN-3/3A took place during Phrygian construction. In these soundings, moreover, the earlier Early Bronze levels recognized stratigraphically produced only a few ceramic artifacts from undisturbed deposits. As a result, only a tentative relative ordering of the material can be proposed via presence or absence of fabrics, shapes, and details of attributes (Table 5).

Typologically the earliest ceramic evidence appears in the cist grave below Tumulus F. The primitive bowl and fragmentary jar (**1, 2**) find a similar pre-"Copper Age" companion in the two-handled vessel from burial H 28 in the Hittite Cemetery.[11] This material does not correspond to any occupation level yet reached on the City Mound, but it documents an early phase of third-millennium occupation at the site.

Most of the Early Bronze pottery comes from soundings on the City Mound. Correlation of the levels begins with the stratification reviewed in chapter I, the burned layer traced over the Early Bronze levels in both soundings. Similarities among the ceramic assemblages confirm their general contemporaneity. All contexts produced handmade pottery of tan and orange grit-tempered fabrics with red or orange burnished slip. Other common traits include shapes (handleless bowls, dippers, pitchers) and forms of attributes or decoration (lug handles, knobbed or angular vertical handles, impressed ornament).

---

11. *Hitt. Cem.*, 6-7, pl. 16h.

Stratigraphic evidence in Trench PN-3 for successive periods of occupation provides a potential basis for tracing ceramic developments within the Early Bronze deposits. Given the very limited samples available for Levels 10 to 8, however, and the generally mixed nature of the Early Bronze contexts in this vicinity, little internal development can be documented. Vessels from Levels 10 to 8 find close parallels in shape and manufacture with the Level 7 assemblage, including dippers (6-8), and vessels perhaps formed on the wheel (5-7, 10). The similarity between the earlier and later levels may be misleading, resulting from the very small quantities of pottery available. At present it documents unmistakable ceramic continuity between the levels, suggesting that they follow in close succession and represent a relatively brief duration.

Pottery of Megaron 12 Level VI shares traits with both the earlier and later levels just discussed and probably overlaps them. Important for these correlations is the closed group of vessels found together in a pithos (92). This consisted of dippers with flat and rounded bases and handles rising above the rim (88-90), a bowl with lug handles (87), a small beaked pitcher with angular handle (94), and a vessel lid (96). The dippers resemble specimens from PN-3 Level 9 (6, 7) and

Level 7 (47); the bowl with lug handles is similar to a larger version from PN-3 Level 7 (38). Among other finds from Level VI are a coarse pan (95) with exact counterparts from PN-3 Level 7 (43, 44).

Level VI produced no bowls or dippers with indented bases, painted pottery, examples of fine incised or relief decoration, or wheelformed vessels. The absence of such features, which are characteristic of PN-3 Level 7, may reflect the much smaller sample from Level VI or perhaps may indicate chronological differences now disguised by the overlying burned layer that implies approximate contemporaneity. Further investigation of less disturbed occupation levels may clarify the relative sequence within the various areas of the City Mound.

Early Bronze items from miscellaneous contexts seem to coincide with pottery from the uppermost level recognized in Trench PN-3. A bowl with a red-striped interior (99) is most closely related to the group defined by examples from PN-3 Level 7 (33, 63, 65). Incised multiple chevron ornament on a pitcher or jar fragment (100) resembles a fragment from PN-3 Level 7 (68). The animal figurine (101) may also belong to the Early Bronze Age.[12]

External Correlations and Chronology

Specific comparisons between the Gordion Early Bronze finds and those from other Anatolian sites are noted in the catalogue. It remains to assemble these for each level and to consider the settlement of this period as a unit, establishing a series of synchronisms with well-defined sequences elsewhere in central and western Anatolia. This framework is summarized in Table 1 (see p. 107).

The cist grave group beneath Tumulus F, together with the jar from burial H 28 in the Hittite Cemetery, finds parallels with pre- "Copper Age," or "Chalcolithic," pottery of Ališar Level 12M, placing the earliest documented occupation at Gordion in Early Bronze I.[13] Extramural burial is rare in this period in the regions between the Kızıl Irmak and Sakarya rivers. Mixed practices, including cist graves and pithoi, are attested in intramural location at Polatlı, Karayavşan, and Ahlatlıbel in Early Bronze II-III contexts.[14] The closest available comparison is the Early Bronze I cemetery at Kusura near Afyon, dominated by pithoi but also containing cist and earth burials.[15] Whether

extramural burials in mixed forms continued at Gordion during Early Bronze II or III times is unknown.[16]

Early Bronze levels on the City Mound appear to correspond to sequences at nearby Polatlı Hüyük, where soundings in 1950 produced a stratified Early and Middle Bronze Age deposit that remains the principal regional source for correlations during this period. Soundings in separate trenches in the habitation mound at Polatlı yielded occupation levels, which the excavators considered to form a continuous sequence comprising four ceramic phases. Relevant to the Gordion Early Bronze Age are Phase I (Levels I-X), characterized by handmade red polished or "local ware"; Phase II (Levels XI-XV), containing wheelmade beakers and the "multiple-crossed" bowl linked to Troy V; and Phase III (Levels XVI-XXII), with painted pottery likened to "Cappadocian Ware" and wheelmade red and brown burnished ware.[17] The Polatlı sequence was subsequently restudied by W. Orthmann, who postulated a hiatus in the Early Bronze stratification based on the finds from levels in trenches B and C.

---

12. Animal figurines 81 and 101 are discussed by I.B. Romano in her forthcoming monograph on the Gordion terracotta figurines.

13. *OIP* 28, 52-54, for description of "Chalcolithic" plain ware.

14. T.S. Wheeler, *AJA* 78 (1974) 424, Appendix I.

15. W. Lamb, *Archaeologia* 86 (1936) 55.

16. See M.J. Mellink, Appendix, p. 107.

17. *AnatSt* 1 (1951) 53-54.

He divided Phase I into "Period Ia" (Levels I-IV) dating to early Early Bronze II, and "Period Ib" (Levels V-XI) dating to Middle Bronze I. The intervening periods, Early Bronze IIIa and IIIb, were represented only by stray finds, not a stratified cultural deposit. Middle Bronze I continued with "Period II" (Levels XII-XV), correlated with Kültepe Karum Levels IV and III.[18]

Polatlı Phase I provides close parallels for the Early Bronze sequence at Gordion. As Orthmann noted in his division of Levels I-X into Periods Ia and Ib, Phase I comprises an earlier and later phase. Traits characteristic of Period Ia occur principally in Megaron 12 Level VI and in material from PN-3 Pits H and I: bowls with lug handles (38, 87), and pans (43, 44, 95). Polatlı Period Ib furnishes numerous and specific parallels for PN-3 Level 7: bowls and jars with horizontal fluting (28, 55), cups (74) and bowls (17, 25, 28) with indented ("dimple") base, and pitchers (76-78) and dippers (48, 50) with knobbed or twisted handle decoration. Bridging the transition to Phase II (Levels XI-XV), Orthmann's Period II (Levels XII-XV) are "multiple-crossed" bowls with red and white painted interiors, found at Gordion in PN-3 Level 7 (33, 63). Phase II also witnesses the first appearance of wheel-made beakers, one of which occurs at Gordion in PN-3 Level 7, Pit G (53). Phase III (XVI-XVII), overlapping with Orthmann's Period III (Levels XVI-XVIII), embraces close relatives of painted "Intermediate Ware," which actually begin in Phase II; examples of this occur in PN-3 Level 7 (56).

The Gordion Early Bronze sequence thus appears to follow closely that at Polatlı, but suggests that no significant hiatus occurred between Periods Ia and Ib, as Orthmann proposed. Features characteristic for these two phases are found in the same level or in overlapping levels at Gordion. If these sites prove to follow a closely parallel sequence, Polatlı may ultimately help to furnish a context for unstratified material recovered from Gordion. A fragmentary depas amphikypellon retrieved during the Körte excavations in 1900 most likely belongs in the period represented by PN-3 Level 7, since the shape occurs at Polatlı with the characteristic traits of Period Ib noted above.[19]

Close connections with other sites in the Polatlı-Ankara region are also evident. Bowls with horizontal fluting, dippers and bowls with indented base, and red and white painted bowl interiors link Gordion with Asarcık Level V, and Karayavşan near Haymana. Gordion shares with the Ankara sites of Ahlatlıbel and Etiyokuşu a preference for red-polished pottery in pitchers and dippers embellished with fluted and ribbed ornament. Farther afield, connections with Boğazköy Nordwesthang-Büyükkale Level 9 are indicated by large vessels with rim-impressed ornament, jars of "Intermediate Ware," and wheelmade tan ware beakers.[20] To the southwest, plastic and incised ornament in red-polished pottery and wheelmade beakers supply correlations with Beycesultan VIa and VIb.

A relative chronology for Gordion's Early Bronze Age occupation is furnished by the synchronisms with Anatolian sequences cited above, linked to Trojan and Cilician relative chronologies by cross-dating.[21] PN-3 Level 7, encompassing most of the finds from Pits H and I, belongs in Early Bronze IIIb. The earlier occupation, represented by PN-3 Levels 10 to 8, and part of Megaron 12 Level VI, can be assigned tentatively to the preceding Early Bronze IIIa or possibly even slightly earlier, to the end of Early Bronze II. Additional investigation of suitably stratified levels at sites in west central Anatolia should help to define Early Bronze II and III occupation through more refined ceramic sequences.

Catalogue of the Early Bronze Age Finds

The earliest evidence recovered to date comes from the cist grave beneath Tumulus F and its associated pottery. This material is catalogued first, followed by the bulk of the Early Bronze pottery from the excavated contexts reviewed in chapter I. Early Bronze Age pottery from miscellaneous contexts on the City Mound is described last.

Most of the catalogued items have been assigned an excavation inventory number, given in the individual entries; those few items without this identification are designated as "not inventoried."

18. *Keramik aus Inneranatolien*, 28-31; *Frühe Keramik*, 49-50.

19. Körte, *Gordion*, 196, fig. 193; *AnatSt* 1 (1951) 45-46.

20. A. Öktü, *Die Intermediate-Keramik in Kleinasien* (Berlin 1973), 98-100, considers the Polatlı and Gordion samples as a western variant of "Intermediate Ware," citing also an unpublished example from Karayavşan. Cf. *Keramik aus Inneranatolien*, 22-23. More recently, specimens of "Intermediate Ware" have been reported from Karahüyük-Konya by S. Alp, "Karahüyük," *Belleten* 38 (1974) 545.

21. M.J. Mellink in R.W. Ehrich, ed., *Chronologies in Old World Archaeology* (Chicago 1965), 110-117; cf. D.F. Easton, *AnatSt* 26 (1976) 145-173, and J. Yakar, *AnatSt* 29 (1979) 51-67, all with additional bibliography. The forthcoming publication of Early Bronze Age pottery from the recent excavations at Demirci Hüyük should contribute important new information for ceramic correlations and relative chronologies in west central Anatolia.

Tumulus F Cist Grave **(1-4)**

The Early Bronze cist grave below Tumulus F contained two vessels (1, 2), both of coarse handmade fabric. Additional grave gifts were a copper or bronze object (3) and a flint blade (4).

BOWL (1)

1 Hemispherical bowl
P 253   Cist burial beneath Tumulus F
H. 0.097; D. rim 0.223 m.
Fig. 1; Pl. 10
Not examined.
 Complete; mended from two pieces. Rim chipped and abraded; interior scratched. Some surface incrustation.
 Hemispherical form with straight upper wall, plain rim, flat base.
 Reddish brown clay with many visible inclusions, heavily grit- and vegetal-tempered. Handmade.

JAR (2)

2 Jar
P 528   Cist burial beneath Tumulus F
GPH. 0.23; Est. D. neck 0.0915 m.
Fig. 1; Pl. 10
 Mended section preserves part of neck and shoulder of jar. Double convex body, straight cylindrical neck.
 Gray clay, heavily grit- and vegetal-tempered. Traces of dark red slip (10R 5/4) on the exterior; fired black at core, pinkish buff and gray at surface. Handmade.
 Alişar Level 12 M, "Chalcolithic Age" (*OIP* 28, 67, fig. 74); Alaca Hüyük (*Alaca 1936*, pl. 33).

NONCERAMIC ARTIFACTS (3 and 4)

3 Copper or bronze hook-shaped object
ST 64b   Cist burial beneath Tumulus F
L. 0.032 m.
Pl. 10
 Hook corroded; broken at both ends.
 Found touching one end of 4, perhaps part of haft or container.

4 Flint blade
ST 64a   Cist burial beneath Tumulus F
L. 0.1315; W. 0.02 m.
Pl. 10
 Complete.
 Flint blade; smooth on one face, two facets on second face. Striking platform preserved. Secondary pressure flaking used to blunt it near haft for finger hold and to sharpen it near point.

City Mound **(5-101)**

TRENCH PN-3   **(5-83)**

LEVEL 10   **(5)**

BOWL (5)

5 Four-handled bowl
P 3391   Level 10, against Wall II
H. 0.065; Est. D. 0.14; Est. D. rim 0.13; D. base 0.038 m.
Fig. 1; Pl. 10
 Mended section preserves less than one-half of bowl.
 Squat globular form with flat rim, slightly everted collared neck, indented base. Four horizontal handles, grooved over top and pierced, placed at maximum diameter of vessel.
 Fine light reddish brown clay with many inclusions; fired gray at core. Red to reddish brown slip (10R 5/8, 2.5YR 5/6), burnished, on both surfaces. Handmade?
 Polatlı Level VIII, with two handles (*AnatSt* 1 [1951] 47, fig. 11a:2).

LEVEL 9   **(6-11)**

DIPPERS (6-8)

6 Dipper
P 3407   Level 9, W of Wall I, N room intermediate floor
GPH. at rim 0.059; Est. D. rim 0.155; W. handle 0.02 m.
Fig. 1; Pl. 10
 Mended section preserves handle and part of rim and wall.
 Hemispherical form with tapered rim. Handle, vertically ribbed on upper surface, rises above rim.
 Fine light red (2.5YR 5/6) clay with many inclusions. Red (2.5YR 5/6) slip, burnished and lustrous, on both surfaces. Handmade?
 Polatlı Level XII (*AnatSt* 1 [1951] 38, fig. 7a:14).

7 Dipper
P 3392   Level 9, W of Wall I, N room intermediate floor
H. 0.06-0.064; D. rim 0.142 m.
Fig. 1; Pl. 10
 Circa one-half preserved; mended. Handle broken.
 Hemispherical form with plain, slightly incurved rim, rounded base. Handle, round in section, attached on and just below rim.
 Fine orange (5YR 6/6) clay, with many tiny inclusions. Red (2.5YR 5/8) slip on both surfaces; some burnish strokes visible on base. Surfaces well smoothed. Handmade?
 Polatlı Level XII (*AnatSt* 1 [1951] 38, fig. 7a:13).

8 Dipper
P 3406   Level 9, W of Wall I, N room intermediate floor
GPH. 0.105; Est. D. rim 0.20 m.
Fig. 1; Pl. 10
 Mended and restored section preserves part of rim and wall, with handle scar below rim.
 Hemispherical form with slightly outturned rim.
 Fine light brown (5YR 6/3) clay with many inclusions. Red to reddish brown (10R 5/8) slip on both surfaces, worn on exterior. Handmade.

VESSEL STAND (9)

9   Vessel stand
P 5317   Level 9
H. 0.106; GPW. 0.0951; GTh. 0.011 m.
Fig. 1; Pl. 10
Section mended from two joining sherds preserves upper and lower finished edges of flaring cylindrical vessel. Broken at upper and lower rims and along wall on both sides. Surfaces incrusted; some discoloration.

Pot stand, with flat upper surface, wall of cylindrical vessel tapering inward to lower rim forming base. Outer edge at base decorated with cabled torsional plastic surface. Upper rim crimped. Vessel walls preserve finished edges of cut-out patterns, five diagonal ovals spaced evenly around stand.

Brown clay, gritty; fired gray at core. Surfaces covered with brown slip, smoothed, with matt finish. Handmade.

No close parallels. Stand with oval perforations: Boğazköy Nordwesthang-Büyükkale Level 9 (*Frühe Keramik*, 30, no. 167, pl. 4); similar form but without perforation: surface find from Çerkezhüyük near Ankara (*Keramik aus Inneranatolien*, 170, no. 31/06, pl. 89).

HANDLE (10)

10   Vertical handle
Not inv.   Level 9, N and S rooms W of Wall I
GPL. 0.12; GPW. 0.125; W. handle 0.032; GTh. 0.016 m.
Pl. 11
Large section broken from vessel wall preserves handle in full. Broken on side of handle, cracked and damaged on lower side; surface worn, slightly incrusted.

Vertical handle, concave in section.

Coarse, gritty, reddish brown (2.5YR 5/4) clay. Exterior slipped and burnished reddish brown (2.5YR 4/6), now mostly matt and worn. Vessel handmade?

NONCERAMIC ARTIFACT (11)

11   Whetstone
ST 562   Level 9, W of Wall I, N room intermediate floor
L. 0.202; GW. 0.10; D. perforation 0.0125; GTh. 0.02 m.
Pl. 11
Complete, with some gouges. Surfaces well smoothed by wear.

Flat palettelike stone, elliptical except for sharpened ends of ellipse. In one end, suspension hole drilled from each face, meeting at center with smaller hole. Valleys worn obliquely across by sharpening of blades.

LEVEL 8   (12 and 13)

CUP   (12)

12   Cup
P 3380   Level 8, floor levels below Pits H and I
H. at rim 0.018; D. rim 0.056 m.
Fig. 1; Pl. 11
Mended across bowl; handle restored. Base area blackened.

Small flat cup with plain rim, probably with vertical handle rising above rim (drawn as restored).

Fine buff (7.5YR 7.5/4) clay with hand-burnish strokes over all, fired gray at core. Handmade.
Asarcık Level Va (*IstMitt* 16 [1966] 69, fig. 9:11, 12).

NONCERAMIC ARTIFACT (13)

13   Whetstone
ST 561   Level 8, fill N of Wall II
PL. 0.055; W. 0.023; Th. 0.006-0.008 m.
Pl. 11
Broken across one end; some flaws in stone.

Flattened strip of stone trimmed squarely at preserved end and along edges. Well worn on flat faces and thin edges.

LEVEL 7   (14-83)

BOWLS (14-41)

14   Bowl
Not inv.   Level 7
Est. D. rim 0.10; GTh. 0.004 m.
Fig. 1
Fragmentary bowl mended from two joining sherds.

Plain rim, tapered profile, rounded base.

Fine orange clay, apparently well fired. Red slip on both surfaces; horizontal and oblique burnish marks visible. Handmade.
Asarcık Level V (*IstMitt* 16 [1966] 61, fig. 1:7); Etiyokuşu Level I (EY.173, *Etiyokuşu*, 68, fig. 63).

15   Shallow bowl
Not inv.   Level 7, Pits H and I
Est. D. rim 0.20; GTh. 0.004 m.
Fig. 1
Rim sherd of shallow hemispherical bowl, plain rim. Some greenish incrustation on interior.

Medium orange clay, gritty. Light red (10R 6/8) slip, worn, on both surfaces. Burnish marks visible on exterior; lustrous on exterior and near rim on interior. Handmade?

16   Hemispherical bowl
P 3385   Level 7
H. 0.068-0.074; Est. D. 0.165; D. base 0.042 m.
Fig. 1; Pl. 11
Circa one-half preserved.

Bowl of hemispherical form with plain, slightly incurved rim; flat or indented base.

Fine light red (2.5YR 6/8) clay with many small inclusions. Light red (2.5YR 6/8) slip on both surfaces; burnish strokes over all. Handmade.

17   Hemispherical bowl
P 2626   Level 7, top of floor and in burned material above
H. 0.09-0.107; D. rim 0.197 m.
Fig. 1; Pl. 11
Circa two-thirds preserved; mended to complete.

Hemispherical form with rim tapered on interior; indented base.

Fine, clean pink to light brown clay. Red (2.5YR 5/6) slip on both surfaces, mostly worn on exterior. Well smoothed and polished. Wheelformed, finished by hand.

18   Hemispherical bowl
Not inv.   Level 7
Est. D. rim 0.18; GTh. 0.008 m.
Fig. 1
Rim sherd of bowl preserves most of profile, with plain, slightly incurved rim. Area near base slightly blackened.

Fine light red clay, with some gritty inclusions; well fired. Light red slip on interior and exterior, horizontal and oblique burnish strokes on both surfaces. Handmade?

19 Hemispherical bowl
Not inv.   Mixed Level 7
Est. D. rim 0.18; GTh. 0.004 m.
Fig. 2
Rim sherd of bowl with plain rim.
Fine, clean orange clay, well fired. Reddish brown to light red mottled slip on both surfaces, well smoothed. Handmade?

20 Hemispherical bowl
Not inv.   Mixed Level 7
Est. D. rim 0.14; GTh. 0.004 m.
Fig. 2
Rim sherd of bowl with slightly tapered rim.
Fine orange clay, well fired. Reddish brown (2.5YR 4/8) slip, burnished, on both surfaces. Probably wheelmade.

21 Hemispherical bowl
Not inv.   Level 7, Pits H and I
D. rim 0.20; GTh. 0.004 m.
Fig. 2
Rim sherd; worn, some blackened spillage around rim. Hemispherical bowl with rim slightly tapered on inside.
Medium clay, gritty; fired gray at core, light red near surfaces. Light red (10R 6/8) slip on both surfaces. Hand-burnish marks visible on interior. Handmade?

22 Hemispherical bowl
P 3387   Level 7, in burnt floor W of Wall I
H. 0.068; D. rim 0.17 m.
Fig. 2; Pl. 11
Circa three-fourths preserved.
Hemispherical form with slightly incurved rim, rounded base.
Fine orange clay with many tiny inclusions; well fired. Red (2.5YR 5/8) slip on both surfaces, burnish strokes over all. Handmade?

23 Hemispherical bowl
P 2625   Level 7, top of floor and in burned material above
H. 0.097; D. rim 0.14 m.
Fig. 2; Pl. 11
Mended from many sherds; restored to complete with plaster. Some blackening on exterior near rim.
Hemispherical form with tapered, slightly everted rim, flat base.
Fine orange clay. Dark red-brown (10R 4/4) slip both interior and exterior; base reserved. Exterior lustrous, interior fired to shiny black. Horizontal and oblique burnish marks on both surfaces. Handmade.

24 Hemispherical bowl
Not inv.   Level 7
Est. D. rim 0.18; GTh. 0.007 m.
Fig. 2
Fragmentary bowl, mended from three sherds.
Shallow hemispherical form, outturned rim.
Fine orange clay well fired. Red (7.5R 4/8) slip on both surfaces, highly lustrous. Wheelmade?

25 Deep bowl
P 3378   Level 7, burnt floor under Phrygian pavement (floor 3)
H. 0.091-0.106; D. 0.16; D. rim 0.142; D. base ca. 0.035 m.
Fig. 2; Pl. 11
Almost fully preserved; mended and plastered to complete.
Deep bowl with S-shaped profile, plain rim, indented base.
Fine buff (7.5YR 7/4) clay with some inclusions. Red (7.5R 5/6) slip both surfaces, well smoothed and polished; base reserved. Burnish strokes visible. Handmade.
Polatlı Levels VIII and XI (AnatSt 1 [1951] 47, fig. 11a:4, 5).

26 Deep bowl
Not inv.   Level 7
Est. D. rim 0.24; GTh. 0.008 m.
Fig. 2
Rim fragment of bowl with S-shaped profile, plain rim. Mended from five sherds.
Fine tan (5YR 7/4) clay, slightly gritty; well fired. Brown (7.5YR 5/6) slip on exterior, slightly worn, extending inside rim. Clay-colored slip on interior. Burnish strokes visible on both surfaces. Handmade?

27 Deep bowl
Not inv.   Fill in disturbed area between Levels 7 and 8
Est. D. rim 0.26; GTh. 0.012 m.
Fig. 2
Rim and adjoining upper wall sherd of bowl with slightly outturned rim. Blackened along one edge of sherd, inner rim worn.
Tan clay with some grit and vegetal temper. Exterior covered with red-brown slip, burnished; interior below rim with tan "self-slip." Handmade.

28 Hemispherical bowl
P 5281   Level 7, burned clay layer and on top of paving slabs
H. 0.039; D. rim 0.10; GTh. 0.004 m.
Fig. 2; Pl. 11
Mended with some gaps and chips from several joining sherds. Preserves ca. one-half bowl (rim and body; all of base).
Small circular base, indented and rising slightly on interior. Shallow hemispherical form, rising almost vertically on upper wall to plain rim. Shallow horizontal fluting on exterior upper wall formed by four low ridges, continuing around circumference.
Orange (5YR 6/6) clay, fine and clean. Both surfaces covered with reddish brown (2.5YR 5/8) slip, highly burnished and still lustrous. Handmade.
Polatlı, Levels VII-VIII and XI (Keramik aus Inneranatolien, 132, nos. 8/40-8/41, pl. 35; AnatSt 1 [1951] 47, fig. 11a:16); Asarcık Level V (IstMitt 16 [1966] 67, fig. 7:1-2).

29 Hemispherical bowl
P 5279   Level 7
GPH. 0.059; Est. D. rim 0.13; GTh. 0.006 m.
Fig. 2; Pl. 12
Mended section preserves less than one-half of bowl, with rim and adjoining wall.
Hemispherical form, plain rim. On wall below rim, three parallel short, shallow grooves, each ca. 0.015 m. in length; a similar set on opposite side of bowl.
Orange clay, fine and clean. Reddish brown slip on exterior and on inner rim, heavily burnished and lustrous. Handmade.
Beycesultan Level XVI, similar decoration on red burnished dipper (Beycesultan I, 146, fig. P.24:14); Level VII, similar ornament on buff wash bowl (Beycesultan I, 224, fig. P.58:14).

30 Hemispherical bowl
P 5311   Level 7, Pits H and I
H. 0.076; Est. D. rim 0.14; GTh. 0.011 m.
Fig. 2
Section mended from two joining sherds preserves entire height of bowl, part of rim and base. Some blackening near rim. Slip worn.
Rim tapered on interior. Walls rise rather steeply to straight upper wall, forming deep hemispherical bowl. Base flattened.
Tan clay, gritty. Thin orange-red (10R 5.5/8) slip on both surfaces, smoothed, with matt finish. Handmade.
Larger examples from Polatlı Level III (Keramik aus Inneranatolien, 131, no. 8/17, pl. 33); Asarcık Level V (IstMitt 16 [1966] 61, fig. 1:4).

31   Bowl
P 5296   Level 7, Pits H and I
Est. D. rim *ca.* 0.23; GPL. 0.061; GPW. 0.062; GTh. 0.0065 m.
Fig. 2; Pl. 12
Rim sherd and adjoining wall. Rim worn; fresh scratch
across exterior (pick mark?).
Bowl with S-shaped profile, slightly outturned rim, tapered
on inside. On outer wall between rim and greatest diameter,
horizontal row of small oblique slashes (each *ca.* 0.004 m. in
length) formed by incision. Row and intervals between
slashes slightly irregular.
Light brown (5YR 5/6) clay, clean, with few inclusions.
Light brown (5YR 6/6) slip, well smoothed and lustrous, on
both surfaces. Wheelmade or wheelformed and finished by
hand.
Etiyokuşu (*Keramik aus Inneranatolien*, 129-130, no.
6/41, pl. 32); Boğazköy, Nordwesthang-Büyükkale Level 9
(*Frühe Keramik*, 15, no. 15, pl. 8).

32   Small bowl
P 5298   Level 7, Pits H and I
GPL. 0.035; GPW. 0.047; GTh. 0.0055 m.
Fig. 2; Pl. 12
Rim sherd and adjoining wall.
Small bowl with S-shaped profile, slightly outturned rim.
On exterior, horizontal row of oblique slashes, formed by in-
cision, just below rim. Row and intervals between slashes
slightly irregular.
Tan (5YR 6/4) clay, gritty. Light brown (5YR 6/6) slip,
smoothed with matt finish, on both surfaces. Probably wheel-
made.
Ahlatlıbel, similar decoration on small dipper (*TTAED* 2
[1934] 24).

33   Painted hemispherical bowl
P 5313   Level 7, Pits H and I
Est. D. rim 0.20; GPL. 0.0375; GPW. 0.041 m.
Pl. 12
Rim sherd and adjoining wall. Worn and abraded; some
discoloration.
Hemispherical bowl with plain rim. On interior, red
painted band around inner rim; below, red diagonal stripes
extend from rim to inside bottom of bowl (three bands
preserved in part, spaced at slightly irregular intervals).
Tan clay, clean. Exterior, solid red slip, smoothed. Handmade.
Similar decoration: Polatlı Levels XI-XIII (*AnatSt* 1 [1951]
52, figs. 13, 14); also Karahüyük-Konya, with horizontal
handle and intersecting incised lines on exterior (*Belleten* 22
[1958] 321-323, pl. I:4).

34   Lug-handled bowl
P 5290   Level 7, Pits H and I
Est. D. rim 0.16; GPL. 0.048; GPW. 0.126; GTh. 0.0045 m.
Fig. 2; Pl. 12
Section mended from several joining sherds preserves part
of rim and adjoining wall. Surfaces worn and scratched.
Shallow hemispherical form, rim tapered on interior. Mini-
ature lug handle on upper wall, *ca.* 0.02 m. below rim.
Red-brown (10R 5/6) clay, some grit temper but generally
clean. Well fired. Both surfaces covered with orange-red (10R
4.5/8) slip, burnished, with lustrous finish. Handmade.
Below, 37, with comparanda.

35   Lug-handled bowl
P 5291   Level 7, Pits H and I
Est. D. rim 0.17; GPL. 0.054; GTh. 0.005 m.
Fig. 2; Pl. 12
Section mended from two joining sherds preserves part of
rim and wall. Some discoloration and incrustation on both
surfaces.

Shallow hemispherical form, plain rim. Miniature lug
handle on upper wall, *ca.* 0.017 m. below rim.
Reddish brown (2.5YR 5/6) clay, fine and clean. Both surfaces covered with lustrous slip fired to a mottled reddish
brown (10R 5/8, 2.5YR 5/8) to tan. Handmade.
Below, 37, with comparanda.

36   Lug-handled bowl
P 5292   Level 7, Pits H and I
GPL. 0.053; GPW. 0.063; GTh. 0.003 m.
Pl. 12
Section mended from two joining sherds preserves part of
rim and adjoining wall. Very slight blackening on both sur-
faces.
Bowl with nearly vertical wall, plain rim. Miniature lug
handle on upper wall below rim preserved at edge of sherd.
Orange clay, gritty; much "gold" and "silver" mica visible
on surfaces. Both surfaces covered with light red (10R 6/6)
slip, mostly matt finish. Probably handmade.
Below, 37, with comparanda.

37   Lug-handled bowl
P 5293   Level 7, Pits H and I
GPL. 0.037; GPW. 0.039; GTh. 0.004 m.
Pl. 12
Part of rim and adjoining wall.
Small bowl with plain rim. Miniature lug handle, *ca.* 0.02
m. below rim.
Light red (2.5YR 6/6) clay, clean, with few gritty in-
clusions. Red-brown (10R 4/8) slip, lustrous, on both sur-
faces. Probably handmade.
34-37: Asarcık Level V (*IstMitt* 16 [1966] 62, fig. 2:2).

38   Lug-handled bowl
P 5316   Level 7, Pit E
GPH. 0.133; Est. D. rim 0.27; GTh. 0.011 m.
Fig. 3; Pl. 12
Circa one-fourth of rim preserved. Mended section of rim
and adjoining body; lug handle preserved in full. Some gaps
and chips; handle abraded.
Bowl of deep hemispherical form, plain rim. Lug handle
on upper wall above greatest diameter.
Light brown clay, grit- and vegetal-tempered; medium to
coarse ware. Brown slip, worn, now with matt appearance on
exterior and rim. Tan slip on interior below brown-slipped
area. Handmade.
Polatlı Level III (*AnatSt* 1 [1951] 43, fig. 10:5); Asarcık Level
V (*IstMitt* 16 [1966] 66, fig. 6:4).

39   Bowl with horizontal handles
P 5289   Level 7, fill over surface of floor
Est. D. rim 0.37; GPW. 0.17; Th. handle: 0.023 m.
Fig. 3; Pl. 12
Mended section preserves part of rim, adjoining wall, and
all of horizontal handle near rim. Surfaces slightly incrusted,
scratched and worn; some black discoloration.
Deep, wide-mouthed vessel with relatively straight walls
rising to flattened rim. Horizontal handle, round in section,
extends from upper wall to just below rim.
Orange (5YR 6/6) clay, coarse and gritty; "gold" and "sil-
ver" mica visible on surface. Both surfaces covered with slip
varying from red-brown to dark orange. Burnish strokes
visible. Handmade.
Polatlı Level XVIII (*AnatSt* 1 [1951] 43, fig. 10:14); Asarcık
Level V (*IstMitt* 16 [1966] 66, fig. 6:6).

40   Bowl with horizontal handles
P 3404   Level 7, burnt soil N of Wall P
GPH. 0.132; Est. D. rim 0.24; Est. D. 0.28 m.
Fig. 3; Pl. 12
Mended and restored section preserves *ca.* one-half bowl
with horizontal handle.

Deep bowl with tapered rim. Horizontal pierced lug handle set obliquely on wall just above maximum diameter.

Red-brown (2.5YR 5/6) clay with many inclusions. Red-brown (2.5YR 5/6) slip on both surfaces, smoothed and burnished. Handmade.

Asarcık Level V (*IstMitt* 16 [1966] 62, fig. 2:6; 63, fig. 3:1); Boğazköy, Nordwesthang-Büyükkale Level 9 (*Frühe Keramik*, 25, no. 101, pl. 2).

41 Bowl with horizontal handles
P 5306   Level 7, Pits H and I
D. rim unknown; GPL. 0.082; GPW. 0.112; W. handle 0.028; Th. rim 0.011 m.
Fig. 3

Handle, part of rim and adjoining wall from large vessel. Surfaces slightly incrusted; interior surface cracked. Exterior somewhat blackened at rim and on lower handle area.

Large vessel with relatively straight wall rising to plain rim. On upper wall a horizontal handle, oval in section.

Reddish brown (2.5YR 5/4) clay, gritty. Plum red slip on exterior, continuing just inside rim. Both surfaces smooth, with matt finish. Handmade.

PLATE (42)

42 Plate
Not inv.   Mixed Level 7
Est. D. rim 0.31; GTh. 0.014 m.
Fig. 3

Rim fragment mended from two joining sherds. Some dark discoloration on rim.

Shallow open vessel with rim thickened on exterior.

Coarse reddish brown (2.5YR 5/8) clay with many gritty inclusions; well fired. Interior covered with tan-orange (5YR 6/8) slip; exterior with red (10R 5/8) paint, mostly worn; probably originally solid red, although where worn, a tan (5YR 7/4) slip is visible. Paint carelessly applied. Handmade.

PANS (43 and 44)

43 Pan
P 5310   Level 7, Pits H and I
H. 0.49-0.051; D. rim unknown; GPW. 0.095 m.
Fig. 3

Single piece preserves part of rim, full height and part of base. Blackened on rim and outer wall, interior.

Shallow, flat vessel, probably oval in form. Base flat, roughened. Wall rises at *ca.* 70° angle towards plain rim.

Brown clay, grit- and vegetal-tempered. Brown slip, smoothed, on exterior and interior surfaces; some luster preserved. Handmade.

Below, **44**, with comparanda.

44 Pan
P 5309   Level 7, Pits H and I
H. 0.044-0.046; D. rim unknown; GPW. 0.087 m.
Fig. 3; Pl. 12

Single piece preserves part of rim, full height, and part of base. Blackened slightly on outer rim.

Shallow, flat vessel, probably an oval or subrectangular shape. Base flat, wall nearly vertical, angling out slightly towards plain, flattened rim.

Light brown clay, gritty and coarse. Covered with "self-slip" on exterior, rim, and interior; roughened surface on base. Handmade.

Below, **95**.

43 and 44: Polatlı Levels II, VII (*AnatSt* 1 [1951] 43, fig. 10:22, 23); Etiyokuşu (*Keramik aus Inneranatolien*, 129, no.

6/40, pl. 32); Ahlatlıbel (*ibid.*, 126, nos. 5/70 and 5/71, pl. 27); Demirci Hüyük (*IstMitt* 27/28 [1977/78], figs. 8:5, 11:7, 13:2); Alaca Hüyük (*Keramik aus Inneranatolien*, 142, no. 11/89, pl. 47); Boğazköy, Nordwesthang-Büyükkale Level 9 (*Frühe Keramik*, 37, no. 257, pl. 27).

DIPPERS (45-50)

45 Dipper
P 5304   Level 7, Pits H and I
Est. D. rim 0.16; GPL. 0.052; GPW. 0.11; W. handle 0.015; GTh. 0.004 m.
Fig. 3; Pl. 13

Section mended from several joining sherds preserves all of handle, part of rim, and adjoining wall where handle attached. Some chips.

Bowl of shallow hemispherical form, wall curving in gently towards rim, slightly tapered on inside. Vertical loop handle, slightly concave in section, set below rim.

Light reddish brown (2.5YR 6/6) clay, clean. Both surfaces covered with reddish brown (10R 5/8) slip, smoothed and burnished, lustrous. Handmade?

46 Dipper
P 2627   Level 7, top of floor at -4.65 m. and in overlying burned material
H. 0.11; Est. D. rim 0.19 m.
Fig. 3; Pl. 13

Less than one-half preserved; mended and restored to complete.

Hemispherical form with plain rim, nearly flat base; handle, vertically ribbed on upper surface, set below rim.

Fine orange clay with many inclusions. Red (10R 4/8) slip, somewhat worn and streaky, on both surfaces. Handmade, or wheelformed and finished by hand.

Asarcık Level V (*IstMitt* 16 [1966] 62, fig. 2:4).

47 Dipper
P 5305   Level 7, Pits H and I
Est. D. rim *ca.* 0.21; GPL. 0.113; GPW. 0.138; W. handle 0.034 m.
Fig. 3; Pl. 13

Single large sherd preserves entire handle, part of rim and adjoining wall of large bowl. Interior and most of handle blackened.

Deep hemispherical form, plain rim. Vertical handle, oblong in section, rises above rim.

Tan clay, gritty. Exterior and lower part of handle preserve thin orange (7.5YR 7/6) slip. Surfaces well smoothed, burnish strokes visible. Handmade.

Polatlı Level XII, buff clay, unburnished (*AnatSt* 1 [1951] 3, fig. 7a:17); Asarcık Level Va (*IstMitt* 16 [1966] 69, fig. 9:1-2); Demirci Hüyük Phase L (*IstMitt* 29 [1979] fig. 11:5); Demirci Hüyük Phase K (*IstMitt* 30 [1980] pl. 5:1, 3).

48 Dipper handle
P 5303   Level 7, Pits H and I
GPL. 0.435; W. handle 0.011; GTh. 0.0065 m.
Fig. 3; Pl. 13

Loop handle preserved in full, with place of attachment to bowl. Some discoloration on upper handle.

Handle, approximately triangular in section, set at rim. Upper part of handle decorated with eight parallel ridges forming diagonal fluting, neatly executed. Lower part of handle undecorated. Handle attached to bowl by means of clay dowel, made separately and inserted into handle "socket."

Orange (5YR 6/6) clay, relatively clean. Handle and both surfaces covered with reddish brown (2.5YR 5/6) slip, burnished and lustrous; very well smoothed and polished. Bowl wheelmade.

Polatlı Level X (*AnatSt* 1 [1951] 47, fig. 11b:11); Etiyokuşu (EY.196, *Etiyokuşu*, fig. 68); Demirci Hüyük Phase O (*IstMitt* 27/28 [1977/78] fig. 14:7).

49 Dipper handle
Not inv.   Level 7, Pits H and I
GPL. 0.048; W. handle 0.0135 m.
Pl. 13

Loop handle of dipper. Broken at both ends; preserves lower place of attachment to vessel. Surfaces chipped, slightly incrusted. Exterior, four parallel grooves along length.

Orange (2.5YR 6/8) clay, fine and clean. Both surfaces covered with red slip, well smoothed and polished.

50 Dipper handle
P 5302   Level 7, Pits H and I
GPL. 0.07; W. handle 0.0125 m.
Pl. 13

Handle and place of attachment at rim. Faint blackening on handle.

Handle, round in section, rises above rim. Softly modeled, twisted decoration on upper part, continuing approximately to center of loop. Lower part undecorated.

Light red clay, gritty. Handle and interior covered with orange (10R 6/6) slip, burnished; some luster preserved.

Similar ornament: Demirci Hüyük, Phase O or P (*IstMitt* 27/28 [1977/78] fig. 16:4).

CUPS (51 and 52)

51 Cup
P 5603   Level 7
H. 0.04; Est. D. rim 0.07; GTh. 0.01 m.
Fig. 3; Pl. 13

Fragmentary cup preserves part of rim, entire profile, and base.

In center of base a circular depression, *ca.* 0.018 m. across. Base of handle preserved on upper part of vessel wall.

Reddish brown clay, gritty. Surfaces covered with reddish brown slip, worn and matt. Handmade.

52 Painted cup
P 5287   Level 7
GPH. 0.042; Est. D. rim 0.07; W. handle 0.009; GTh. 0.006 m.
Fig. 3; Pl. 13

Single section preserves *ca.* one-third of vessel, including part of rim, entire height of vessel wall, and part of base. Handle broken at place of attachment. Some blackening on both surfaces.

Cup has small flat base, conical lower body, slightly globular at maximum diameter, continuing vertically to plain rim. Small horizontal handle or pierced lug, round in section, set below rim.

Painted red band on inner rim. Vertical red bands, *ca.* 0.01 m. wide, extend into center of cup from rim; two bands preserved, one crossed by two short horizontal lines.

Tan clay with some grit and vegetal temper. Exterior covered with reddish brown (5YR 4/4) slip; interior is tan-slipped with red painted decoration. Surfaces well smoothed with little luster. Handmade.

BEAKER (53)

53 Beaker
P 3401   Level 7, Pit G
GPH. 0.035; D. base 0.036; GPW. 0.055 m.
Fig. 4; Pl. 14

Flat base with visible stringmarks; part of body flaring towards top of vessel. Green spots on interior and exterior; exterior slightly blackened.

Fine, clean light brown (7.5YR 6.5/4) clay, surfaces smoothed and plain. Wheelmade.

Polatlı, beginning in Level XI (*AnatSt* 1 [1951] 50, fig. 12:5); Ahlatlıbel (Ab. 560, *TTAED* 2 [1934] 27); Boğazköy, Nordwesthang-Büyükkale Level 9 (*Frühe Keramik*, 13, nos. 1-5, pls. 1, 7); Boğazköy Unterstadt Level 5 (*Heth. Keramik*, 114, no. 144, pl. 11); Beycesultan Level VIa (*Beycesultan* I, 236, fig. P.64:9).

JARS (54-57)

54 Jar or pitcher handle
P 5276   Mixed Level 7
GPH. 0.14; W. of handle 0.034 m.
Pl. 13

Handle fully preserved; broken where attached to wall. Surfaces somewhat worn and scratched.

Probably from large pitcher or two-handled jar.

Brown (5YR 4/4) clay, clean, with some "silver" mica. Surface and handle covered with highly lustrous dark brown (2.5YR 3/4) slip, burnished. Vessel wheelmade?

55 Miniature jar
P 5280   Level 7
H. 0.05; Est. D. rim 0.04; GTh. 0.007 m.
Fig. 4; Pl. 14

Mended section preserves part of rim, full height of wall, and part of base.

Small, closed, globular vessel with plain rim. On exterior wall between rim and greatest diameter, four shallow parallel ridges forming horizontal fluting, continuing around vessel in slightly torsional direction.

Orange (5YR 7/6) clay, fine and clean. Red-brown (10R 5/6) slip on rim and exterior, well smoothed and burnished. Base reserved. Handmade.

Perhaps a spouted jar, as Polatlı, unstratified example (*AnatSt* 1 [1951] 47, fig. 11b:3, pl. Vf); also unstratified teapot (?) from Boğazköy (*Frühe Keramik*, pl. 37:12).

56 Globular jar
P 5283a-d   Level 7
a Est. D. rim 0.20; GPL. 0.076; GPW. 0.0855; GTh. 0.01;
b GPL. 0.135 m; GPW. 0.11; GTh. 0.01;
c GPL. 0.08; GPW. 0.094; GTh. 0.009;
d GPL. 0.073; GPW. 0.063; GTh. 0.0075 m.
Fig. 4; Pl. 14

Four fragments of one or more vessels, consisting of: *a* rim and adjoining shoulder; *b* vertical handle and adjoining wall, mended from two joining sherds; *c* body sherd which probably belongs to same vessel as *a* and *b*, although nonjoining; *d* body sherd similar to *c* but more likely to be from another vessel of like shape and decoration. Fragments *a-c* slightly blackened on both surfaces. Some chips and incrustation.

Globular jar, base uncertain, "collared" neck flaring out slightly to plain rim. Vertical handles, oblong in section, on body at maximum diameter. Exterior below neck covered with tan slip and brown matt painted decoration: row of multiple chevrons, apex toward neck, continuing around handle area. Chevrons cross one another over body of vessel. Handle has single diagonal painted lines over upper surface.

Tan (7.5YR 6/6) clay, gritty, with some "gold" mica. Solid brown (2.5YR 5/4) matt paint on neck, both surfaces. Interior plain below neck. Handmade.

Polatlı Levels XV-XVII, XXII (*AnatSt* 1 [1951] 52, fig. 13: 1-8); Boğazköy, Nordwesthang-Büyükkale Level 9 (*Frühe Keramik*, 22, no. 65, pl. 5).

57 Hole-mouth jar
P 5278 Level 7
GPH. 0.12; Est. D. rim 0.32; GTh. 0.014 m.
Fig. 4; Pl. 14

Mended section preserves part of rim, adjoining wall, and base of horizontal handle. Interior surface incrusted, heavily worn and pitted.

Hole-mouth jar with fairly straight walls, plain rim slightly flattened across top. Handle, circular to oval in section, swings out from wall near rim. Restored in drawing as two-handled vessel.

Brown (5YR 6/3) clay, grit- and vegetal-tempered. Light brown (7.5YR 6/4) or tan slip on both surfaces, smoothed and matt on exterior. Handmade.

PITCHERS (58-61)

58 Pitcher[22]
P 2595 Level 7, in burned layer at -4.65 m.
H. 0.145; D. rim 0.077; D. 0.119; D. base 0.05 m.
Fig. 4; Pl. 15

Intact. Several abrasions; surface blackened from secondary burning.

Pitcher with short cylindrical neck, upturned spout, double conical body, flat base; handle from rim to shoulder.

Fine orange (7.5YR 6/6) clay, slightly gritty, fired gray at core. Red slip on exterior and interior to base of neck; burnish strokes visible over all. Handmade.

Compare Asarcık Level V (IstMitt 16 [1966] 64, fig. 4:1-2; Polatlı Level VI (AnatSt 1 [1951] 47, fig. 11b:7); Ahlatlıbel, with plastic ornament (TTAED 2 [1934] 27); Etiyokuşu, with plastic ornament (Etiyokuşu, fig. 74).

59 Pitcher
P 2606 Level 7, in burned layer at -4.65 m.
H. 0.365; D. 0.395; D. rim 0.16; D. base 0.11 m.
Fig. 4; Pl. 15

Almost fully preserved; mended to complete.

Short cylindrical neck, upturned spout, ovoid body; vertical handle from rim to shoulder.

Red clay, gritty; fired gray at core. Red-brown (7.5YR 5/4) slip mottled with cream on exterior and just inside rim, preserving oblique burnish strokes. Interior well smoothed. Handmade.

Ahlatlıbel (TTAED 2 [1934] 27); Etiyokuşu (Etiyokuşu, fig. 74).

60 Pitcher
P 3334 PN-3, earth fallen from scarps
GPL. 0.051; D. tube 0.014; Th. tube and handle 0.028 m.
Pl. 15

Tubular spout broken at body attachment and across handle.

Short tube, round in section, cut off obliquely at outer end. Small handle, round in section, attached at inner end of opening perpendicular to spout. Grooved decoration around spout at base of strut and tube; faceted spirally around handle.

Orange clay, fine and clean; fired light gray-brown at core. Red slip on exterior over clay-colored slip visible in grooves. Handmade.

61 Pitcher
P 5315 Level 7, Pits H and I
GPL. 0.071; GPW. 0.096; GTh. 0.0125 m.
Pl. 15

Single piece preserves part of rim and adjoining neck of pitcher with rising spout. Rim and exterior worn.

Fragment indicates cylindrical neck; rim everted and rolled outward from neck.

Brown clay, gritty. Dark red slip, smoothed and highly lustrous, on exterior rim and continuing just inside vessel. Remainder of interior finished with tan "self-slip." Handmade.

Asarcık Level V (IstMitt 16 [1966] 64, fig. 4:1-2; Polatlı Level VI (AnatSt 1 [1951] 47, fig. 11b:7); Ahlatlıbel, with plastic ornament (TTAED 2 [1934] 27); Etiyokuşu, with plastic ornament (Etiyokuşu, fig. 74).

PYXIS(?) (62)

62 Pyxis(?)
P 5312 Level 7, Pits H and I
H. 0.044; D. base 0.095; Est. D. upper opening 0.05 m.
Fig. 4; Pl. 15

Single piece preserves full height of vessel, and part of rim, interior base, and bottom. Broken on all sides. Surfaces worn and slightly incrusted.

Cylindrical vessel with flat base, flangelike rim at top and bottom; upper rim almost flat across top.

Fine, clean red clay. Upper rim, exterior, and base covered with red slip, burnished and glossy. Interior surface, cream to red slip, smoothed without luster. Handmade.

Asarcık Level V (IstMitt 16 [1966] 63, fig. 3:13); Ahlatlıbel (TTAED 2 [1934] 39).

SHERDS WITH PAINTED DECORATION (63 and 64)

63 Painted body sherd
P 5286 Level 7
GPL. 0.026; GPW. 0.032; GTh. 0.0065 m.
Pl. 15

Single body sherd, possibly from a small cup. Scratched and worn.

Interior surface decorated with red painted lines forming multiple chevrons; part of three preserved, pointing towards bottom of vessel. Not very neatly painted.

Tan-orange (7.5YR 6/6) clay, fine, with few gritty inclusions. Exterior with red slip preserving some luster. Interior with red paint on tan-slipped (7.5YR 6/4) surface. Handmade.

64 Painted body sherd
P 5288 Level 7
GPL. 0.059; GPW. 0.078; GTh. 0.006 m.
Fig. 4; Pl. 15

Single sherd from upper body wall of hemispherical or globular vessel. Some incrustation on interior; surfaces scratched and worn. Upper edge of sherd preserves transition to more vertical section, probably neck or shoulder.

On exterior extending to just below maximum diameter of vessel: net pattern of painted lines in brown with matt finish.

Orange clay (5YR 6/6), gritty, with some "gold" and "silver" mica. Exterior covered with light brown slip, painted decoration in dark brown. Interior plain. Wheelmade.

Alişar Levels 6M, 12T (OIP 28, fig. 233: d 138; fig. 235 c 366).

---

22. Previously published by R.S. Young, AJA 66 (1962) pl. 48, fig. 28.

SHERDS WITH GROOVED DECORATION (65-69)

65   Rim sherd
P 5284   Level 7
Est. D. rim 0.08; GPL. 0.025; GPW. 0.037; GTh. 0.004 m.
Fig. 4; Pl. 15
Sherd preserves rim and adjoining wall of cup or small bowl with gently curved profile, slightly outturned rim.
On exterior, grooved decoration in three lines forming reserved chevron, apex towards rim. On interior, red painted decoration on buff slip: thin bands extending from rim diagonally towards bottom of cup (part of two bands preserved).
Buff clay, fine, with some inclusions. Red slip on rim and exterior, lustrous. Interior surface covered with tan slip. Handmade.

66   Rim sherd
P 5297   Level 7, Pits H and I
Est. D. rim 0.065; GPL. 0.045; GPW. 0.053; GTh. 0.008 m.
Fig. 4; Pl. 15
Rim and adjoining wall of small closed vessel, probably jar or teapot. Surfaces slightly blackened, discolored. Rim plain.
On exterior just below rim, row of tiny oblique slashes; below on wall, two sets of parallel incised lines forming chevron, apex towards rim; bands thus formed contain row of oblique slashes. Incisions spaced at slightly irregular intervals.
Tan clay, gritty. Brown (2.5YR 5/4) slip on rim and exterior, smoothed and matt. Interior plain. Wheelmade.
Polatlı Level XII (AnatSt 1 [1951] 52, fig. 13:19); similar ornament on pitcher, Boğazköy, Nordwesthang-Büyükkale Level 9 (Frühe Keramik, 26, no. 116, pls. 13, 41a); related ornament in Beycesultan Level VIa (Beycesultan I, 250, fig. P.71:9).

67   Body sherd
P 5275   Mixed Level 7
GPH. 0.089; GPW. 0.108; GTh. 0.017 m.
Pl. 16
Sherd from upper wall of vessel, probably jar. Some dark discoloration on exterior.
Vessel with wide neck, large globular body; flaring out at neck.
On wall, three parallel grooves forming pendent semicircles, turning downward to right.
Brown (2.5YR 5/4) clay, coarse and gritty; some "silver" mica. Plum red slip, burnished, on both surfaces. Handmade.
Asarcık Level V (IstMitt 16 [1966] 67, fig. 7:6, 11).

68   Body sherd
P 5285   Mixed Level 7
GPL. 0.035; GPW. 0.036; GTh. 0.0065 m.
Fig. 4; Pl. 16
Mended section preserves part of wall from vessel, perhaps a teapot or jar.
On exterior, grooved decoration in three parallel lines forming reserved chevron. Interior solid red without decoration.
Orange clay, some inclusions. Both surfaces covered with red slip, burnished and lustrous. Handmade.

69   Body sherd
P 5299   Level 7, Pits H and I
GPL. 0.037; GPW. 0.019; GTh. 0.006 m.
Pl. 16
Body sherd of small vessel, broken on all sides. Some blackening on both surfaces. Most of surface slip rotted away.
Vessel shape unknown. Upper end of sherd surface smooth; remainder decorated with shallow grooved decoration, set in slight diagonal to left. Ridges ca. 2.8 mm. in width.

Tan clay with few gritty inclusions. Exterior covered with purplish brown slip, now worn but probably originally lustrous, preserved in several places. Interior surface plain, uneven. Handmade.
Similar ornament above brown painted panel: Polatlı Level XIX (AnatSt 1 [1951] 52, fig. 13:11).

SHERDS WITH RELIEF DECORATION (70-73)

70   Body sherd
P 5308   Level 7, Pits H and I
GPW. 0.07; GTh. 0.0085 m.
Fig. 4; Pl. 16
Single sherd broken on all four sides, from flat area of large vessel, perhaps a jar. Partly blackened on both surfaces.
On exterior, part of design modeled in low relief. Two parallel ridges, irregular, meet approximately in oval shape, resembling part of a petal design. Between ridges, lines, barely palpable, may represent uneven surface of vessel rather than intentional decoration.
Orange clay, very gritty. Interior preserves some orange slip, mostly rotted away. Exterior covered with slip mottled from red to brown, smoothed, with some luster preserved. Handmade.

71   Rim sherd
P 5282   Mixed Level 7
GPL. 0.046; GPW. 0.04; GTh. 0.0125 m.
Pl. 16
Rim and plastic decoration. Worn; lug damaged; some greenish discoloration.
From vessel of hemispherical form, upper wall rising almost vertically to plain rim. On exterior surface a plastic lug in the shape of a crescent extends onto and just above rim.
Orange-red (2.5YR 6/6) clay, gritty. Both surfaces covered with slip fired from tan to red (10R 5/6). Handmade.
Below, 72.

72   Rim sherd
P 5295   Level 7, Pits H and I
GPL. 0.062; GPW. 0.051; GTh. 0.0055 m.
Fig. 4; Pl. 16
Rim and adjoining upper wall. Some fresh chips on surface.
Bowl(?) with fairly straight sides, plain rim. On upper wall, plastic crescent of irregular relief, extending to just below rim. Slipped and smoothed as rest of surface.
Orange clay, gritty. Both surfaces covered with light orange red slip, smoothed, and preserve some luster. Handmade.
71, 72 Asarcık Level V (IstMitt 16 [1966] 61, fig. 1:8; 62, fig. 2:5,8); Karayavşan (AJA 70 [1966] 148; vessel on display in Museum of Anatolian Civilizations, Ankara); Demirci Hüyük (IstMitt 27/28 [1977/78] fig. 12:2, Phase L) and (IstMitt 30 [1980] pl. 4:5, Phase G); Boğazköy, Nordwesthang-Büyükkale Level 9 (Frühe Keramik, 25, nos. 97, 99-100; pls. 2, 12, 19); Alaca Hüyük (Alaca 1935, A1-758); Beycesultan Level VIb (Beycesultan I, 234, fig. P.63:4).

73   Rim sherd
P 5294   Level 7, Pits H and I
GPL. 0.058; GPW. 0.05; GTh. 0.006 m.
Pl. 16
Rim sherd and adjoining wall.
Possibly from bowl, but rim curves inward as if forming a trefoil mouth. Rim plain. On upper wall, part of a plastic addition, probably beginning of crescent lug: part of handle?
Light red (2.5YR 6/6) clay with gritty inclusions. Red (10R 6/6) slip on both surfaces, smoothed, with matt finish. Probably handmade.

BASE (74)

74 Base
P 5314   Level 7, Pits H and I
GPH. 0.02; GPW. 0.048; GTh. 0.005 m.
Fig. 5

Base and adjoining lower body, probably from small bowl or cup. Broken on all sides; scratched and slightly discolored.

In center of base a circular depression, *ca.* 0.015 m. across, as if pressed with index finger.

Light brown clay, fine and clean, with no visible inclusions. Both surfaces covered with red slip, smoothed and lustrous. Handmade.

Probably to be restored as a tiny dipper: Alaca Hüyük (*Alaca 1936*, pl. 71); Ahlatlıbel (Ab. 109, *Keramik aus Inneranatolien*, 124, no. 5/37, pl. 23).

HANDLES (75-78)

75 Horizontal handle
P 5277   Mixed Level 7
GPW. 0.173; Th. handle 0.025; GTh. 0.017 m.
Fig. 5; Pl. 16

Handle, broken from vessel wall on all sides. Blackening near edges; handle worn.

Shape probably large vessel with two horizontal handles. Horizontal handle, oval in section, swings upward at maximum diameter. Diagonal impression across lower surface of handle as if worn through by a string attaching vessel lid.

Light red (2.5YR 6/6) clay, gritty; exterior with red (10R 5/8) and tan mottled slip, originally lustrous. Hand-burnish strokes visible. Interior unslipped. Handmade.

Asarcık Level V (*IstMitt* 16 [1966] 66, fig. 6:2); Boğazköy, Nordwesthang-Büyükkale Level 9 (*Frühe Keramik*, 20, 27, nos. 48, 121-124, pls. 2-4).

76 Vertical loop handle
P 5301   Level 7, Pits H and I
GPL. 0.081; W. handle 0.028 m.
Fig. 5; Pl. 16

Handle, fully preserved, broken at either end and from place of attachment to vessel. Surfaces slightly incrusted. Slip worn, especially on ridges. Probably from a pitcher.

Handle forms vertical loop. On spine, series of diagonal parallel plastic ridges. Smoothed and free of ridges at upper and lower ends.

Orange (5YR 6/6) clay, gritty. Surfaces of handle and adjoining wall covered with plum red slip; smoothed, with matt finish. Handmade.

Polatlı Level XII, pitcher handle (*AnatSt* 1 [1951] 41, fig. 9b:10).

77 Vertical knobbed handle
P 5300   Level 7, Pits H and I
D. rim unknown; GPL. 0.061; W. handle 0.021 m.
Fig. 5; Pl. 16

Vertical handle, mended from two joining sherds; broken at either end at place of attachment. Preserves part of rim where handle attached, probably from pitcher. Surfaces slightly incrusted.

On spine of handle, vertical row of six knobs, pinched up from rim and handle and smoothed with rest of surface.

Orange (5YR 6/6) clay, gritty. Surfaces covered with cherry red slip, burnished, with some luster preserved.

78 Vertical handle
P 5307   Level 7, Pits H and I
D. rim unknown; GPL. 0.111; W. handle 0.0295 m.
Fig. 5; Pl. 16

Handle fragment mended from two joining sherds, preserves most of handle and part of adjoining rim of vessel, probably pitcher. Broken at lower end. Surfaces slightly incrusted and discolored.

On spine of handle, shallow vertical depression in center of area joining rim. Below this, shallow parallel grooves—two oblique, two horizontal—formed by impressing instrument; edges smoothed. Handle approximately round in section.

Light red (2.5YR 6/6) clay, gritty. Surfaces covered with red (10R 5/8) slip, smoothed.

SPINDLE WHORLS (79 and 80)

79 Spindle whorl
MC 185   Level 7
H. 0.015; D. 0.028; D. hole 0.006 m.
Fig. 5; Pl. 16

Almost fully preserved; one side broken.

Double convex whorl with maximum diameter off center. Incised around edges with three groups of concentric semicircles, six in each group.

Fine clay, fired gray at core and black at surfaces; well burnished.

Related incised decoration, Etiyokuşu Level II (EY 257, *Etiyokuşu*, 100-101, fig. 90). Similar form among examples. from the Hittite Cemetery (*Hitt. Cem.* 43, MC 84: pl. 24c,p and MC 86: pl. 24d,i).

80 Spindle whorl
MC 245   Level 7
H. 0.017; D. 0.023; D. hole 0.007 m.
Pl. 17

Complete. Squat spherical form. Decoration on surface in short incisions forming overlapping arches of multiple lines (four, five, and six). Single incised line around perforation at both ends.

Fine clay, fired gray and black; surfaces well smoothed and polished.

FIGURINE (81)

81 Animal figurine
T 125   Earth fallen from scarps
GPH. 0.043; W. of head 0.018 m.
Pl. 17

Neck and part of head preserved; broken across neck. Blackened area on top of snout and along neck behind right ear (from secondary burning?).

Head and neck of animal with snout, long neck; two ears formed by small plastic bumps. Right ear slightly larger than left.

Tan clay, gritty; light brown slip on surface. Handmade.

Possibly Middle or Late Bronze Age; resembles an unstratified example from Boğazköy (*Heth. Keramik*, 159, pl. 137, no. 1325).

NONCERAMIC ARTIFACTS (82 and 83)

82 Copper or bronze pin
B 1366   Top of Level 7
PL. 0.037; D. head 0.007; Th. shaft where round in section 0.0016 m.
Pl. 17

Slightly corroded; broken across shaft.

Straight shaft, round in section at top and flattened at tip. Spherical head, flattened on top, attached to shaft without visible join.

83   Stone blade
ST 467   Burned clay overlying Level 7 paving slabs
L. 0.067; W. 0.018; GTh. 0.005 m.
Pl. 17
Apparently complete; polished from use along both sides of cutting edges.
Thin straight flake, smooth on one face where percussion platform remains. Second face has two facets, one plain, other with secondary pressure flaking to sharpen.
White chert.

SOUNDING BENEATH MEGARON 12
84-96

LEVEL VI (84-96)

BOWLS (84-87)

84   Hemispherical bowl
Not inv.   Level VI
D. rim 0.13; GTh. 0.008 m.
Fig. 5
Rim sherd of bowl with hemispherical form, plain rim. Much of surface, especially exterior, blackened.
Medium clay with noticeable inclusions, fired orange at surface, black elsewhere. Red (10R 5/8) slip on rim and exterior surface; interior fired reddish brown. Handmade.

85   Hemispherical bowl
Not inv.   Level VI
D. rim 0.108; GTh. 0.004 m.
Fig. 5
Rim sherd of bowl with hemispherical form, plain rim. Exterior blackened in places.
Fine, gritty orange clay; well fired. Clay-colored slip on both surfaces. Handmade.

86   Hemispherical bowl
Not inv.   Level VI
Est. D. rim 0.20; GTh. 0.008 m.
Fig. 5
Rim sherd of bowl with hemispherical form, slightly incurved rim.
Orange-red (2.5YR 6/8) clay, gritty; well fired. Orange-red slip, or "self-slip," on both surfaces. Hand-burnish marks visible on exterior. Surfaces smoothed, with matt finish. Handmade.

87   Lug-handled bowl
P 228   Level VI, in pithos **92**
H. 0.122; D. rim 0.146 m.
Fig. 5; Pl. 17
Almost fully preserved; mended and restored to complete. Surfaces blackened and cracked.
Deep hemispherical form, flattened base, rim tapered on inside. Two small lug handles opposite one another below rim.
Brown (5YR 4/6) clay with many inclusions. Brown (5YR 4/4) slip on both surfaces; burnish strokes on exterior, and on interior near rim. Handmade.
Polatlı Level III (*AnatSt* 1 [1951] 43, fig. 10:5).

DIPPERS (88-91)

88   Dipper
P 225   Level VI, in pithos **92**
H. at rim 0.065-0.067; D. rim 0.153 m.
Fig. 5; Pl. 17

Circa one-half preserved; restored to complete.
Hemispherical form with tapered rim, flat off-center base. Vertical handle, concave in section, rises above rim.
Fine orange-red (2.5YR 5/8) clay with gritty inclusions. Red (2.5YR 6/8) slip on both surfaces, burnished over all; exterior lustrous. Handmade.
Polatlı Level XII (*AnatSt* 1 [1951] 38, fig. 7a:14); Demirci Hüyük Phase K (*IstMitt* 30 [1980] pl. 5:1); small example, red polished: Demirci Hüyük Phase L (*IstMitt* 29 [1979] fig. 11:5).

89   Dipper
P 226   Level VI, in pithos **92**
H. at rim 0.074; D. rim 0.155 m.
Fig. 5; Pl. 17
Mended to complete. Interior and base blackened.
Hemispherical form with round base, plain rim. Vertical handle, round in section, rises above rim; handle is angular in profile near lower end.
Fine red (2.5YR 5/6) clay with many inclusions. Red slip, mottled to red-brown and orange (2.5YR 5/8) on both surfaces. Horizontal and oblique burnish strokes visible; lustrous finish. Handmade.

90   Dipper
P 227   Level VI, in pithos **92**
H. at rim 0.081; D. rim 0.152 m.
Fig. 5; Pl. 17
Upper body with handle preserved; restored to complete with rounded base.
Hemispherical form with tapered rim. Vertical handle, oval in section, is angular on top.
Fine tan (2.5YR 6/4) clay, fired gray at core. Orange-red (2.5YR 5/8) slip both surfaces, burnished and lustrous. Handmade.

91   Dipper handle
P 5272   Level VI
GPH. 0.048; GPW. 0.057; Th. rim 0.006 m.
Fig. 5; Pl. 18
Single sherd preserves vertical handle and part of adjoining rim. Handle broken at both ends.
Handle, oblong in section, attached at rim and rises above at oblique angle.
Orange (5YR 6/6) clay, with some grit. Red (10R 5/6) slip, burnished, on both surfaces; well smoothed but little luster preserved. Handmade.
Polatlı Level XXX (*AnatSt* 1 [1951] 40, fig. 8a:1).

PITHOI (92 and 93)

92   Pithos
P 789   Level VI
H. 0.78; D. 0.63; D. rim 0.48; D. base 0.48 m.
Pl. 18
Circa one-half preserved; mended and restored.
Short cylindrical neck with slightly everted rim; oval body, flat base. At shoulder two horizontal loop handles, concave in section.
Brown clay with many gritty inclusions. Red slip on exterior, burnished; interior slipped brown, well smoothed. Handmade.
Related to example from Beycesultan Level VII (*Beycesultan* I, 232, fig. P. 62:2).

93   Pithos(?)
P 5273   Level VI
GPL. 0.103; GPW. 0.091; GTh. 0.012 m.
Fig. 5; Pl. 18
Rim sherd and adjoining wall. Blackened on exterior, on interior near rim. Surfaces worn, slightly incrusted.

Large, straight-sided vessel, flat rim. Row of impressed circles *ca.* 0.01 m. below rim on exterior, as if pressed by index finger, continues across sherd; three and one-half impressions preserved.

Reddish brown (5YR 4/6) clay, very gritty; some "gold" mica. Exterior originally slipped? Surface now matt. Handmade.

Polatlı Levels XVI, XXX (*AnatSt* 1 [1951] 43, fig. 10:3, 10); Asarcık Level V (*IstMitt* 16 [1966] 68, fig. 8:3); Boğazköy, Nordwesthang-Büyükkale Level 9 (*Frühe Keramik*, 29, nos. 159-163, pls. 7, 16); Beycesultan Level VIII (*Beycesultan* I, 232, fig. P.62:1).

PITCHER (94)

94 Pitcher
P 229 Level VI, inside pithos **92**
H. 0.119; Max. D. 0.085 m.
Fig. 5; Pl. 18
Intact, with a few cracks and chips mended with plaster; spout chipped. Blackened around base.

Tall narrow neck with beaked spout, double conical body, flattened base. Vessel leans in direction of spout. Vertical handle with angular profile extends from rim to shoulder.

Fine orange (5YR 6/6) clay, slightly gritty. Brown (5YR 4/4) slip, mottled to reddish brown (5YR 4/6), on exterior and inside spout; lustrous finish, burnish strokes visible. Handmade.

Related to Demirci Hüyük Phase K (*IstMitt* 29 [1979] fig. 12:1); similar shape but much larger, Asarcık Level V (*IstMitt* 16 [1966] 64, fig. 4:3).

PAN (95)

95 Pan
P 5274 Level VI
H. 0.054; D. rim unknown; GPW. 0.067 m.
Fig. 5; Pl. 18
Rim sherd preserves adjoining wall and complete profile with part of base. Some blackening on rim and base; base eroded. Grayed on interior rim.

Shallow vessel with flat base; interior bottom flat.

Coarse brown clay, grit- and vegetal-tempered. Claycolored "slip" covering both surfaces; roughly finished. Handmade.

Above, **43** and **44**, with comparanda.

LID (96)

96 Lid
P 230 Level VI, in pithos **92**
H. 0.091; Est. D. 0.235 m.
Fig. 5; Pl. 18
Circa one-third preserved; mended and restored to complete. Blackened in places on both surfaces.

Circular form with rounded edge; handle, approximately round in section, across top center. Steam hole formed by irregular perforation to one side of handle, away from which handle leans slightly.

Buff (7.5YR 7/4) clay, gritty. Light brown (7.5YR 6/4) slip, unevenly applied, on exterior; burnish strokes visible. Interior also slipped, now worn and cracked. Handmade.

Etiyokuşu (EY 153, *Etiyokuşu*, fig. 97); Boğazköy, Nordwesthang-Büyükkale Level 9 (*Frühe Keramik*, 30, nos. 165-166, pls. 4, 16); Alaca Hüyük (*Alaca 1935*, pl. 77; *Alaca 1937-1939*, fig. 26); Karataş-Semayük, Early Bronze III

(*AJA* 72 [1968] 253, pl. 82, fig. 21); Tarsus Early Bronze III (*Tarsus* II, 157, nos. 644, 645, fig. 279); Aphrodisias (*AJA* 75 [1971] pl. 30, fig. 41).

SOUNDING BENEATH MEGARON 10
97 and 98

LAYER 15 (97)

BOWL (97)

97 Painted bowl
P 5462 Layer 15
D. rim *ca.* 0.20; GPL. 0.055; GPW. 0.0585; GTh. 0.095 m.
Fig. 6; Pl. 18
Rim sherd and adjoining wall of bowl with plain, slightly incurved rim. Both surfaces worn, slightly incrusted. Rim chipped.

On inner surface, red paint around rim circumference, from which bands of red paint *ca.* 0.012 m. in width form triangles, with base of triangle at rim; part of three bands preserved.

Orange-buff (7.5YR 6/6) clay, gritty; some "gold" mica. Exterior and inner rim covered with red slip, smoothed and polished; some luster preserved. Interior covered with tan (7.5YR 7/4) slip (or "self-slip"), decorated with solid red paint. Handmade; fired gray at core.

Polatlı Level XVI (*AnatSt* 1 [1951] 52, fig. 13:17).

LAYER 16 (98)

DIPPER (98)

98 Dipper handle
Not inv. Layer 16
GPL. 0.0585; W. handle 0.0145 m.
Pl. 18
Loop handle, preserved in full, probably from rim of dipper. Handle oval or subrectangular in section.

Orange (5YR 6/6) clay, gritty; fired gray at core. All surfaces covered with red (10R 5/8) slip, worn but well smoothed and polished.

EARLY BRONZE FINDS FROM
MISCELLANEOUS CONTEXTS
99-101

BOWL (99)

99 Painted bowl
P 3703 Above open area north of TB 8: Hellenistic well, masonry lining
GPH. 0.08; Est. D. rim 0.18; GPW. 0.105 m.
Fig. 6; Pl. 19
Single large rim sherd from hemispherical bowl with plain rim.

Red (2.5YR 5/6) slip on exterior and rim. Interior slipped red with light red stripes hung from rim, forming multiple chevrons. Both surfaces well smoothed and polished; handburnish strokes visible.

Light reddish brown (5YR 6/4) clay with gritty inclusions, medium ware; fired gray at core. Handmade.

INCISED SHERD (100)

100   Incised sherd
P 3610   Megaron 6, leveling-up fill against NE wall
GPW. 0.054; GPL. 0.0435; GTh. 0.0055 m.
Fig. 6; Pl. 19

Sherd from shoulder of closed shape, probably jar. Broken on all sides.

Shoulder rounded, wide spherical or ovoid body. Interior surface preserves finger impressions made while clay wet; these are not smoothed over, suggesting a rather small closed shape difficult to reach inside to smooth interior. On exterior incised decoration: standing triangle formed by triple outline.

Fine brown (5YR 5/3) clay, fired grayish on interior. Plum red slip on exterior, well smoothed and highly burnished. Fired grayish on inside surface. Handmade.

FIGURINE (101)

101   Animal figurine
T 98   Above cella of TB 8, pit in floor 4 (above Clay Layer)
GPH. 0.035; GPL. 0.057; GPW. 0.032 m.
Pl. 19

Lacking head and lower parts of four legs; mended at center. Animal figurine, quadruped of unidentifiable species.

Coarse gritty clay, slipped and originally polished; fired black throughout

Compare "Copper Age" animal figurines from Alişar Hüyük (*OIP* 28, 182, fig. 185).

Middle and Late Bronze Age Pottery

Ceramic finds dating to the Middle and Late Bronze Ages were recovered from the sounding below Megaron 10, in Layers 18-5. The sounding below Megaron 12 produced pottery of Middle to Late Bronze Age date in Level VC-VA, above the Early Bronze Age occupation in Level VI. In both soundings, the end of Late Bronze Age occupation was signaled by an overlying layer containing a few examples of handmade tan and gray pottery (Megaron 10 Layer 4 and Megaron 12 Level IVB). These latter levels are transitional between Late Bronze and Early Iron Age occupation. Since their associated pottery consists almost exclusively of Late Bronze Age types, these later levels have been included in this chapter which charts Middle and Late Bronze Age ceramic developments at Gordion.

Analysis of the Material

Middle and Late Bronze Age levels have produced approximately 7,000 sherds, and a few well-preserved or restorable vessels. The bulk of the ceramic finds from both soundings consists of very fragmentary samples. As with fragmentary material from the Early Bronze levels, the selection of items for inclusion in the catalogue is confined principally to diagnostic sherds illustrating rim, profile, base, or handle developments, or painted, applied, or incised ornament. A selection of examples from each level illustrates the principal shapes represented. Additional information on the individual assemblages, including mention of items too fragmentary to be catalogued, is given in the description of material recovered from each level.

Examples located or recorded in 1985 could not be incorporated into the catalogue sequence. These have been grouped as Supplementary entries, given a number beginning with **S**, and listed separately at the end of the catalogue in chapter III (pp. 85-91). The information they contribute to the assemblage from each level is included in the description of each level in the two deep soundings.

Most of the pottery from these levels is extremely fragmentary; about 70% of the collection from each level consists of body sherds of unknown shapes. Diagnostic sherds generally can be assigned to broad shape categories, but many resist classification and most leave uncertain the original appearance of the complete vessel. As a result, it is often difficult to match Gordion fragments with better-preserved specimens from other sites without the risk of introducing misleading comparisons. Specific parallels for individual items are given in catalogue entries only for those vessels or diagnostic features that are sufficiently well preserved or distinctive to support detailed comparisons. The relationship of the Gordion material to broader ceramic categories of this period in Anatolia is outlined in the following descriptions of fabrics, shapes, and forms of decoration. This analysis provides the basis for the external correlations and chronology proposed at the end of this chapter.

Description of the Pottery

FABRICS

The introduction of wheelmade pottery marks the beginning of the Middle Bronze Age in central Anatolia and, accordingly, at Gordion. The ceramic repertory of the second-millennium levels displays a continuity in fabrics and shapes, and thus is treated as a unit.

WHEELMADE BUFF

This category forms the principal fabric throughout the second-millenium levels. Two wares are distinguished here, the basic buff and the red-slipped variant.

WHEELMADE BUFF AND ORANGE

This fabric, basically identical with the ware of the red-slipped fabric, first appears in Middle Bronze contexts (Megaron 10 Layer 17). As the red slip is gradually given up, it becomes the dominant ware in the Late Bronze Age (Megaron 10 Layers 11-5, Megaron 12 Levels VB-VA) and Transitional levels (Layer 4, Level IVB). It is of micaceous clay, fired buff to orange (Munsell 7.5YR 7/4, 10YR 7/3, 2.5YR 6/6, 5YR 6/6), often lighter at the surface. A small percentage of examples in all levels is fine and thin-walled, of clean, well-fired clay with no visible temper. These examples are usually finished with a "self-slip" of clean clay which adheres well to the surfaces and is customarily smoothed and polished. Medium ware examples are consistently gritty in temper, containing inclusions ranging from 2-5 mm. in size. Such vessels are sometimes "self-slipped" but more often simply fired without further surface treatment. Buff and orange pottery becomes increasingly coarse in temper during the second millennium. By the latest Bronze Age levels of the Megaron 10 and Megaron 12 sequences, this ware is normally very gritty in temper, smoothed only in cursory fashion, and often fired gray at the core.

The characteristic shape in this fabric is the shallow bowl or plate. Other shapes include bowls, jars, pitchers, pithoi, and lids. Decoration may be stamped or incised. Zoomorphic vessels and figurines also occur. Individual examples are discussed below under the appropriate shape or type categories.

The general affinities of the wheelmade buff and orange fabric are with those of Middle and Late Bronze Age levels from Boğazköy, Alaca Hüyük, and Tarsus, supplemented by more recent excavations at Korucutepe, Maşat Hüyük, and Porsuk.[1]

WHEELMADE RED-SLIPPED

This category, the so-called "Hittite" pottery, forms the principal ware in the Middle Bronze Age levels and continues to appear, although in decreasing quantities, throughout the Late Bronze Age. The clay is tan, orange, or light red in color (Munsell 2.5YR 6/6, 7.5YR 6/6-7/6, 5YR 6/6), often micaceous, and usually contains sandy or gritty temper, rarely vegetal. Surfaces are finished with a slip fired red to brown (Munsell 10R 6/8, 5YR 5/8, 2.5YR 6/4), customarily well smoothed and polished with a lustrous finish; wheel-burnishing marks are occasionally preserved. In Middle Bronze levels, open vessels of this fabric are most often slipped on both surfaces. During the Late Bronze Age there is a tendency increasingly to cover only the exterior or part of the exterior of a vessel—normally upper body, rim, and handles—with a slip. Fine and medium wares are distinguished on the basis of temper. Fine examples are of clean, well-fired clay, thin-walled, with no visible gritty inclusions. Medium designates samples with consistently gritty temper, the inclusions ranging from 2-5 mm. in size. Red-slipped and polished wares occur in a variety of shapes, principally bowls, jars, and pitchers. There is some plastic, impressed, or incised decoration on the pottery, but it is rare. Zoomorphic vessels and attachments are represented in some samples. Specific examples are listed below in the descriptions of vessel shapes and types.

Red- or brown-slipped and burnished "Hittite" pottery has been identified as a distinctive category since the initial investigations at Boğazköy, followed by excavations at Alişar Hüyük, Kültepe, and Tarsus.[2]

WHEELMADE BUFF-SLIPPED "ENAMEL" WARE

A few sherds of buff and orange fabric are distinguished by a thick cream or pale buff slip with lustrous, "enamel" finish on the exterior (320, 358) or on both surfaces (419). They are of exceptionally fine, clean clay and differ from the standard buff and orange products also in their unusual shapes (320, jar with flanged handle; 358, cup or beaker; 419, sharply carinated bowl). A flask fragment from Megaron 10 Layer 1 (584) may belong to the same group, and is likewise from a shape rare at Gordion. These examples may represent a category of white- or cream-slipped ware known from Kültepe and Boğazköy, and from Late Bronze II levels at Tarsus.[3]

Another pale buff-slipped specimen is a fine bowl from Megaron 10 Layer 14 (166). Its distinctive "clinky" sound produced when sherds are tapped together links it with fragments of a large oval vessel

1. *Heth. Keramik*, esp. 31-32, 34-84, describes the pottery and its sequence at Boğazköy, reviewing also the relevant material from Alaca Hüyük, Tarsus, Beycesultan, and other second-millennium sites. Also *Korucutepe* 3, 5-6, 70-76; *Porsuk* I, 23-25, 29-39; *Maşat* II, 95-110.

2. *Heth. Keramik*, 10-32, 34-84, reviews the history of investigation of "Hittite" pottery and its development at Boğazköy, also A. C. Gunter,

"The Old Assyrian Colony Period Settlement at Boğazköy-Hattuša in Central Turkey: A Chronological Reassessment of the Archaeological Remains," Ph.D. diss. (Columbia University 1980), 62-89. The use of the term "Hittite" for archaeological remains is discussed below, pp. 103-105, with further references.

3. *Kültepe-Kaniş* II, pl. F:1-2; *Heth. Keramik*, 32; *Tarsus* II, 203.

from Megaron 12 Level VA (not catalogued). The fabric of the Level VA sample is also unusual in having a gray core; it is almost certainly an import.[4]

PAINTED WARES

Pottery with painted decoration forms only a small percentage of the second-millennium ceramic assemblage. The principal type is a red-on-buff ware with geometric designs—net pattern or solid triangles—on the vessel exterior. Examples from Gordion are found in well-stratified contexts in Megaron 10 Layers 8-7 (**270, 332, 333**). Additional specimens come from miscellaneous contexts (**515, 516**). Since the painted group is rare and generally very fragmentary, few shapes are clearly documented: one is a jar (**270**), another a handled vessel, probably a jar or a teapot (**515**). A Bronze Age painted fragment from a 6th-5th century context (North Central Trench Level IIB) documents a carinated bowl with thickened rim, similar in profile to an unpainted example from Megaron 10 Layer 10 (**232**). The paint is matt red (Munsell 10R 5/6, 5YR 5/6), often somewhat carelessly applied, on a buff or cream slip (Munsell 10YR 8/2, 7.5YR 7/4) which covers the gritty buff clay of the vessel. This decoration appears on the buff and orange wheelmade fabric described above, which is the common ware of all Hittite pottery with the exception of cooking pots.

Pottery painted in red geometric patterns on a cream or buff surface is represented in Hittite Empire levels at Boğazköy (Büyükkale Level III), Maşat Hüyük Level I, and Korucutepe Phase I.[5]

Three other examples also display red painted decoration, but should be distinguished from the group just described. Two sherds have a cream-slipped exterior and a solid red band *ca.* 0.01 m. wide (Megaron 10 Layer 10, **252**; Layer 7, **331**). In their fine, clean clay, careful execution, and painted design, they differ from the patterned red-on-buff group. From Megaron 10 Layer 13 is a jar with vertical handle (**202**), painted in a solid red zone above the handle.

A sherd with dark brown painted decoration from Megaron 10 Layer 13 (**203**) may be an import from North Syria, as related specimens form Boğazköy and Kültepe suggest. Another unusual piece is a buff-slipped sherd with brown zone, from Megaron 10 Layer 7 (**S41**). Its unusually smooth, matt surfaces also suggest nonlocal manufacture.[6]

COOKING POT WARE

This fabric forms a small but distinct category, appearing in a restricted range of shapes throughout the Middle and Late Bronze Age levels of both soundings. The clay is coarse with gritty temper, often with large flakes of "gold" mica, and contains inclusions larger than 5 mm. Normally the exterior is covered with a thin clay-colored "self-slip," frequently cracked and flaking. Both clay and slip are brown or reddish brown (Munsell 2.5YR 5/4, 5YR 6/4), fired dark, often black, at the core. Most examples are blackened or smoke-stained from use. The typical shape is a two-handled jar of hole-mouth form, or with thickened rim; handle shapes show some development.

Cooking pot ware is well represented as a distinct ceramic category at other second-millennium sites in Anatolia, where it likewise appears in a restricted range of shapes.[7]

WHEELMADE BUFF OR ORANGE MICACEOUS

A small group of ceramic fragments is characterized by a biscuit or surface displaying a heavy concentration of "silver" mica. Examples are fired buff (Munsell 7.5YR 7/4) or orange (5YR 6/6). Usually the exterior is carefully finished, with a clay-colored, light brown, or red slip, often burnished; the interior is left plain or simply smoothed. The "silver" mica concentration on the surface can be distinguished from the mica film or slip that occurs frequently on the Phrygian pottery from Gordion. The earlier, pre-Phrygian group is also distinguished by its shapes. Only a few display any overlap with the types favored among the wheelmade buff wares of Hittite tradition, such as the plate (**354**), and the jar with lid rest (**340**). The other examples of the fabric represent a different repertory: bowls with profile indented below the rim (**390**), which is sometimes flat; a small jar with trefoil rim (**S60**); a jar or wide-mouthed jug (**398**). Samples with "silver" micaceous biscuit or surface concentration appear only in Megaron 10 Layers 6-4 (**340, 354, 390, 391, 394, 398, S60, S62**), Megaron 12 Level IVB (**S65**), and in the overlying Iron Age levels in both soundings (**542, 545, 553, 582, 583, 585**).

Since clay sources with similar mineral components were extensively exploited for manufacture of Phrygian pottery at Gordion, the heavy "silver" mica content alone does not call for interpretation of these pieces as imports. Yet local production seems unlikely

4. White- or buff-slipped examples of local manufacture are not especially fine nor are they fired gray at the core.

5. *Heth. Keramik*, 32-34; *Maşat* II, fig. 32; *Korucutepe* 3, 6 and 74 with pls. 14C, 27G.

6. References cited in catalogue, under **203**. Also C. Hamlin, "The

Habur Ware Ceramic Assemblage of Northern Mesopotamia: An Analysis of Its Distribution," Ph.D. dissertation (University of Pennsylvania 1971) 1-5, 253-255, with rich bibliography. A fragmentary example of Habur ware from Boğazköy, Unterstadt 4 (*Heth. Keramik* 151, no. 1147, pl. 125).

7. References cited below under cooking pots, p. 34 with n. 42.

at least for the initial examples because of their small quantity and difference in fabric and surface treatment from the prevailing ceramic tradition at the site. Moreover, a source for the pottery in terms of a regional home is suggested by examples related in fabric and shape recovered from surface surveys in the Akhisar-Manisa area of western Anatolia, dated generally to the late second millennium.[8] The importance of the group in the overall sequence at Gordion is analyzed in a preliminary way in the section on internal chronology (pp. 46-47) and in chapter IV (pp. 92-101).

WHEELMADE TAN OR ORANGE COARSE

A few examples from Megaron 12 Level IVB are of gritty fabric (**S64**, **S66-S68**). They are distinguished from the standard local buff and orange wheelmade ware principally by their coarse, dense manufacture and generally darker hues. Their shapes display some overlap with prevailing Hittite forms (shallow bowl, **S66**; jar with broad rim indented on the upper surface, **S68**). The other examples of the Level IVB group are not paralleled among the pottery from the Late Bronze Age levels: heavy bowl (**S64**); small hole-mouth jar (**S67**). Whether these few samples constitute a distinct fabric is uncertain, but they merit isolation from the dominant local ceramic tradition.[9]

HANDMADE TAN AND GRAY

This group is catalogued comprehensively as "Early Phrygian Handmade" ware and analyzed in detail in the forthcoming volume by G. Kenneth Sams on the Pre-Kimmerian Phrygian pottery at Gordion.[10] Only a brief mention of this fabric is, therefore, included here. The handmade pottery is usually coarse and gritty, fired tan, dark gray, or intermediate shades. Surfaces may be left plain, smoothed, or slipped. Characteristic of this group is decoration on rim or body, often in a row of incised or impressed designs; plastic ornament also occurs.

A few examples of the handmade group first appear in the transitional levels, Megaron 10 Layer 4 and Megaron 12 Level IVB, in assemblages dominated by Late Bronze Age buff and orange wares. Samples continue to appear in Early Iron Age levels, always a minority and in very small quantities. The general af-finities of the handmade pottery with alien ceramic products of Troy Level VIIb2 have been observed by M. J. Mellink.[11] More recent excavations of Late Bronze and Early Iron Age levels at sites in Greece, Bulgaria, and Yugoslavia reveal a related phenomenon, whose precise relationships are beginning to be defined and understood.[12]

SHAPES

Given the fragmentary nature of the pottery and the limited corpus produced from the soundings, no detailed typology can be attempted here. Most diagnostic sherds, unless unusually well preserved or of distinctive types, allow no more than rudimentary identifications, and uncertainty regarding classification is a frequent problem. Samples have been assigned to broad shape categories, aided by comparisons with better-preserved vessels in ceramic sequences excavated at Kültepe, Alişar, Boğazköy, and Tarsus. Within each shape division, more detailed classification and internal chronology are based principally on the Megaron 10 sequence. In general, the Gordion pottery displays close affinities with the repertory of Hittite shapes recovered from the sites noted above and others in central and southeastern Anatolia. Further excavations at Gordion should produce additional material from suitably stratified contexts, enabling a more refined classification and more detailed comparisons with other excavated sequences.

The order of presentation in the catalogue, within each level as appropriate, is in the following sequence.

BOWLS

Bowls, generally open hemispherical vessels with rim diameters greater than 0.10 m., form the dominant category in all second-millennium levels. Since evidence for complete shapes is meager, bowls, as defined here, may overlap with vessel types distinguished from bowls in larger, better-preserved assemblages from other Bronze Age Anatolian sites.[13]

A sequence of shapes and characteristic surface treatment, defined principally by rim sherds, can be discerned in both soundings.

---

8. D. H. French, *AnatSt* 17 (1967) 64-65; *AnatSt* 19 (1969) 72; ware listed as "second millennium buff." My thanks to D. H. French for discussing the material with me and permitting me to examine samples from the survey collection, now housed in the British Institute of Archaeology at Ankara.

9. G. K. Sams, personal communication, notes that these pots may not belong to the Phrygian categories.

10. *Ibid.*

11. *BibOr* 17 (1960) 251.

12. H. A. Bankoff and F. A. Winter, *JIES* 12 (1984) 1-30, with extensive bibliography. The chronology of the Gordion handmade group is presented in the forthcoming volume by G. K. Sams, together with an assessment of its significance for local ceramic developments. See also below, pp. 92-95.

13. *Heth. Keramik*, 63-68, encompassing bowls and a subdivision of generally large, deep open vessels distinguished as *Schüsseln*. See also below, p. 31 n. 17.

Among carinated bowls, a few distinct types can be recognized. A common one is the carinated bowl, partially or entirely red-slipped, with thickened rim and upswung horizontal handles; it is introduced in Megaron 10 Layers 17 and 16 (**109, 110, 120**). Fragments in Layers 17-15 displaying a similar carinated profile and thickened rim, but without evidence for handles, may belong to bowls of this type (**108, 118, 119, 136-140**). The type continues, generally with sloping rim, in Megaron 10 Layers 11-7 (**217, 231, 232, 268, 301-303, S26, S27**) and in Megaron 12 Level VC (**409**). Examples with buff-slipped surfaces from Megaron 10 Layer 14 (**174-176**) and one without slip from Layer 13 (**194**) may represent a handleless variety. A well-preserved example of the two-handled type was found in the Hittite Cemetery.[14] It is well known from other sites in central and western Anatolia, particularly in Middle Bronze levels.[15]

Carinated bowls with thickened, sloping rim, partially red-slipped or plain, are a standard component of the bowl repertory in Megaron 10 Layers 12-7 (**227, 228, 230, 297, 298, S19**) and Megaron 12 Level VC-VA (**406, 408, 453**). They may indicate a substantial presence of the two-handled type attested in some of these levels.[16] Several carinated specimens (**229, 267, 299, 407**) may belong to examples of the deep bowls or *Schüsseln* popular at Boğazköy during most of the second millennium.[17]

Another carinated type, usually with partial red slip, has an upper wall that is vertical (**107, 133-135**, perhaps **419**) or angled slightly inwards (**171, 172**), and a plain rim. A carinated bowl from Megaron 10 Layer 11 (**216**) has a narrow vertical ridge from rim to carination, a feature paralleled on bowls from Polatlı, Asarcık, and Ilıca.[18]

Bowls without carination may also be subdivided. Fine red-slipped bowls with incurved rim appear in Megaron 10 Layers 18-15 (**102, 106, 129**). Red-slipped bowls with curved profile and thickened rim (**132, 400**) represent a type with a wide distribution in Middle Bronze contexts in central and southwestern Anatolia.[19] Buff or orange bowls with plain or thick-

ened rim are found in Megaron 10 Layers 15-12 (**130, 159-162, 193, 204, S8, S13, S14**). Similar bowls, plain or partially red-slipped, occur in several burials of the Hittite Cemetery, with rounded (**494, 495**), pointed, or slightly raised (**496**) base.[20] Fine examples with partial red slip are found in Megaron 10 Layers 15, 14 and 11 (**129, 158, 212**) and Megaron 12 Level VB (**423**); **255** and **422** are spiral-burnished. In Megaron 10 Layer 14 there are red- or brown-slipped bowls with everted rim (**168, 169**); shallower bowls with everted rim, matt buff-slipped or unslipped, are in Layers 10 and 7 (**224, 296**). Fine buff bowls appear in Megaron 10 Layers 5-4 (**348, 385, S51**).

Two groups enjoy long lives in both soundings, becoming the most common varieties in the later levels. One consists of handleless bowls with inverted rim, occurring with red or buff slip or with plain, often wheelmarked surfaces. Examples begin in Megaron 10 Layer 14 (**163-165, S3**) and continue in Layers 11-4 (**214, 233, 234, 260-262, 288, 290, 293, 294, 387, 388, S15, S43, S45, S46**); they also appear in Megaron 12 Levels VC-IVB (**403, 425-430, 432, 448, 451, 478, 479**). Rim diameters are generally between 0.23-0.30 m. There is a general trend towards shallower forms and increasingly thick, vertical rims. By the latest levels of both soundings, red-slipped versions are extremely rare; these bowls share the plain, heavily wheelmarked surfaces of other ceramic products of the latest levels. A late variant of the inverted rim group has a rim that overhangs the upper wall of the bowl, thus projecting both above and below the upper wall (Megaron 10 Layers 7-6 and 4: **290, 292, 389, S46**).

Bowls with inverted rim display some overlap with the broad-rimmed group described below and especially with the shallow vessels classified separately as plates; as small fragments they can be difficult to orient correctly and thus to assign to a particular category. Bowls with inverted rim are a category well represented at a number of central and southern Anatolian sites.[21]

The second group has a thickened, generally broad rim, and surfaces either left unslipped or finished with red or buff slip (Megaron 10 Layers 12-4: **213, 215, 223,**

14. *Hitt. Cem.*, 27, pls. 15b, 29b.

15. Polatlı Level XXIV [*AnatSt* 1 [1951] 40, fig. 8b:5, 8; Asarcık Level IV (*IstMitt* 16 [1966] 71, fig. 11:1, 2); Boğazköy, Nordwesthang-Büyükkale Level 8a (*Heth. Keramik*, 144, no. 956, pl. 108; *Nordwesthang-Büyükkale*, 44, no. 35, pl. 24); *Maşat* Level V (*Maşat* II, fig. F:5-10); Beycesultan Levels V and IVb (*Beycesultan* II, 86, fig. P.2:4; 120, fig. P.24:24). For fragments without evidence for handles, compare example from Boğazköy, Nordwesthang-Büyükkale Level 8a (*Nordwesthang-Büyükkale*, 44, no. 30, pl. 24), and from Beycesultan Level V (*Beycesultan* II, 84, fig. P.1:15, with reddish buff wash).

16. Compare handleless bowls with similar profile from Asarcık, unstratified (*IstMitt* 16 [1966] 87, fig. 27:10); Boğazköy, Unterstadt Level 3 and Büyükkale Level IVc (*Heth. Keramik*, 142, nos. 901, 904,

pl. 99); Maşat Levels V and III (*Maşat* II, figs. 40, B:23); also Porsuk Level V (*Porsuk* I, 47, no. 97, pl. 16).

17. Boğazköy, Unterstadt Level 3 (*Boğazköy* VI, 78, fig. 11:109; 81, fig. 13:116); Büyükkale Level IVb (*Heth. Keramik*, 144, no. 972, pl. 109).

18. References cited in catalogue, under **216**.

19. References cited in catalogue, under **400**.

20. Additional examples: *Hitt. Cem.*, 27-28, pls. 15d-l, 16a-d, 30a-g.

21. Boğazköy, perhaps beginning in Unterstadt Level 4 (*Heth. Keramik*, 139, no. 760, pl. 88, slipped); Unterstadt Level 3, unslipped or partially slipped, with variations in rim (*Boğazköy* VI, 76, fig. 10b:65; 79, fig. 12:90-91, 95, 97-98); Beycesultan Level IVa, red-slipped (*Beycesultan* II, 134, fig. P.33:36); Asarcık, unslipped examples, unstratified (*IstMitt* 16 [1966] 87, fig. 27:2, 7, 9); Maşat Level I, unslipped (*Maşat* II, figs. A:1-2 and 25; pl. 101, for a suggestion that some bowls with sharply inverted rim were used as lids).

225, 259, 263, 287, 291, 295, 296, S16-S18, S36; Megaron 12 Levels VC- IVB: 402, 404, 431, 452, 474, 477). The lip may be rounded or angular. Bowls are hemispherical or shallow; rim diameters range from 0.23-0.36 m. By the later levels of both soundings, the bowls are generally quite shallow, their rims less broad (351, 384, 473, 475, 476 , 480, S47, S53, S54). A few very shallow examples, such as S52 and S66, closely resemble in form and gritty, wheelmarked ware the vessels grouped below as plates. The red slip gradually yields entirely to buff slip or to unadorned, strongly wheelmarked surface treatment. Two examples of the bowl with thickened, broad rim occur in the Hittite Cemetery.[22] This general type also appears at other sites in central Anatolia.[23]

A few unusual forms deserve note. Ridged decoration on the outer wall or rim of bowls is a feature of Megaron 10 Layer 8 (264, 265). A spouted bowl with horizontal handle from the same layer (269) is a rare type.[24] Also from Layer 8 is a votive bowl (277) with close parallels at most Hittite Empire centers.[25] A red-slipped vessel with vertical handle, a bowl or jar, appears in Megaron 10 Layer 7 (S37). Sieved bowls, or colanders, found in Megaron 10 Layers 7 and 6 (300, 339), represent a vessel type known from second-millennium levels at Beycesultan, Tarsus, and Korucutepe.[26]

Several examples from Megaron 10 Layer 4 and Megaron 12 Layer IVB differ from earlier and contemporary bowl fashions both in their profiles and in their heavily micaceous fabric (390, 391, S64, S65). They are related in fabric to a small group of vessels from Megaron 10 Layers 6-4 (340, 354, 394, 398, S60, S62). Bowls similar in profile and fabric to 390 and S65 have been recovered from Megaron 10 Layers 2-1 (545, 553, 569, 578).

There is little evidence for the lower part of bowls. Examples with ring base and red-slipped interior appear in Megaron 10 Layers 17-13 (104, 111, 178) and in Megaron 12 Level VB (fragment, not catalogued), and seem to represent a relatively short-lived type. A bowl with red-slipped interior on a pedestal base, 105, is a re-lated form.[27] Pedestal base fragments from Megaron 10 Layers 16-15 (126, S2) could belong to bowls on tall pedestals, a type from Polatlı, Beycesultan, and Tarsus.[28] A tan ring base fragment smoothed on the vessel interior (149) probably belongs to a bowl. Disk base fragments, probably from bowls, appear in Megaron 10 Layers 16 and 13.[29]

PLATES

This category overlaps in shape some of the shallow bowls of Late Bronze Age levels discussed above, and in fragmentary form they are often difficult to distinguish from each other. Plates are very shallow bowls, probably not intended to hold liquids. They become a principal component of the Late Bronze Age and Transitional assemblages in Megaron 10 Layers 7-4 (304, 305, 354-357, 392, 393, S48), and appear in Early Iron Age layers (3-1) of the same sounding. Rim diameters are difficult to obtain, but suggest a range of 0.22-0.35 m.

A subdivision consists of large plates, perhaps used as serving platters, sometimes made with a wide rim around the circumference. They are found in Megaron 10 Layers 8-5 (257, 344, 353, S38-S39), and also in Early Iron Age levels (561). Most examples are of coarse, unslipped ware, but two from Megaron 10 Layer 7 preserve red slip (S38, S39); one (S38) has a grooved upper surface. Fragments indicate a wide range of rim diameters from this group, from *ca.* 0.38-0.60 m.

Both varieties of plates are known from second-millennium levels at Boğazköy, Tarsus, Maşat, Korucutepe, and Porsuk.[30] Examples from Maşat are identified as lids; perhaps some of the Gordion vessels here classified as plates were also used as lids.

JARS

As employed in the present study, this category encompasses a wide assortment of shapes and sizes, mostly oval or globular vessels whose height exceeds their greatest diameter. Very few well-preserved or restorable

22. *Hitt. Cem.*, 29, pls. 16f-g, 30j, with "rolled rim."

23. Boğazköy, Unterstadt Level 3 (*Boğazköy* VI, 79, fig. 12:88); Polatlı Level XXV (*AnatSt* 1 [1951] 36, fig. 6c:1-2).

24. Bowls with spouts are unusual, and do not appear to have been equipped with a handle. Compare example from Boğazköy, Büyükkale IVb (*Heth. Keramik*, 145, no. 1000, pl. 113); also Maşat Level V, buff-slipped and polished (*Maşat* II, 104, fig. 42).

25. References cited in catalogue, under 277.

26. Beycesultan Level IVc (*Beycesultan* II, 108, fig. P.16:27); Tarsus Late Bronze II (*Tarsus* II, 218-219, nos. 1235-1237, figs. 325, 387); Korucutepe Phase J (*Korucutepe* 3, 102, pl. 21J).

27. Compare the bowls on tall pedestals, or "fruitstands," cited in n. 28.

28. Polatlı Level XXII (*AnatSt* 1 [1951] 50, fig. 12:7); Beycesultan, a very popular shape; closest parallels are from Beycesultan Levels V (*Beycesultan* II, 94, fig. P.6:7, 10) and IVc (*Beycesultan* II, 106, fig. P.14:3, with buff wash). Also Tarsus Late Bronze I (*Tarsus* II, 188-189, nos. 974-976, fig. 377).

29. A bowl from Middle Bronze Tarsus shows the base type (*Tarsus* II, 167, no. 758, figs. 293, 367).

30. Boğazköy, Unterstadt Levels 3, 1b and Büyükkale Levels IVb, III (*Heth. Keramik*, 142, 909-910, 914, 916; pls. 100, 101). Tarsus Late Bronze II (*Tarsus* II, 210, nos. 1121-1124; figs. 316, 384); Maşat Levels III-II, "lids" (*Maşat* II, figs. 8, 10-12); Korucutepe, in Phase I, red-slipped with wide rim; and in Phase J, wheelmarked platter (*Korucutepe* 3, pl. 5:199-201; pl. 4:171); Porsuk Level V (*Porsuk* I, 33, pls. 20-21). Example from Beycesultan Level I, with wide rim, grooved decoration on rim underside (*AnatSt* 5 [1955] 87, fig. 20:14-15).

examples have been recovered from the soundings, leaving as the principal basis for identification or classification a comparison with better-preserved vessels from other sites in central Anatolia. This category includes vessels sometimes classified separately as pots.[31]

Certain specific features recur in successive levels in both soundings, surviving a gradual transition from red-slipped to buff-slipped or plain surfaces. Jars with sharply everted rim begin in Megaron 10 Layer 18 (**103**) and reappear in most levels through Layer 6 (**141, 179, 180, 196, 219, 241, 242, S49**); they are also present in Megaron 12 Levels VB-VA (**441, 459**). Rim diameters range from 0.20-0.45 m., most falling between 0.20 and 0.30 m. Vessels with similar rim form from Asarcık and Boğazköy furnish the most likely type for reconstructing most of the Gordion fragments.[32] To judge by intact or restorable specimens from other sites, jars with everted rim commonly have a globular to oval body and a flat base (rarely, rounded or ring). Flat bases occur in most levels of both soundings and are candidates for jars with everted rim (**124, 327, 345, 376, 416, 444, 463, 464, S34**). Among well-preserved jars, ring bases are usually fairly large, 0.09-0.15 m. in diameter. This criterion of size may serve to distinguish fragments in this range from ring bases of pitchers or teapots, which normally measure less than 0.09 m. in diameter.[33] At Gordion, fragments of large ring bases (**125, 188, 189, 201, 209, 329, 378-380, 418, 445, 465**, perhaps **490, 491, S35, S59**), generally unslipped, are found in Megaron 10 Layers 16-5 and Megaron 12 Levels VC-IVB. Some of these may belong to jars with everted rim. A variation on the everted rim, with a slanted outer surface, is a feature of Megaron 10 Layers 5 and 4 (**361, 395, S56**).

Another group of jars displays an everted rim thickened on the outside; these may be subdivided into red- or buff-slipped examples with rim diameter less than 0.30 m. (**360, 438, 455**) and a group of larger dimensions, with plain surfaces (**439, 440, 483-485**). Two sherds from Megaron 10 Layer 7 have everted rims that turn downwards (**314, 316**).[34] A thickened, sometimes rounded rim occurs on red- or buff-slipped jars in

Megaron 10 Layer 7 (**308, 309, 311**), one (**308**) preserving a stamped design on the vessel wall. In Megaron 12 Level VB are two examples of large, rather coarse jars with thickened, rounded rim (**457, 458**); similar rims are found among a number of examples from Porsuk Level V, where most served as cooking pots.[35] Gordion has produced a cooking pot fragment with this form of rim (**461**).

Jars with cylindrical neck and gently outturned rim resemble jugs, but generally have larger rim diameters than jugs and lack the thickened rim characteristic of the latter group. Surface treatment varies considerably, and no single vessel type can be discerned among these fragments (**270, S5**; with larger diameter, **243, 454**; diameter unknown, **186, 271**). Sharply outflaring rims (**251, 315**) may belong to vessels with narrow neck and oval body, a type attested in the Hittite Cemetery.[36] Since their rim diameters can seldom be estimated, however, it is difficult to assign them to a particular shape. Jars with gently outturned or outflaring rims are present in the second-millenium repertory at a number of Anatolian sites, furnishing a range of possibilities for classifying the Gordion fragments.[37]

A category of vessel with basket handles, identified by handle fragments, occurs in Megaron 10 Layers 15-12 (**S11, S12**; additional fragments, not catalogued). To judge by better-preserved specimens from sites in central Anatolia, some may be restored as basket-handled jars, usually made as teapots with trough or tubular spout.[38] Small to medium jars, some carinated, in plain buff or with good red slip (**115, 144, 145, 237, 306, 307, 411, 436, 437, S1, S21, S24**), may belong to teapots or to one-handled jars such as those found in the Hittite Cemetery.[39] A handle fragment from Megaron 10 Layer 16 (**127**) should be assigned to a one-handled jar or teapot.

A few distinctive forms or features are attested in only one or two examples. Megaron 10 Layer 11 produced a small jar with vertical handle, perhaps belonging to a type with ring base as exemplified in the Hittite Cemetery.[40] It is not otherwise definitely attested in the stratified series. Layer 11 also yielded two

---

31. *Heth. Keramik*, 53-55, pots; *Porsuk* I, 35-37, distinguishing pots and jars.

32. Asarcık Level IV (*IstMitt* 16 [1966] 73, fig. 13:1); well-preserved examples from Boğazköy Unterstadt 4, Nordwesthang-Büyükkale Level 8a, Büyükkale Levels IVd, IVa (*Heth. Keramik*, 129-130, nos. 505-506, 522-523, 532, 534-535, pls. 54-55).

33. *Hitt. Cem.*, 22-24, diameters 0.05-0.08 m.; generally less than 0.09 m. among pitchers and teapots from Boğazköy (*Heth. Keramik*, 118-124). Small pots may also have ring bases less than 0.09 m. in diameter, but these seem to be uncommon; see examples from Gordion (*Hitt. Cem.*, 26, pl. 15a) and Boğazköy (*Heth. Keramik*, 130, no. 520, pl. 52). At Boğazköy, well-preserved jars with everted rim, or deep, basinlike bowls (*Schüsseln*), may have ring bases with diameters between 0.09-0.15 m. (*Heth. Keramik*, 131, no. 553, pl. 53; 144, no. 972, pl. 109).

34. Compare rim on unslipped pot from Boğazköy, Unterstadt Level 3 (*Boğazköy* VI, 73, fig. 9:52).

35. *Porsuk* I, 25-26, pls. 27-31.

36. *Hitt. Cem.*, 26, pls. 14g-h, 29.

37. Compare rim fragments from Boğazköy, Unterstadt Levels 4-2 (*Heth. Keramik*, 131, nos. 539-540, 545-546, 551-552, pls. 59-60).

38. Examples cited below, n. 50.

39. *Hitt. Cem.*, 24-25, pls. 14b-c, with slightly everted rim; 14e, with plain rim. Teapots with plain rim are found in most second-millennium levels at Boğazköy, from Unterstadt Levels 4-1 (*Heth. Keramik*, 123-124, nos. 351-352, 356, 362-363, 365-366, 376, 378, pl. 35, for well-preserved examples; catalogued specimens later than the period of Unterstadt 3 rarely have red slip).

40. *Hitt. Cem.*, 26-27, pl. 15a; further discussion of the type in *Heth. Keramik*, 53, with bibliography.

red- or brown-slipped jars with horizontal ridges on the exterior wall (**218**, **S28**). A kraterlike vessel with one or more vertical handles (**245**) is unique at Gordion. Jars with everted and indented (**317**, **394**) or grooved rims (**318**, **364**), or with lid rest (**319**, **340**), are features of Megaron 10 Layers 7-4. From Megaron 12 Level IVB came a small hole-mouth jar (**S67**) and a large jar with deeply indented upper surface (**S68**). Neither has a close parallel at Gordion.

A painted vessel preserved in several fragments in the clay packing over the Destruction Level documents a bucket-shaped jar with horizontal handles (**515**).

COOKING POTS

This category is defined principally by the coarse, gritty fabric of the vessels, as described above (p. 29), but is also recognizable by a few distinctive forms. Most common is a simple hole-mouth vessel, occurring in a broad range of sizes (**113**, **114**, **121**, **123**, **142**, **143**, **206-208**, **220**, **246**, **462**, **487**, **S4**, **S29**). A few examples of this type preserve a lug or vertical handle below the rim (**122**, **156**, **S30**). The hole-mouth cooking pot is found, with little variation, in all second-millenium levels at Gordion. Examples from the Hittite Cemetery, used as burial containers, display a deep form and flat base.[41] The hole-mouth form also occurs among pithoi, distinguished by their greater dimensions (**341**, **499**, **S22**). Another, less common form of cooking pot displays a thickened rim and narrowing shoulder (**S50**) or globular body (**461**). Both hole-mouth and thickened-rim types are known from second-millennium levels at sites in central and southeastern Anatolia, where they likewise exhibit little chronological development.[42]

PITHOI

This term designates a group of large vessels with flat base, oval body, and two vertical handles placed between neck and body on opposite sides of the vase. At Gordion most examples are wheelmade; their surfaces are finished with a buff or red slip, or left plain. In the stratified series only small fragments of rims, handles, or relief bands allow the identification of the type,

making it difficult to compare them with examples from other sites. Pithoi occur in two main forms: with hole-mouth rim, like the dominant cooking pot shape (**341**, **499**, **S22**), or with a broad or everted rim, often banded (**181-183**, **247**, **248**, **342**, **497**, **498**). They are the principal burial containers of the Hittite Cemetery at Gordion, which yielded restorable examples of both forms (**497-499**).[43]

PITCHERS

Common to pitchers are a spout and a handle located opposite it. A variety of spout forms occurs at Gordion, representing types known from other second-millennium sites in Anatolia. Beginning in Megaron 10 Layer 14 are beak spouts of good red-polished fabric (**184**), occurring again in Layer 7 (**S40**). A distinctive variety of the beak spout, with tip curved downward, is documented by fragments in Megaron 10 Layers 14 through 12 (**197**). Examples of this variety occur in Old Assyrian Colony Period contexts in central Anatolia, but the duration of the type has not been determined; fragments also appear in Hittite Empire levels at several sites.[44] Another form, the spout with "bearded" underside, is attested in a late, mixed context (**506**). The strainer spout first appears in Megaron 10 Layer 14, for the squat teapot form (**185**); strainers are also present in Layer 5 (**366**) and in Megaron 12 Level VA (**460**). The large storage pitcher or *Pithosschnabelkanne* occurs in Megaron 10 Layers 14 (red-brown slipped, **184**) and 13 (buff fragments, not catalogued). Buff or orange trefoil rims are present in most levels from Megaron 10 Layers 15-4, but rarely sufficiently preserved to be catalogued (**198**, **273**, **322**, **367**; additional fragments in Layers 14, 11-10, 4). One example (**322**) preserves part of the vertical handle attached at the rim.[45] A buff handle and rim from Layer 12 (**S23**) is from a simple type with gentle carination.

Evidence for the body or base of pitchers is scanty. Well-preserved beak-spouted examples from the Hittite Cemetery at Gordion are characterized by a low-placed, weak carination and minimal brown slip.[46] Vessels with sharply carinated body and pedestal base, preserving a good red slip (Megaron 10 Layer 14, **190**; Megaron

41. *Hitt. Cem.*, 20-21, pls. 12c-i, 25c-d.

42. Hole-mouth pots from Polatlı Level XXV (*AnatSt* 1 [1951] 41, fig. 9:6-7) and Asarcık Level IV (*IstMitt* 16 [1966] 73, fig. 13:5). Beycesultan Level IVb, hole-mouth and globular examples, both with vertical handles (*Beycesultan* II, 126, fig. P.29:4-5). Korucutepe Middle and Late Bronze levels, in globular jars with thickened rim and vertical handles (*Korucutepe* 3, 5, pls. 17D, 19A-C, E). Porsuk Level V, hole-mouth and globular examples (*Porsuk* I, 23, 35-37, pls. 27-35). Tarsus Middle and Late Bronze cooking pot shapes are different from those at Gordion (*Tarsus* II, 181, 198, 219).

43. *Hitt. Cem.*, 19-22, pls. 11-12. Banded pithoi are also used for burial at Yanarlar near Afyon (*Yanarlar*, fig. 11) and Bağbaşı near Karataş-Semayük, Elmalı (*AJA* 71 [1967] pl. 78, fig. 27).

44. *Heth. Keramik*, 36-38, favoring a relatively brief duration for the popularity of the type. More recent excavations document production in Old Hittite times: *Boğazköy* VI, 67, fig. 4. A spout of this type is from Tarsus Late Bronze I (*Tarsus* II, 192, no. 1012, fig. 309).

45. Some fragments may belong to jars with quatrefoil rim, as in an example from the Hittite Cemetery (*Hitt. Cem.*, 25, pls. 14d, 28c-d). At Boğazköy, pitchers with trefoil rim are not certainly attested before Old Hittite levels; but examples from Kültepe and Alişar are earlier (*Heth. Keramik*, 46-47, with further references). Buff pitchers with bifoil or trefoil rim are popular at Beycesultan in Levels IVb and IVa (*Beycesultan* II, 125, fig. P.28:13; 136, fig. P. 25:9-10). Buff trefoil rims from Asarcık, unstratified (*IstMitt* 16 [1966] 88, fig. 28:7, 8).

46. *Hitt. Cem.*, 23, pls. 13a, 13c-d, 26a-e.

12 Level VA, **466**), indicate the coexistence and succession of the form, associated with central Anatolian sites.[47] Some other red-slipped pedestal base fragments in Megaron 10 Layers 18-13 may also belong to pitchers, suggesting the early popularity of this type (perhaps **150, S6, S7**).[48] An unslipped example from Megaron 10 Layer 5 (**377**) may belong to a carinated pitcher or large teapot.

A handle fragment from Megaron 10 Layer 16 should be assigned to a one-handled jar or teapot (**127**). Rim fragments of small to medium vessels in Megaron 10 Layers 17-7 (**115, 144, 145, 237, 306, 307, S1, S20, S21, S24**) and in Megaron 12 Levels VC and VB (**411, 436, 437**), here classified generally as jars, are good candidates for teapots. Well-preserved teapots are found in the Hittite Cemetery, and are well documented at other sites in central and western Anatolia.[49] Given the popularity of the shape at Boğazköy, a healthy presence in the occupation sequence at Gordion may be postulated. Jars or teapots with basket handle are attested as small fragments in Megaron 10 Layer 15 and in Layer 13 (**S11, S12**, buff specimens). Examples from the Hittite Cemetery and other Anatolian sites suggest that this type of handle often accompanies teapots with strainer spout.[50]

JUGS

Jugs are vessels with narrow cylindrical neck and oval body, usually with a vertical handle from neck to shoulder. Similar vessels with trefoil rims are treated here as pitchers. Gordion has produced intact examples of jugs from the Hittite Cemetery, but only fragmentary specimens from the soundings in the City Mound.[51] Among these, rim diameters range from 0.08 to 0.14 m.; a few examples preserve a vertical handle attached at the neck. In the stratified sequence, jugs may begin in Megaron 10 Layer 14, where rim fragments belong to jugs or jars (**186, S5**?). A version characteristic of Layer 11 has a vertical handle, oval in section, just below the gently outturned rim (**S32**; second fragment, not catalogued). Layer 11 also witnesses the form that becomes standard, and increasingly popular, in Layers

8-4: a jug with large thickened rim, in gritty buff or orange fabric, generally left plain but occasionally with red or buff slip applied on rim and exterior (**274, 326, 343, 368, 369, S57**). Jugs of this type occur in Megaron 12 Levels VC-VB and IVB (**412, 442, 488**). Comparisons with better-preserved examples from the Hittite Cemetery and other second-millennium sites in Anatolia furnish a range of possibilities for restoring the Gordion fragments, with oval body, and pointed or gently rounded base. A base fragment from Megaron 12 Level VB (**446**) probably represents the lower part of a large jug.[52]

The Gordion evidence indicates that jugs appear in both burial and habitation contexts, and that they become increasingly common during the late second millennium. Both of these developments are paralled at Boğazköy.[53]

A few specimens may be from vessels closely related in shape to jugs. One is a red-slipped neck fragment from Megaron 10 Layer 7 (**323**) that belongs to a jug or bottle. It has no exact parallels, but resembles in its highly constricted neck and neck ridge the "spindle bottles" from Boğazköy and Korucutepe.[54] The Gordion example bears an unusual plum red slip, but is not clearly identifiable as an import.

Two fragments belong to flasks, which are distinguished from jugs by their lentoid body; sometimes they have vertical handles on the shoulder in addition to a neck handle. Gordion has produced only two fragments of this vessel type, both from Early Iron Age levels (**584**; second fragment, not catalogued, from Megaron 10 Layer 1). Both have a pronounced rib along the "seam" of the vessel, and are embellished with a good cream slip and enamel-like finish. They are from unusually flat varieties of this vessel type.[55]

VESSELS WITH POINTED BASE

This type is named for the distinctive form of the lower part of the vessel. They belong to two groups. Those with conical to ovoid lower body and pointed to gently rounded base, such as **330**, probably represent the lower part of large jugs with narrow cylindrical

47. The Gordion examples of the sharply carinated type seem also to have a low-placed carination. *Heth. Keramik*, 36-41, for discussion of the beak pitcher type (compare esp. nos. 242, 247, 248, pls. 23-24).

48. Compare the tall pedestals of bowls or "fruitstands": above, n. 28.

49. *Hitt. Cem.*, 24-25, pl. 14b-c. *Heth. Keramik*, 41-46, for the vessel type and further references.

50. Teapots with strainer spout: *Hitt. Cem.*, 25, pls. 14e, 28g, with vertical and basket handles; also *Heth. Keramik*, 124, no. 391, pl. 38; *Nordwesthang-Büyükkale*, 53, no. 179, pl. 40. Beycesultan Level V, with basket handle (*Beycesultan* II, 97, fig. P.8:5-6). Maşat Level V, red-slipped; and Level III (*Maşat* II, fig. 53, D:2). Basket handle fragments, red-slipped from Polatlı Level XXIV (*AnatSt* 1 [1951] 50, fig. 12:14, 15) and Boğazköy, Nordwesthang-Büyükkale Level 8b (*Frühe Keramik* 40, nos. 303-305, pl. 32).

51. *Hitt. Cem.*, 23-24, pl. 13e-f.

52. The base **446** resembles an example from Korucutepe Phase J (*Korucutepe* 3, 98, pl. 18N).

53. *Heth. Keramik*, 47-50.

54. Ibid., 73-74, with bibliography; Korucutepe Phase J (*Korucutepe* 3, pl. 18N).

55. *Heth. Keramik*, 50-53, for the type; also Bilgi, M. ö. II. *binyılında Anadolu'da bulunmuş olan matara biçimli kaplar* (Istanbul 1982), collects examples of the type and analyzes distribution and development. A flat variety similar to the Gordion examples is found at Beycesultan Level II (*AnatSt* 5 [1955] 71, fig. 14:3).

neck and vertical handle. Vessels of this form are found in the Hittite Cemetery at Gordion and in second-millennium levels at Boğazköy, Tarsus, Maşat, and Korucutepe.[56] The second group displays a conical lower body and pointed or small flat base; examples are few but persistent, occurring in small fragments in most levels from Megaron 10 Layers 14-5 (**374, 375** are the best preserved) and in Megaron 12 Level IVB. Comparisons with better-preserved vessels from other sites suggest possible reconstructions for these Gordion fragments, as small two-handled vessels or as large, juglike vessels.[57]

VESSEL LIDS

Three ceramic objects from the soundings are identified as lids. One, a perforated lid with spool handle (**370**) from Megaron 10 Layer 5, has close counterparts at Boğazköy.[58] The fragmentary flat clay objects (**325** and **413**) are probably flat vessel lids with central steam-hole. Presumably they were equipped with a handle, like the Early Bronze lid (**96**).

VESSELS WITH PLASTIC, INCISED, OR IMPRESSED DECORATION

Surface ornament is very rare, and confined almost exclusively to the red-slipped category. Examples occur in Megaron 10 Layers 16-7 and in Megaron 12 Levels VC and VA, primarily on jars. Incised marks and stamped designs on vessels are discussed below in separate sections.

Plastic ornament occurs as a pellet (**S24**), on a jar with two low swellings (**306**), and as a low ridge on the neck of pitchers or teapots (**S1**); similar features are found on vessels in the Hittite Cemetery.[59] A pitcher from Megaron 10 Layer 14 has plastic imitation of metal rivets on the upper end of the handle (**184**). The presence of horizontal ridges on the shoulders of jars is a feature of Megaron 10 Layer 11 (**218, S28**). A bowl from Megaron 10 Layer 11 with pinched vertical ridge (**216**) has relatives at Polatlı, Asarcık, and the Ilıca cemetery.[60] An unslipped handle from Megaron 12

Level VA (**467**) bears a plastic ropelike pattern on its upper surface, a form of decoration that has no parallels at other second-millennium sites in central Anatolia.

Parallel grooves decorate jars in Megaron 10 Layer 10 (**238**) and Megaron 12 Level VC (**411**), also a plate rim (**S38**) and body sherds (**S42**), all from Layer 7. Incised patterns are unusual. From Megaron 10 Layer 14 are decorated body sherds (**191, 192**); **469**, from Megaron 12 Level VA, is probably a jar or teapot. An unslipped handle from Megaron 12 Level VA (**468**) bears an incised line linking it to handle treatment of vessels in western and southwestern Anatolia.[61]

BATHTUBS

This term refers to large quasi-rectangular clay containers with a wide opening and deep form. They occur in better-preserved examples at Kültepe, Alişar, Tarsus, and Korucutepe.[62] Gordion has produced candidates for bathtubs in fragments from Megaron 10 Layers 8 and 7 (**275, 324**). Bathtubs appear in the Late Bronze I period at Tarsus and in Korucutepe Phases I and J, suggesting the continued production of such vessels throughout most of the second millennium. Whether they served as bathtubs is not known. Some examples preserved an interior shelf that could have accommodated a seated person.[63]

ZOOMORPHIC VESSELS AND FIGURINES

Examples from stratified deposits and miscellaneous contexts, although few and very fragmentary, document the production of vessels embellished with animal forms and animal-shaped vessels and figurines throughout most of the second millennium at Gordion. Only a single example of a zoomorphic vessel from a stratified context (**254**), from Layer 9 under Megaron 10, is included in the catalogue. Additional fragments from Megaron 10 Layers 16, 12, and 7, not catalogued, indicate continuous local production from the Middle to Late Bronze Age. Other examples come

56. *Hitt. Cem.*, 24, pls. 13b, 27d. *Heth. Keramik*, 47-50, for the type; example from Nordwesthang-Büyükkale, probably Level 7 (*Nordwesthang-Büyükkale*, 45, no. 48, pl. 27); also from Unterstadt Level 2 and Büyükkale Level III (*Heth. Keramik*, 126, nos. 422, 442, 444, pls. 38, 40).

57. Small two handled vessels ("goblets") from Maşat (*Maşat* II, 106, fig. 58; pls. 49:6-8, 50:1-2; with further references). Compare a group of small votive vessels from Boğazköy, Büyükkale Level IIIa (*Heth. Keramik*, nos. 1047-1052, 1055, pl. 119) and similar vessels from Hittite Empire Alaca and Tarsus Late Bronze II (*Heth. Keramik*, 69, with discussion and bibliography); also from Korucutepe Phase K (two-handled juglet) and Phase J (one-handled) (*Korucutepe* 3, 102, pl. 21M-N).

58. Boğazköy examples cited in catalogue, **370**. Related objects from Tarsus are a perforated "brazier" lid, Late Bronze I (*Tarsus* II, 197, no.

1057, figs. 308, 383) and a lid with spool handle, Late Bronze II (*Tarsus* II, 219, no. 1238, figs. 327, 387).

59. *Hitt. Cem.*, 22, pl. 13g (pitcher with neck ridge and clay warts); 24, pls. 14b, 28a (jar with swellings). For the applied pellet on **S24**, see also comparanda cited in catalogue.

60. References cited in catalogue, **216**.

61. Beycesultan, example from Level IVa (*Beycesultan* II, 130, fig. P.31:11); Aphrodisias, Late Bronze sherds from West Acropolis excavations (*AJA* 80 [1976] 398, fig. 7; 402, fig. 14).

62. *Tarsus* II, 197, no. 1054, with further references; also Korucutepe Phases I and J (*Korucutepe* 3, 98, pls. 17E, 18P, 18Q).

63. *Tarsus* II, 197, no. 1054.

from miscellaneous contexts on the City Mound (**508-514**), which also yielded several fragmentary figurines (**522-525**).[64]

Two examples of unslipped barrel-shaped animal vessels preserve a hole in the center of the back (**511, 512**); a third, red-slipped fragment (**510**) belongs to the same type. Small fragments similar to **510** were found in Layers 16, 12, and 7 under Megaron 10; Layer 7 also produced an unslipped fragment, as **511, 512**. Comparison of the barrel-shaped rhyta with better-preserved examples from excavations in central Anatolia suggests that they were equipped with spouts in the form of an animal's head. Spout fragments **508** and **509** may have belonged to similar vessels or to jugs with zoomorphic attachments. The ram's head from Megaron 10 Layer 9 (**254**) is not a spout, and its place of attachment and original vessel type are not so easily determined. Vessels with zoomorphic decoration from Kültepe and Boğazköy, for example, demonstrate that such protomes were used on a wide variety of vessel forms.[65] The Gordion examples suggest that zoomorphic rhyta of the same type were made during both Middle and Late Bronze Ages. Since they are few and poorly stratified, however, no chronological or typological sequence can be established.[66]

Two examples, **513** and **514**, are vessel handles with animal attachments in the shape of a ram's head. The figurines (**522-525**) represent animal types also favored at Boğazköy.

The provenience of the animal vessels and figurines in habitation contexts on the City Mound—none were found in any burial in the Hittite Cemetery—corresponds to practices observed elsewhere in west central Anatolia. Vessels with zoomorphic spouts or attachments occur only once in the cemetery of pithos burials at Yanarlar, and seldom among the burials, mostly cremations, at Ilıca.[67]

VESSEL MARKS

Incised marks on Bronze Age vessels are examined by Lynn E. Roller in a comprehensive analysis of the Phrygian nonverbal graffiti from Gordion.[68] Only a few comments on the types of marks represented and their chronological significance are therefore given here.

All six Bronze Age vessel marks catalogued here are graffiti, that is, incised before firing. Five occur on unslipped vessels, only one on a red-slipped handle (**500**). They can be divided into three groups. First are the incised triangular signs with interior perpendicular, mostly retrieved from miscellaneous contexts on the City Mound (**517-520**); one was recovered from Megaron 12 Level VB (**447**) and one from a pre-Level IC context in the North Central Trench (**493**). The triangular marks are found on the vessel wall—on one example near the base—in a generally prominent location. No specific vessel type seems to be associated with this graffito, but most fragments belong to closed vessels of simple form, probably jars, without further surface adornment.

A second graffito type is a double arrow, known from a single example recovered from Küçük Hüyük (**521**). It has no parallels among examples from second-millennium contexts elsewhere in Anatolia, and may instead belong to a coarse ware Iron Age vessel. The location of the double arrow on the underside of the base also contrasts with the general Hittite practice of placing graffiti on easily visible parts of the vessel.[69]

The function of the vessel marks is not fully understood. The triangular marks found on sherds at a number of sites have been likened to the Hittite hieroglyphic sign for "king" or "royal."[70] Their occurrence on vessels may thus refer to a centrally distributed commodity or container.[71] Yet an example also occurs on a burial pithos from Yanarlar, where no evidence for Hittite imperial control is known.[72] Nevertheless, the marks are found throughout a wide area of Anatolia between *ca.* 1400 and 1200 B.C., and must have had a common meaning understood by inhabitants at the various sites. That they refer to some aspect of centrally administered production or distribution of vessels or contents remains the most likely hypothesis.

---

64. The Bronze Age figurines are discussed in detail by Irene Bald Romano in *Gordion Special Studies* II: *The Terracottas and Figural Vessels*, forthcoming.

65. K. Bittel, *Die Hethiter* (Munich 1976), figs. 50, 53, 55, 59, 70, 71. A strainer spout from Tarsus Late Bronze II preserves traces of a plastic animal paw (*Tarsus* II, 217, no. 1225, fig. 325).

66. Most of the Boğazköy examples were recovered from fill or much disturbed contexts and do not offer reliable evidence for establishing a chronology of production or style.

67. *Yanarlar*, 117, fig. 98, jug with antelope head spout; rhyton with ram's head from Ilıca, illustrated in K. Bittel, *Die Hethiter* (Munich 1976), fig. 166. Further discussion of zoomorphic rhyta in *Kültepe-Kaniş* II, 63-69. Textual information on zoomorphic vessels is given in L. Rost, *MIO* 8 (1961) 161-217 and *MIO* 9 (1963) 175-239; O.

Carruba, *Kadmos* 6 (1967) 88-97; also B. Rosenkranz, in *Festschrift für H. Otten* (Wiesbaden 1973), 283-289.

68. *Gordion Special Studies* I, 1-2, 4-5, 1A-1 to 1A-10.

69. Marks on the underside of the base are found at Tarsus, Late Bronze IIa-b, inscribed with Linear B(?): *Tarsus* II, 229, no. 1372, fig. 328. Also on a Red Lustrous Ware bottle from Porsuk Level V (*Porsuk* I, 26, 53, no. 247; pls. 41, 43).

70. *Gefässmarken*, 76, with further references. Compare the raised triangle on a red-slipped vessel from Tarsus, Late Bronze I (*Tarsus* II, 198, no. 1065, fig. 312).

71. This is also suggested by L. E. Roller (see *Gordion Special Studies* I, 2).

72. *Yanarlar*, fig. 101. The cemetery as a whole is dated to the Old Hittite period, although the presence of this mark suggests a slightly later date for some of the burials.

A red-slipped handle fragment bearing an incised beaked jug illustrates a third graffito type (**500**). It was recovered from the area of the Hittite Cemetery, in fill of Phrygian structures that occupied part of the ancient burial ground. As noted in the catalogue, its parallels are with examples from Boğazköy and Alişar Hüyük.

Vessels with stamped concentric circle pattern are discussed below under seals and seal impressions.

SEALS AND SEAL IMPRESSIONS

This category of material has been treated in part by Hans G. Güterbock and will be analyzed in detail by Edith Porada in her forthcoming study of the entire corpus of Gordion seals.[73] Only a few comments are therefore given here on the sources and chronological value of the excavated examples.

Seals and seal impressions occur at Gordion in second-millennium contexts on the City Mound and in the Hittite Cemetery. In stratified deposits they are found in Megaron 10 Layer 5 (**381, 382**) and Megaron 12 Level VA (**470**). From miscellaneous contexts come a hieroglyphic seal impression (**532**) and a bead seal (**533**) Of Old Hittite date is the bulla from a miscellaneous context on the City Mound (**532**).[74] A Hittite hieroglyphic impression on a jar handle (**381**) and a faience cylinder seal (**382**), were recovered from Megaron 10 Layer 5. Comparisons with excavated examples from more reliable contexts can be used to establish a general chronology for the other seals. The bead seal (**533**) is an unusual type. Related examples indicate a date no later than the first half of the second millennium, thus also probably in the Old Hittite period. The impression of a foot on a vessel handle (**470**) finds most parallels for the design in the later Old Assyrian Colony Period. Kültepe Karum Level Ib, at Boğazköy and Kültepe.[75] A slightly later date, in the Old Hittite period, would be consonant with the earliest material represented in this level, Megaron 12 Level VA.

A separate category of seal impression is found on the group of vessels stamped with concentric circles (**253, 308**). This ornament is well attested on vessels, and by examples of metal and clay stamps with this pattern, from early second-millennium levels at sites in central and western Anatolia; it first appears in the later Old Assyrian Colony Period.[76] Its occurrence at Gordion in levels of the later Old Hittite and Hittite Empire periods indicates continuous use during most of the second millennium B.C. An example from Maşat Hüyük Level I, a stratum assigned to the 13th century B.C., seems to corroborate the Gordion evidence for the chronological range of this stamped design.[77]

Description of Sequences

SOUNDING BELOW MEGARON 10

The 1965 sounding under the anteroom of Phrygian Megaron 10 yielded approximately 5,400 sherds of second-millennium date in Layers 18 to 4. With the exception of Early Bronze specimens in the lowest layers, the deposits were almost entirely free of earlier or later admixture, representing undisturbed, stratified accumulation. In Layer 4 appeared a few sherds of handmade dark pottery and two of gray Phrygian ware, unmistakable products of post-Hittite, Iron Age potters. The overlying Layers 3-1 also yielded Late Bronze Age and handmade pottery, with an increasing percentage of Phrygian gray ware. Bronze Age pottery from these later, essentially Iron Age levels, is catalogued separately in chapter IV.

LAYER 18 (102-105)

The lowest level in the sounding reached the water table. Among the 35 sherds recovered from Layer 18 were a few extrusive Early Bronze body sherds. Most of the second-millennium specimens are wheelmade buff and orange gritty fabrics, red or red-slipped on both surfaces or on part of the vessel. Identifiable shapes include a bowl with incurved rim (**102**), a jar with wide everted rim (**103**), a bowl with ring base and matt, red-slipped interior (**104**), and a vessel with a pedestal base (**105**), probably a bowl. A red-slipped pitcher handle documents this vessel type (fragment, not catalogued).

LAYER 17 (106-117)

This layer approached the water table; its horizontal exposure was restricted to an area of the trench lying west of the Layer 15 wall, producing some 85 sherds. Except for a few extrusive Early Bronze sherds, Layer 17 contained pottery of wheelmade buff and orange gritty fabric, red-slipped entirely or in part, burnished but with little luster now evident. Some sherds preserve a thin clay-colored "self-slip." Fabrics range from fine,

73. H. G. Güterbock in *Young Symposium*, 51-63.

74. *Ibid.*, 51, 55; also two stamp seals from the Hittite Cemetery, 51, with further references.

75. References cited under **470**.

76. References cited under **253**.

77. References cited under **253**.

clean, thin-walled (**106**) to coarse, gritty cooking pot ware (**113, 114**).

Fine red-slipped bowls with incurved rim (**106**), and examples with ring base and red-slipped interior (**111**) continue; the lower bowl profile of the ring base is not flattened. Other bowl types have carinated profiles, and plain (**107**) or thickened rims (**108-110**); **109** and **110** preserve horizontal handles. Jars are of rounded shape with narrow openings, their rims gently everted (**112**). Open mouth vessels with red slip may be small jars (**115-117**). Cooking pots have thickened hole-mouth rims (**113, 114**).

LAYER 16   (118-128, S1)

As in the preceding layers, buff and orange gritty fabrics with partial red slip predominate among the 145 fragmentary samples. Early Bronze extrusive specimens include cup rims and a dipper handle (**98**).

Large carinated bowls with thickened rim (**118-120**) continue, some preserving upswung (**120**) or outswung horizontal handles. Another type attested previously are fine red-slipped bowls with incurved rims (fragments, not catalogued). Bases of bowls now are simply flattened, or made as disks, rings, or pedestals (**126**, from bowl?). Among jar shapes are examples with flat (**124**) and ring bases (**125**). Of the hole-mouth cooking pots (**121-123**), **122** has an arrised lug handle.

Pitchers are represented by a teapot handle (**127**). Sherds with neck ridge (**S1**; second fragment, not catalogued) are from small jars, possibly teapots. Additional teapot fragments document the shape in plain buff ware or with partial, thin red slip. A pedestal base (**126**), and a carinated vessel fragment may belong to teapots or pitchers. A cylindrical red-slipped pottery fragment, not catalogued, may represent a barrel-shaped animal vessel or rhyton, similar to the examples recovered from miscellaneous contexts (**510-512**).

Nonceramic artifacts include a copper or bronze tool fragment, probably a chisel (**128**).

LAYER 15   (129-150, S2)

Layer 15 produced approximately 400 sherds, mostly very fragmentary. Handmade Early Bronze sherds continued to appear, both fine and medium red-slipped and painted specimens (**97**), and coarse wares. Of Middle Bronze pottery, buff and orange fabrics with well-polished red-slipped surfaces are increasingly represented; unadorned buff and orange wares continue in the minority.

Bowl types already documented in earlier levels include a fine red-polished example with incurved rim (**129**), buff bowls with simple carination, plain rims, and partial red slip (**133, 134**), red-slipped carinated

bowls with thickened rim (**135-140**). Highswung horizontal handles are still a regular feature of the carinated, thickened rim group (fragments, not catalogued). A pedestal base (**S2**) may belong to a bowl. A vessel fragment with ring base (**149**) smoothed on the vessel interior is probably from a bowl. New bowl shapes include hemispherical red-slipped bowls (**132**) and red-slipped open vessels, some probably deep bowls (**131, 144, 145**). Another deep bowl rim fragment, not catalogued, documents a type that reappears in Layer 14 (**170**).

Jars are represented by large red-slipped examples with everted rim (**141**). Small jars, not catalogued, are red-slipped and display incurved shoulders or profiled rims; a basket-handled jar, perhaps a teapot, is also represented. Rims of open vessels with thickened rims (**146, 147**) may belong to simple jars. Cooking pots continue in large and small versions of the standard hole-mouth shape (**142, 143**, perhaps **148**).

Pitchers, not catalogued, are documented by a buff trefoil rim and a red-polished handle from a beaked type. A few fragments of banded pithoi also occur.

LAYER 14B   (151-157)

An area labeled 14B lay below the level of floor 15, but was not sealed by this floor; it produced some 70 sherds. These were principally red-slipped wares, generally coarse and often handmade, and thus probably include extrusive Early Bronze examples. Well-preserved specimens include small handmade bowls or "pinch pots" (**151, 152**), a plain red-slipped bowl (**153**), orange or buff or partially red-slipped jars with everted rim (**154, 155**), a hole-mouth cooking pot with vertical handle (**156**), and a red-polished pitcher beak-spout (**157**). A single fragment of a buff shallow bowl with inverted rim, not catalogued, heralds the appearance of this important type, well represented in subsequent levels.

LAYER 14   (158-192, S3-S7)

Layer 14 yielded a much larger sample than earlier levels in the Megaron 10 sounding, approximately 1,380 specimens. The ceramic assemblage is still dominated by slipped and polished orange and buff wares, the slip now more often fired reddish brown or light brown than brilliant red. Plain orange and buff wares are increasingly represented, however, forming together with the buff-slipped subgroup up to 40% of the total assemblage.

Bowl shapes continuing from earlier levels are the simple form with plain rim (**158**); red-slipped deep bowls (**167-170**), carinated with plain rim and partial red slip (**171, 172**); carinated with thickened rim, now fewer, and showing a slight change in profile (174-176). Bowls with ring base and red-slipped interior (178) are still represented, as are pedestal bases, mostly with red slip but occurring occasionally in plain buff ware. New to the bowl category are inverted rims with red-slipped surfaces (163-165) and a profile with distinct carination (173). A shallow brown-slipped bowl with inverted rim (S3) is a type closely paralleled by examples from Layers 13 and 12. Buff or orange bowls with incurved rim (160-162) gain in popularity and continue to appear in subsequent levels. An unusual piece is 166, a fine bowl with cream ring-burnished slip, whose "clinky ware" may link it to samples from Megaron 12 Level VA.

Jars also represent both old and new types. Ring bases (188, 189) continue from lower levels, as do small red-slipped jars (not catalogued). New are the everted rim types of 179 and 180, appearing in both red-slipped and buff finish in medium and large sizes, and a wide, indented buff rim (187) probably belonging to a large jar.

In the category of pitchers are small red-slipped teapot fragments with neck ridge, continuing a type attested in Layer 16. Pedestal bases, red-slipped or plain (S6, S7), may belong to teapots or pitchers. A buff trefoil rim, not catalogued, illustrates a variety documented in Layer 15 and continuing in subsequent levels. New are *Pithosschnabelkannen* (184) with plastic ornament, strainer-spouted teapots (185) and red- and brown-slipped curved beak spouts (fragments, not catalogued) better preserved in Layer 13. Pedestaled, carinated shapes (190) document further the new varieties in this category. Narrow-necked vessels with outturned rim (186, S5) may be restored as either jugs or jars. A pointed base fragment, not catalogued, represents the first appearance of this vessel form, which recurs in later levels.

Pithoi are of the old, banded type, in buff or orange ware with hard fabric (181-183). Cooking pots continue in traditional hole-mouth form (S4), one (fragment, not catalogued) with an arrised vertical lug represented in Layer 16. Two sherds from vessels of unknown form (191, 192) have incised ornament on slipped surfaces.

LAYER 13 (193-203, S8-S12)

A small quantity of pottery, *ca.* 200 sherds, documents ceramic developments in Layer 13. By this time red-slipped wares have declined, and buff and orange wares dominate the assemblage.

Very few of the bowl shapes prevalent in earlier levels continue: large bowls with thickened rim are now produced in plain buff ware with a gentler carination (194, S9, S10). Disk and ring bases are also manufactured in plain buff. Other types continue Layer 14 trends, such as buff or orange bowls with in-

curved, thickened rims (S8) and carinated profiles, here with partial red slip (195). A ring base fragment with red-slipped interior (example from Pit A, not catalogued) continues an earlier type. Fine shallow bowls with brown or red slip, not catalogued, are inherited from Layer 14 and reappear in Layer 12. Jars with ring bases continue (201), as do those with everted rims, now occurring in a more sharply everted fashion (196). A large jar with vertical handles and red painted shoulder (202) is new.

Pitchers also document previously attested types, some with new variations. Red-slipped beak spouts (197) display a curved tip. Buff trefoil rims are wider (198). Buff teapots probably with basket handle, suspected earlier, now occur (S11, S12). Banded pithoi continue, as do hole-mouth cooking pots (200).

A painted sample (203), a single sherd of unusually fine, clean fabric, has bands in dark brown or black paint on a light brown slip. Similar finds from Boğazköy and Kültepe suggest that this may be an import from North Syria.

A pit dug through the floor of Layer 13 produced some 20 sherds of red-slipped and plain buff pottery, including a buff *Pithosschnabelkanne* spout, a banded pithos sherd, a jar with ring base (201), and a bowl ring base with red-slipped interior. It also yielded a flint scraper (ST 554).

LAYER 12 (204-211, S13-S24)

As in Layer 13, buff and orange wares continued to prevail among the sherds, approximately 240 in all, retrieved from Layer 12. A relatively large quantity of traditional red-slipped shapes, such as bowls with thickened rim with horizontal handles, together with handmade samples of this ware, suggest that some of the material was extrusive.

Simple buff and orange bowl types continue; forms with incurved rims either plain or thickened (204, S13, S14) are now common. Descendants of the carinated bowl with thickened rim and horizontal handles appear in plain buff ware or red-slipped, with new, squatter proportions (S19). Plain buff or orange bowls with broad rim are now popular (S15-S18). A red-slipped pedestal base fragment may illustrate a reappearance of the shape or an extrusive specimen. Jars retain everted rim (205, if not a deep bowl) and ring base (209). Hole-mouth cooking pots (206-208) and pithoi of hole-mouth (S22) or broad-rimmed, banded type demonstrate continuity with previous developments.

Pitcher fragments include Layer 13 types: a curved tip of a reddish brown-slipped beak spout and a buff *Pithosschnabelkanne* spout. A large buff handle and neck section (S23) suggests a gently carinated variety. Teapots continue in the form of red- and brown-slipped rims (S20, S21); a sherd with plastic decoration

(**S24**) may belong to this category. A fragment of a vessel with pointed base suggests the continued production of this type. A red-slipped cylindrical fragment similar to one from Layer 16 may belong to an animal vessel or rhyton with barrel-shaped body, a type documented by examples retrieved from miscellaneous contexts (**510-512**).

Two pits dug through the floor of Layer 12, labeled A and B, produced fragmentary pottery and other finds. From Pit A came the rim of a carinated bowl (**S19**), coarse but thin-walled buff bowls, large jars with vertical handles, hole-mouth cooking pots, and a lead ring (**211**). Pit B yielded slightly more pottery, some 20 sherds, including buff or orange bowls (**S13-S18**), a pitcher handle (**S23**), a pithos rim (**S22**), and a copper or bronze pin (**210**).

LAYER 11   (212-220, S25-S35)

Layer 11 furnished *ca.* 225 sherds, among which buff and orange wares represent about 60% of the total assemblage. Bowls include a few examples of the carinated, thickened rim type with upswung horizontal handles, generally smaller than in earlier levels, plain or with red-slipped treatment (**S26, S27**); **217** may also belong to this group. Relatively shallow bowls with broad (**213, 215**) or new inverted rim (**214**) occur frequently. A shallow bowl with incurved rim (**S25**) continues an earlier form. One bowl has a vertical ridge between rim and carination (**216**). Fine bowls are now adorned with partial red slip (**212**).

Among jars the everted rim variety still appears, now commonly in plain buff or orange or with red slip (**219** is, exceptionally, gray). New are tan-slipped jars with a horizontal ridge below the rim (**218, S28**). New features are flat wheel-turned bases (**S34**), supplementing the older ring bases (**S35**). A small jar with vertical handles (**S33**) is also new. Cooking pots continue the hole-mouth variety in several sizes (**220, S29**), including a large example with vertical handle (**S30**).

Pitchers appear increasingly often with trefoil rims, in buff and orange, rather coarse fabrics. Two handmade spout fragments may belong to *Pithosschnabelkannen*. Jugs with narrow cylindrical neck, with buff slip and large vertical neck handle of oval section (**S32**) seem to be especially characteristic of Layer 11. The jug neck with thickened rim (**S31**) inaugurates a type increasingly common throughout the second millennium. The basket-handled teapot also occurs, as do teapot rim and body fragments in buff and red-slipped versions. A buff pedestal base fragment may represent a teapot or pitcher.

A red-slipped sherd with ornamental graffito seems to be a Phrygian contaminant.

LAYER 10   (221-253)

The approximately 350 sherds from Layer 10 again documented a majority of buff and orange wares, comprising some 65% of the total assemblage. Among inherited bowl shapes are fine samples with plain or gently outturned rims (**221**), and carinated forms with horizontal handles (**231, 232**). Buff bowls with thickened, sloping rims continue from earlier levels (**222, 223, 225**). Shallow bowls with inverted to vertical (**233, 234**) or broad (**235, 236**) rims now become more common and increase in popularity throughout the remaining second-millennium levels. Medium and coarse wares now predominate in the bowl category.

In jars types, the large, buff or orange variety with everted rims (**239-242**) continue, as do examples with flat or ring bases (fragments, not catalogued) attested in earlier levels. New are small jars with grooved exterior (**238**), jars with relief medallion (**253**) that recur in Layer 7, and a kraterlike vessel with vertical handle (**245**). Pitchers preserve trefoil rims, now thickened (not catalogued). Cooking pots perpetuate the hole-mouth variety, small with vertical handle (**244**) and large (**246**). Pithoi continue in the banded type, with red slip (**247, 248**). A sherd from a vessel of unknown form (**252**) has a painted red band.

LAYER 9   (254)

No context pottery was saved and labeled from Layer 9. The excavator recorded at least five boxes of sherds, described as "still Hittite."[78] This indicates close resemblance to the pottery retrieved from the overlying levels, dominated by gritty buff and orange wares. A single item, a zoomorphic vessel fragment, has been catalogued from this level (**254**).

LAYER 8   (255-282)

Layer 8 yielded 485 sherds. Gritty buff and orange ware is now markedly prevalent, about 70% of the assemblage. This is left plain or covered with a thin "self-slip," with wheelmarks clearly visible.

Among bowls, traditional types are few: reddish brown-slipped carinated forms with highswung horizontal handles (**268**), a fine red-slipped type with tapered rim and spiral-burnished surface (**255**). Buff and orange shallow bowls are increasingly represented, with a variety of rims: slightly thickened (**256**), inverted or vertical (**258, 260-262**), and broad (**259, 263**). Bowls with articulated features also occur, including a double ridged profile (**264**) and ridged rims (**265, 266**). One example has a spout and horizontal handle (**269**). A category of coarse plate ware makes its initial ap-

---

78. R. S. Young, Gordion Notebook 117, 94-95.

pearance in the form of large platters with broad upper rims (257), continuing through Megaron 10 Layer 5 and occurring also in Early Iron Age levels in both deep soundings.

Orange and buff jars continue to be characterized by everted rims (272), broad rims, flat wheelturned and sturdy ring bases (fragments, not catalogued). Two examples preserve painted decoration. A small specimen painted in red-on-cream geometric patterns (270) represents a style that continues in Layer 7. A rim with brown interior band (271) may be associated with similar decoration on a large jar rim fragment from Megaron 12 Level IVA (593). Pitchers have trefoil rims (273). The narrow-necked jug with thickened rim (274) continues from previous levels. "Bathtub" fragments appear in red- and buff-slipped versions (275, 276). A shape not otherwise represented at Gordion is a small votive cup with string-cut base (277), a vessel type well known from Hittite Empire centers in central and southeastern Anatolia.

Pits A and B, cut through floor 8, contained some 60 ceramic fragments (255-257, 261, 263, 275, 276, 278) as well as metal and stone tools and ornaments (279-282). A variety of pottery shapes were encountered: shallow bowls, a platter, "bathtub" fragments, and a handle from a very large jug.

LAYER 7   (283-337, S36-S42)

A relatively large ceramic sample, some 1,200 fragments and restorable vessels, was recovered from Layer 7. Buff and orange wares, most often now gritty and strongly wheelmarked, continue to dominate the ceramic repertory. A few red-slipped examples are Early Bronze extrusive specimens.

The typical bowl shapes seen in lower levels continue recent trends. Most common are shallow buff or red-slipped bowls with broad, sometimes angled rims (287, 289, 291, S36) and shallow buff or red-slipped bowls with inverted or vertical rims (286, 288, 293, 294, 304). A distinctive inverted rim projects both above and below the upper wall (290, 292). Continuing from Layer 8 are coarse plates (305, S39), one with grooved upper surface (S38), and large buff bowls with broad rim (295). The now standard carinated bowl with thickened, sloping rim and horizontal handle, plain buff, or rarely, red-slipped, remains popular (297-299, 301), supplemented by the "bead" rim version (302, 303). A buff example with related profile (300) introduces the sieved bowl, recurring in Layer 6. Fine buff or orange bowls continue in small quantities (283), some with ring bases (not catalogued). A red-slipped rim fragment with spiral-burnish follows a Layer 8 example (255) in technique. A shape not attested in previous levels is a red-slipped bowl with vertical handle (S37).

Well-established jar types also continue: large buff or orange examples with everted rims (314), flat (327) and ring bases (328 and 329). Red-slipped jars (or teapots?, 306, 307) are probably to be restored with basket handles (fragments, not catalogued). More recent developments are also retained, such as buff or orange jars with strongly outturned rims (310-313), a red-slipped jar with relief medallion (308), vessels with red-painted geometric patterns (331-333), "bathtubs" (324?; also rim fragment, not catalogued). New is the repertory of profiled jar rims—grooved, ledged, or indented rather than simple everted forms. Such rims occur in brown-slipped examples (317, 319) as well as in plain orange or with buff slip (315, 316, 318). One with lid-rest (319) has a pierced lug attachment. A small, fine buff jar with flanged vertical handle (320) is unusual in its shape and "enamel" slip.

Pitchers are still furnished with trefoil rims (322) and red-slipped curved beak spouts (S40), now also with tubular spouts (321). Narrow-necked jugs continue in buff or with partial red slip (326). Vessels with pointed base are represented by a lower body fragment (330), probably from a jug of elongated oval form, and by a base fragment. Hole-mouth cooking pots are found, as are examples of pithoi in hard fabric and giant size (fragments, not catalogued).

As noted above, painted sherds with red-on-cream geometric patterns (331-333) continue a Layer 8 fashion. Another painted sherd, from a closed vessel of globular form, is highly distinctive in its smooth, matt surfaces with buff and brown painted decoration and may be an import (S41). Two brown-slipped vessel fragments have grooved surface decoration (S42). Fragments of a red-slipped and an orange animal vessel or rhyton of barrel shape resemble better-preserved specimens from miscellaneous contexts (510-512). A crescent loomweight in gritty buff ware (334) has exact counterparts from miscellaneous contexts (526-529).

Nonceramic finds include a copper or bronze blade (335), a copper or bronze hook (336), and a stone axhead (337).

LAYER 6   (338-347, S43-S50)

Only a small number of sherds, about 40, were kept from Layer 6. Buff and orange wares are again in the majority. The few shapes preserved exhibit a close resemblance to examples from Layers 8 and 7. Shallow bowls in plain buff or orange, or with dull red polish, are again common. These perpetuate the inverted or vertical (S43, S45, S46) and broad rims (S47) of previous levels. A sieved bowl (339) continues a Layer 7 innovation; large coarse plates also recur (344; S48). Jars retain everted rims (S49), flat (345) and ring bases. A small cooking pot has a gradually narrowing shoulder and thickened rim (S50). Pithoi of hole-mouth (341) and everted rim types (342) continue. Jugs with vertical handle (343) are mostly in plain buff or orange, rarely with a red-brown slip.

An unusual item is a jar with rim grooved for lid rest (340). Similar rims appear in the preceding Layer 7, but this example is of entirely different fabric, fine with heavy "silver" mica concentration in the biscuit and on the outer surface. This marks the first appearance at Gordion of pottery with micaceous fabric and surface finish that continues in Layers 5 through 1 of the Megaron 10 sounding and appears in Megaron 12 Level IVB.

Nonceramic artifacts include a copper or bronze nail or pin (346) and a glass bead (347).

LAYER 5 (348-383)

From Layer 5 came ca. 350 ceramic fragments, again strongly dominated by buff and orange wares. These are usually gritty, hard-fired, and heavily wheel-marked, with occasional attention to smoothing of surfaces. Shallow bowls continue to be common, even characteristic, normally with broad, angled rim (351). Plates too are popular, buff- or red-slipped (354-356); large coarse versions (353) continue from preceding levels. Fine buff ware is still manufactured in small quantities, in thin-walled bowls (348, 352) and in a cup or beaker with "enamel" slip (358). Descendants of the carinated bowl with thickened rim have finally disappeared, and red-slipped specimens now appear rarely (plate, 354; jar with outturned rim, 372). The red-slipped plate (354) is further distinguished by a surface concentration of "silver" mica, linking this sample with a jar in Layer 6 (340) and with several vessel fragments in Layer 4 (390, 391, 394, 398, S60, S62) and in Megaron 12 Level IVB (S65).

Buff and orange wares prevail among other previously attested shapes as well, including large jars with everted rims (359-361), gently rounded (373) and ring bases (378-380). Jars with ridged rims (364) and outturned rims (371, 372) continue recent fashions. A large jar with broad and flat, or faintly profiled rim (362, 363, 365) is popular. Pitchers retain trefoil rims (367) and strainer spouts (366); jugs are plain or buff-slipped (368, 369). A pedestal base (377) and a flat base (376) remain popular. Vessels with pointed base (374, 375) may represent jugs with conical lower body, in various sizes. A lid with spool handle is perforated (370). A jar handle has a hieroglyphic Hittite seal impression (381). Artifacts other than pottery include a faience cylinder seal (382) and a copper or bronze pin (383).

A small trefoil rim sherd of Phrygian gray ware also occurs.[79]

LAYER 4 (384-398, S51-S63)

About 120 sherds are available from Layer 4. The ceramic repertory of this layer closely resembles that of the preceding Layer 5. By now the buff and orange pottery has reached nearly 90% of the assemblage.

Bowls continue fashions of Layer 5 along with their relative frequencies: a few fine, thin-walled bowls (385, 386, S51); a dominating proportion of shallow bowls with broad (384, S53-S54) or inverted rims (S53, 387-389); and large plates (392, 393). Jars likewise follow types of preceding levels, with everted rims (395, S55, S56), gently rounded (S58) and heavy ring bases (S59). Pitchers with trefoil rims continue, as do jugs (S57) and coarse cooking pots of hole-mouth form. A vessel fragment with lug (S61) may be of the cooking pot category. A black-polished spindle whorl, not catalogued, resembles undecorated examples from the Hittite Cemetery.[80]

In addition to the buff and orange pottery, Layer 4 also produced several small groups of alien ceramic tradition. The first, a wheelmade group, consists of plain buff or orange, tan- or red-slipped vessels of unusual shape, often of distinctive micaceous fabric or surface treatment, burnished or with micaceous concentration. These include a buff bowl of heavy appearance (390), whose profile and fabric closely resemble an example from Megaron 12 Level IVB (S65). Other members of this group are a large red-slipped bowl (391), a large jar (394), a wide-mouthed jug(?) (398), a trefoil rim (S60), and a red-slipped handle (S62). The burnished exterior and micaceous concentration link this group to the examples that appeared in Layers 6 and 5 (above, 340, 354) and recur in Layers 3-1 of the deep sounding, and Layers 2-1 under the Main Room of Megaron 10.

Handmade pottery forms a second group. A handmade gray bowl rim displays a row of incised notches across the outer rim;[81] a dark gray body sherd of handmade manufacture has impressed ornament. Handmade samples of closely related type, tan or gray with incised or impressed ornament, are also represented in Layers 3-1 and in Megaron 12 Levels IVB and IVA. The cooking pot with lug noted above (S61) may in fact belong to this group. A handmade vessel with ribbed handle (S63) finds closest counterparts in ware and shape with Early Bronze samples at Gordion and probably is an isolated extrusion.

79. G. K. Sams interprets the presence of this sherd as evidence for the post-Bronze Age, mixed nature of the deposit (personal communication).

80. *Hitt. Cem.*, 43, pls. 24a, d; these examples are also undecorated, of buff clay.

81. G. K. Sams, *Gordion* IV, P 5732.

Finally, two sherds of wheelmade gray ware also appear. This category is likewise a component of Megaron 12 Level IVB, suggesting that the combined occurrence of the various ceramic classes there and in Layer 4 represents a contemporaneous deposit.

SOUNDING BELOW MEGARON 12

The initial deep sounding in 1950 produced approximately 1,400 sherds from Levels VC-VA through IVB, nearly all of second-millennium date. A few extrusive Early Bronze samples from the underlying Level VI were present in small quantities in all of the levels. With these exceptions, the deposit appeared to represent relatively undisturbed, stratified accumulation. As in the Megaron 10 sequence, the final Late Bronze Age level is signaled by the appearance in small quantities of three new ceramic groups: wheelmade pottery of unusual shape or with surface mica concentration, handmade tan and gray ware, and gray Phrygian pottery.

LEVEL VC (399-418)

Level VC produced some 400 ceramic fragments, of which buff and orange wares constitute about 70% of the total assemblage. Among buff and orange bowls are a small plain specimen (399), carinated examples with outturned (405), thickened, or sloping rims (406-408) and horizontal handles (409), and shallow bowls with inverted or broad rims (401-404). Their surfaces are often covered with a matt buff slip. A round base with buff-slipped surfaces may belong to a bowl (415). Red-polished bowls occur with different profiles, including an example with S-curved profile (400). A very fine buff cup rim with punched dot design also preserves traces of reddish-brown slip (414).

Jars are buff or buff-slipped, with round, flat, or ring bases (416-418); a small red-slipped jar with everted rim (410) is unusual. A jar or teapot rim (411) has horizontal grooves on its red-slipped surface. A red-slipped handle fragment may belong to a basket type, from a jar or teapot. Pitchers are represented by fragments: red-slipped handles with triangular section, and a shoulder fragment of a carinated red-slipped pitcher (not catalogued). Jugs are also found (412). Cooking pots occur in standard hole-mouth form. A flat ceramic object (413) may be a disk-shaped lid with central steam-hole.

LEVEL VB (419-447)

As in the preceding level, buff and orange gritty fabrics account for ca. 70% of the 535 sherds in Level VB. Some extrusive Early Bronze samples continue to appear.

The carinated red-slipped bowl with thickened sloping rim is still in evidence (435). Red-polished treatment is also given to carinated bowls with plain rim (433, 434), and shallow or hemispherical specimens with plain or incurved rims (422, with spiral burnish; 423, 424). Shallow bowls with broad or inverted rims are now popular, occurring with partial red slip (425), but ordinarily with plain or buff slipped surfaces (420, 426-432). A fine bowl with carinated profile has "enamel" slip (419). A ring base fragment with red-slipped interior, not catalogued, represents a type known from Megaron 10 Layers 18-13 (104, 111, 178).

Most jar rims belong to large examples with everted rims, of gritty orange or buff fabric with little attention to surface treatment (439-441); an example with red slip (438) is unusual. Small buff- or red-slipped jars (436, 437) are probably teapots; a red-slipped basket handle fragment indicates that some were thus equipped. Round, flat, and ring bases may belong to jars or pitchers (443-445). Pitchers are represented by a reddish brown-slipped handle with spine ridge, probably from a large, elegant example with curved beak spout. Buff or orange jugs (442) continue, some perhaps to be restored with a large oval body and base, as 446. A large red-slipped pithos handle fragment also occurs. Cooking pots are of the hole-mouth type.

Level VB also yielded a sherd with graffito (447), the only example recovered from a defined Bronze Age level at Gordion. The incised triangular mark is closely paralleled by an example retrieved from an unspecified pre-Level I context in the North Central Trench (493) and from miscellaneous deposits at the site (517-520).[82]

LEVEL VA (448-471)

Level VA produced a total of 255 sherds, roughly 80% of them buff and orange fabrics. As in preceding levels, a few extrusive Early Bronze sherds continued to appear.

Bowl types of earlier levels reappear. Shallow bowls with broad or inverted rims (448-452), in buff or with rare red-brown slip (450), are now popular. Carinated bowls with horizontal handles still occur (red-slipped handle fragment, not catalogued), along with their buff-slipped descendants with thickened, sloping rim (453). Gently rounded bases, in plain buff or orange, belong to bowls or jars. Loop handle fragments with matt buff or polished red slip may represent one-handled bowls, or possibly teapots.

Jar rims are commonly of thickened, usually everted form, in coarse gritty ware (457-459) or with partial red slip (455, 456). A jar with cylindrical neck (454) occurs

---

82.   Above, pp. 81, 84; *Gordion Special Studies* I, 2, 5, fig. 1.

in gritty coarse ware. A teapot rim sherd, slipped light reddish brown and burnished, documents this shape. Flat and ring bases from jars or pitchers continue (463-465). Pitchers include a red-slipped carinated example with pedestal base (466) and a buff strainer spout (460). Jugs occur in plain buff with vertical handle or in brown-slipped versions. Cooking pots continue large hole-mouth types (462) and appear in a rarer form with rounded, thickened rim (461).

Incised or impressed ornament occurs on several examples. A red-slipped carinated sherd, perhaps from a teapot, is decorated with rows of incision (469). A red-slipped handle preserves a foot-shaped seal impression (470); another, very similar handle fragment, unadorned (its mate?), is also from this level. Two other handles with unusual surface treatment deserve special mention: 467, with plastic, ropelike ornament; 468, with incised line.

Several fragments of a large closed vessel perhaps of oval form are of unusually fine, clean, "clinky" ware, fired mostly gray at the core; they are slipped on the exterior in buff with some pale red streaks. This pottery may be linked to an example from Megaron 10 Layer 14 (166) but has no certain parallels at Gordion.[83]

A black polished spindle whorl with incised decoration also occurs (471).

LEVEL IVB   (472-492, S64-S68)

Buff and orange wares form about 85% of the 250 sherds from Level IVB. Shallow bowls with thickened or broad (473-477, 480) or inverted (478, 479) rims continue and gain in popularity. Other bowl types are retained in characteristically small quantities, such as fine bowls (472) and the carinated bowl with thickened, sloping rim (482). Large flat plates are also represented (probably 489). Jars again are characterized by everted rims (483-485) and ring bases (490, 491). Cooking pots include hole-mouth examples (487), some with lugs or vertical handles (486). A large buff-slipped pithos knob belongs to a "bathtub" of the type better preserved in Megaron 10 Layers 8 and 7. Jugs (488), some certainly with vertical handles, are also retained from earlier levels. A fragment of a large vessel with pointed base probably belongs to a jug.

As in Megaron 10 Layers 4 and 3, Megaron 12 Level IVB produced additional, alien ceramic groups. First is a wheelmade buff pottery distinguished by its burnished surface and "silver" mica concentration. This is represented by a bowl (S65) with indented profile similar to examples in Megaron 10 Layer 4 (390) and Main Room Layer 1 (578). Another wheelmade group is of dark tan or orange gritty fabric, without "silver" mica but of unusually dense, coarse manufacture (shal-

low bowl, S66) or in previously unattested forms (S64, S67, S68). This may represent a Hittite subgroup but merits isolation from prevailing ceramic tradition.

Two additional categories are also found in both Megaron 12 Level IVB and Megaron 10 Layer 4. One is a handmade group, tan or dark fired, with incised or plastic decoration, some of which can be mended with joining fragments from Level IVA.[84] Finally, Phrygian gray wheelmade pottery mainly in large coarse jars forms about 5% of the total assemblage.

PRE-LEVEL IC   (493)

A small selection of pottery from the North Central Trench labeled "pre-Level IC" consisted mostly of plain buff or orange and a little red-slipped Bronze Age pottery, mixed with Phrygian gray ware. From this deposit came a sherd with incised triangular mark (493), closely related to graffiti from Level VB (447) and from miscellaneous contexts (517-520).

BURIALS (494-505)

The burials recovered in 1962 from the Museum Site extension of the Hittite Cemetery were poorly preserved and contained little pottery or other grave gifts. Besides the burial pithoi themselves (497-499), only buff or orange bowls are represented (494-496). Nonceramic finds included copper or bronze pins (501, 502), silver ring fragments (505), and collections of knuckle bones (503, 504).

A red-slipped jar handle with incised design was recovered from fill over the cemetery, but could not be associated with a particular burial (500).

MISCELLANEOUS CONTEXTS (506-533)

In addition to finds from the stratified deposits under Megaron 10 and Megaron 12, further finds of Middle and Late Bronze date were recovered from other contexts on the Gordion City Mound. Their principal source is the clay packing, 2.4-4 m. thick, overlying the Kimmerian Destruction Level of ca. 696 B.C. Some of the finds are closely paralleled among examples from stratified contexts. Painted red-on-buff pottery (515, 516) is also found in Megaron 10 Layers 8 and 7, crescent loomweights (526-529) are similar to examples from Layer 7, and a hieroglyphic Hittite sealing (532) has a parallel in Layer 5. Incised vessel marks of triangular form (517-520) are matched by an example from Megaron 12 Level VB (447) and another from a pre-Level IC context in the North Central Trench (493).

---

83. Compare buff-slipped "enamel" ware, above, pp. 28-29.

84. G. K. Sams, *Gordion* IV, P 5667 and P 5668, and see Pl. 32A.

Fragments of barrel-shaped animal vessels or rhyta similar to **510-512** have been identified among sherds from Megaron 10 Layers 16, 12, and 7. Other categories have little or no representation among the stratified finds, such as zoomorphic spouts and handles (**508, 509, 513, 514**). Figurines are represented by several ex-amples (**522-525**), while a single well-preserved animal head from a vessel was recovered from a stratified context, in Megaron 10 Layer 9 (**254**). From miscellaneous deposits are also a few highly unusual artifacts, including a double arrow graffito (**521**) and a rare bead seal (**533**).

Internal Correlations and Chronology

Since the deep soundings under Megaron 10 and under Megaron 12 could not be directly linked, correlation of the Middle and Late Bronze Age levels at Gordion depends on ceramic comparisons. This task is hampered by the disparity in quantities of pottery between the two soundings, Megaron 10 having yielded a considerably larger corpus. Moreover, the fragmentary nature of the material makes it difficult to follow closely the development of particular shapes or judge the relative importance of unusual traits. Nevertheless, gradual changes in the fabrics and shapes within the assemblage from each level in both soundings suggest a successive accumulation with little disturbance or admixture. An internal chronology is established by comparing the proportion of different fabrics within each level and the presence of common shapes. The sequence outlined for the occupation levels permits a relative dating of finds from miscellaneous contexts on the City Mound as well as those from the Hittite Cemetery.

The second-millennium sequence at Gordion begins with the lowest levels under Megaron 10. Layer 18 is the earliest defined stratum, although extrusive Early Bronze sherds retrieved in small quantities from Layers 18-15 demonstrate the presence of a still earlier settlement underneath it. These levels follow in succession, with some mixing of material principally in Layers 15 and 14B. Layers 18-15 comprise a ceramic phase dominated by red-slipped, gritty buff and orange fabrics in a variety of shapes, characteristically the carinated bowl with thickened rim and horizontal handles. Layer 14B, reached below Layer 15, appears to belong with the period represented by Layer 16, although the available samples exhibit little overlap.

In Layer 14 appears a complex of shapes that dominates the Megaron 10 repertory for the remainder of its duration: shallow bowls with broad or angled rims, narrow-necked jugs, and jars with sharply everted rims. With Layers 13-12 buff and orange wares have reached a commanding proportion in the assemblage, one that continues to increase in later layers. By this time the standard profiles and types of Layers 18-15 are only minimally represented. Instead, orange or buff jars with everted rims and ring bases, pitchers with trefoil rims, and narrow-necked jugs occur frequently. Layer 13 also furnishes the first examples of painted pottery, one of them (**203**) probably an import from North Syria.

A predominance of buff and orange wares in similar shapes, forming roughly 60% of the assemblage, characterizes the ceramic phase represented by Layers 11 and 10. New elements include white- or red-slipped "bathtub" rims, a vessel stamped with concentric circles, and the first appearance of a painted pottery with red-on-cream designs. Layer 9 occupies an uncertain place in the Megaron 10 sequence because its sherds were not kept. Observations by the excavator suggest that it belongs with the subsequent ceramic phase, but this cannot be confirmed. An animal vessel fragment from this level, **254**, provides the only well-preserved, stratified second-millennium example of this type.

Layers 8-5 can be grouped as a homogeneous assemblage, which also documents a steady increase in the proportion of buff and orange wares to the red-slipped alternative. Gritty, coarse fabrics exhibiting little attention to surface treatment are characteristic of this phase. Roughly 10-15% of the buff specimens are covered with a thin, clay-colored "self-slip" which is usually given no additional smoothing or finish. A new shape is the large coarse plate. "Bathtub" fragments and painted pottery with red-on-cream designs, both in minute quantities, link Layers 8 and 7. The shallow bowl with thickened or vertical rim is the typical shape for this phase, its popularity continuing into Layer 4. Plates increase in frequency in Layer 5 and continue into Layer 4, along with fine buff bowls.

In Layer 6 a jar rim of unusual micaceous fabric (**340**) introduces a wheelmade tradition external to the prevailing Late Bronze Age pottery. This continues in one example in Layer 5 (**354**), then increases to several specimens in Layer 4 (**390, 391, 394, 398, S60, S61**). Otherwise the assemblages from these layers share most component types, including shallow bowls and plates, and jars with everted rims, in gritty buff and orange wheelmarked wares. Layer 4 also produced two examples of handmade pottery with incised ornament, and two Phrygian gray sherds.

As noted above, the Megaron 12 sequence is known through a considerably smaller corpus of sherds. The pottery from each level in this sounding appears to reflect a wider chronological range, thus perhaps containing a greater proportion of extrusive material, than assemblages from the Megaron 10 stratigraphic units. Approximate equations will refer to the latest material from the Megaron 12 levels. Comparisons of the percentages of wares together with specific vessel shapes and their relative frequency within each level furnish the basis for correlations between the two sequences. Megaron 12 Level VC, the earliest stratified deposit above the Early Bronze Level VI, finds common ceramic ground with Megaron 10 Layers 11 and 10, the phase following domination by the bead-rim bowl. Approximately 70% of the VC assemblage is composed of buff and orange plain wares, occurring in shallow bowls with thickened or vertical rims, jars, and jugs. A jar rim, **405**, resembles an example in Megaron 10 Layer 10 (**226**). Horizontal grooves in the upper wall of a jar in Layer 10 (**238**) and one in Level VC (**411**), are a rare trait, again providing a link. The assemblages of VC and Layers 11-10 do not correspond precisely, however. A red-slipped bowl (**400**) resembling an example from Megaron 10 Layer 15 (**132**) suggests that Level VC incorporates earlier material from a period not recognized stratigraphically, or calls for a somewhat earlier beginning, perhaps overlapping with Megaron 10 Layer 12.

Megaron 12 Level VB contains a proportion of wares similar to that of Megaron 12 Level VC, suggesting gradual chronological progression. Connections in certain shapes with Megaron 10 Layer 8 form an additional basis for associating these assemblages (buff and orange bowls, **263, 431**). At its beginning Level VB may overlap the elusive Megaron 10 Layer 9, whose pottery is virtually unknown. The end of the phase is signaled by an unusual jar profile (**437**) which resembles an example in Megaron 10 Layer 7 (**307**). Level VB and

Layer 7 also share the initial popularity of carinated bowls with sloping rim (**297, 298, 435**) and shallow bowls with vertical rim (**290, 292-294, 427-430**).

In Megaron 12 Level VA the predominance of buff and orange wares reaches about 80% of the assemblage, including the "self-slipped" variety. Both specific shapes and the general impression of coarse, gritty mass-production point to correlation with Megaron 10 Layers 7 and 6. A form of jar with narrowing shoulder and thickened rim (**455, 456**) closely resembles an example in Megaron 10 Layer 7 (**308**), the latter preserving a stamped pattern of concentric circles. These levels also share carinated bowls with sloping rim (**297, 298, 453**). Flat jar bases (**463, 464**) find a counterpart in Megaron 10 Layer 6 (**345**).

Megaron 12 Level IVB continues the fabric and shape repertory of VA, with another increase in the proportion of buff and orange to red-slipped wares. The buff plate with barely raised rim gains in popularity, linking IVB with Megaron 10 Layer 4. These levels also exhibit a similar repertory of shapes as a whole, including large coarse plates, shallow bowls, jugs, and jars of coarse cooking pot fabric. Finally, in both IVB and 4 a few sherds of coarse handmade pottery with notched rim decoration make their appearance (see Pl. 32).

Some of the ceramic artifacts retrieved from miscellaneous contexts have close parallels in the stratified series. Painted pottery with red-on-buff geometric designs occurs only in Megaron 10 Layers 8 and 7, furnishing a temporal association for the similar examples **515** and **516**. Crescent loomweights, well represented in the clay layer over the Destruction Level, appear only once in the stratified sequence, in Megaron 10 Layer 7 (**334**). Another category with few stratigraphic associations is the group of vessels with graffiti (**517-521**). The four examples of the triangular sign (**517-520**), are matched by one from Megaron 12 Level VB (**447**). The remainder of the items from miscellaneous contexts requires the aid of comparisons from other sites to establish the periods they represent. Parallels from dated contexts are cited in the catalogue entries for these examples (**506, 511, 512, 522-529**).

External Correlations and Chronology

Only a small ceramic sample represents the earliest second-millennium levels at Gordion, Megaron 10 Layers 18-15, but the affinities of shapes and fabrics are sufficiently clear for general correlations. The period is Middle Bronze I to II, the inaugural era of wheelmade

red-slipped, well-burnished pottery of "Hittite" style. Shapes in this fabric, including fine bowls and carinated bowls with thickened rims often with horizontal handles, point to Polatlı Phase III (Levels XVI-XXII), and early levels of Phase IV (XXIII-XXIV), secondarily to Nordwesthang-Büyükkale 8d-8b, and Büyükkale IVd.[85] Ties to Beycesultan V are indicated by the red-slipped and polished wares, popular two-handled carinated bowls, and pedestaled vessels.[86] Some elements of Megaron 10 Layer 14B should be placed in this period as well. The small handmade bowls from this level show affinities with Asarcık Va.[87] Pitchers with rising beak spout and small buff jars with everted rim, however, point to a Middle Bronze III connection.[88]

Megaron 10 Layer 14 continues the partially red-slipped carinated bowls with thickened rims and horizontal handles. It also introduces teapots with strainer spout, and buff or orange bowls with thickened or angled rims that become second-millennium staples. The Layer 14 assemblage corresponds to Polatlı Phase IV (Levels XXIII-XXXI), generally Middle Bronze III.[89] Its counterpart in fully literate Anatolia is the later Old Assyrian Colony Period or Kültepe Karum Level Ib, at Boğazköy represented by Unterstadt 4, Nordwesthang-Büyükkale 8a, and Büyükkale IVd; but overlaps with the following period of Unterstadt 3, Nordwesthang-Büyükkale 7, and Büyükkale IVc.[90]

An Old Hittite ceramic assemblage commences with the following ceramic phase, Megaron 10 Layers 13-12. The relatively small collections from these two levels limit specific correlations, but broad associations and some details can be established. In archaeological terms the period is Middle Bronze IV, corresponding to Asarcık Level IV and the Boğazköy levels Unterstadt 3, Nordwesthang-Büyükkale 7, and Büyükkale IVc. Common to these assemblages are pitchers with beak spouts, trefoil or straight rims, and jars with everted rims.[91] A painted jar from Level 13 (**202**) is closely matched by examples from Alişar Levels 11-10T and Maşat Level V. Another painted specimen from this layer may be an import from North Syria (**203**).

With Megaron 10 Layers 11 and 10, correlated also with the later material of Megaron 12 Level VC, synchronisms become available over a wider area of Anatolia. Near Gordion itself only unstratified pottery from Asarcık Hüyük fits this ceramic phase.[92] The precise relation of the Gordion levels to the Boğazköy sequence is more difficult to define. Similarities between the pottery from Layers 11 to 10 and that of Old Hittite Boğazköy (Unterstadt 3, Nordwesthang 7, Büyükkale IVc) have been noted in the catalogue. They imply a strong ceramic continuity between these phases, one which is difficult to document at Boğazköy itself, where the Old Hittite assemblage is known in more detail than that of the following early Empire. At Tarsus the ceramic repertory of Late Bronze I resembles Megaron 10 Layers 11-10 and Megaron 12 Level VC.[93] In the southeast, similar shapes and fabrics characterize Korucutepe Phase I.[94] In western Anatolia the period is represented by some of the material from Beycesultan Levels II and I.[95]

Megaron 10 Layers 9-5 form a relatively unified ceramic phase, although the Megaron 12 sequence corroborates the implication that a subdivision may be needed. The latest material in Megaron 12 Level VB finds parallels with Megaron 10 Layers 9-7; similarly, the latest material from VA overlaps with Megaron 10 Layers 6-5. The incised triangular sign preserved on a sherd from Megaron 12 Level VB (**447**) links the pottery of this level with Büyükkale IVb, Maşat III-II, Tarsus Late Bronze II, Alaca Empire levels, and Korucutepe Phases I-J.[96] Red-and-cream painted pottery with geometric motifs (**270, 332, 333**) supplies a synchronism between Megaron 10 Layers 8-7 and Büyükkale III, Maşat I, and Korucutepe Phase I.[97] By this time the ceramic assemblage at all pertinent sites deserves the epithet "drab" the Tarsus excavators bestowed on it at first sight.[98] The mass-produced, grim appearance of the Gordion pottery contributes its testimony to that observed for Büyükkale III, Maşat I, and Korucutepe Phase J.[99]

Megaron 10 Layer 4 and Megaron 12 Level IVB continue the direction of preceding levels in fabrics and shapes, but few precise parallels can be named from the major Hittite centers. Gordion seems to preserve in this

85. *AnatSt* 1 (1951) 36, fig. 6b:14-15, 17-21; *Frühe Keramik*, 31, no. 191, pl. 21; 39-40, nos. 291, 295, pl. 31; *Heth. Keramik*, no. 707, pl. 84; *Boğazköy* VI, 18, fig. 3:39-40, 43.

86. *Beycesultan* II, 86, fig. P.2:1-3; 92, fig. P.5:29; 94 fig. P.6:8-11.

87. *IstMitt* 16 (1966) 69, fig. 9:10.

88. Büyükkale Level IVd (*Boğazköy* VI, 43, fig. 16:158; p. 46, fig. 18:176).

89. *AnatSt* 1 (1951) 36, fig. 6c:1-3.

90. *Frühe Keramik*, pls. 34:356; 36:340, 352, 355; *Heth. Keramik*, pls. 36:385; 85:721; 89:776, 778; *Boğazköy* VI, 73, fig. 9:35; 75, fig. 10a:60-62; 76, fig. 10b:65, 69-72.

91. *IstMitt* 16 (1966) 70-73, figs. 12:10-11; 13:1-2, 6; *Nordwesthang-Büyükkale*, pls. 30:77, 80; 35:128; *Heth. Keramik*, pl. 58:514; *Boğazköy* VI, 73, fig. 9:33-39.

92. *IstMitt* 16 (1966) 87-88, figs. 27-28.

93. *Tarsus* II, 183-184, figs. 375:959-960, 991; 376:profiles E, I; 378:984; 379:1015, 1036, 1038; 382:1040.

94. *Korucutepe* 3, 71, pls. 10G, 15N, 16B.

95. Cf. J. Mellaart, *AnatSt* 20 (1970) 55-67, with further bibliography. The forthcoming complete publication of the pottery from Beycesultan Levels III-I will provide additional documentation for assessing their relative chronology.

96. References are cited in catalogue, under **447**.

97. *Heth. Keramik*, pl. 16:177-181; *Maşat* II, fig. 32 (*Maşat* I, pl. 48:3); *Korucutepe* 3, 74, pls. 14C, 26G.

98. *Tarsus* II, 203.

99. *Heth. Keramik*, 109; *Maşat* II, 101; *Korucutepe* 3, 76.

stratum a period following the destruction of Boğazköy and possibly other sites in *ca.* 1200 B.C. Additional chronological information is supplied by the few sherds of handmade tan- or dark-fired pottery recovered from both levels. The affinities of the alien pottery with the handmade "Knobbed Ware" of Troy VIIb2 have long been noted.[100] At Troy the intrusive handmade arrivals are associated with Mycenaean IIIC pottery, furnishing a date in the 12th century B.C.[101] How long the Hittite ceramic domination at Gordion continued, and when the users of handmade pottery arrived, cannot be more precisely determined. This question is discussed in chapter IV with reference to Late Bronze Age pottery from Early Iron Age levels at Gordion (see pp. 92-95).

Hittite Cemetery: Internal and External Correlations

As already described in chapter I, the 1962 Museum Site excavations added eight pithos graves to the Hittite Cemetery. The place of the cemetery in Anatolian chronology and history has been extensively analyzed by M.J. Mellink. Drawing on comparative ceramic material available principally from Kültepe, Boğazköy, and Ališar Hüyük, she suggested that the cemetery dated to the Old Assyrian Colony and early Old Hittite periods, in archaeological terms Middle Bronze III and IV. She also noted the unusual character of the Gordion extramural necropolis dominated by pithos burials in early second-millennium Anatolia, linking the practice to third-millennium burial customs of western Anatolia.[102] Subsequent investigations at Gordion and other sites provide new information for assessing the date and significance of the cemetery, largely supporting Mellink's suggestions and interpretation.

The sequences on the City Mound now furnish a local context for the ceramic repertory displayed in the cemetery. Burial pithoi and pottery included as tomb gifts are closely associated with the assemblages of Megaron 10 Layers 14-12. These share fabrics, preference for partial red-slip surface treatment, and a variety of characteristic shapes: bowls with thickened rim and horizontal handles, pitchers with trefoil rim or beak spout, teapots with strainer spout, jugs, banded pithoi, and hole-mouth shapes. Bowls with broad, thickened rims make an appearance in the cemetery but do not form a significant percentage of the repertory, as they do in the subsequent ceramic phase represented by Megaron 10 Layers 11-10 and Megaron 12 Level VC. As detailed above in the section on external correlations, the period is Middle Bronze III and IV. Whether the burials coincide neatly with the beginning and end of this chronological division is not certain.

The general form of extramural burial in pithoi, with simple accompanying gifts of metal ornaments and pottery vessels, now has decisively western Anatolian associations in both third- and second-millennium manifestations. To the Early Bronze Kusura pithos burials can now be added a cemetery at Yanarlar near Afyon, dating generally to the Old Hittite period.[103] Middle Bronze Age pithos burials at Karataş-Semayük and Bağbaşı near Elmalı continue local third-millennium customs and help to define the geographical range of the practice, extending to that area of southwest Anatolia.[104] In central Anatolia, however, the Gordion cemetery remains an isolated phenomenon in this period. By Old Hittite times cremation is introduced at nearby Ilıca and farther east in the Osmankayası cemetery at Boğazköy.[105] Extramural pithos burial in Hittite territory is otherwise attested only at Ferzant/Büget near Çorum, where it occurs together with burial in stone cists.[106] Here, as well as at nearby Kazankaya where the deceased were placed in long pits, the burials appear to antedate the cremation burials at Osmankayası and Ilıca.[107]

100. M. J. Mellink, *BibOr* 17 (1960) 251.

101. N. K. Sandars in J. Boardman, M. A. Brown, T. G. E. Powell, eds., *The European Community in Later Prehistory* (London 1971), 17-22, citing southeast European parallels. H. W. Catling and E. A. Catling, *BSA* 76 (1981) 71-82, with bibliography, for the 'barbarian' pottery of LH IIIC:1 date that is pertinent to the Anatolian material; also K. A. Wardle, *BSA* 75 (1980) 262-263. H. A. Bankoff and F. A. Winter, *JIES* 12 (1984) 1-30, review the material systematically; also J. Bouzek, *The Aegean, Anatolia and Europe: Cultural Interrelations in the Second Millennium B.C.*, SIMA XXIX (Göteborg 1985), 182-195.

102. *Hitt. Cem.*, 55-57.

103. *Yanarlar*, esp. 73-88.

104. Mellink, *AJA* 71 (1967) 257, idem, *AJA* 73 (1969) 330-331. T. S. Wheeler, *AJA* 78 (1974) 415-425, for the Early Bronze Age pithos burials at Karataş-Semayük.

105. *Ilıca*, esp. 10-38, 59-64; *Osmankayası*, 3-10.

106. *Maşat* I, 87-88.

107. *Maşat* I, 69-88. The Middle Bronze II-III necropolis at Ikiztepe near Bafra included a single pithos burial in a cemetery otherwise composed of inhumations: *AnatSt* 29 (1979) 202. The pithos burials of late second-millennium date currently under investigation near Beşiktepe in the Troad suggest continuity of the practice in western Anatolia (M.J. Mellink, *AJA* 89 [1985] 552-553).

Catalogue of the Middle and Late Bronze Age Finds

Middle and Late Bronze Age pottery and nonceramic artifacts from the sounding below Megaron 10 are catalogued first, followed by pottery from the Megaron 12 sounding, the burials, and miscellaneous contexts. Well-preserved items or unusual diagnostic fragments have been assigned an excavation inventory number; the majority is designated as "not inventoried."

Ceramic finds located or recorded in 1985 could not be incorporated into the catalogue sequence. They have been grouped as Supplementary entries, given a number beginning with **S** (**S1-S68**), and listed separately at the end of the chapter III catalogue (pp. 85-91,

Figs. 28-31, Pls. 30 and 31). The information they contribute to the assemblage from each level and the overall ceramic development at Gordion is included in the description of the fabrics, shapes, and levels given above, pp. 27-46.

Vessel profiles are illustrated in line drawings, supplemented as needed by photographs. Editorial considerations limited the detailed illustration of vessels in most cases to examples with rim diameters of 0.30 m. or less; examples with larger diameters generally appear as abbreviated profiles.

City Mound   *(102-493)*

MEGARON 10   (102-398)

LAYER 18   (102-105)

BOWL (102)

102   Shallow bowl
Not inv.   Layer 18
Est. D. rim 0.25; GTh. 0.009 m.
Fig. 6
Rim sherd of shallow bowl with incurved rim.
Fine light brown (7.5YR 5/4) clay, slightly micaceous; well fired. Light reddish brown (5YR 5/4) slip on both surfaces; wheel-burnish marks faintly visible on inside of rim; low luster.

JAR (103)

103   Jar
Not inv.   Layer 18
Est. D. rim 0.20; GTh. 0.01 m.
Fig. 6
Rim sherd; worn on rim and interior.
Jar with everted rim. Shoulder narrows gradually towards neck; profile of lower rim ridged.
Reddish brown (2.5YR 6/4) clay, coarse and gritty, micaceous. Red (10R 5.5/6) slip on exterior continues to just inside rim; smoothed and polished, with matt finish. Interior plain.

BASES (104 and 105)

104   Ring base
Not inv.   Layer 18
GPH. 0.025; D. base 0.05 m.
Fig. 6
Base and adjoining lower body of vessel with ring base. Base fully preserved. Probably from a bowl.
Fine orange (5YR 6/6) clay, micaceous, with few tiny inclusions; well fired. Red slip on interior, smoothed, with matt finish. Exterior mostly smoothed, but wheelmarks clearly visible.

105   Pedestal base
Not inv.   Layer 18
GPH. 0.033; GTh. 0.0045 m.
Fig. 6
Base and lower body of bowl with pedestal base. Broken across base.
Fine, clean gray clay, slightly micaceous. Light brown (7.5YR 6/4) slip applied to exterior, thickly in places, to *ca.* 0.02 m. from base. Interior covered with red-orange slip, mottled black and brown in one area. Both surfaces well smoothed and polished.

LAYER 17   (106-117)

BOWLS (106-111)

106   Shallow bowl
Not inv.   Layer 17
Est. D. rim 0.14; GTh. 0.004 m.
Fig. 6
Rim sherd of shallow bowl with incurved rim.
Fine tan (2.5YR 6/4) clay, slightly micaceous; fired clean. Reddish brown (2.5YR 5/6) slip, smoothed and polished, on both surfaces.
Boğazköy, Unterstadt Level 4 (*Heth. Keramik*, 139, no. 769, pl. 88).

107   Carinated bowl
Not inv.   Layer 17
Est. D. rim 0.228; GTh. 0.0045 m.
Fig. 6
Rim and adjoining upper wall, mended from two joining sherds.
Carinated bowl with straight upper wall, plain rim.
Fine buff (7.5YR 7/6) clay, with some gritty inclusions; well fired. Traces of dull light red slip on rim and exterior above carination. Well smoothed both surfaces, few wheelmarks visible.

108   Carinated bowl
Not inv.   Layer 17
Est. D. rim 0.28; GTh. 0.008 m.
Fig. 6

Rim sherd of bowl, mended from two joining sherds. Slip worn, especially on rim.

Thickened rim; base of sherd preserves beginning of slight carination.

Fine brown (7.5YR 5/6) clay, with some gritty inclusions; well fired. Red (10R 5.5/6) slip on exterior, extending inside rim. Interior plain, wheelmarks clearly visible. Traces of original luster on rim; now with matt finish.

109 Carinated bowl with horizontal handles
P 5464   Layer 17
D. rim unknown; GPL. 0.086; GPW. 0.136; Th. handle 0.02; GTh. 0.0125 m.
Fig. 6; Pl. 19

Mended section preserves rim, handle, place of attachment, and part of adjoining wall. Some chips; slightly grayed in places.

Bowl with thickened rim, carination at point where handle is attached. Horizontal handle, approximately triangular in section, rises well above rim.

Buff (7.5YR 7/4) clay, gritty; fired gray at core. Interior mostly plain. Exterior, lower part of handle and inner rim preserve red (10R 6/8) slip. Smoothed; slightly lustrous to matt finish.

110 Bowl with horizontal handles
P 5465   Layer 17
D. rim unknown; GPL. 0.051; GPW. 0.064; Th. handle 0.019; GTh. 0.0085 m.
Pl. 19

Single sherd preserves part of rim, base of handle and place of attachment on vessel wall. Some slight greenish discoloration.

Bowl with thickened rim, perhaps carinated at point where handle is attached. Handle, oval in section, rises probably just above rim.

Buff (7.5YR 7/4) clay, with gritty inclusions; some "gold" and "silver" mica. Surfaces appear "self-slipped" and smoothed; fired buff to orange.

111 Ring base of bowl
Not inv.   Layer 17
GPH. 0.059; D. base ca. 0.055; GTh. 0.0049 m.
Fig. 6

Base and adjoining wall of bowl, mended from six sherds. Base slightly damaged.

Bowl with ring base, wall rising gradually to carinated upper wall.

Buff (7.5YR 7/4) clay, with some inclusions; fired gray at core. Red-orange (2.5YR 6/8) slip applied on interior surface of bowl. Exterior upper wall perhaps originally covered with tan slip, of which little remains; well smoothed and polished.

JAR (112)

112 Jar
Not inv.   Layer 17
Est D. rim 0.14; GTh. 0.006 m.
Fig. 6

Rim sherd of jar with gently everted rim, flaring shoulder. Some grayish and greenish discoloration on exterior.

Fine, clean buff (10YR 7/3) clay with very few gritty inclusions; well fired. Surfaces well smoothed.

COOKING POTS (113 and 114)

113 Cooking pot
Not inv.   Layer 17

Est. D. rim 0.24; GTh. 0.012 m.
Fig. 6

Rim sherd of cooking pot of hole-mouth form.

Orange (5YR 6/6) clay, coarse and gritty. Surfaces partly smoothed.

114 Cooking pot
Not inv.   Layer 17
Est. D. rim 0.25; GTh. 0.012 m.
Fig. 6

Rim sherd of cooking pot of hole-mouth form. Blackened on exterior and outside rim.

Orange clay, coarse and gritty. Exterior and rim smoothed, plain; interior roughly finished.

OPEN MOUTH VESSELS (115-117)

115 Open mouth vessel
Not inv.   Layer 17
Est. D. rim 0.16; GTh. 0.006 m.
Fig. 6

Rim sherd of open mouth vessel. Damaged on exterior.

Buff clay, slightly gritty; red slip on both surfaces, wheel-burnished, with slight luster preserved on interior. Exterior matt.

116 Open mouth vessel
Not inv.   Layer 17
Est. D. rim 0.22; GTh. 0.006 m.
Fig. 6

Rim sherd of open mouth vessel with thickened rim. Two shallow parallel grooves at lower edge of rim on exterior.

Fine orange clay, slightly micaceous, with few tiny inclusions. Red-orange (2.5YR 6/6) slip, mostly worn but visible on both surfaces; wheel-burnish marks preserved on inside rim.

117 Open mouth vessel
Not inv.   Layer 17
D. rim unknown; GTh. 0.012
Fig. 6

Rim sherd of jar(?) with rim thickened on outside, probably from a carinated shape.

Fine orange clay, slightly micaceous with some inclusions; fired gray at core. Red slip on both surfaces, wheel-burnish marks visible. Smoothed, with slight luster.

LAYER 16   (118-128, S1)

BOWLS (118-120)

118 Carinated bowl
Not inv.   Layer 16
Est. D. rim 0.22; GTh. 0.007 m.
Fig. 7

Rim sherd of bowl with thickened rim, slight carination.

Fine orange clay, with some gritty inclusions; well fired. Orange-red (5YR 6/6) slip, unevenly applied in streaks; better preserved on interior than exterior. Exterior well smoothed.

119 Carinated bowl
Not inv.   Layer 16
Est. D. rim 0.22; GTh. 0.0078 m.
Fig. 7

Rim sherd of bowl with thickened rim, slight carination.

Fine buff (10YR 7/3) clay, with some gritty inclusions. Pale red (10R 6/4) slip on exterior, continuing inside rim. Surfaces smoothed, with matt finish.

120 Bowl with horizontal handles
P 5463   Layer 16
GPH. 0.096; D. rim unknown; GPW. 0.14; Th. handle 0.002;
GTh. 0.011 m.
Fig. 7; Pl. 19
Mended section preserves part of rim and adjoining wall,
most of handle and one place of attachment.
Bowl with thickened rim, probably slight carination.
Horizontal handle, roughly triangular in section, rises above
rim.
Tan clay, rather gritty. Red slip preserved on exterior, part
of handle, and inner rim. Slipped area smoothed, with matt
finish.

COOKING POTS (121-123)

121 Cooking pot
Not inv.   Layer 16
Est. D. rim 0.25; GTh. 0.0136 m.
Fig. 7
Rim sherd of hole-mouth cooking pot with thickened rim.
Exterior blackened.
Reddish brown clay, coarse and gritty with noticeable in-
clusions; fired dark at core. Wheelmarks somewhat smoothed
from exterior surface.

122 Lug-handled cooking pot
Not inv.   Layer 16
Est. D. rim 0.25; GTh. 0.016 m.
Fig. 7
Rim sherd of hole-mouth cooking pot with arrised vertical
lug. Exterior blackened; lug damaged.
Reddish brown clay, coarse and gritty; well fired. Wheel-
marks mostly smoothed.

123 Cooking pot
Not inv.   Layer 16
D. rim unknown; GTh. 0.012 m.
Fig. 7
Rim sherd of hole-mouth cooking pot, thickened rim.
Reddish brown (2.5YR 5/4) clay with gritty inclusions;
fired gray at core. Pale red slip poorly preserved on both sur-
faces, mostly smoothed.

BASES (124-126)

124 Base
Not inv.   Layer 16
GPH. 0.028; Est.D. base 0.08 m.
Fig. 7
Base fragment, probably from jar with flat base. Mended
from two joining sherds.
Buff (7.5YR 7/4) clay, gritty; fired darker at core. Buff slip
on exterior surface, mottled darker in places. Exterior
smoothed; wheelmarks visible.

125 Ring base
Not inv.   Layer 16
GPH. 0.025; Est. D. base 0.09 m.
Fig. 7
Base fragment of jar or pitcher with ring base.
Medium to coarse orange clay, gritty. Wheelmarks mostly
smoothed or worn.

126 Pedestal base
Not inv.   Layer 16
Est. D. base 0.10; GTh. 0.0004 m.
Fig. 7

Fragment preserves edge of pedestal base, probably from
bowl or pitcher.
Fine buff ware, clean and well fired. Surfaces smoothed.
Upper surface may have originally had thin red slip.

HANDLE (127)

127 Handle
Not inv.   Layer 16
GPL. 0.0805; GPW. 0.051; Th. handle 0.013 m.
Pl. 19
Vertical handle, broken at both ends; surfaces worn, slight-
ly incrusted.
Handle probably from a one-handled jar or teapot, attached
to rim of vessel. Handle triangular in section, sharply arrised
along top surface.
Fine, clean orange (5YR 6/6) clay. Red (10R 4/8) slip cover-
ing all surfaces; well smoothed and polished, with some luster
preserved.

METAL (128)

128 Copper or bronze chisel or stylus fragment
B 1591   Layer 16
PL. 0.022; GW. 0.006; GTh. 0.005 m.
Pl. 19
Shaft broken across close to sharpened end. Edge chipped;
roughened by corrosion.
Shaft flat, rectangular in section; flattening out gradually
to a slightly splayed sharpened edge.
Boğazköy, Büyükkale Level IVd (*Kleinfunde*, 76, no. 209,
pl. XIII; of "Type Ia," also represented in Levels IVc-III,
76-77).

LAYER 15   (129-150, S2)

BOWLS (129-140)

129 Bowl
Not inv.   Layer 15
Est. D. rim 0.14; GTh. 0.027 m.
Fig. 7
Rim sherd of bowl with slightly incurved rim.
Fine, clean red clay; well fired. Red slip on both surfaces,
slightly mottled on exterior. Well smoothed and polished; lit-
tle luster preserved.

130 Shallow bowl
Not inv.   Layer 15
D. rim unknown; GTh. 0.005 m.
Fig. 7
Rim sherd of shallow bowl with thickened rim. Surfaces
discolored, slightly incrusted.
Orange (5YR 6/6) clay with some gritty inclusions. Sur-
faces left plain, rather roughly finished.

131 Deep bowl
Not inv.   Layer 15
Est. D. rim 0.24; GTh. 0.0061 m.
Fig. 7
Rim section mended from two joining sherds. Deep bowl
with straight upper wall and slightly outturned, thickened
rim.
Fine orange clay, micaceous, with few gritty inclusions;
well fired. Red slip on both surfaces, well smoothed and
polished; little or no luster preserved.

132   Hemispherical bowl
Not inv.   Layer 15
Est. D. rim 0.28; GTh. 0.0058 m.
Fig. 7
Rim sherd of bowl of hemispherical form, slightly out-turned rim. Worn and chipped on exterior.
Fine, clean orange clay, well fired. Red (10R 5/8) slip on both surfaces. Well smoothed on exterior, somewhat less carefully on rim and interior.
Related to type as below, **400**, with comparanda.

133   Carinated bowl
Not inv.   Layer 15
Est. D. rim 0.20; GTh. 0.0061 m.
Fig. 7
Rim sherd of carinated bowl with plain rim.
Orange clay, slightly gritty and micaceous; fired gray at core. Red (10R 5/8) slip on exterior, with matt finish; plain, or slipped in dull tan, smoothed, on interior.

134   Carinated bowl
Not inv.   Layer 15
Est. D. rim 0.16; GTh. 0.0062 m.
Fig. 7
Rim sherd of carinated bowl with plain rim.
Fine orange clay, well fired. Red slip on interior and on exterior to *ca.* 0.01 m. below carination. Well smoothed; slipped surfaces polished.
Boğazköy, Nordwesthang-Büyükkale Level 8a (*Nordwesthang-Büyükkale*, 44, no. 27, pl. 24).

135   Carinated bowl
Not inv.   Layer 15
Est. D. rim 0.25; GTh. 0.006 m.
Fig. 7
Rim sherd of carinated bowl, rim thickened slightly on outside.
Fine orange clay, well fired. Orange-red (2.5YR 6/6) slip on interior, streakily applied, and near rim and carination on exterior. Exterior surface well smoothed.

136   Carinated bowl
Not inv.   Layer 15
Est. D. rim 0.28; GTh. 0.006 m.
Fig. 7
Rim sherd of bowl with thickened rim, gently carinated profile.
Orange clay, slightly micaceous and gritty; fired gray at core. Dull tan (7.5YR 6/4) slip on exterior, smoothed and polished. Interior plain and smoothed.

137   Carinated bowl
Not inv.   Layer 15
Est. D. rim 0.28; GTh. 0.007 m.
Fig. 7
Rim sherd of carinated bowl with thickened rim.
Tan clay, slightly gritty and micaceous; fired gray at core. Red (10R 5/8) slip on exterior and just inside rim; interior plain, smoothed. Rim and exterior preserve wheel-burnish strokes.

138   Carinated bowl
Not inv.   Layer 15
Est. D. rim 0.28; GTh. 0.0071 m.
Fig. 8
Rim sherd of carinated bowl with thickened rim.
Orange clay, micaceous and slightly gritty; well fired. Dull orange (5YR 6/6) slip on both surfaces; traces of redder slip below rim and below carination on exterior. Both surfaces well smoothed and polished.

139   Carinated bowl
Not inv.   Layer 15
Est. D. rim 0.40; GTh. 0.008 m.
Fig. 8
Rim sherd of carinated bowl with concave profile below thickened rim.
Orange clay, with some gritty inclusions. Red (10R 5.5/6) slip on exterior and just inside rim. Interior plain.

140   Carinated bowl
Not inv.   Layer 15
D. rim unknown; GTh. 0.0093 m.
Fig. 8
Rim sherd of carinated bowl with thickened rim. Mended from two joining sherds.
Fine orange clay with gritty inclusions. Red (10R 5.5/6) slip on exterior, extends just inside rim; smoothed. Interior plain.

JAR (141)

141   Jar
Not inv.   Layer 15
Est. D. rim 0.24; GTh. 0.0098 m.
Fig. 8
Rim sherd of jar with everted rim.
Coarse, gritty orange clay; fired gray at core. Light red slip unevenly preserved on exterior, rim, and just below rim. Interior plain, surface pitted.

COOKING POTS (142 and 143)

142   Cooking pot
Not inv.   Layer 15
Est. D. rim 0.28; GTh. 0.014 m.
Fig. 8
Rim sherd of hole-mouth cooking pot with rim thickened on inside. Exterior blackened.
Light brown (5YR 6/4) clay, coarse and grit-tempered. Fired dark throughout.

143   Cooking pot
Not inv.   Layer 15
Est. D. rim 0.36; GTh. 0.0138 m.
Fig. 8
Rim sherd of hole-mouth cooking pot with thickened rim. Exterior blackened.
Coarse light orange clay; fired gray at core. Surfaces partly smoothed of wheelmarks.

RIM SHERDS FROM OPEN VESSELS (144-148)

144   Rim sherd
Not inv.   Layer 15
Est D. rim 0.20; GTh. 0.006 m.
Fig. 8
Rim sherd of open vessel with straight sides, plain rim. Perhaps from a jar or deep bowl.
Fine buff clay. Orange (2.5YR 6/6) slip on both surfaces, unevenly applied on interior. Smoothed on outside, with dull finish.

145   Rim sherd
Not inv.   Layer 15
Est. D. rim 0.20; GTh. 0.0048 m.
Fig. 8

Rim sherd of open vessel with straight sides, slightly thickened and outturned rim. Perhaps from a jar or deep bowl.

Fine, clean orange clay. Red (10R 5/6) slip on both surfaces, worn slightly on rim and interior.

146 Rim sherd
Not inv.   Layer 15
Est. D. rim 0.30; GTh. 0.006 m.
Fig. 8
Rim sherd of open vessel with straight sides, rim thickened on outside.

Fine orange clay, fired gray at core. Dull orange-tan (5YR 7/4) slip on both surfaces, well smoothed and polished especially on exterior.

147 Rim sherd
Not inv.   Layer 15
Est D. rim 0.28; GTh. 0.0077 m.
Fig. 8
Rim sherd of open vessel with straight upper wall, thickened outcurved rim. Slip worn. Possibly a jar.

Orange clay, slightly gritty and micaceous. Light red (10YR 6/6) slip on both surfaces, well smoothed.

148 Rim sherd
Not inv.   Layer 15
Est. D. rim 0.36; GTh. 0.02 m.
Fig. 8
Rim sherd of large hole-mouth vessel. Probably a large jar or cooking pot.

Tan clay, coarse and gritty. Surfaces rough.

BASES (149 and 150)

149 Ring base
Not inv.   Layer 15
GPH. 0.025; Est. D. base 0.05 m.
Fig. 8
Fragment of ring base, possibly a bowl.

Tan clay, gritty. Smoothed on interior, roughened on outside.

150 Pedestal base
Not inv.   Layer 15
D. base 0.06; GTh. 0.004 m.
Fig. 8
Fragment of vessel with pedestal base, slightly thickened at lower edge. Exterior worn.

Light brown (5YR 5/6) clay, with orange (2.5YR 6/6) slip, burnished, on both surfaces. Exterior lustrous; interior well smoothed.

LAYER 14B   (151-157)

PINCH POTS (151 and 152)

151 Pinch pot
P 3332   Layer 14B
H. 0.077-0.08; D. 0.084; D. rim 0.04-0.05 m.
Pl. 19
Not examined.
Intact. Rim chipped, slip flaking off.
Spherical pinch pot with small irregular flattening for base, plain hole for mouth.

Clay gritty and slightly micaceous, fired dark gray. Surface slipped and fired to pale gray. Handmade.
Below, 152.

152 Pinch pot
P 3333   Layer 14B
H. 0.045; D. rim 0.083 m.
Pl. 19
Mended; chipped.
Pinch pot of hemispherical form with plain rim; stands unevenly.

Buff (7.5YR 6/4) clay; fired buff at surfaces which may have been slipped. Pink on bottom and in two areas near rim. Well smoothed; handmade.
151 and 152: perhaps related to group of miniature vessels from Asarcık Level Va (*IstMitt* 16 [1966] 69, esp. fig. 9:10).

BOWL (153)

153 Hemispherical bowl
Not inv.   Layer 14B
Est. D. rim 0.22; GTh. 0.0063 m.
Fig. 8
Rim sherd of bowl with hemispherical form, plain rim.
Orange clay, somewhat gritty. Both surfaces covered with burnished red slip, worn on exterior.

JARS (154 and 155)

154 Jar
Not inv.   Layer 14B
Est D. rim 0.14; GTh. 0.012 m.
Fig. 8
Rim sherd of jar with everted rim. Blackened on one edge. Upper wall tapers gradually towards neck, then turns out at rim.
Coarse orange clay, well fired.

155 Jar
Not inv.   Layer 14B
Est D. rim 0.24; GTh. 0.017 m.
Fig. 8
Rim sherd of jar with gently everted rim. Some greenish and black discoloration on exterior.
Orange clay, coarse and gritty. Traces of dull red slip on inside rim. Exterior and inside rim somewhat smoothed; interior surface rough.

COOKING POT (156)

156 Cooking pot with vertical handle
Not inv.   Layer 14B
Est. D. rim 0.22; GTh. 0.007 m.
Fig. 8
Rim sherd of hole-mouth cooking pot with rim thickened on inside. Upper wall on exterior preserves top end of vertical handle. Blackened on exterior, including base of handle; black traces on interior.
Reddish brown clay, coarse and very gritty.

PITCHER (157)

157 Trough spout
P 5461   Layer 14B
GPL. 0.099; GPW. 0.044 m.
Pl. 19
Trough spout of pitcher with rising beak spout, *ca.* three-fourths preserved; broken at tip of spout and base. Surfaces worn and somewhat incrusted.

Orange clay, relatively fine and clean. Trough rims and exterior of spout covered with red slip, well smoothed. Matt finish, with some luster.

LAYER 14 (158-192, S3-S7)

BOWLS (158-178)

158 Small bowl
Not inv. Layer 14
Est. D. rim 0.12; GTh. 0.0051 m.
Fig. 8
Rim sherd of small bowl with plain rim. Slip worn.
Fine orange-tan (2.5YR 6/4) clay, micaceous; well fired. Dull red slip on exterior and rim, unevenly applied and mottled to orange. Well smoothed and polished.

159 Bowl
Not inv. Layer 14
Est. D. rim 0.18; GTh. 0.0048 m.
Fig. 8
Rim sherd of bowl with upper wall gradually thickening below plain. Some green discoloration on both surfaces.
Buff (10YR 7/3) clay, slightly micaceous and gritty. Wheelmarks faintly visible on exterior.

160 Small bowl
Not inv. Layer 14
Est. D. rim 0.12; GTh. 0.0052 m.
Fig. 8
Rim sherd of small bowl with slightly thickened, incurved rim. Surfaces pitted.
Buff clay, slightly micaceous and gritty; wheelmarks visible.

161 Bowl
Not inv. Layer 14
Est. D. rim 0.20; GTh. 0.0057 m.
Fig. 8
Rim sherd of bowl with slightly thickened, incurved rim.
Fine buff (10YR 7/3) clay. Smoothed, wheelmarks visible both surfaces.

162 Bowl
Not inv. Layer 14
Est. D. rim 0.24; GTh. 0.0078 m.
Fig. 9
Rim sherd of bowl with upper wall gradually thickened, incurved rim. Green discoloration on both surfaces.
Buff clay, rather coarse and gritty; fired darker at core. Surfaces plain.

163 Bowl
Not inv. Layer 14
Est. D. rim 0.26; GTh. 0.0059 m.
Fig. 9
Rim sherd of bowl with inverted rim. Slightly blackened on both surfaces; rim worn.
Orange clay, micaceous and slightly gritty; fired darker at core. Red slip, spiral-burnished, on both surfaces.

164 Bowl
Not inv. Layer 14
Est. D. rim 0.24; GTh. 0.0058 m.
Fig. 9
Rim sherd of bowl with inverted rim.
Orange clay, slightly gritty. Red-brown burnished slip on both surfaces.

165 Bowl
Not inv. Layer 14
Est. D. rim 0.22; GTh. 0.0048 m.
Fig. 9
Rim sherd of bowl with inverted rim. Surfaces slightly blackened.
Orange clay, slightly micaceous and gritty. Red slip on both surfaces, burnished.

166 Shallow bowl
Not inv. Layer 14
Est. D. rim 0.24; GTh. 0.004 m.
Fig. 9
Rim sherd of shallow bowl with vertical rim.
Fine, clean, orange (2.5YR 5/8) clay, well fired; "clinky" ware. Pale buff (10YR 8/3) ring-burnished slip on exterior and interior at rim; interior below rim apparently plain.

167 Deep bowl
Not inv. Layer 14
Est. D. rim 0.28; GTh. 0.0048 m.
Fig. 9
Rim sherd of large deep bowl with slightly everted, thickened rim.
Tan (5YR 6/3) clay, micaceous; clean and well fired. Reddish brown (2.5YR 5/6) slip on both surfaces, smoothed and polished but not lustrous.

168 Deep bowl
Not inv. Layer 14
Est. D. rim 0.20; GTh. 0.007 m.
Fig. 9
Rim sherd of deep bowl with thickened, slightly everted rim.
Fine tan-orange clay (5YR 6/4) slightly gritty. Red (10R 5/6- 5/8) slip on both surfaces, unevenly applied and worn on rim. Exterior well smoothed, polished but not lustrous.

169 Deep bowl
Not inv. Layer 14
Est. D. rim 0.30; GTh. 0.012 m.
Fig. 9
Rim sherd of large deep bowl with thickened, slightly everted rim. Slightly blackened on both surfaces.
Orange (5YR 6/8) clay, somewhat gritty. Reddish brown (2.5YR 5/4) burnished slip on both surfaces, smoothed, with little luster.

170 Deep bowl
Not inv. Layer 14
Est. D. rim 0.32; GTh. 0.008 m.
Fig. 9
Rim sherd of large deep bowl with gentle carination. Traces of incrustation on both surfaces.
Pale orange (5YR 6/6) clay, somewhat gritty; well fired. Slight "silver" dusting. Both surfaces well smoothed, covered with good orange (5YR 6/6) slip; not lustrous.

171 Carinated bowl
Not inv. Layer 14
Est. D. rim 0.20; GTh. 0.0055 m.
Fig. 9
Rim sherd of carinated bowl with plain rim.
Orange (5YR 7/6) clay, relatively clean. Dull orange (2.5YR 6/6) slip on interior and on exterior above carination, tan (5YR 7/3) below carination. Well smoothed, especially exterior above carination.

172 Carinated bowl
Not inv. Layer 14
Est. D. rim 0.24; GTh. 0.0058 m.
Fig. 9

Rim sherd of carinated bowl with plain rim.

Orange-tan (2.5YR 6/4) clay, slightly micaceous and gritty. Dull red slip on exterior above carination; reddish brown (2.5YR 5/6) on interior above and below carination. Wheel-burnish marks visible on both surfaces; unslipped interior well smoothed.

173   Carinated bowl
Not inv.   Layer 14
D. rim unknown; GTh. 0.006 m.
Fig. 9

Rim sherd of carinated bowl with slightly everted plain rim. Some surface discoloration.

Fine buff (7.5YR 7/6) clay, with few gritty inclusions. "Self-slip" on both surfaces, smoothed and polished.

174   Carinated bowl
Not inv.   Layer 14
Est. D. rim 0.24; GTh. 0.0088 m.
Fig. 9

Rim sherd of carinated bowl with thickened rim.

Light brown (2.5YR 5/4) clay, micaceous and slightly gritty. Tan-orange (2.5YR 6/6) slip on both surfaces, mottled on interior; smoothed and polished.

175   Carinated bowl
P 5457   Layer 14
GPH. 0.091; Est. D. rim 0.32; GTh. 0.08 m.
Fig. 9; Pl.19

Mended and plastered section preserves approximately one-third of rim circumference, adjoining body and vessel profile. Section restored with fragments from different vessels so that profile and diameter are approximate only. Rim chipped and abraded; some discoloration on interior.

Large carinated bowl with thickened rim.

Buff-tan clay, clean, with few gritty inclusions. Buff (7.5YR 7/6) slip on both surfaces, well smoothed; slightly lustrous to matt finish.

176   Carinated bowl
P 5458   Layer 14
GPH. 0.06; GPW. 0.14; Est. D. rim 0.32; GTh. 0.008 m.
Fig. 9

Mended section preserves part of rim, adjoining body and most of profile. Some gaps and chips; slightly incrusted on exterior.

Carinated bowl, similar to **175**.

Buff-tan clay with some gritty inclusions. Buff (7.5YR 7/6) slip on both surfaces, fired slightly reddish in places. Surfaces well smoothed, with matt finish.

Beycesultan Level V (*Beycesultan* II, 84, fig. P.1:12, with polished red wash).

177   Bowl
P 3331   Layer 14
GPH. 0.12; GPW. 0.27; Est. D. rim 0.45 m.
Pl. 20

Large mended section preserves part of rim and adjoining wall of bowl. Rim thickened and slightly everted. Burned material on exterior.

Clay fine and clean; fired orange at surfaces, gray-brown at core. Both surfaces slipped red to orange (2.5YR 6/8), burnished smooth and lustrous.

178   Ring base of bowl
Not inv.   Layer 14
GPH. 0.03; D. base 0.06 m.
Fig. 9

Base of lower adjoining body of bowl with ring base. Base fully preserved; some surface incrustation.

Buff (7.5YR 7/6) clay, relatively clean; few visible inclusions. Some mica. Base left plain; interior surface covered with red (10R 6/6) slip, worn and matt but well smoothed.

JARS (179 and 180)

179   Jar
Not inv.   Layer 14
Est. D. rim 0.27; GTh. 0.008 m.
Fig. 9

Rim sherd of jar with everted rim. Mended from two joining sherds. Slip worn.

Orange (5YR 6/6) clay, gritty. Dull red (10R 6/6) slip, on rim and exterior, including upper rim. Interior plain.

180   Jar
Not inv.   Layer 14
Est. D. rim 0.45; GTh. 0.016 m.
Fig. 9

Rim sherd of jar with everted rim. Some surface discoloration.

Orange (5YR 6/6) clay, gritty. Pale buff (10YR 8/4) slip on rim and exterior.

PITHOI (181-183)

181   Pithos
Not inv.   Layer 14
Est. D. rim 0.45; GTh. 0.022 m.
Fig. 10

Rim sherd of pithos with broad, everted rim. Some discoloration and incrustation. Narrow ridge on outer wall below rim.

Orange (5YR 6/6) clay, gritty and coarse; fired buff (7.5YR 7/4) at surfaces. Wheelmarks visible on exterior, worn on interior.

182   Pithos
Not inv.   Layer 14
Est. D. rim 0.40; GTh. 0.02 m.
Fig. 10

Rim sherd of pithos with wide, sloping rim. Narrow horizontal bands on outer wall below rim.

Orange clay, coarse and gritty; smoothed on exterior.

183   Pithos
Not inv.   Layer 14
Est. D. rim 0.50; GTh. 0.019 m.
Fig. 10

Rim sherd of pithos with broad, flat rim. Upper wall tapering sharply towards vessel neck. Narrow horizontal band on outer wall below rim.

Dark buff clay, gritty and coarse; surfaces plain.

PITCHERS (184 and 185)

184   Pitcher
P 3393   Layer 14
GPH. 0.22; Max. D. rim 0.103 m.
Fig. 10; Pl. 20

Mended neck and rim of large pitcher.

Sloping shoulder, short neck, troughlike beak spout. Vertical handle, oval in section, attached at rim; two small knobs, one on either side of place of attachment, imitating metal rivets, separated by circular depression.

Buff (7.5YR 7/4) clay, fine and clean; well fired. Red slip on exterior, and on interior of neck.

185 Pitcher
P 5460 Layer 14
GPH. 0.087; Est. D. rim 0.30; GPW. 0.094; W. spout 0.035;
GTh. 0.0105 m.
Fig. 10; Pl. 20
Rim and spout fragment from spouted vessel of teapot
form. Rim and spout chipped; strainer area damaged. Surfaces and spout interior discolored.
Wide, flat rim; just below this is spout opening, with
trough ending in short downward curve. Opening in vessel
wall preserves strainer perforations at base of trough and on
upper side of opening. Probably the entire opening was perforated, now broken through.
Buff clay with some gritty inclusions. Rim and exterior
covered with brown slip, now worn, with matt finish. Interior
apparently plain. All surfaces well smoothed.

RIMS (186 and 187)

186 Rim sherd
Not inv. Layer 14
D. rim unknown; GTh. 0.012 m.
Fig. 10
Rim sherd. Upper wall gradually turning outward to thickened rim; perhaps from cylindrical neck of jug.
Orange (5YR 6/6) clay, slightly micaceous and gritty. Buff
(7.5YR 7/4) slip on rim and exterior; slip worn, or surface
plain, on interior.

187 Rim sherd
Not inv. Layer 14
Est. D. rim 0.44; GTh. 0.021 m.
Fig. 10
Rim sherd with indentation below outer rim; wide rim.
Probably from a large jar. Green discoloration on both surfaces.
Buff-orange clay, coarse and gritty; fired lighter at surface.
Both surfaces roughly finished.

BASES (188-190)

188 Ring base
Not inv. Layer 14
GPH. 0.036; Est. D. base 0.09 m.
Fig. 10
Base fragment and adjoining lower body of vessel with ring
base. *Circa* one-third of circumference preserved. Ring
chipped. Possibly a jar or pitcher.
Buff (7.5YR 7/6) clay, relatively clean, with few gritty inclusions. Surfaces mostly smoothed, plain.

189 Ring base
Not inv. Layer 14
GPH. 0.032; Est. D. base 0.11 m.
Fig. 10
Fragment of ring base. Almost one-half of circumference
preserved. Probably a jar or pitcher.
Tan (7.5YR 6/6) clay, gritty. Wheelmarks visible on exterior and base, worn smooth on ring.

190 Pedestal base
P 5459 Layer 14
GPH. 0.057; Est. D. base 0.05; GTh. 0.007 m.
Fig. 10; Pl. 20
Mended section preserves *ca.* one-third of base circumference and part of adjoining lower body. Some darkened and
incrusted areas on both surfaces. Base blackened on bottom, as
if entire vessel burnt secondarily and unevenly.

Pedestal base and carinated lower body suggest beakspouted pitcher of sharply carinated form.
Buff clay, with some gritty inclusions. Both surfaces
covered with red (10R 5/6, 10R 4/6 interior) slip, well
smoothed and polished, with lustrous finish.

INCISED BODY SHERDS (191 and 192)

191 Incised sherd
P 5456 Layer 14
GPL. 0.11; GPW. 0.055; GTh. 0.0135 m.
Pl. 20
Body sherd from vessel of unknown shape. Exterior worn,
slightly incrusted.
On exterior, incised parallel lines in groups of three forming a chevronlike pattern; at wider end of sherd, crossed lines.
Incised lines are shallow, flat, and neatly formed.
Orange (5YR 6/6) clay with some gritty inclusions but relatively clean. Exterior originally slipped, probably reddish
brown; now worn and discolored. Interior covered with thin
buff "self-slip."

192 Incised sherd
P 5455 Layer 14
GPL. 0.475; GPW. 0.0625; GTh. 0.015 m.
Pl. 20
Body sherd from vessel with rounded shoulder. Exterior
worn; interior slightly incrusted.
On exterior, incised lines in groups of three forming chevron pattern. On interior, a few indented lines preserved in
part at upper edge of sherd.
Buff clay with some gritty inclusions. Exterior covered with
brown (5YR 5/8) slip, well smoothed and polished. Interior
left plain, roughly finished.

LAYER 13 (193-203, S8-S12)

BOWLS (193-195)

193 Hemispherical bowl
Not inv. Layer 13
Est. D. rim 0.22; GTh. 0.012 m.
Fig. 11
Rim sherd of bowl with hemispherical form; upper wall
gradually thickens and curves inward at rim. Green discoloration on both surfaces.
Orange clay, rather gritty; fired buff at surface.

194 Bowl
Not inv. Layer 13
Est. D. rim 0.32; GTh. 0.086 m.
Fig. 11
Rim sherd of bowl with gently carinated profile; thickened,
sloping rim. Mended from two joining sherds.
Buff (7.5YR 7/4) clay, gritty; surfaces plain. Wheelmarks
mostly smoothed except on inside rim.

195 Carinated bowl
Not inv. Layer 13
D. rim unknown; GTh. 0.012 m.
Fig. 11
Rim sherd of carinated bowl, slightly outturned rim thickened on interior.
Buff (7.5YR 7/6) clay, gritty and rather coarse. Red (10R
5/6) slip, very worn, on exterior surface and on interior to just
above carination.
Related profile, in unslipped ware: Boğazköy, Nordwesthang-Büyükkale Level 7 (*Nordwesthang-Büyükkale*, 48, no.
111, pl. 33).

JAR (196)

196   Jar
Not inv.   Layer 13
Est. D. rim 0.22; GTh. 0.0065 m.
Fig. 11
Circa one-fourth of rim circumference preserved. Some green discoloration both surfaces; interior incrusted.
Rim sherd of jar with sharply everted rim, flaring shoulder.
Orange (5YR 7/6) clay, gritty. Pale buff (10YR 8/3) slip, smoothed, on both surfaces.

PITCHERS (197 and 198)

197   Spout fragment
P 5346   Layer 13
GPL. 0.073; GPW. 0.026; Th. trough wall 0.0175 m.
Fig. 11; Pl. 20
Beak spout fragment, broken irregularly across trough. Spout end worn and slightly chipped; some dark discoloration.
Shallow, V-shaped trough, terminates in beak with tip curved downward.
Orange (5YR 6/6) clay, fine, containing little grit and mica. Red (10R 5/8) slip on spout exterior continues just inside trough. Well smoothed, lustrous in places.
Boğazköy, Büyükkale Level IVc (*Heth. Keramik*, 118, no. 252, pl. 30).

198   Trefoil pitcher
P 5347   Layer 13
GPH. 0.048; GPL. 0.091; GTh. 0.005 m.
Pl. 20
Neck and rim fragment from pitcher with trefoil mouth, broken on three sides. Some green and dark discoloration. Bottom edge of sherd preserves junction with shoulder, where vessel begins to flare out.
Buff (7.5YR 7/4) clay, relatively clean. Both surfaces plain, wheelmarks mostly visible.

RIM SHERDS (199 and 200)

199   Rim sherd
Not inv.   Layer 13
Est. D. rim 0.32; GTh. 0.007 m.
Fig. 11
Rim sherd of large open vessel with thickened rim.
Orange clay, gritty. Light reddish brown slip on both surfaces; well smoothed and polished, especially on exterior.

200   Rim sherd
Not inv.   Layer 13
D. rim unknown; GTh. 0.0084 m.
Fig. 11
Rim sherd with rim thickened on interior. Grayed throughout. Probably from a hole-mouth jar or cooking pot.
Gritty, coarse clay, now fired gray throughout. May originally have been slipped buff.

BASE FRAGMENT (201)

201   Ring base
Not inv.   Layer 13
GPH. 0.032; Est. D. base 0.09 m.
Fig. 11
Sherd preserving base and adjoining lower body. *Circa* one-third circumference preserved.
Ring base, possibly from a jar.
Clean buff clay (7.5YR 7/4), with few gritty inclusions; surfaces smoothed.

HANDLE (202)

202   Vertical handle
P 5344   Layer 13
GPL. 0.13; GPW. 0.154; W. handle 0.023; GTh. 0.011 m.
Fig. 11; Pl. 20
Vertical handle and adjoining body wall from large vessel. Surfaces worn; greenish discoloration on interior.
Large vessel with vertical handle, triangular in section with palpable spine ridge, located on body wall perhaps at area of greatest diameter. Possibly a large storage jar. Exterior painted in solid matt red (10R 5/6) zone above handle; paint thinly and not very neatly applied.
Buff (7.5YR 7/6) clay, gritty. Interior and handle area covered with worn, pale buff (10YR 8/4) slip.
Alişar Levels 11-10T (*OIP* 29, fig. 197, c 2377, c 2744; fig. 198, e 2302; pl. 7, c 2377); Maşat Level V (*Maşat* II, 75, pl. 94:1). See also Kültepe example with hieroglyphic inscription, *Belleten* 18 (1954) 373 ff., fig. 6.7.37.

PAINTED BODY SHERD (203)

203   Painted body sherd
P 5345   Layer 13
GPL. 0.056; GPW. 0.045; GTh. 0.0055 m.
Pl. 20
Body sherd from a constricted vessel, probably a jar. Exterior scratched; interior discolored.
Exterior, solid background of light brown (7.5YR 6/4) slip, over which horizontal bands in dark brown (5YR 3/2) paint. Three bands at regular intervals preserved, each band *ca.* 0.003 m. wide; below, wider band or perhaps solid painted area, in which break occurs. Interior plain.
Orange-red (2.5YR 6/6) clay, fine and clean, with few inclusions.
Compare Habur ware (B. Hrouda, *Die bemalte Keramik des zweiten Jahrtausends in Nordmesopotamien und Nordsyrien*, pl. 7:8; 8:1-20).

LAYER 12   (204-211, S13-S24)

BOWL (204)

204   Bowl
Not inv.   Layer 12
Est. D. rim 0.19; GTh. 0.0059 m.
Fig. 11
Rim sherd of bowl with thickened, incurved rim.
Tan clay, coarse and gritty; surfaces left plain and rough.

BOWL OR JAR (205)

205   Bowl or jar
Not inv.   Layer 12
Est. D. rim 0.19; GTh. 0.0061 m.
Fig. 11
Rim sherd of deep bowl or jar with upper wall narrowing at neck, gently everted rim.
Gritty buff ware, rough both surfaces.

COOKING POTS (206-208)

206   Cooking pot
Not inv.   Layer 12
Est. D. rim 0.35; GTh. 0.013 m.
Fig. 11

Rim sherd of hole-mouth cooking pot with rim thickened on inside.

Coarse, gritty ware, blackened on exterior, interior buff.

207 Cooking pot
Not inv.   Layer 12
Est. D. rim 0.28; GTh. 0.01 m.
Fig. 11
Rim sherd of hole-mouth cooking pot with rim thickened on inside.

Brown clay, rather coarse and gritty. Brown slip, burnished, on both surfaces.

208 Cooking pot
Not inv.   Layer 12
Est. D. rim 0.36; GTh. 0.016 m.
Fig. 11
Rim sherd of large hole-mouth cooking pot with rim thickened on inside.

Coarse, gritty ware, fired black throughout.

BASE (209)

209 Ring base
Not inv.   Layer 12
GPH. 0.041; Est. D. base 0.14 m.
Fig. 11
Ring base fragment. Possibly from large jar.
Buff-orange clay, gritty; surfaces rough and plain.

METAL (210 and 211)

210 Copper or bronze pin
B 1644   Layer 12, Pit B
PL. 0.04; D. head 0.006 m.
Pl. 20
Point and part of shaft broken away. Right-angled bend just below head.

Spherical head, flattened on top. Thin shaft, round in section. Parallel or spiral grooves on shaft just below head, poorly preserved.

Boğazköy, examples without grooves below head, from Unterstadt Level 3 and Büyükkale Level IVb (*Kleinfunde Unterstadt*, 14, no. 2666, pl. IX; *Kleinfunde*, 89, no. 402, pl. XIX).

211 Lead ring
ILS 461   Layer 12, Pit A
Th. 0.003 m.
Pl. 20
Complete; twisted and opened.

Lead wire, round in section, originally bent into a circle. Ends carefully rounded off.

Hittite Cemetery (*Hitt. Cem.*, 35-36, pl. 20h-m; also Boğazköy, Büyükkale Levels IVd and III, Unterstadt Levels 3-2 (*Kleinfunde*, 166, nos. 1726-27, 1729-30A, pl. LIX; *Kleinfunde Unterstadt*, 37, nos. 3502, 3507, 3510; pl. XXIII).

LAYER 11   (212-220, S25-S35)

BOWLS (212-217)

212 Small bowl
Not inv.   Layer 11
Est. D. rim 0.21; GTh. 0.0027 m.
Fig. 11
Rim sherd of small, thin-walled bowl with plain rim. Exterior scratched.

Orange (5YR 7/6) clay, very fine and clean. Red-brown (2.5YR 5/6) slip on exterior and applied in band, *ca.* 0.01 m. wide, on interior rim. Smoothed and polished.

213 Shallow bowl
Not inv.   Layer 11
Est. D. rim 0.23; GTh. 0.0055 m.
Fig. 11
Rim sherd of shallow bowl with broad, rounded rim. Surfaces discolored and slightly incrusted.

Orange (5YR 6/6) clay, relatively clean, with few gritty inclusions. Fired paler at surfaces, gray at core. "Self-slipped" or finished without slip.

214 Bowl
Not inv.   Layer 11
Est. D. rim 0.23; GTh. 0.0054 m.
Fig. 11
Rim sherd of bowl with inverted rim thickened on interior. Surfaces discolored green.

Buff (7.5YR 7/6) clay, gritty. Pale buff (10YR 8/3) slip on both surfaces, roughly finished.

215 Shallow bowl
Not inv.   Layer 11
Est. D. rim 0.30; GTh. 0.0091 m.
Fig. 11
Rim sherd of shallow bowl with rounded, thickened rim. Slightly darkened on both surfaces.

Buff (7.5YR 7/4) clay, somewhat gritty. Surfaces plain.

216 Carinated bowl
Not inv.   Layer 11
Est. D. rim 0.22; GTh. 0.004 m.
Fig. 12
Rim sherd of bowl with carinated profile, slightly everted, thickened rim. Pinched-up vertical ridge *ca.* 0.005 m. wide, from rim to carination.

Buff-orange (7.5YR 7/6) clay, somewhat gritty. Traces of very thin orange-red slip on exterior rim and above carination. Surface roughly finished.

Tarsus Late Bronze I (*Tarsus* II, 188, fig. 376: profile E); for ridge, Ilıca cemetery (*Ilıca* pl. 3: 21, 22); Polatlı Level XXV (*AnatSt* 1[1951] 50, fig. 12:10-11).

217 Carinated bowl with horizontal handles
Not inv.   Layer 11
D. rim unknown; GTh. 0.008 m.
Fig. 12
Rim sherd of carinated bowl with sloping, thickened rim: one edge of sherd preserves base of horizontal handle. Outer rim chipped.

Orange (5YR 6/6) clay, gritty. Orange-red slip on exterior and rim, traces preserved on interior. Originally polished.

JARS (218 and 219)

218 Jar
Not inv.   Layer 11
D. rim 0.264; GTh. 0.0079 m.
Fig. 12
Rim sherd of small jar with upper wall tapering inward at neck, flat thickened rim. Horizontal ridge below rim on exterior.

Tan (5YR 6/4) clay with some grit and surface mica. Tan (5YR 6/4) slip, very worn, on exterior; probably not originally slipped on interior.

219 Jar
Not inv.   Layer 11
Est. D. rim 0.50; GTh. 0.017 m.
Fig. 12
Rim sherd of large jar with sharply everted rim.
Gray clay, somewhat gritty. Surfaces left plain, smoothed inside and outside.

COOKING POT (220)

220 Cooking pot
Not inv.   Layer 11
Est. D. rim 0.29; GTh. 0.008 m.
Fig. 12
   Rim sherd of hole-mouth cooking pot. Exterior blackened.
   Orange (5YR 6/6) clay with relatively large inclusions,
coarse, gritty and micaceous. Surfaces plain.

LAYER 10   (221-253)

BOWLS (221-236)

221 Small bowl
Not inv.   Layer 10
Est. D. rim 0.11; GTh. 0.0035 m.
Fig. 12
   Rim sherd of small, shallow bowl with gently curved
profile; plain, slightly outturned rim.
   Fine, clean orange clay with very few inclusions. Surfaces
well smoothed and plain.

222 Bowl
Not inv.   Layer 10
D. rim unknown; GTh. 0.009 m.
Fig. 12
   Rim sherd of shallow bowl with sloping, thickened rim.
   Orange (5YR 7/6) clay, somewhat gritty. Pale buff (10YR
8/3) slip on both surfaces.

223 Large bowl
Not inv.   Layer 10
Est. D. interior rim 0.27; GTh. 0.018 m.
Fig. 12
   Rim sherd of large bowl with sloping, thickened rim.
Scratches on interior; rim chipped.
   Orange-buff (5YR 6/6-7/6) clay, gritty; some mica visible
on surface. Fired slightly paler at surfaces; plain.

224 Bowl
Not inv.   Layer 10
D. rim unknown; GTh. 0.01 m.
Fig. 12
   Rim sherd of bowl with curved profile, everted rim. Sur-
faces discolored.
   Tan (7.5YR 6/4) clay, with some gritty inclusions; pale buff
(7.5YR 8/4) slip on both surfaces.

225 Bowl
Not inv.   Layer 10
D. rim unknown; GTh. 0.0095 m.
Fig. 12
   Rim sherd of bowl with rounded, thickened rim. Green dis-
coloration on both surfaces.
   Orange (5YR 6/6) clay, gritty. Surfaces fired buff (7/5YR
7/4), plain.

226 Carinated bowl
Not inv.   Layer 10
D. rim unknown; GTh. 0.012 m.
Fig. 12
   Rim sherd of bowl with slight carination, everted and
slightly thickened rim. Green and rust discoloration.
   Buff clay, gritty; fired darker at core. Buff slip on both sur-
faces.

227 Carinated bowl
Not inv.   Layer 10
D. rim unknown; GTh. 0.009 m.
Fig. 12

Rim sherd of carinated bowl with sloping, thickened rim.
Some surface discoloration.
   Orange (5YR 7/6) clay, somewhat gritty. Pale buff (10YR
8/3) slip on both surfaces.

228 Carinated bowl
Not inv.   Layer 10
Est. D. rim 0.32; GTh. 0.0098 m.
Fig. 12
   Rim sherd of bowl with slight carination, rounded and
thickened rim.
   Orange (5YR 7/6) clay, rather coarse and gritty. Traces of
orange-red (2.5YR 6/6) slip on exterior, almost completely
worn away.

229 Carinated bowl
Not inv.   Layer 10
Est. D. rim 0.272; GTh. 0.009 m.
Fig. 12
   Rim sherd of deep carinated bowl with sloping, thickened
rim.
   Orange clay, with few gritty inclusions and some mica.
Surfaces plain.

230 Carinated bowl
Not inv.   Layer 10
D. rim unknown; GTh. 0.014 m.
Fig. 12
   Rim sherd of carinated bowl with sloping, thickened rim.
Slightly blackened on interior and inner rim.
   Orange (5YR 6/6-7/6) clay, gritty. Thin buff (10YR 8/3)
slip on both surfaces; wheelmarks smoothed but still visible.

231 Carinated bowl with horizontal handles
Not inv.   Layer 10
Est. D. rim 0.26; GTh. 0.012 m.
Fig. 12; Pl. 21
   Rim sherd of bowl with carinated profile, thickened rim.
Base of horizontal handle preserved in part at edge of sherd.
   Orange (5YR 6/6) clay with some gritty inclusions. Tan-
orange (5YR 7/6) slip, rather worn, on outer rim and above
carination on exterior.

232 Carinated bowl with horizontal handles
Not inv.   Layer 10
Est. D. rim 0.29; GTh. 0.0088 m.
Fig. 12; Pl. 21
   Rim sherd of bowl with carinated profile; sloping, thick-
ened rim. Base of horizontal handle preserved in part at one
edge of sherd.
   Orange (5YR 6/6) clay, somewhat gritty. Red-orange
(2.5YR 6/6) slip on both surfaces, smoothed and lightly
polished.

233 Shallow bowl
Not inv.   Layer 10
D. rim unknown; GTh. 0.0055 m.
Fig. 12
   Rim sherd of shallow bowl with inverted, almost vertical
rim.
   Fine, clean orange (5YR 7/6-6/6) clay, well fired. Red
(2.5YR 5/8) slip on both surfaces, smoothed and lightly
polished.

234 Shallow bowl or plate
Not inv.   Layer 10
D. rim unknown; GTh. 0.0067 m.
Fig. 12
   Rim sherd of shallow bowl or plate with inverted, almost
vertical rim.

Orange (5YR 6/6) clay, gritty. Red (10R 5/8) slip preserved on exterior and on interior below rim. Slip rather thinly and carelessly applied; dull and worn.

235 Shallow bowl
Not inv.   Layer 10
D. rim unknown; GTh. 0.011 m.
Fig. 12
Rim sherd of shallow bowl with broad, everted rim. Surfaces slightly discolored.
Orange (5YR 7/6) clay, gritty. Matt buff (7.5YR 8/4) slip on both surfaces.

236 Shallow bowl
Not inv.   Layer 10
D. rim unknown; GTh. 0.0091 m.
Fig. 12
Rim sherd of shallow bowl with broad, inverted rim. Exterior indented where rim joins bowl, with corresponding bump on interior.
Orange clay, gritty. Buff slip, or "self-slip," on both surfaces.

JARS (237-245)

237 Jar
Not inv.   Layer 10
Est. D. rim 0.14; GTh. 0.0059 m.
Fig. 12
Rim and adjoining wall of small jar with slightly everted rim. Slip worn, especially on outer rim.
Orange (5YR 6/6) clay, gritty. Red (10R 5/6) slip on exterior and on interior to just below rim. Interior surface smoothed, matt; wheelmarks visible on interior.

238 Jar
Not inv.   Layer 10
D. rim unknown; GPL. 0.068; GPW. 0.0795; GTh. 0.009 m.
Fig. 13; Pl. 21
Rim sherd of small jar with everted, sloping rim. Some discoloration on both surfaces; much worn and abraded. Four parallel grooves separated by ridges, 0.003-0.004 m. wide, on outer wall ca. 0.025 m. below rim.
Orange (5YR 6/6) clay, gritty. Traces of red (10R 5/6) slip preserved on rim and exterior.

239 Jar
Not inv.   Layer 10
D. rim unknown; GTh. 0.0134 m.
Fig. 13
Rim sherd of jar with everted rim.
Gritty clay, fired gray throughout. Perhaps originally slipped buff on both surfaces.

240 Jar
Not inv.   Layer 10
Est. D. rim 0.308; GTh. 0.0068 m.
Fig. 13
Rim sherd of jar with everted rim. Rim chipped.
Orange (5YR 7/6) clay with gritty inclusions, some mica. Surfaces plain.

241 Jar
Not inv.   Layer 10
Est. D. rim 0.316; GTh. 0.012 m.
Fig. 13
Rim sherd of jar with everted rim. Inner rim and surface pitted; surfaces discolored green.
Buff (7.5YR 7/6) clay with some gritty inclusions. Both surfaces apparently covered with paler buff (10YR 8/4) slip.

242 Jar
Not inv.   Layer 10
Est. D. rim 0.38; GTh. 0.016 m.
Fig. 13
Rim and adjoining upper wall of large jar with everted rim. Surfaces pitted, especially interior.
Orange (5YR 7/6) clay, gritty. Buff (7.5YR 8/4) slip on exterior and rim; interior perhaps self-slipped (thin, cracked coating).

243 Jar
Not inv.   Layer 10
D. rim 0.26; GTh. 0.01 m.
Fig. 13
Rim sherd of jar with everted rim. Outer rim chipped; inner surface pitted.
Orange (5YR 6/6) clay, gritty. Traces of orange (5YR 6/6) slip on rim.

244 Jar with vertical handles
Not inv.   Layer 10
Est. D. rim 0.32; GPL. 0.122; GPW. 0.134; L. handle 0.115; GTh. 0.0135 m.
Fig. 13
Rim, adjoining upper wall, and handle of jar. Surfaces incrusted; much greenish discoloration.
Hole-mouth jar with rim thickened on inside, vertical handle, oblong in section, preserved in full.
Buff clay, gritty. Both surfaces appear "self-slipped," although wheelmarks are visible on interior; surfaces rough.

245 Jar with vertical handle
Not inv.   Layer 10
Est. D. rim 0.272; GPL. 0.121; GPW. 0.082; L. handle 0.075; GTh. 0.01 m.
Fig. 13
Single sherd preserves rim, upper wall, and entire handle. Surfaces incrusted; interior heavily abraded; much greenish discoloration.
Jar of kraterlike form, with outturned rim; vertical handle, oblong in section, is attached at rim and rises above it.
Reddish brown (2.5YR 5/4) clay, coarse and very gritty. Both surfaces appear "self-slipped," although wheelmarks are visible on interior; surfaces rough.

COOKING POT (246)

246 Cooking pot
Not inv.   Layer 10
Est. D. rim 0.35; GTh. 0.015 m.
Fig. 13
Rim sherd of large hole-mouth cooking pot with rim thickened on inside. Inner rim blackened; inside of vessel grayed.
Orange (5YR 6/6) clay, coarse and gritty. Surfaces apparently covered with thin "self-slip" (5YR 7/4).

PITHOI (247 and 248)

247 Pithos
Not inv.   Layer 10
D. rim unknown; GTh. 0.015 m.
Fig. 13
Rim sherd of large pithos with thickened band rim. Rim chipped.
Orange (5YR 6/6) clay, gritty and coarse. Traces of red (10R 6/4) slip on rim and exterior.
Below, **248**.

248   Pithos
Not inv.   Layer 10
Est. D. rim 0.46; GTh. 0.040 m.
Fig. 13
Rim sherd of pithos with band rim. Green discoloration on rim and inner surface; inner rim chipped.
Orange (2.5YR 6/6) clay, gritty; traces of red (10R 5/6) slip on exterior.
247 and **248**: compare "bathtub," Tarsus Late Bronze I (*Tarsus* II, no. 1054, fig. 381).

RIM SHERDS (249-251)

249   Rim sherd
Not inv.   Layer 10
D. rim unknown; GTh. 0.0065 m.
Fig. 13
Rim sherd of vessel with thickened rim. Some green discoloration on interior, darker on exterior. Probably from a small jar.
Buff (7.5YR 6/6) clay, gritty. Orange (5YR 6/6-5/6) slip on exterior and on interior just inside rim. Smoothed and polished on exterior; wheelmarks smoothed but faintly visible on interior.

250   Rim sherd
Not inv.   Layer 10
D. rim unknown; GTh. 0.013 m.
Fig. 13; Pl. 21
Rim sherd from large open vessel. Green discoloration on both surfaces.
Rim indented on interior. Probably from large bowl or jar.
Orange (5YR 7/6) clay, somewhat gritty. Buff (7.5YR 8/4) slip on both surfaces. Shallow horizontal impressions, as if from a string, preserved across exterior; a second row as if impressed from a knotted length of string.

251   Rim sherd
Not inv.   Layer 10
D. rim unknown; GTh. 0.013 m.
Fig. 13
Rim sherd of jar with strongly everted, sloping rim. Interior surface damaged at bottom of sherd.
Tan-orange (2.5YR 6/6) clay, gritty. Red (10R 5/6) slip on both surfaces, on interior to just above break, rather carelessly applied.

PAINTED BODY SHERD (252)

252   Painted body sherd
P 5343   Layer 10
GPL. 0.043; GPW. 0.0395; GTh. 0.009 m.
Pl. 21
Body sherd from vessel of unknown shape. Exterior worn, slightly chipped; some incrustation on interior.
Exterior covered with cream (10YR 8/2) paint. Across this near edge of sherd, a solid red band *ca.* 0.01 m. wide.
Tan (7.5YR 7/4) clay, clean, with few gritty inclusions. Exterior smoothed, with matt finish; interior left plain.
Below, **331**.

SHERD WITH IMPRESSED DESIGN (253)

253   Sherd with impressed design
P 5342   Layer 10
GPL. 0.0755; GPW. 0.046; GTh. 0.015 m.
Pl. 21

Body sherd broken on all sides from fairly straight vessel wall. Surfaces worn; some incrustation.
On exterior near edge of sherd: part of an impressed design of concentric circles. Part of three grooves preserved, each *ca.* 0.004 m. wide; stamped evenly.
Dark orange (2.5YR 6/6) clay, gritty; "gold" mica visible on surface. Thin red (10R 6/6) slip on exterior, smoothed, with a matt finish.
Below **308**.
Stamped design: Alaca (Al.e.73, *Belleten* 19 [1965] no. 51); Karahöyük-Konya Level II and later (*Karahöyük-Konya Damga*, pl. 27:66, 28:71); Maşat Level I (*Maşat* II, pl. 101:28). Stamps with concentric design are known in metal from Gordion (*Hitt. Cem.*, 42, pl. 23k,l) and Alişar Hüyük Levels 11-10T (*OIP* 29, 213, d 747; also 417, fig. 478, lower row 1-4), and in clay from Alişar (*ibid.*, 222, fig. 258) and Kusura (*Archaeologia* 86 [1936] 30, fig. 12:16).

LAYER 9   (254)

ZOOMORPHIC VESSEL (254)

254   Ram's head from vessel
P 3329   Layer 9
GPL. 0.075; L. head 0.046; W. head 0.047 m.
Pl. 21
Head and neck complete, broken at shoulder.
Long cylindrical neck, tapering towards head. Flattish head with curled-in horns, pierced pellet eyes, snoutlike nose grooved across end for mouth and pierced for nostrils. Interior hollowed roughly halfway up neck.
Fine buff (7.5YR 6/4-7/4) clay, with few gritty inclusions; surface well smoothed.

LAYER 8   (255-282)

BOWLS (255-269)

255   Bowl
Not inv.   Layer 8, Pit A
Est. D. rim 0.32; GTh. 0.0036 m.
Fig. 14
Rim sherd of thin-walled bowl with tapered rim.
Fine orange (5YR 6/6) clay, fired darker at core. Orange-red (2.5YR 6/8) slip on both surfaces, spiral-burnished in narrow horizontal bands.

256   Shallow bowl
Not inv.   Layer 8, Pit A
Est. D. rim 0.32; GTh. 0.012 m.
Fig. 14
Rim sherd of shallow bowl with slightly thickened rim. Surfaces grayed and much of core black.
Orange-buff (5YR 7/6) clay, gritty, with some "gold" mica. Surfaces left plain.

257   Shallow bowl or plate
Not inv.   Layer 8, Pit A
Est. D. rim 0.60; GTh. 0.02 m.
Fig. 14
Rim sherd of large shallow bowl or plate with broad rim. Lower outer surface blackened; upper surface pitted; both worn and flaking.
Orange (5YR 6/6) clay, coarse and gritty. Surfaces plain.

258 Shallow bowl
Not inv. Layer 8
Est. D. rim 0.23; GTh. 0.09 m.
Fig. 14
Rim sherd of shallow bowl with thickened, almost vertical rim.
Orange (5YR 6/6) clay, somewhat gritty. Light red (2.5YR 6/6) slip on upper wall of exterior; preserved on interior also but very worn.

259 Shallow bowl
Not inv. Layer 8
Est. D. rim 0.256; GTh. 0.0088 m.
Fig. 14
Rim sherd of shallow bowl with broad, thickened rim, marked by indentation on inner surface. Mended from two joining sherds.
Buff (7.5YR 7/4) clay, gritty; apparently fired gray at core. Surfaces plain; lower surface roughly finished.

260 Bowl
Not inv. Layer 8
Est. D. rim 0.32; GTh. 0.011 m.
Fig. 14
Rim sherd of bowl with upper wall gradually thickened towards inverted, almost vertical rim.
Orange (5YR 7/6) clay, gritty. Matt buff (10YR 8/3) slip on both surfaces; thinner, less carefully applied on exterior.

261 Bowl
Not inv. Layer 8, Pit A
Est. D. rim 0.28; GTh. 0.009 m.
Fig. 14
Rim sherd of bowl with inverted rim.
Fine orange (5YR 6/6) clay, with some "gold" mica. Surface plain; wheelmarks visible.

262 Bowl
Not inv. Layer 8
Est. D. rim 0.30; GTh. 0.009 m.
Fig. 14
Rim sherd of bowl with inverted rim. Rim chipped.
Orange clay, somewhat gritty. Red slip on rim and on interior along a band *ca.* 0.02 m. wide, and on exterior along a band 0.01 m. wide. Streaks of slip below exterior band.

263 Shallow bowl
Not inv. Layer 8, Pit A
Est. D. rim 0.36; GTh. 0.014 m.
Fig. 14
Rim sherd of large shallow bowl with broad, thickened rim.
Fine orange (5YR 7/6) clay; surfaces plain.

264 Bowl
Not inv. Layer 8
Est. D. rim 0.24; GTh. 0.0068 m.
Fig. 14
Rim sherd of bowl with slightly thickened, rounded rim; two parallel ridges on exterior below rim.
Orange (5YR 6/6) clay, gritty and micaceous. Thin buff (7.5YR 7/4) slip on both surfaces.

265 Bowl
Not inv. Layer 8
Est. D. rim 0.21; GTh. 0.006 m.
Fig. 14
Rim sherd of shallow bowl with inverted, ridged rim. Rim chipped.
Light reddish brown (2.5YR 5/4) clay, somewhat gritty. Surfaces plain.

266 Bowl
Not inv. Layer 8
Est. D. rim 0.24; GTh. 0.01 m.
Fig. 14
Rim sherd of bowl with grooved, thickened rim. Broken at bottom of sherd; inner rim chipped.
Orange (5YR 6/6) clay, somewhat gritty; fired lighter at surface. Wheelmarks smoothed away on exterior.

267 Carinated bowl
Not inv. Layer 8
Est. D. rim 0.40; GTh. 0.011 m.
Fig. 14
Rim sherd of large, deep bowl with slight carination, thickened rim.
Orange (5YR 7/6) clay, with some gritty inclusions. Surfaces plain, mostly smoothed of wheelmarks on exterior.

268 Carinated bowl with horizontal handles
P 5340 Layer 8
GPH. 0.091; D. rim unknown; GPW. 0.12; W. handle 0.019; GTh. 0.013 m.
Fig. 14; Pl. 21
Part of rim, adjoining wall, and part of handle with place of attachment preserved. Handle broken across middle. Surfaces worn; some incrustation.
Bowl with slight carination, thickened rim. Horizontal loop handle, circular in section, swings high above rim from place of attachment at maximum diameter.
Buff (7.5YR 6/6) clay, gritty. Both surfaces covered with reddish brown (2.5YR 5/6) slip, smoothed, with matt finish. Slip does not extend underneath handle.

269 Spouted bowl
Not inv. Layer 8
GPH. 0.088; GPW. 0.108; Th. handle 0.028; GTh. 0.011 m.
Pl. 21
Rim, adjoining wall of bowl, base of horizontal handle. Rim chipped; surfaces slightly incrusted.
Thickened and uneven rim indicating spout. Profile carinated below base of handle attachment; handle oblong in section.
Buff (7.5YR 7/6) gritty clay. Both surfaces covered with thin, pale buff (10YR 8/4) slip.

JARS (270-272)

270 Painted jar
P 3344 Layer 8
GPH. 0.07; Est. D. rim 0.12; GTh. 0.006 m.
Fig. 14; Pl. 21
Sherd with rim and adjoining neck of jar. Wide, cylindrical neck tapers towards gently outturned rim.
Cream (10YR 8/2) slip on exterior; row of hourglasses painted at top of neck in reddish orange paint. Below this is additional painted decoration of uncertain pattern.
Clay gritty; fired brown at core, buff on surface.

271 Jar
Not inv. Layer 8
D. rim unknown; GTh. 0.008 m.
Fig. 14
Rim sherd of jar. Upper wall curving inward from shoulder, gradually thickening towards rim.
Buff (7.5YR 7/6) clay, gritty. Buff (10YR 8/2) slip on exterior and on interior below rim; interior rim slipped brown (7.5YR 4/2) in band *ca.* 0.055 m. wide, now quite worn but perhaps originally polished.

272   Jar
Not inv.   Layer 8
Est. D. rim 0.36; GTh. 0.011 m.
Fig. 14
  Rim and adjoining upper wall of jar with everted, thickened rim.
  Orange (5YR 7/6) clay, gritty and rather coarse, with some mica. Surfaces plain.

PITCHER (273)

273   Pitcher
P 5341   Layer 8
GPH. 0.102; GTh. 0.011 m.
Pl. 21
  Single sherd preserves part of rim, cylindrical neck, and shoulder of large trefoil pitcher. Surfaces worn; some incrustation especially on interior. Roughly finished at rim.
  Orange (5YR 7/6) clay, gritty. Surfaces plain, wheelmarks visible.

JUG (274)

274   Jug
Not inv.   Layer 8
Est. D. rim 0.12; GTh. 0.0067 m.
Fig. 14
  Rim sherd of jug with thickened rim.
  Orange (5YR 7/6) clay, somewhat gritty. Surfaces plain; wheelmarks visible on exterior.

BATHTUBS (275 and 276)

275   Knob from bathtub?
P 5338   Layer 8, Pit B
GPL. 0.077; GPW. 0.095; D. knob 0.068; GTh. 0.0534 m.
Fig. 14; Pl. 21
  Single sherd broken on all sides preserves knob or boss, and place of attachment to vessel wall. Surfaces slightly chipped, with thin incrustation.
  Originally attached to large flat surface. Depression on knob surface worn away at either side (ca. 0.0175 wide, 0.005 m. deep).
  Orange (5YR 6/6) clay, gritty and rather coarse. Surface of knob and wall covered with a thin buff (10YR 8/2) slip, matt finish. Appears handmade.
  Below, **324**.
  Compare knobs on brazier from Boğazköy, Nordwesthang-Büyükkale Level 7 (*Nordwesthang-Büyükkale*, 56, no. 218, pl. 43).

276   Bathtub rim?
P 5339   Layer 8, Pit B
GPL. 0.0515; GPW. 0.745 m.
Pl. 21
  Single sherd broken on all sides preserves finished surface (top or bottom), corner and flat lower finished surface. Much worn; slip eaten away.
  On flat surface is a perpendicular band section, 0.041 m. wide, preserving a corner. Perhaps from rim band or rib of large vessel or bathtub.
  Orange (5YR 6/6) clay, gritty. Flat surface has thin tan slip; band with corner and other surface covered with thin red (10R 6/6) slip, matt finish. Handmade.
  Compare large clay tub with corners from Tarsus Late Bronze I (*Tarsus* II, 197, no. 1054, figs. 310, 381). Also top

corner fragment from Korucutepe Phase I (*Korucutepe* 3, 98, pl. 18Q).

VOTIVE BOWL (277)

277   Votive bowl
P 3390   Layer 8
H. 0.018; D. base 0.04; D. rim 0.06 m.
Pl. 21
  One-half of bowl preserved, broken across.
  Flat, string-cut base, shallow bowl flaring to plain rim. Base roughened so stands unevenly.
  Light reddish brown (5YR 6/4) clay, somewhat gritty; some "gold" mica. Formed on wheel and finished by hand.
  Boğazköy, Büyükkale Levels IVc-III, especially III and Unterstadt 1 (*Heth. Keramik*, 146-147, nos. 1032-1041, pls. 119-120, with further references to Alaca, Tarsus Late Bronze II, Beycesultan Level II); also Maşat Level III (*Maşat* II, figs. 2-5), 2-5), and Korucutepe Phase J (*Korucutepe* 3, 101, pl. 21A).

SPINDLE WHORL (278)

278   Spindle whorl
MC 230   Layer 8, Pit A
H. 0.0215; D. 0.028; D. hole 0.005-0.006 m.
Fig. 14; Pl. 21
  Complete.
  Cylindrical form, flattened on top and bottom. Incised lines on exterior and outside hole.
  Fine clay, with "gold" and "silver" mica, fired to mottled red and gray-brown.

NONCERAMIC ARTIFACTS (279-282)

279   Copper or bronze stylus and eraser
B 1582   Layer 8, Pit B
L. 0.173; D. shaft 0.007; W. eraser end 0.015 m.
Pl. 22
  Mended; complete when recovered, pointed end now broken off.
  Rod, round in section, tapering to point at one end; at the other, beyond a swelling in shaft, a short flattened chisel-like end, for erasing in wax or clay.
  Boğazköy, Unterstadt Level 1 (*Kleinfunde Unterstadt*, 31, no. 3395, pl. XIX); also an unstratified example (*Kleinfunde*, 133-134, no. 1214, with discussion and further references on use of styli).

280   Copper or bronze knife
B 1578   Layer 8, bottom of Pit A
L. 0.28; L. blade 0.185; GW. blade 0.031 m.
Pl. 22
  Mended many times but complete; some corrosion present.
  Long straight blade, with very slight concavity to spine and long reverse curve to cutting edge, probably from use. Tang begins at gentle setback and continues margined by sharp flanges on both faces to contain half-cylindrical pieces of handle. Butt notched out to triangular cut, rivet hole near it.
  Boğazköy, Nordwesthang-Büyükkale Level 7 or 6 (*Kleinfunde*, 79, no. 258).

281   Copper or bronze pin
B 1657   Layer 8, Pit A
PL. 0.07; D. head 0.01 m.
Pl. 22
  Broken and mended approximately at center of shaft, where bent to L-shape. Point broken off; slightly corroded.

Head solid double-convex. Shaft below head is square in section, becomes round as it thins towards point.

282   Stone polisher
ST 547   Layer 8, Pit A
H. 0.05; GW. 0.055; D. suspension hole 0.007-0.008 m.
Fig. 14
Apparently intact; a few scratches and chips.
Nearly regular five-faced stone, with two flat-square faces, one convex-square face, and two flat-triangular faces. Neatly pierced for suspension through centers of the flat-triangular faces.
Hard, glossy black stone. All surfaces smoothed by rubbing.

LAYER 7   (283-337, S36-S42)

BOWLS (283-304)

283   Bowl
Not inv.   Layer 7
D. rim unknown; GTh. 0.0055 m.
Fig. 15
Rim sherd of bowl with rim tapered on inside.
Fine orange (5YR 6/6) clay with few gritty inclusions, fired lighter at surface. Wheelmarks mostly smoothed away on exterior.

284   Shallow bowl
Not inv.   Layer 7
D. rim unknown; GTh. 0.008 m.
Fig. 15
Rim sherd of shallow bowl; upper wall gradually thickens to rounded rim.
Orange (5YR 6/6) clay, somewhat gritty. Buff (10YR 8/4) slip on both surfaces, beneath which wheelmarks are partly visible.

285   Bowl
Not inv.   Layer 7
D. rim unknown; GTh. 0.006 m.
Fig. 15
Rim sherd of bowl with straight upper wall, plain rim.
Buff (7.5YR 7/4) clay, gritty, with some mica. Dull red (2.5YR 6/6) slip preserved on rim and upper exterior wall.

286   Shallow bowl
Not inv.   Layer 7
D. rim unknown; GTh. 0.0035 m.
Fig. 15
Rim sherd of small shallow bowl with angled, almost vertical rim.
Orange (5YR 6/6) clay, fine and clean, surfaces well smoothed. Red (10R 5/6) slip, originally polished, on outer rim and interior surface.

287   Shallow bowl
Not inv.   Layer 7
D. rim unknown; GTh. 0.006 m.
Fig. 15
Rim sherd of shallow bowl with broad, thickened rim. Outer rim chipped.
Orange-red (2.5YR 5/8) clay, relatively fine and clean. Red (10R 5/6) slip, burnished and originally lustrous, on both surfaces; streakily applied on exterior.

288   Shallow bowl
Not inv.   Layer 7
D. rim unknown; GTh. 0.01 m.
Fig. 15
Rim sherd of shallow bowl with thickened, almost vertical rim.

Orange clay, gritty, with some mica. Surface plain; wheelmarks visible, mostly worn smooth on rim.

289   Shallow bowl
Not inv.   Layer 7
D. rim unknown; GTh. 0.0075 m.
Fig. 15
Rim and adjoining wall of shallow bowl with broad, angled rim. Surfaces discolored.
Buff (7.5YR 6/6) clay, gritty. Surfaces left plain or covered with thin "self-slip," fired lighter than core.

290   Shallow bowl
Not inv.   Layer 7
D. rim unknown; GTh. 0.006 m.
Fig. 15
Rim sherd of shallow bowl with inverted rim projecting above and below vessel edge.
Orange clay, relatively fine and clean. Matt red slip, worn, preserved on rim and upper surface; perhaps originally applied on lower surface as well.

291   Shallow bowl
Not inv.   Layer 7
D. rim unknown; GTh. 0.009 m.
Fig. 15
Rim sherd of shallow bowl with thickened, broad rim rounded on top. Slight surface incrustation.
Orange (5YR 7/6) clay, gritty, with dusting of "silver" mica. Surfaces plain.
Close to Tarsus Late Bronze II example (*Tarsus* II, 209, no. 1119, fig. 384).

292   Bowl
Not inv.   Layer 7
D. rim 0.308; GTh. 0.01 m.
Fig. 15
Rim and adjoining wall of bowl with inverted rim projecting above and below edge of vessel. Slip flaking; surfaces worn; rim chipped.
Orange clay, gritty. Clay-colored slip thinly applied on both surfaces.

293   Bowl
Not inv.   Layer 7
Est. D. rim 0.30; GTh. 0.01 m.
Fig. 15
Rim sherd of bowl with inverted rim. Slight incrustation on both surfaces.
Orange (5YR 7/6) clay, gritty. Buff (7.5YR 7/4-8/4) slip on rim and exterior; stringmarks visible on lower surface.

294   Shallow bowl
Not inv.   Layer 7
Est. D. rim 0.23; GTh. 0.007 m.
Fig. 15
Rim sherd of shallow bowl with inverted, almost vertical rim, tapered on interior. Outer rim chipped.
Orange (5YR 6/6) clay, gritty and micaceous. Red (10R 6/6) slip on interior and exterior rim; traces preserved on lower surface.

295   Bowl
P 3405   Layer 7
D. rim 0.328; GTh. 0.009 m.
Fig. 15; Pl. 22
Circa two-thirds of upper part of bowl preserved; mended, with remainder restored in plaster.
Broad, thickened rim, rounded on top. Base restored as flat.
Fine buff (7.5YR 7/4) clay with few gritty inclusions. Surfaces smoothed, plain.

296 Bowl
Not inv. Layer 7
D. rim unknown; GTh. 0.007 m.
Fig. 15
Rim sherd of bowl with everted rim. Some incrustation especially on interior.
Orange clay, gritty. Surfaces plain; wheelmarks mostly smoothed away on exterior, visible on rim and interior.

297 Carinated bowl
Not inv. Layer 7
D. rim unknown; GTh. 0.01 m.
Fig. 15
Rim sherd of carinated bowl with thickened, gently sloping rim.
Orange clay, gritty. Matt buff slip on both surfaces, beneath which wheelmarks are partly visible.

298 Carinated bowl
Not inv. Layer 7
D. rim unknown; GTh. 0.008 m.
Fig. 15
Rim sherd of carinated bowl with thickened, sloping rim.
Reddish orange (2.5YR 6/6) clay, gritty. Surfaces plain, wheelmarks visible.

299 Carinated bowl
Not inv. Layer 7
Est. D. rim 0.33; GTh. 0.0075 m.
Fig. 15
Sherd preserves rim and adjoining wall. Deep bowl with carinated profile; thickened, sloping rim. Surfaces incrusted.
Fine orange (5YR 6/6) clay with few gritty inclusions. Surfaces plain.

300 Carinated bowl with sieve
P 5330 Layer 7
Est. D. rim 0.272; GPL. 0.045; GPW. 0.063; GTh. 0.009 m.
Fig. 15; Pl. 22
Sherd preserves rim and adjoining wall. Surfaces slightly incrusted; interior abraded.
Bowl with slight carination, thickened rim. Two circular perforations through wall just below rim, *ca.* 0.008 across and 0.02 m. apart.
Light orange (5YR 6/6) clay, gritty; fired lighter at surfaces. Wheelmarks mostly visible.
Below, **339**.

301 Carinated bowl with horizontal handles
Not inv. Layer 7
D. rim unknown; GTh. 0.009 m.
Fig. 15
Rim sherd of bowl with slight carination, sloping, thickened rim. Base of horizontal handle preserved on one side of sherd.
Orange (5YR 6/6) clay, with few gritty inclusions. Red (10R 5/6) slip, carelessly applied, on inner rim and exterior, mottled with cream (10YR 8/3).

302 Carinated bowl with horizontal handles
P 5323 Layer 7
D. rim unknown; GPL. 0.07; GPW. 0.087; GTh. 0.005 m.
Fig. 15; Pl. 22
Part of rim and handle with adjoining wall and place of attachment. Slip worn on handle.
Bowl with slight carination, thickened, rounded rim. Handle, round in section, rises from area of maximum diameter, swinging well away from rim and forming wide horizontal loop.
Orange-red (10R 6/8) clay, relatively clean with some gritty inclusions; fired darker at core. Red (10R 5/8) slip on exterior and inner rim, smoothed, with matt finish.

303 Carinated bowl with horizontal handles
P 5324 Layer 7
GPL. 0.053; GPW. 0.07; Th. handle 0.02; GTh. 0.0065 m.
Fig. 15; Pl. 22
Sherd preserves part of rim, handle and adjoining wall with place of handle attachment.
Profile of bowl like **302**. Handle, oval in section, rises above rim.
Orange-buff (7.5YR 6/6-7/6) clay, gritty; handle fired dark at core. Light red (10R 6/8) slip on exterior wall, extending to base of handle. Handle, rim and interior slipped tan or with "self-slip." All surfaces smoothed, with matt finish.

PLATES (304 and 305)

304 Plate
Not inv. Layer 7
Est. D. rim 0.23; GTh. 0.005 m.
Fig. 15
Rim sherd of plate with vertical rim.
Orange (5YR 7/6) clay, relatively clean. Red (10R 5/8) slip on both surfaces, somewhat worn and dull.
Close to Tarsus Late Bronze II (*Tarsus* II, fig. 384: profile B).

305 Plate
Not inv. Layer 7
D. rim unknown; GTh. 0.011 m.
Fig. 15
Rim and adjoining body of plate.
Reddish brown (2.5YR 6/6) clay, gritty. Surfaces plain, roughly finished, especially lower surface.

JARS (306-320)

306 Jar
P 5328 Layer 7
Est. D. rim 0.11; GPL. 0.065; GPW. 0.083; GTh. 0.006 m.
Fig. 15
Rim and adjoining wall sherd of jar or teapot. Surface worn, slightly incrusted and discolored.
Biconical vessel, slightly outturned rim. Two small swellings pressed from inside jar, on upper wall, *ca.* 0.05 m. apart, with corresponding depressions on interior.
Orange (5YR 7/6) clay, very gritty. Exterior and inner rim covered with red (10R 5/8) slip, mostly worn now but probably originally lustrous.
Jar from Hittite Cemetery with similar swellings: Old Hittite (*Hitt. Cem.*, 24, pl. 28a).

307 Jar
Not inv. Layer 7
D. rim unknown; GTh. 0.005 m.
Fig. 15; Pl. 22
Rim sherd of jar (teapot?) with relatively thin walls; everted, thickened rim. Rim chipped.
Orange clay, with few gritty inclusions. Dull orange-red slip on interior rim and exterior, somewhat casually applied. Interior surface plain.
Below, **437**.

308 Jar with impressed design
P 5329 Layer 7
Est D. rim 0.28; GPL. 0.066; GPW. 0.10; GTh. 0.0085 m.
Fig. 15; Pl. 22
Rim and adjoining shoulder of jar. Worn; slight discoloration.

Rim slightly everted and thickened on outside; rounded shoulder. Groove on exterior at junction with shoulder. Part of an impressed pattern of concentric circles preserved on vessel wall below rim. Circles are of uneven width, decreasing towards center of design.

Buff-tan (7.5YR 6/6) clay, gritty. Red (10R 5/8) slip on rim and exterior, now worn but originally lustrous. Interior plain.

For impressed design: above, **253**, with further references.

309 Jar
Not inv. Layer 7
Est. D. rim 0.35; GTh. 0.01 m.
Fig. 16
Rim and adjoining upper wall of jar. Some thin incrustation on exterior.

Thickened rim; upper wall sloping inward to neck.

Orange (5YR 6/6) clay, gritty. Buff (10YR 8/3) slip, thin and matt, on exterior and perhaps on both surfaces.

310 Jar
Not inv. Layer 7
D. rim unknown; GTh. 0.011 m.
Fig. 16
Rim sherd of jar with everted, faintly grooved rim. Some green discoloration on interior.

Orange (5YR 7/6) clay, gritty. Thin buff (10YR 8/3) slip on both surfaces; wheelmarks mostly smoothed on interior, visible on exterior.

311 Jar
Not inv. Layer 7
Est. D. rim 0.23; GTh. 0.007 m.
Fig. 16
Rim sherd of jar with outturned, thickened rim.

Buff (7.5YR 7/6) clay, gritty. Pale buff (10YR 8/4) slip thinly applied on both surfaces, beneath which wheelmarks are visible.

312 Jar
Not inv. Layer 7
D. rim unknown; GTh. 0.007 m.
Fig. 16
Rim sherd of jar with outturned, gradually thickened rim. Somewhat incrusted, especially on exterior.

Orange (2.5YR 6/8) clay with gritty inclusions, some mica. Surfaces plain.

313 Jar
Not inv. Layer 7
D. rim unknown; GTh. 0.0061 m.
Fig. 16
Rim sherd of jar with sharply outturned, thickened rim. Green discoloration on both surfaces.

Light red (2.5YR 6/6) clay, gritty; surfaces plain.

314 Jar
Not inv. Layer 7
Est. D. rim 0.26; GTh. 0.012 m.
Fig. 16
Rim and adjoining upper wall of jar with everted, thickened rim. Interior surface pitted.

Orange clay, gritty; fired lighter at surfaces.

315 Jar
Not inv. Layer 7
Est. D. rim 0.29; GTh. 0.01 m.
Fig. 16
Rim sherd of jar with sharply outturned rim.

Buff-orange (5YR 7/6) clay, gritty. Thin buff (7.5YR 8/4) slip on both surfaces, worn on outer rim.

316 Jar
Not inv. Layer 7
Est. D. rim 0.28; GTh. 0.009 m.
Fig. 16
Rim and adjoining wall of jar with everted rim. Rim chipped.

Orange (5YR 6/6) clay with gritty inclusions; some mica visible on surface. Surfaces plain.

317 Jar
Not inv. Layer 7
Est. D. rim 0.25; GTh. 0.009 m.
Fig. 16
Rim and adjoining upper wall of straight-sided jar with sharply outturned, wide rim. Shallow indentation in upper surface of rim.

Orange-buff (5YR 7/6) clay, gritty. Brown (5YR 4/3) slip on upper surface of rim and on exterior, with wheel- and stroke-burnish marks preserved. Interior plain.

318 Jar
Not inv. Layer 7
Est. D. rim 0.20; GTh. 0.011 m.
Fig. 16
Rim sherd of jar with ledged rim, grooved on exterior. Surfaces somewhat incrusted.

Orange (5YR 6/6) clay, gritty. Buff (10YR 8/4) slip on both surfaces.

319 Jar with pierced lug handles
P 5327 Layer 7
GPH. 0.054; Est. D. rim 0.11; GTh. 0.0055 m.
Fig. 16; Pl. 22
Section mended from two joining sherds preserves part of rim and adjoining wall, most of lug.

Small globular jar; ledged rim, probably a rest for vessel lid. Lug, pierced vertically, on outer wall above maximum diameter.

Orange-buff (7.5YR 6/6) clay, gritty; some "gold" mica. Exterior, rim, and rim ledge covered with brown (5YR 5/8) slip, worn; some luster preserved. Interior plain.

320 Jar with vertical handle
P 5336 Layer 7
GPH. 0.057; GPW. 0.071; W. handle 0.0135; GTh. 0.0045 m.
Pl. 22
Single sherd preserves part of shoulder, body, and vertical handle near lower place of attachment. Exterior surface slightly incrusted and scratched.

Small jar with constricted neck. Vertical handle, flanged, with edges thicker than center; wider at base than in center.

Fine, clean buff (7.5YR 7/6) clay. Exterior covered with thin buff (10YR 8/4) "enamel" slip; interior plain.

PITCHERS (321 and 322)

321 Pitcher spout
P 5325 Layer 7
GPL. 0.115; GPW. 0.127; D. spout 0.046; GTh. 0.008 m.
Fig. 16; Pl. 23
Tubular spout and adjoining body at place of attachment. Spout broken at upper opening; vessel wall section broken on all sides. Surfaces slightly incrusted.

Spout rises steeply from vessel, with short trough turned out slightly at opening; lip of spout thickened.

Orange-buff (7.5YR 6/6) clay, gritty; fired slightly darker at core in spout area. Some "gold" mica. Surfaces plain, fired buff.

322   Trefoil pitcher
P 5335   Layer 7
GPH. 0.0546; GPW. 0.098; W. handle 0.036; GTh. 0.008 m.
Fig. 16; Pl. 23
    Single section preserves part of rim, handle, and adjoining neck of pitcher. Surfaces slightly incrusted.
    Cylindrical neck; thickened, everted trefoil rim. Handle, oblong in section, attached at rim; broken off where extends vertically to vessel shoulder.
    Tan-buff (7.5YR 7/4) clay, gritty; fired buff at surfaces. Surfaces rather cursorily smoothed and finished. Fingerprint impressions preserved on interior at place of handle attachment.

JUG OR BOTTLE (323)

323   Jug or bottle
P 5326   Layer 7
GPH. 0.0535; Est. D. upper opening 0.023; Est. D. opening at shoulder 0.041; W. handle 0.014 m.
Fig. 16; Pl. 23
    Part of neck and vertical handle from narrow-necked jug or bottle. Surfaces incrusted; worn and abraded especially on upper area near opening.
    Narrow cylindrical neck with two relief rings at junction with shoulder. Handle, oval in section, extends down from neck to form vertical loop.
    Orange-buff (7.5YR 6/6) clay, gritty. Exterior and handle covered with light plum red slip, matt finish.

BATHTUB (324)

324   Knob from bathtub?
P 5332   Layer 7
GPL. 0.101; GPW. 0.133; D. knob 0.082; GTh. 0.0315 m.
Fig. 16; Pl. 23
    Fragment from wall of large bathtub, with knob attached to exterior surface. Sherd broken on all sides. Knob chipped and abraded.
    Knob is circular, rising at slightly lopsided angle from vessel wall. May be a knob from a bathtub or a pithos wall, for ornament or for use in attaching lid, as a sort of lug.
    Orange (7.5YR 6/6) clay, gritty. Knob and exterior surface covered with buff (10YR 7/4) slip, smoothed, matt finish. Interior surface fired lighter; mostly smoothed of wheelmarks.
    Above, **275**, with comparanda.

LID (325)

325   Lid
P 5337   Layer 7
GPL. 0.07; GPW. 0.067; GTh. 0.022 m.
Pl. 23
    Part of finished rim and adjoining wall of flat vessel, perhaps lid with central steam-hole. Surfaces grayed, worn. Blackened on inner central hole and in a few places on exterior.
    Orange clay, very coarse and gritty; surfaces plain, fired tan-orange.
    Below, **413**.

RIM SHERD (326)

326   Rim sherd
Not inv.   Layer 7
Est. D. rim 0.12; GTh. 0.008 m.
Fig. 16

Rim and adjoining wall probably from jug with cylindrical neck, thickened rim. Rim chipped.
    Orange (5YR 6/6) clay, relatively fine and clean, with few gritty inclusions. Red (10R 4/6) slip on lower rim and exterior; very worn, especially on rim. Interior plain.

BASES (327-330)

327   Base
Not inv.   Layer 7
GPH. 0.045; D. base 0.06; GTh. 0.0075 m.
Fig. 16
    Base and adjoining lower wall of vessel with flat base. Base fully preserved. Surface discolored; base worn.
    Tan (5YR 6/4) clay, gritty and rather coarse. Surfaces plain.

328   Ring base
Not inv.   Layer 7
GPH. 0.048; D. base 0.085; GTh. 0.008 m.
Fig. 16
    Base and adjoining lower body. Base fully preserved. Blackened slightly on interior and exterior.
    Orange (5YR 6/6) clay, gritty and rather coarse. Surfaces plain, with some wheelmarks visible on exterior.

329   Ring base
Not inv.   Layer 7
GPH. 0.047; Est. D. base 0.15; GTh. 0.007 m.
Fig. 16
    Fragment of ring base, probably from large jar or pitcher.
    Orange (5YR 6/6) clay, gritty. Buff (10YR 8/3) slip preserved on both surfaces.

330   Base
P 5331   Layer 7
GPL. 0.104; GPW. 0.115; GTh. 0.0235 m.
Fig. 16; Pl. 23
    Part of base and adjoining lower vessel wall. Surfaces abraded, worn and scratched.
    Base is a rounded area; walls rise steeply to form conical lower part of vessel. Perhaps from lower part of large jug.
    Orange-red (2.5YR 5/6) clay, coarse and gritty, with some "gold" and "silver" mica. Fired somewhat darker on exterior. Wheelmade? Interior roughly finished by hand.

PAINTED SHERDS (331-333)

331   Painted body sherd
P 5334   Layer 7
GPL. 0.055; GPW. 0.063; GTh. 0.006 m.
Pl. 23
    Body sherd from vessel of unknown shape. Interior slightly incrusted.
    Exterior painted in cream (10YR 8/2) and red-brown (2.5YR 4/8), smoothed and slightly lustrous. Painted decoration consists of solid cream background; on this a solid red band, ca. 0.01 m. in width, across sherd.
    Orange clay (5YR 6/6), fine and clean, with few gritty inclusions. Interior plain.
    Above, **252**.

332   Painted body sherd
P 3301   Layer 7
GPL. 0.06; GPW. 0.046; GTh. 0.006 m.
Pl. 23
    Body sherd from shoulder(?) of closed shape, perhaps jar.
    Painted decoration on exterior, in matt red-brown (2.5YR 4/8) on light buff (7.5YR 8/4) background: parallel lines and

lines crossing at oblique angles to form plain and hatched triangles.

Fine buff (7.5YR 7/4) clay with gritty inclusions; fired gray at core.

Below, **333**.

333   Painted body sherd
P 5333   Layer 7
GPL. 0.042; GPW. 0.038; GTh. 0.007 m.
Fig. 16; Pl. 23
Body sherd from vessel of unknown shape. Exterior chipped.

Exterior painted in matt red (10R 5/6) on a light buff-slipped surface: painted lines form pattern of crossing triangles, bordered by a solid red band. Lines of triangles 0.004, band 0.008 m. wide. Interior plain.

Orange-red (2.5YR 6/6) clay, fine and clean, with few gritty inclusions.

Also below, **515** and **516**.

332 and **333**: related to examples from Maşat Level I (*Maşat* II, fig. 32) and Korucutepe Phase I (*Korucutepe* 3, pls. 14C, 27G).

LOOMWEIGHT (334)

334   Loomweight
MC 312   Layer 7
GPL 0.083; GPW. 0.044; GTh. 0.028 m.
Pl. 23
Fragmentary crescent loomweight preserves one end with perforation; broken across at *ca.* one-third of full length. Surfaces pitted and abraded.

Nearly oval at preserved end; slightly concave in section. Perforation *ca.* 0.01 m. across.

Orange-buff (7.5YR 7/6) clay, gritty. Hand-formed.
Below, **526-529**, with comparanda.

NONCERAMIC ARTIFACTS (335-337)

335   Copper or bronze blade
B 1577   Layer 7
GPL. 0.052; GPW. 0.01 m.
Pl. 23
Broken at proximal end, approximately in middle of blade. Roughened by corrosion.

Flat, thin, sharpened on convex edge; spine has concave curve.

336   Copper or bronze hook
B 1635   Layer 7
GPL. 0.063; W. lashing head 0.009 m.
Pl. 23
Complete; originally attached at straight end.

Large hook formed from metal rod round in section. Hook is in form of semicircle ending in plain barbless point. Shaft has slight reverse curve; lashing head is curved and flattened.

337   Stone ax head
ST 546   Layer 7
GPL. 0.048; GPW. 0.055; GTh. 0.043 m.
Pl. 24
Half of a double or cutting portion only of single ax. Cutting edge chipped.

Wide at point where hafting hole was bored (striations are horizontal and parallel in hole). Side profile of ax tapers back from convex cutting edge to a narrower (i.e., shorter) neck around the hafting hole. Very smooth on all surfaces, as if used as whetstone after breakage.

Gray-black, fine-grained stone.

LAYER 6   (338-347, S43-S50)

BOWLS (338 and 339)

338   Shallow bowl
Not inv.   Layer 6
Est. D. rim 0.20; GTh. 0.007 m.
Not. illus.
Rim sherd of shallow bowl with profile indented on outer wall, flattened rim.

Orange clay, relatively clean, with few tiny inclusions. Matt red slip on both surfaces, rather thinly and carelessly applied on interior. Some burnish strokes visible.

339   Sieved bowl
Not inv.   Layer 6
Est. D. rim 0.16; GTh. 0.008 m.
Fig. 17
Rim sherd of sieved bowl with gently carinated profile, thickened rim. Row of circular perforations below rim, part of five preserved; exterior diameter of perforations 0.0045 m.

Orange (2.5YR 6/6) clay, generally clean, with few tiny inclusions; some "silver" mica.

Above, **300**.

Tarsus Late Bronze II (*Tarsus* II, 218-219, nos. 1235-37; figs. 325, 387); Korucutepe Phases I-J (*Korucutepe* 3, 102, pl. 21J).

JAR (340)

340   Jar
Not inv.   Layer 6
Est. D. rim 0.22; GTh. 0.011 m.
Fig. 17
Rim sherd of jar with tapered neck and broad, ledged rim. Blackened along inner and outer rim; rim chipped.

Orange (2.5YR 5/6) clay, relatively clean, with few tiny inclusions; dense "silver" mica concentration in biscuit and on surfaces. Surfaces covered with clay "self-slip" and wiped; burnish strokes visible. Import?

PITHOI (341 and 342)

341   Pithos
Not inv.   Layer 6
Est. D. rim 0.60; GTh. 0.025 m.
Fig. 17
Rim sherd of pithos of hole-mouth form, with rim thickened on inside. Blackened on rim and interior.

Reddish brown (2.5YR 5/4) clay, very coarse and gritty. Wheelmarks smoothed on exterior.

342   Pithos
Not inv.   Layer 6
Est. D. rim 0.70; GTh. 0.031 m.
Fig. 17
Rim sherd of pithos with everted rim. Blackened on rim and broken edges of sherd.

Coarse orange (5YR 6/6) clay, with many gritty inclusions; some "gold" and "silver" mica. Outer surface perhaps smeared with slip, now flaking. Apparently handmade.

JUG (343)

343   Jug
Not inv.   Layer 6
Est. D. rim 0.10; GTh. 0.016 m.
Fig. 17

Rim sherd of jug with cylindrical neck, thickened rim. Bottom edge of sherd on exterior preserves stub of vertical handle.

Buff (7.5YR 6/6) clay, gritty; fired lighter at surfaces. Exterior wet-smoothed or lightly "self-slipped."

RIM SHERD (344)

344 Rim sherd
Not inv.   Layer 6
Est. D. rim 0.38; GTh. 0.01 m.
Fig. 17

Rim sherd probably from large plate, with thick straight rim.

Gritty orange (5YR 6/6) clay, with "gold" and "silver" mica.

BASE (345)

345 Flat base
Not inv.   Layer 6
GPH. 0.044; Est. D. base 0.08 m.
Fig. 17

Base and adjoining lower wall. Broken across base near center and along upper wall.

Jar with flattened base.

Orange (5YR 6/6) clay, somewhat gritty. Exterior preserves some reddish brown slip, now worn; interior plain.

NONCERAMIC ARTIFACTS (346 and 347)

346 Copper or bronze nail or pin
B 1576   Layer 6
PL. 0.05; head 0.006 m.
Pl. 24

Complete? Shaft perhaps broken; roughened by corrosion.

Fairly straight pin, with thin shaft, round in section, and double convex solid head. Point blunt.

347 Glass bead fragment
G 311   Layer 6
D. 0.022; Th. 0.01; hole 0.005 m.
Pl. 24

Badly crushed remains of a bead with gaps and chips.

Squat spherical bead, plain around outer edges; depressions around stringhole on both faces.

Milky, very light green glass with large bubbles.

Boğazköy, Unterstadt Level 1 (Kleinfunde Unterstadt, 43, no. 3588, pl. XXVI).

LAYER 5   (348-383)

BOWLS (348-352)

348 Bowl
Not inv.   Layer 5
Est. D. rim 0.16; GTh. 0.0045 m.
Fig. 17

Rim sherd of bowl with rim tapered slightly on inside. Some dark discoloration and scratches on exterior.

Orange (5YR 7/6) clay, fine and clean; fired buff on interior. Surfaces plain; wheelmarks smoothed on lower outer surface.

Tarsus Late Bronze II (Tarsus II, 209, no. 1113, fig. 384).

349 Bowl
Not inv.   Layer 5
Est. D. rim 0.20; GTh. 0.0077 m.
Fig. 17

Rim sherd of bowl with plain rim.

Orange (5YR 7/6) clay, gritty, with some mica. Surfaces plain; somewhat roughly finished.

350 Shallow bowl
Not inv.   Layer 5
Est. D. rim 0.16; GTh. 0.008 m.
Fig. 17

Rim sherd of shallow bowl with flattened base, plain rim. Interior surface uneven.

Orange (5YR 6/6) clay, gritty. Buff slip on both surfaces, well smoothed.

351 Bowl
Not inv.   Layer 5
D. rim unknown; GTh. 0.088 m.
Fig. 17

Rim sherd of bowl with broad, thickened rim.

Orange (5YR 6/6) clay, gritty and rather coarse; some mica visible on surface. Surfaces plain, exterior roughly finished.

352 Carinated bowl
Not inv.   Layer 5
Est. D. rim 0.18; GTh. 0.0026 m.
Fig. 17

Rim sherd of thin-walled bowl with slightly carinated profile, plain rim.

Orange (5YR 7/6) clay, fine and clean. Buff (7.5YR 7/4) slip on exterior and just inside rim, somewhat carelessly applied.

PLATES (353-357)

353 Plate
Not inv.   Layer 5
Est. D. rim 0.36; GTh. 0.0185 m.
Fig. 17

Rim sherd of large plate with tapered rim. Exterior surface blackened.

Orange (5YR 7/6) clay, gritty; some mica visible on surface. Buff (10YR 8/3) slip preserved on interior surface, perhaps originally also present on exterior surface.

354 Plate
Not inv.   Layer 5
D. rim unknown; GTh. 0.01 m.
Fig. 17

Rim sherd of plate with raised rim.

Orange (5YR 6/6) clay, gritty; much "silver" mica visible on surface. Red slip on both surfaces, somewhat worn and mottled.

355 Plate
Not inv.   Layer 5
D. rim unknown; GTh. 0.008 m.
Fig. 17

Rim sherd of plate with slightly thickened rim.

Orange (5YR 6/6) clay, gritty. Surfaces plain; lower surface roughly finished.

356 Plate
Not inv.   Layer 5
D. rim unknown; GTh. 0.0075 m.
Fig. 17

Rim sherd of plate with flattened rim.

Buff (7.5YR 7/6) clay, with some gritty inclusions. Pale buff slip on both surfaces.

357 Plate
Not inv.   Layer 5
D. rim unknown; GTh. 0.01 m.
Fig. 17

Rim sherd of plate with vertical rim. Some blackening on lower surface.

Orange-red (2.5YR 6/6) clay, gritty. Surfaces plain.

CUP (358)

358 Cup
Not inv. Layer 5
Est. D. rim 0.06; GTh. 0.005 m.
Fig. 17
Rim and adjoining wall of cup or beaker with slight carination; plain, outturned rim.

Orange (5YR 7/6) clay, very fine and clean. Buff (10YR 8/3) slip of "enamel" type on exterior, mostly worn. Fine, smooth surfaces, especially exterior.

JARS (359-364)

359 Jar
Not inv. Layer 5
Est. D. rim 0.40; GTh. 0.019 m.
Fig. 17
Rim and adjoining upper wall of large jar with thickened, everted rim, rounded on top. Blackened along inner rim.

Orange (5YR 6/6) clay, very gritty. Surfaces plain.

360 Jar
Not inv. Layer 5
Est. D. rim 0.29; GTh. 0.009 m.
Fig. 18
Rim sherd of jar with everted rim, thickened on inside.

Orange-red (2.5YR 6/6) clay, gritty and rather coarse, with much surface mica. Surfaces left plain or covered with thin "self-slip," now flaking off interior.

361 Jar
Not inv. Layer 5
Est. D. rim 0.38; GTh. 0.0122 m.
Fig. 18
Rim and adjoining upper wall of large jar with narrowing shoulder, everted rim faintly grooved across top.

Orange (5YR 6/6) clay, gritty, with some "gold" mica. Surfaces plain.

362 Jar
Not inv. Layer 5
Est. D. rim 0.38; GTh. 0.0152 m.
Fig. 18
Rim sherd of large jar with broad, everted rim.

Orange (5YR 6/6) gritty clay with some mica. Exterior covered with thin, pale buff (10YR 8/2) slip?

363 Jar
Not inv. Layer 5
Est. D. rim 0.50; GTh. 0.015 m.
Fig. 18; Pl. 24
Rim and adjoining wall fragment of large jar preserves base of vertical handle. Some surface incrustation.

Broad rim. Below rim, base of handle, round in section.

Very faint, horizontal ridges preserved on either side of handle.

Tan (5YR 6/4) clay, gritty; surfaces plain, wheelmarks mostly smoothed away.

364 Jar
Not inv. Layer 5
Est. D. rim 0.37; GTh. 0.007 m.
Fig. 18
Rim sherd of large jar; some surface discoloration. Upper rim grooved and ridged.

Orange (5YR 7/6) clay, gritty, with some mica. Pale buff (10YR 8/3) slip on both surfaces.

COOKING POT (365)

365 Cooking pot
Not inv. Layer 5
D. rim unknown; GTh. 0.016 m.
Fig. 18
Rim sherd of large jar with broad rim. Blackened both interior and exterior.

Orange (2.5YR 6/8) clay, gritty, with some "gold" and "silver" mica. Exterior surface perhaps originally covered with thin buff slip.

PITCHERS (366 and 367)

366 Sieve-spouted pitcher
P 5322 Layer 5
GPL. 0.078; GPW. 0.068; GTh. 0.007 m.
Fig. 18; Pl. 24
Single sherd preserves part of strainer spout, trough, and adjoining wall of pitcher. Broken across trough and on all sides. Surfaces slightly incrusted.

Perforations in wall at end of trough, in rows and along trough curve; each ca. 0.0045 m. in diameter.

Orange (5YR 6/6) clay, gritty; some "gold" mica. Both surfaces covered with thin buff (7.5YR 8/4) slip, smoothed on exterior, with matt finish.

Tarsus Late Bronze II, with trace of plastic animal at spout (*Tarsus* II, 217, no. 1225, fig. 325).

367 Trefoil pitcher
P 5320 Layer 5
GPH. 0.072; Est. D. rim 0.08; W. handle 0.025; Th. handle 0.015; GTh. 0.06 m.
Fig. 18
Single sherd preserves part of rim and handle, and adjoining shoulder of pitcher with trefoil rim.

Vertical handle, flat and oblong in section, preserved at upper end where attached to trefoil rim of vessel. Surfaces have slight gray incrustation.

Buff (7.5YR 7/6) clay, gritty, with some "gold" mica. Exterior covered with thin coat of clay or "self-slip," fired to lighter buff (10YR 8/4).

JUGS (368 and 369)

368 Jug
Not inv. Layer 5
Est. D. rim 0.09; GTh. 0.007 m.
Fig. 18
Rim sherd of jug. Some surface discoloration; worn on rim.

Thickened rim, rounded at lip; cylindrical neck preserves beginning of transition to flaring shoulder.

Orange clay, with gritty inclusions but relatively clean. Surfaces well smoothed, plain.

369 Jug
Not inv. Layer 5
Est. D. rim 0.10; GTh. 0.012 m.
Fig. 18
Rim sherd of jug with tapered neck, thickened rim. Some surface discoloration.

Orange (5YR 6/6) clay, gritty. Surfaces apparently covered with poorly preserved buff (7.5YR 7/4) slip.

LID (370)

370 Lid
P 5321 Layer 5
GPH. 0.037; GPW. 0.049; GTh. 0.009 m.
Pl. 24

Upper part of perforated vessel lid, broken on all sides, with intact spool handle attached to lid. Surfaces slightly incrusted; handle abraded.

Oblong spool handle placed upright in center of lid. Perforations through lid arranged roughly in concentric circles around handle, *ca.* 0.01 m. apart.

Orange-red (2.5YR 6/6) clay, gritty, with some "gold" mica. Surfaces covered with thin "self-slip," dull finish. Handmade.

Boğazköy, Unterstadt Level 2 and Büyükkale Level III (*Heth. Keramik*, 146, nos. 1018, 1031, pls. 116, 118).

RIMS (371 and 372)

371   Rim sherd
Not inv.   Layer 5
D. rim unknown; GTh. 0.01 m.
Fig. 18
Rim sherd with outturned rim. Possibly from a jar or jug.
Orange (5YR 7/6) clay, gritty. Pale buff (10YR 8/3) slip on both surfaces.

372   Rim sherd
Not inv.   Layer 5
D. rim unknown; GTh. 0.01 m.
Fig. 18
Rim sherd of jar or bowl with everted, slightly thickened rim. Break on exterior, perhaps indicating base of handle.
Orange-red (2.5YR 6/6) clay, gritty. Traces of orange-red (2.5YR 5/6) slip preserved on exterior.
Below, **405**.

BASES (373-380)

373   Base
Not inv.   Layer 5
GPH. 0.056; D. base 0.08; GTh. 0.007 m.
Fig. 18
Mended section preserves complete base and adjoining lower wall. Gently rounded base, possibly from bowl or jar.
Orange (5YR 6/6) clay, gritty. Buff (7.5YR 7/4) slip on both surfaces; wheelmarks mostly smoothed away, not very neatly, on exterior.

374   Base
P 5319   Layer 5
GPH. 0.08; D. base 0.02; GTh. 0.0125 m.
Fig. 18; Pl. 24
Single sherd preserves base and adjoining lower wall. Some incrustation on exterior; both surfaces slightly grayed.
Small flat base, wall rising rather steeply to form conical lower body of vessel.
Orange-red (2.5YR 6/6) clay, gritty, with "gold" mica visible on surface. Exterior roughly finished with thin layer of clay, matt finish. Interior lumpy; fingerprint impressions from pressing out by hand.

375   Base
P 5318   Layer 5
GPH. 0.186; Max. D. 0.16; GTh. 0.009 m.
Fig. 18; Pl. 24
Mended section preserves base and lower part of vessel. Thin, streaky white bands on both surfaces may be incrustation.

Small flat base; walls rise steeply to form cone comprising lower part of vessel. Interior near base, lumpy and unfinished.
Orange-red (2.5YR 6/6) clay, gritty, with "gold" mica. Exterior apparently "self-slipped," smoothed; interior left plain.

376   Base
Not inv.   Layer 5
GPH. 0.035; D. base 0.05; GTh. 0.009 m.
Fig. 18
Base and adjoining lower wall. Base *ca.* three-fourths preserved; blackened on interior. Base nearly flat but rises slightly in center. Possibly from pitcher or jar.
Orange (5YR 6/6) clay, micaceous; rather coarse and gritty. Surfaces fired lighter.

377   Pedestal base
Not inv.   Layer 5
GPH. 0.059; Est. D. base 0.06; GTh. 0.013 m.
Fig. 18
Base and adjoining lower body.
Base fully preserved. Interior roughly hollowed out. Probably from a pitcher or large teapot.
Orange-red (2.5YR 6/6) clay, relatively clean. Surfaces plain, with wheelmarks visible.

378   Ring base
Not inv.   Layer 5
GPH. 0.047; D. base 0.10; GTh. 0.019 m.
Fig. 18
Base and adjoining lower body of large jar or pitcher; walls rising rather steeply from ring base.
Orange-red (2.5YR 6/6) clay, gritty. Buff (7.5YR 8/4) slip on exterior, worn on edges of base.

379   Ring base
Not inv.   Layer 5
GPH. 0.066; Est. D. base 0.14; GTh. 0.011 m.
Fig. 18
Base and adjoining lower body of large jar or pitcher with ring base. *Circa* one-third of circumference preserved. Interior slightly blackened and pitted; hole in wall near base.
Orange (5YR 6/6) clay, gritty. Surfaces plain; wheelmarks visible on exterior.

380   Ring base
Not inv.   Layer 5
GPH. 0.045; Est. D. base 0.15; GTh. 0.012 m.
Fig. 18
Base fragment of large jar with ring base. Surfaces slightly cracked and somewhat discolored; interior surface uneven.
Orange-red (2.5YR 6/6) clay, gritty. Exterior perhaps covered with "self-slip"; wheelmarks visible.

HANDLE WITH SEAL IMPRESSION (381)

381   Handle with seal impression[108]
SS 223   Layer 5
GPL. handle 0.105; D. seal 0.022 m.
Pl. 24
Single sherd preserves part of vessel wall and lower attachment of a vertical handle, oval in section.
At base of handle, impression of a round flat seal, in part obscured by temper flaw and partly broken away.
Coarse clay, micaceous and gritty; fired gray-brown throughout.

---

108. Previous publication: H. G. Güterbock in *Young Symposium*, 51, with further references.

FAIENCE CYLINDER SEAL (382)

382 Cylinder seal
SS 220   Layer 5
L. 0.02; Max. D. 0.011; D. perforation 0.004-0.005 m.
Pl. 25
  Intact; worn.
  Cylinder with incised decoration of oblique crossing lines; pattern bordered by line at either end. Pierced through long axis.
  Faience, pasty white at core, light bluish green on surfaces.

METAL (383)

383 Copper or bronze pin
B 1658   Layer 5
PL. 0.078; D. head 0.005 m.
Pl. 25
  Tip of point broken off. Bent to an L-shape without breaking.
  Head spherical to double-convex with one necking ridge below it. Shaft round in section throughout, tapering very gradually towards point.

LAYER 4   (384-398, S51-S63)

BOWLS (384-391)

384 Shallow bowl
Not inv.   Layer 4
D. rim unknown; GTh. 0.0075 m.
Fig. 19
  Rim sherd of shallow bowl with broad rim. Exterior surface chipped.
  Orange-red (2.5YR 5/6) clay, gritty; fired buff (7.5YR 7/4) at surfaces. String-marks perhaps preserved on base.

385 Bowl
Not inv.   Layer 4
D. rim unknown; GTh. 0.0035 m.
Fig. 19
  Rim sherd of small bowl with gently curved profile, plain rim.
  Buff (7.5YR 7/6) clay, fine and clean. Surfaces plain, well smoothed.

386 Bowl
Not inv.   Layer 4
Est. D. rim 0.15; GTh. 0.003 m.
Fig. 19
  Rim sherd of thin-walled bowl with gently carinated profile, plain rim.
  Fine, clean orange (5YR 6/6) clay. Buff slip on exterior, now mostly worn. Well smoothed and carefully finished.

387 Large bowl
Not inv.   Layer 4
Est. D. rim 0.37; GTh. 0.01 m.
Fig. 19
  Rim sherd of large bowl with inverted, thickened rim.
  Orange (5YR 6/6) clay, gritty. Smeared buff (7.5YR 8/4) slip preserved on bottom surface.

388 Bowl
Not inv.   Layer 4
D. rim unknown; GTh. 0.0095 m.
Fig. 19
  Rim sherd of bowl with inverted rim. Slight incrustation on upper surface.

Orange clay with few gritty inclusions. Red slip preserved on rim and interior, perhaps originally on exterior also.

389 Bowl
Not inv.   Layer 4
Est. D. rim 0.32; GTh. 0.006 m.
Fig. 19
  Rim sherd of bowl with thickened, inverted rim, projecting above and below upper wall. Slightly blackened on exterior rim and part of exterior surface; inner rim chipped.
  Orange (5YR 6/6) clay, micaceous and somewhat gritty; surfaces fired buff (7.5YR 7/4).
  Maşat Level I (*Maşat* II, fig. 21).

390 Bowl
Not inv.   Layer 4
Est. D. rim 0.24; GTh. 0.011 m.
Fig. 19
  Mended from two joining sherds. Rim and adjoining wall of bowl with profile indented just below outside rim. Some blackening on both surfaces.
  Orange-red (2.5YR 6/6) clay, gritty, with "silver" mica. Traces of buff (7.5YR 8/4) slip on rim and exterior. Exterior very well smoothed, originally polished.

391 Large bowl
Not inv.   Layer 4
Est. D. rim 0.29; GTh. 0.0175 m.
Fig. 19
  Rim sherd of large bowl with broad, thickened rim indented on upper surface. Rim chipped.
  Orange-red (2.5YR 6/6) clay, gritty. Red (10R 5/6) slip on both surfaces, mostly worn especially on inner surface. Surfaces smoothed.

PLATES (392 and 393)

392 Plate
Not inv.   Layer 4
D. rim unknown; GTh. 0.0098 m.
Fig. 19
  Rim and adjoining body of plate with indented, rounded rim. Lower surface stained.
  Orange clay, gritty; fired lighter at surface.

393 Plate
Not inv.   Layer 4
D. rim unknown; GTh. 0.0085 m.
Fig. 19
  Rim and adjoining body of plate with rim thickened on outside. Exterior surface incrusted.
  Orange (5YR 6/6) clay, gritty. Surfaces plain, roughly finished. Stringmarks perhaps preserved on bottom.

JARS (394-397)

394 Jar
Not inv.   Layer 4
Est. D. rim 0.29; GTh. 0.0185 m.
Fig. 19
  Rim and adjoining upper wall of large jar narrowing at shoulder; everted rim, broad and indented on upper surface. Outer rim and exterior blackened.
  Orange-red (2.5YR 5/6) clay, gritty and rather coarse, with "silver" mica; surfaces plain.

395 Jar
Not inv.   Layer 4
D. rim unknown; GTh. 0.0105 m.
Fig. 19

Rim and adjoining upper wall of jar narrowing at shoulder; everted rim. Interior slightly blackened.

Orange (5YR 6/6) clay, gritty; surfaces plain.

396 Jar
Not inv.   Layer 4
D. rim unknown; GTh. 0.015 m.
Fig. 19

Rim sherd of jar with gently everted rim; shallow depression on inner rim. Interior blackened.

Orange (5YR 7/6) clay, gritty; surfaces plain.

397 Handle
Not inv.   Layer 4
GPL. 0.15; GPW. 0.09; W. handle 0.029; GTh. 0.01 m.
Pl. 25

Complete handle and part of adjoining vessel wall. Surfaces worn, incrusted, discolored.

Vertical handle, oval in section, with concave upper surface. Probably from a large jar.

Orange (5YR 6/6) clay, gritty, with some "gold" and "silver" mica. Surfaces apparently plain; wheelmarks visible.

JUG? (398)

398 Jug
Not inv.   Layer 4
Est. D. rim 0.27; GTh. 0.0098 m.
Fig. 19

Rim sherd similar to that of a large jug, but unusually wide mouth indicates another vessel shape.

Cylindrical neck, thickened rim. Some incrustation and discoloration; gray on interior and exterior rim.

Orange (5YR 6/6) clay, gritty, with "silver" mica; surfaces plain.

MEGARON 12   (399-492)

LEVEL VC (399-418)

BOWLS (399-409)

399 Shallow bowl
Not inv.   Level VC
Est. D. rim 0.13; GTh. 0.0045 m.
Fig. 19

Rim sherd of small shallow bowl with plain rim.

Orange clay, with some gritty inclusions. Surfaces plain, with wheelmarks mostly visible.

400 Bowl
Not inv.   Level VC
Est. D. rim 0.20; GTh. 0.0058 m.
Fig. 19

Rim sherd of bowl with S-shaped profile, outturned rim thickened on inside. Rim chipped.

Orange clay, fine and relatively clean. Reddish brown slip on both surfaces; well smoothed, with some luster preserved. Boğazköy, Unterstadt Level 4 (*Heth. Keramik*, 142, nos. 882 and 883, pl. 97); Nordwesthang-Büyükkale Levels 8b-8a (*Frühe Keramik*, 40, no. 293, pl. 31; *Nordwesthang-Büyükkale*, 44, no. 31, pl. 24); also Asarcık Level IV (*IstMitt* 16 [1966] 72, fig. 12:1); Ilıca cemetery (*Ilıca*, 40, nos. 6-7, pl.1); Beycesultan Level V (*Beycesultan* II, 86, fig. P.2:7-9).

401 Shallow bowl
Not inv.   Level VC
Est. D. rim 0.25; GTh. 0.0055 m.
Not. illus.

Rim sherd of shallow bowl with profile uneven on interior; inverted, almost vertical rim.

Orange clay, very gritty. Surfaces plain, with wheelmarks mostly visible.

402 Shallow bowl
Not inv.   Level VC
Est. D. rim 0.34; GTh. 0.007 m.
Fig. 19

Rim sherd of shallow bowl with inverted rim.

Orange clay, gritty. Matt buff slip with matt finish on both surfaces. Wheelmarks mostly visible; some smeared with slip on exterior.

403 Bowl
Not inv.   Level VC
Est. D. rim 0.36; GTh. 0.0073 m.
Fig. 19

Rim sherd of bowl with inverted rim. Inner rim abraded.

Orange clay, gritty. Buff slip on both surfaces, applied more thickly on lower surface.

404 Bowl
Not inv.   Level VC
D. rim unknown GTh. 0.013 m.
Fig. 19

Rim sherd of bowl with broad, thickened rim. Surfaces worn; rim abraded.

Orange clay, gritty. Surfaces plain.

405 Carinated bowl
Not inv.   Level VC
Est. D. rim 0.36; GTh. 0.012 m.
Fig. 19

Rim sherd of deep bowl with slight carination; outturned, gradually thickened rim. Rim chipped.

Orange clay, gritty; apparently well fired. Matt buff slip on both surfaces. Wheelmarks mostly visible.

Above, **372**.

406 Carinated bowl
Not inv.   Level VC
Est. D. rim 0.25; GTh. 0.012 m.
Fig. 20

Rim sherd of bowl with slight carination, thickened rim.

Tan (5YR 6/4) clay, gritty; apparently well fired. Surfaces left plain and relatively smooth. Wheelmarks mostly visible.

407 Carinated bowl
Not inv.   Level VC
Est. D. rim 0.36; GTh. 0.012 m.
Fig. 20

Rim and adjoining wall preserves carinated profile, sloping rim. Exterior grooved below rim.

Light red clay, very gritty. Buff slip on exterior and rim; interior with thin "self-slip." Surfaces matt; wheelmarks on exterior smeared away with slip, visible on interior surface.

408 Carinated bowl
Not inv.   Level VC
Est. D. rim 0.34; GTh. 0.011 m.
Fig. 20

Rim sherd of carinated bowl with thickened, sloping rim.

Light red clay, gritty; well fired. Thin buff slip with matt finish on both surfaces; smoothed but wheelmarks visible.

409 Carinated bowl with horizontal handles
P 5468   Level VC
GPL. 0.043; GPW. 0.094; GTh. 0.006 m.
Pl. 25

Part of rim, adjoining wall, and handle with place of attachment. Handle broken above rim. Some grayish incrustation on exterior; interior blackened.

Bowl with slight carination, thickened rim. Horizontal handle, oval in section, rises from maximum diameter to above rim.

Orange clay, gritty. Surfaces covered with "self-slip" or thin coat of clay, fired buff to orange.

JARS (410 and 411)

410 Jar
Not inv. Level VC
Est. D. rim 0.09; GTh. 0.0045 m.
Fig. 20
Rim sherd of small jar with profile tapering sharply towards neck, everted rim.
Fine, clean orange clay. Exterior covered with pale red slip, worn, continuing inside rim. Surfaces well smoothed.

411 Jar
Not inv. Level VC
Est. D. rim 0.15; GTh. 0.006 m.
Fig. 20
Rim sherd of small jar with slightly thickened, sloping rim; parallel horizontal grooves on upper exterior wall.
Red clay, gritty. Matt red slip, smoothed and worn, on exterior; interior plain.
Perhaps a teapot, as example with basket handle from Beycesultan Level IVa (*Beycesultan* II, 137, fig. P.36:11).

JUG (412)

412 Jug
Not inv. Level VC
Est. D. rim 0.09; GTh. 0.006 m.
Fig. 20
Rim sherd of jug. *Circa* one-third of rim circumference preserved.
Cylindrical neck flares outward gradually to thickened rim.
Orange (5YR 6/6) clay, gritty. Pale buff (10YR 8/3) slip on exterior, perhaps extending inside rim; very little preserved on interior.

LID (413)

413 Lid
P 5467 Level VC
GPL. 0.069; GPW. 0.077; GTh. 0.01 m.
Fig. 20; Pl. 25
Part of rim and adjoining wall of flat ceramic object, perhaps a lid. Blackened on outer edge of interior; some incrustation especially on under surface. Central hole with finished edge.
Red-orange clay, very coarse and gritty. Both surfaces seem to be covered with thin "self-slip," matt finish.
Above, **325**.

IMPRESSED RIM SHERD (414)

414 Impressed rim sherd
P 5466 Level VC
GPL. 0.032; GPW. 0.0465; GTh. 0.004 m.
Pl. 25
Rim sherd from thin-walled cup or small bowl.
Steep wall, thin and slightly outturned rim. Two rows of neatly punched dots across sherd below rim. Ten preserved, each *ca.* 0.004 m. across. Corresponding raised circles on interior.

Tan (5YR 6/4) clay, very fine and clean. Reddish brown (5YR 5/4) slip faintly preserved on both surfaces, with matt finish.

BASES (415-418)

415 Base
Not inv. Level VC
GPH. 0.033; GTh. 0.0102 m.
Not illus.
Base and adjoining lower body.
Vessel with rounded base; probably a bowl.
Orange clay, gritty. Buff slip on exterior; interior with similar, paler slip. Wheelmarks smoothed.

416 Base
Not inv. Level VC
D. base 0.09; GTh. 0.0073 m.
Fig. 20
Flat base and adjoining lower wall. Possibly from large jar or storage pitcher.
Orange clay, gritty, with some "silver" mica. Surfaces smoothed and plain.

417 Ring base
Not inv. Level VC
Est. D. base 0.06; GTh. 0.0082 m.
Fig. 20
Part of ring base and adjoining lower body of vessel. Ring worn.
Possibly from jar or pitcher.
Orange clay, gritty. Surfaces smoothed and plain.

418 Ring base
Not inv. Level VC
Est. D. base 0.09; GTh. 0.01 m.
Fig. 20
Fragment of ring base. Almost one-half of base circumference preserved. Grayish discoloration on both surfaces; ring slightly abraded.
Probably from jar or pitcher.
Orange clay, gritty, with some "gold" mica. Surfaces plain.

LEVEL VB (419-447)

BOWLS (419-435)

419 Bowl
Not inv. Level VB
Est. D. rim 0.20; GTh. 0.004 m.
Fig. 20
Rim sherd of thin-walled, carinated bowl with plain rim.
Fine, clean light red clay. Buff "enamel" slip on both surfaces, very well smoothed. Low luster preserved, as if polished smooth on exterior.

420 Shallow bowl
Not inv. Level VB
Est. D. rim 0.24; GTh. 0.007 m.
Fig. 20
Rim sherd of shallow bowl with slightly thickened rim. Rim chipped.
Orange clay, somewhat gritty. Surfaces plain; smoothed but wheelmarks remain visible.

421 Shallow bowl
Not inv. Level VB
Est. D. rim 0.24; GTh. 0.0033 m.
Fig. 20

Rim sherd of shallow bowl with tapered rim.

Fine, clean orange clay. Surfaces plain, well smoothed and polished, with some luster.

422 Bowl
Not inv. Level VB
Est. D. rim 0.18; GTh. 0.0045 m.
Fig. 20

Rim sherd of bowl with wall gradually thickened towards incurved rim.

Fine, clean orange clay, very well fired. Red slip on upper part of exterior, in band *ca.* 0.02 m. wide; plain rim. Interior entirely slipped. Slip is "spiral-burnished" in bands of varying thickness, with most opaque bands plum red. Low to medium luster preserved.

423 Bowl
Not inv. Level VB
Est. D. rim 0.25; GTh. 0.0055 m.
Fig. 20

Rim sherd of bowl with plain rim.

Clean orange clay with little grit temper. Red slip on exterior and inner rim, well smoothed with low luster. Buff slip, rather carelessly applied, on interior surface; matt finish.

424 Bowl
Not inv. Level VB
Est. D. rim 0.21; GTh. 0.007 m.
Fig. 20

Rim sherd of bowl. Upper wall thickening gradually towards plain rim.

Orange clay, gritty. Matt red slip, worn, on both surfaces. Surfaces originally slightly lustrous.

425 Shallow bowl
Not inv. Level VB
Est. D. rim 0.34; GTh. 0.008 m.
Fig. 20

Rim sherd of shallow bowl with inverted, tapered rim.

Orange clay, gritty, with some "gold" mica. Red slip on exterior above carination and on entire interior surface. Worn; originally somewhat lustrous.

426 Shallow bowl
Not inv. Level VB
Est. D. rim 0.22; GTh. 0.0059 m.
Fig. 20

Rim fragment of shallow bowl with broad, thickened rim flattened across top. Rim worn.

Orange clay, gritty. Buff slip on both surfaces; some luster preserved on interior, remainder with matt finish.

427 Bowl
Not inv. Level VB
Est. D. rim 0.21; GTh. 0.008 m.
Fig. 20

Rim sherd of bowl with inverted rim.

Orange clay, rather coarse and gritty. Buff slip on both surfaces, smoothed and matt; wheelmarks visible.

428 Bowl
Not inv. Level VB
Est. D. rim 0.29; GTh. 0.0095 m.
Fig. 20

Rim sherd of large bowl with inverted rim. Surfaces stained, slightly incrusted.

Orange clay, gritty. Surfaces plain; smoothed but wheelmarks mostly remain visible.

429 Bowl
Not inv. Level VB
Est. D. rim 0.27; GTh. 0.01 m.
Fig. 20

Rim sherd of shallow bowl with inverted rim.

Orange clay, very gritty and rather coarse. Buff slip on outer surfaces, stained and cracked; apparently plain on inner surface.

430 Bowl
Not inv. Level VB
Est. D. rim 0.25; GTh. 0.0073 m.
Fig. 20

Rim sherd of shallow bowl with inverted rim.

Orange clay, gritty. Reddened area on exterior (from secondary heating or burning?). Surfaces plain, matt.

431 Bowl
Not inv. Level VB
Est. D. rim 0.39; GTh. 0.0095 m.
Fig. 21

Rim sherd of large bowl with inverted rim.

Red clay, gritty. Thin buff slip, worn, on rim and exterior; interior plain. Wheelmarks mostly visible.

432 Bowl
Not inv. Level VB
D. rim unknown; GTh. 0.007 m.
Fig. 21

Rim sherd of bowl with inverted rim. Rim abraded.

Orange clay, gritty and coarse. Matt buff slip on both surfaces.

433 Carinated bowl
Not inv. Level VB
D. rim unknown; GTh. 0.009 m.
Fig. 21

Rim sherd of carinated bowl; almost vertical upper wall, plain rim.

Orange clay, relatively clean with few gritty inclusions; apparently fired gray at core. Red slip, worn and matt, covers both surfaces. Smoothed, especially exterior. Wheelmarks visible on interior.

434 Carinated bowl
Not inv. Level VB
D. rim unknown; GTh. 0.01 m.
Fig. 21

Rim sherd of carinated bowl with vertical upper wall, plain rim.

Light red, gritty clay. Red slip on exterior above carination and on entire interior surface. Smoothed, especially on exterior; originally with low luster, now somewhat worn.

435 Carinated bowl
Not inv. Level VB
Est. D. rim 0.26; GTh. 0.008 m.
Fig. 21

Rim sherd of carinated bowl with sloping, thickened rim. Slip worn; slightly blackened around carination on exterior. Outer rim worn, somewhat abraded.

Orange clay, gritty. Red slip on both surfaces. Originally perhaps lustrous, now mostly matt finish.

JARS (436-441)

436 Jar
Not inv. Level VB
Est. D. rim 0.14; GTh. 0.006 m.
Fig. 21

Rim sherd of jar (or teapot?) with upper wall narrowing gradually towards plain rim.

Orange clay, gritty. Traces of red slip, very worn, preserved on exterior and inner rim. Interior plain. Surfaces smooth; slipped area preserves low luster.

437 Jar
Not inv.   Level VB
D. rim unknown; GTh. 0.0066 m.
Fig. 21
Rim sherd of jar (or teapot?) with slightly everted rim flattened across top.
Orange clay, gritty. Matt buff slip on both surfaces; wheelmarks mostly visible.
Above, **307**.

438 Jar
Not inv.   Level VB
Est. D. rim 0.30; GTh. 0.0077 m.
Fig. 21
Rim sherd of jar with everted, thickened rim.
Orange clay, gritty. Dull red slip, thin and carelessly applied, on exterior, and interior rim. On rim, lustrous plum red slip. Interior below red slip preserves thin, matt buff slip.

439 Jar
Not inv.   Level VB
Est. D. rim 0.36; GTh. 0.007 m.
Fig. 21
Rim sherd of jar with everted rim thickened on outside.
Orange clay, gritty; surfaces plain.

440 Jar
Not inv.   Level VB
Est. D. rim 0.38; GTh. 0.009 m.
Fig. 21
Rim sherd of jar with everted thickened rim. Blackened on outer rim.
Orange clay, gritty. Surfaces plain; smoothed and worn.

441 Jar
Not inv.   Level VB
D. rim unknown; GTh. 0.013 m.
Fig. 21
Rim sherd of large jar with upper wall tapering towards everted, broad rim. Worn, abraded on inner rim and interior.
Orange clay, gritty; surfaces plain.

JUG (442)

442 Jug
Not inv.   Level VB
Est. D. rim 0.09; GTh. 0.0068 m.
Fig. 21
Rim sherd of jug with cylindrical neck, gradually flaring outward to thickened rim.
Orange clay, gritty. Surfaces plain, smoothed, with wheelmarks mostly visible.

BASES (443-446)

443 Base
Not inv.   Level VB
GPH. 0.034; GTh. 0.0095 m.
Fig. 21
Base fragment of rounded base, probably from jar or pitcher. Small area blackened on interior.
Orange clay, gritty. Surfaces plain; wheelmarks worn on interior.

444 Base
Not inv.   Level VB
GPH. 0.064; D. base 0.05; GTh. 0.0107 m.
Fig. 21
Base and adjoining lower wall of jar or pitcher with flat base. *Circa* two-thirds of base circumference preserved.
Orange clay, gritty. Buff slip, thin and matt, on exterior. Interior plain.

445 Ring base
Not inv.   Level VB
GPH. 0.026; D. base 0.089; GTh. 0.0135 m.
Fig. 21
Ring base fragment; probably from a jar or pitcher. *Circa* two-thirds of base circumference preserved. Ring chipped.
Orange clay, gritty; surfaces plain.

446 Base
P 5469   Level VB
GPH. 0.07; Est. D. base 0.05; GTh. 0.018 m.
Fig. 21; Pl. 25
Single piece preserves most of base and part of adjoining lower wall. Blackened on inside of base and on exterior. Base worn smooth.
Flattened base, wall of varying thickness rising rather steeply to form conical lower part of vessel. Probably from jug.
Orange clay, gritty; fired gray at core. Exterior well smoothed; perhaps this area, now blackened, was originally slipped. Interior unevenly formed and left unsmoothed on inside. Buff clay, relatively clean, with few gritty inclusions. Surfaces left plain; mostly smoothed.

INCISED SHERD (447)

447 Incised body sherd
I 623   Level VB
GPL. 0.075; GPW. 0.057; GTh. 0.012; L. mark 0.0335 m.
Fig. 21; Pl. 25
Body sherd, perhaps from shoulder of vessel. Traces of white incrustation on surfaces.
On exterior, incised before firing: double triangle with short central perpendicular line, partly preserved. Lines somewhat deeply and irregularly incised.
Tan (5YR 6/4) clay with some gritty inclusions and "gold" mica. Exterior covered with tan, probably "self-slip," smoothed, with matt finish. Interior plain.
No exact parallels for graffito except perhaps Maşat Level II (*Maşat* II, pl. 45:8). Resembles group of triangular graffiti with perpendicular line (*Gefässmarken*, 76, with further references); closest parallels are from Yanarlar (*Yanarlar*, fig. 101) and Maşat Levels III-II (*Maşat* II, fig. 14, pl. 45:9). See also below, **493**, **517-520**.[109]

LEVEL VA   (448-471)

BOWLS (448-453)

448 Bowl
Not inv.   Level VA
D. rim unknown; GTh. 0.017 m.
Fig. 22
Rim sherd of bowl with inverted, tapered rim. Blackened all over exterior surface, extending in places to area of rim.
Reddish brown clay, very gritty and coarse. Surfaces plain.

---

109. Above, p. 37; also *Gordion Special Studies* I, 2, 5, fig. 1.

449 Shallow bowl
Not inv.   Level VA
D. rim unknown; GTh. 0.007 m.
Fig. 22
Rim sherd of shallow bowl with broad, thickened rim.
Orange clay, very gritty; surfaces plain, roughly finished.

450 Shallow bowl
Not inv.   Layer VA
D. rim unknown; GTh. 0.01 m.
Fig. 22
Rim sherd of shallow bowl with inverted rim. Rim chipped
and abraded.
Reddish brown clay, gritty. Originally probably lustrous
reddish brown slip on all surfaces, now mostly worn. Surfaces
smoothed.

451 Shallow bowl
Not inv.   Level VA
Est. D. rim 0.22; GTh. 0.0067 m.
Fig. 22
Rim sherd of shallow bowl with inverted rim rounded
across top.
Orange clay, gritty and rather coarse. Surfaces plain, rather
roughly finished.

452 Shallow bowl
Not inv.   Level VA
Est. D. rim 0.26; GTh. 0.0125 m.
Fig. 22
Rim sherd of shallow bowl with broad rim. Lower wall
thickened towards base. Surfaces grayed.
Orange clay, gritty. Surfaces smoothed and left plain.

453 Carinated bowl
Not inv.   Level VA
Est. D. rim 0.37; GTh. 0.008 m.
Fig. 22
Rim sherd of bowl with gentle carination; thickened, slop-
ing rim. Blackened on exterior and upper surface of rim.
Orange clay, gritty. Buff slip, very thin, on both surfaces.

JARS (454-459)

454 Jar
Not inv.   Level VA
Est. D. rim 0.17; GTh. 0.007 m.
Fig. 22
Rim sherd of jar with cylindrical neck, slightly everted rim.
Rim abraded.
Orange clay, gritty and coarse; much "gold" mica. Surfaces
plain.

455 Jar
Not inv.   Level VA
Est. D. rim 0.28; GTh. 0.0085 m.
Fig. 22
Rim sherd of jar with thickened everted rim. Rim slightly
chipped and abraded.
Orange clay, gritty. Rim and exterior preserve traces of red
slip, originally polished and lustrous. Interior plain.

456 Jar
Not inv.   Level VA
Est. D. rim 0.15; GTh. 0.005 m.
Fig. 22
Rim and adjoining wall sherd of small jar with thickened
rim. Outer rim worn.
Orange clay, gritty. Thin, matt red slip, much worn,
preserved on rim and exterior; interior plain. Slipped area
smoothed.

457 Jar
Not inv.   Level VA
Est. D. rim 0.26; GTh. 0.0085 m.
Fig. 22
Rim sherd of jar with thickened rim rounded across top.
Reddish brown clay, gritty and coarse. Surfaces plain,
roughly finished.

458 Jar
Not inv.   Level VA
Est. D. rim 0.38; GTh. 0.009 m.
Fig. 22
Rim sherd of jar with narrowing shoulder, thickened rim
rounded across top.
Reddish orange clay, coarse and gritty. Surfaces plain,
rather roughly finished.

459 Jar
Not inv.   Level VA
Est. D. rim 0.38; GTh. 0.013 m.
Fig. 22
Rim sherd of large jar with wide, everted rim.
Orange clay, rather coarse and gritty. Traces of red slip on
exterior rim and wall below rim. Perhaps "self-slip" on inte-
rior rim, where surface covering appears to be flaking away.

PITCHER (460)

460 Spout fragment with strainer
P 5470   Level VA
GPL. 0.046; GPW. 0.06; GTh. 0.007 m.
Pl. 25
Strainer, broken from spout on sides and bottom. Minor
chips and abrasions.
Four rows of perforations preserved, 0.003-0.005 m. across,
punched from outside at irregular intervals.
Buff (7.5YR 7/6) clay, gritty. Both surfaces covered with
matt buff (10YR 8/4) slip on thin coat of clay that partly
smooths the gritty ware.

COOKING POTS (461 and 462)

461 Cooking pot
Not inv.   Level VA
Est. D. rim 0.27; GTh. 0.012 m.
Fig. 22
Rim sherd of cooking pot with thickened rim, probably
from large globular shape. Rim and exterior mostly black-
ened.
Orange clay, gritty and coarse; some "gold" mica. Fired
lighter on surface; surfaces plain.
Porsuk Level V (*Porsuk* I, 50, pl. 28:173).

462 Cooking pot
Not inv.   Level VA
D. rim unknown; GTh. 0.011 m.
Fig. 22
Rim sherd of large hole-mouth cooking pot. Grayish black
in places on rim, on both surfaces.
Reddish brown clay, very gritty and coarse. Surfaces plain.

BASES (463-466)

463 Base
Not inv.   Level VA
GPH. 0.025; GTh. 0.0075 m.
Fig. 22

Base fragment. Flat base, lower wall rising gradually to vessel body. Probably from jar or pitcher.
Orange clay, gritty. Surfaces plain, somewhat smoothed.

464 Base
Not inv. Level VA
GPH. 0.021; GTh. 0.0084 m.
Fig. 22
Base fragment of jar or pitcher with flattened base.
Orange clay, coarse and gritty. Surfaces plain, roughly finished.

465 Ring base
Not inv. Level VA
GPH. 0.026; Est. D. base 0.09; GTh. 0.008 m.
Fig. 22
Base fragment. Ring base probably from jar or pitcher.
Reddish orange clay, gritty. Exterior surface fired lighter; perhaps vessel preserves "self-slip" here.

466 Pedestal base
Not inv. Level VA
GPH. 0.049; D. base 0.06; GTh. 0.0065 m.
Fig. 22
Sherd preserves base and adjoining wall. Base damaged.
Pedestal base; upper part of fragment preserves carination at maximum diameter. Roughly finished on interior near base. Lower part of small pitcher carinated at maximum diameter.
Orange clay, gritty. Exterior seems to preserve some reddish brown slip; well smoothed. Remainder, including base, plain.

HANDLES (467 and 468)

467 Vertical handle
Not inv. Level VA
GPL. 0.093; GTh. 0.029 m.
Pl. 25
Handle broken at either end of place of attachment. Surfaces worn, chipped, incrusted.
Vertical handle, roughly circular in section. On upper surface, ropelike pattern formed by undulating grooves.
Light brown (2.5YR 5/4) clay, gritty. Core dark gray. Surfaces now grayed.

468 Vertical handle
Not inv. Level VA
GPL. 0.0725; GTh. 0.023 m.
Pl. 25
Section preserves vertical handle, broken at one end, and edge of rim where attached to vessel at other end.
Handle oval in section; on upper surface, incised line along main axis. From one-handled jar or spouted vessel?
Orange (5YR 6/6) clay, gritty; matt buff (10YR 8/4) slip on both surfaces.
If incision is intentional rather than a firing flaw, perhaps it is connected with handle treatment among vessels from Beycesultan IVc-IVb (*Beycesultan* II, 102, fig. P. 14:1; 120, fig. P.26:4) or on Late Bronze Age vessels from Aphrodisias (*AJA* 80 [1976] 402, fig. 14; 406, fig. 260).

INCISED SHERD (469)

469 Incised sherd
P 5471 Level VA

GPL. 0.055; GPW. 0.067; GTh. 0.0075 m.
Fig. 22; Pl. 25
Body sherd from vessel of unknown shape, perhaps teapot; probably from lower body area.
Profile preserves gentle carination near bottom of sherd. Exterior decorated with rows of short incised lines: a horizontal row where profile curves inward; above, three parallel lines meet horizontal row at oblique angle.
Orange (5YR 6/6) clay with some gritty inclusions. Red (10R 5/6) slip on exterior, well smoothed and polished. Interior plain.

HANDLE WITH SEAL IMPRESSION (470)

470 Handle with seal impression[110]
SS 117 Level VA
GPL. 0.093; L. impression 0.019 m.
Pl. 25
Handle fragment of vessel, broken at neck attachment.
Handle, oval in section, from large vessel (pithos?). Deeply impressed near neck: a short right foot, with four toes.
Orange clay, gritty. Red slip, burnished, on both surfaces.
Boğazköy, Büyükkale Level Ib, in debris fill (*Gefässmarken*, 34, fig. 10:A 114). Perhaps already in use as vessel stamp design in the later Old Assyrian Colony period, to judge by stamps from Boğazköy, Nordwesthang-Büyükkale Level 8a and Kültepe Karum Level Ib (*ibid.*, 76, with further references).

SPINDLE WHORL (471)

471 Spindle whorl
MC 41 Level VA
H. 0.012; D. 0.026 m.
Not illus.
Not examined.
Complete.
Profile, rounded face with top central depression larger than central hole; other face is truncated cone. Rounded face incised with four groups of concentric arcs.
Black polished fabric.

LEVEL IVB (472-492, S64-S68)

BOWLS (472-482)

472 Shallow bowl
Not inv. Level IVB
Est. D. rim 0.17; GTh. 0.0055 m.
Fig. 23
Rim sherd of shallow bowl with plain rim. Some surface discoloration.
Fine, clean buff clay. Surfaces plain; well smoothed, with matt finish.

473 Shallow bowl
Not inv. Level IVB
Est. D. rim 0.29; GTh. 0.0095 m.
Fig. 23
Rim sherd of shallow bowl with slightly thickened rim.

110. Previously published, with discussion (*Hitt. Cem.*, 41, pl. 23e).

Orange clay, with some gritty inclusions but relatively clean; "gold" and "silver" mica. Surfaces smoothed, plain, with matt finish.

474 Shallow bowl
Not inv.   Level IVB
Est. D. rim 0.24; GTh. 0.0092 m.
Fig. 23
Rim sherd of large shallow bowl with broad, thickened rim.
Orange clay, coarse and gritty. Surfaces plain.

475 Shallow bowl
Not inv.   Level IVB
Est. D. rim 0.24; GTh. 0.007 m.
Fig. 23
Rim sherd of shallow bowl with slightly thickened rim. Mended from two joining sherds; rim chipped.
Buff clay, gritty. Surfaces smoothed, plain.

476 Shallow bowl
Not inv.   Level IVB
D. rim unknown; GTh. 0.0085 m.
Fig. 23
Rim sherd of bowl with broad rim.
Orange clay, gritty. Buff slip on both surfaces.

477 Shallow bowl
Not inv.   Level IVB
Est. D. rim 0.30; GTh. 0.01 m.
Fig. 23
Rim sherd of shallow bowl with broad rim.
Orange clay, gritty and coarse. Surfaces plain.

478 Shallow bowl
Not inv.   Level IVB
D. rim unknown; GTh. 0.0078 m.
Fig. 23
Rim sherd of shallow bowl with inverted rim.
Light brown clay, gritty. Surfaces smoothed, plain.

479 Shallow bowl
Not inv.   Level IVB
D. rim unknown; GTh. 0.011 m.
Fig. 23
Rim sherd with inverted, almost vertical rim.
Light brown clay, gritty and coarse; well fired. Surfaces plain.

480 Shallow bowl
Not inv.   Level IVB
D. rim unknown; GTh. 0.0085 m.
Fig. 23
Rim sherd of shallow bowl with broad rim.
Orange clay, gritty, with "gold" mica. Surfaces plain.

481 Carinated bowl (jar?)
Not inv.   Level IVB
D. rim unknown; GTh. 0.011 m.
Fig. 23
Rim sherd of bowl or jar with slight carination; everted, thickened rim. Some surface discoloration.
Orange clay, with some gritty inclusions but relatively clean. Matt buff slip on both surfaces.

482 Carinated bowl
Not inv.   Level IVB
D. rim unknown; GTh. 0.014 m.
Fig. 23
Rim sherd of carinated bowl with thickened, sloping rim.
Reddish orange clay, gritty and rather coarse. Buff slip on both surfaces.

JARS (483-485)

483 Jar
Not inv.   Level IVB
Est. D. rim 0.36; GTh. 0.012 m.
Fig. 23
Rim sherd of jar with wide, everted rim.
Reddish orange clay, gritty; surfaces plain.

484 Jar
Not inv.   Level IVB
Est. D. rim 0.37; GTh. 0.0125 m.
Fig. 23
Rim sherd of jar with wide, everted rim.
Orange clay, with some gritty inclusions but relatively clean. Surfaces smoothed, plain.

485 Jar
Not inv.   Level IVB
Est. D. rim 0.37; GTh. 0.0125 m.
Fig. 23
Rim sherd of jar with wide, everted rim.
Reddish orange clay, with some gritty inclusions but relatively clean. Surfaces plain.

COOKING POTS (486 and 487)

486 Cooking pot with vertical handle
Not inv.   Level IVB
Est. D. rim 0.13; GTh. 0.011 m.
Fig. 23
Rim and handle fragment of hole-mouth cooking pot with vertical handle. Handle oval in section, attached below rim.
Light reddish brown clay, coarse and gritty; some "gold" mica. Surfaces plain.

487 Cooking pot
Not inv.   Level IVB
D. rim unknown; GTh. 0.01 m.
Not illus.
Rim sherd of hole-mouth cooking pot with rim thickened on inside. Grayed both surfaces.
Coarse, gritty reddish brown clay with "gold" mica. Surfaces plain.

JUG (488)

488 Jug
Not inv.   Level IVB
Est. D. rim 0.13; GTh. 0.01 m.
Fig. 23
Rim sherd of large jug with cylindrical neck, thickened rim.
Orange clay, with some gritty inclusions but relatively clean. Surfaces plain; exterior and rim partly smoothed.

RIM SHERD (489)

489 Rim sherd
Not inv.   Level IVB
D. rim unknown; GTh. 0.015 m.
Fig. 23
Rim and adjoining wall of large open vessel, probably plate, with broad rim.
Orange clay, gritty and rather coarse. Buff slip on rim and exterior; interior plain.

BASES (490 and 491)

490 Ring base
Not inv. Level IVB
GPH. 0.043; GTh. 0.011 m.
Fig. 23
Fragment of ring base. Probably from jar or pitcher.
Orange clay, gritty; surfaces plain.

491 Ring base
Not inv. Level IVB
GPH. 0.04; GTh. 0.016 m.
Fig. 23
Fragment of ring base. Probably from jar or pitcher.
Orange clay, rather gritty and coarse; surfaces plain.

SPINDLE WHORL (492)

492 Spindle whorl
MC 40 Level IVB
H. 0.01; D. 0.036 m.
Pl. 25
Not examined.
Fragmentary; preserves one face split from remainder.
Circular face with central depression larger than central
hole; incised with six groups of concentric arcs, five in each
group.

Gray-buff clay.
For incised pattern: Polatlı Level XXXI, with four groups
of arcs (*AnatSt* 1 [1951] 62, fig. 15:14).

NORTH CENTRAL TRENCH,
PRE-LEVEL IC (493)

INCISED SHERD (493)

493 Incised sherd
I 624 Pre-Level IC
GPL. 0.097; GPW. 0.079; GTh. 0.008; L. graffito 0.042.
Fig. 24; Pl. 26
Single sherd broken on all sides from vessel, perhaps large
closed shape. Slight surface incrustation and discoloration.
On exterior, incised before firing: triangle with short per-
pendicular line inside from base; lines incised deeply and
regularly. Only lower right corner of mark appears to be com-
plete.
Orange clay, with many gritty inclusions. Exterior
smoothed of wheelmarks, perhaps with a "self-slip"; interior
plain.
Above, **447** with further references, and below, **517-520**.

Hittite Cemetery (494-505)

BOWLS (494-496)

494 Shallow bowl
P 2763 Burial H 52
H. 0.051; D. rim 0.148 m.
Pl. 26
Not examined.
Bowl, mended and plastered to complete. Shallow hemis-
pherical form with round base; plain, slightly incurved rim.
Pale orange porous clay, micaceous. Thin "self-slip" on in-
terior.
Below, **495**.

495 Hemispherical bowl
P 2765 Burial H 50
H. 0.072; D. rim 0.172 m.
Pl. 26
Not examined.
Intact. Hemispherical form with round base; thickened,
slightly incurved rounded rim.
Orange clay, gritty and porous; surfaces plain. Probably
made by coiling on wheel.
494 and **495**: compare handleless bowls, with some varia-
tion in rim and surface treatment, from other Hittite
Cemetery burials (*Hitt.Cem.*, 27-28, pl. 15d-l).

496 Bowl
P 2762 Burial H 50
H. 0.05-0.057; D. rim 0.145; D. base 0.038; GTh. 0.005 m.
Fig. 24; Pl. 26
Mended from many fragments; rim chipped.
Small, slightly raised base, short vertical rim with plain
edge.
Orange-buff (7.5YR 6/4-7/4) clay, porous and gritty. Faint
traces of red slip on exterior near rim. Vessel built on wheel by
coiling; ridges of coils visible on inner surface.

PITHOI (497-499)

497 Pithos
P 2786 Burial H 49
H. 1.15; D. 0.75; D. rim 0.44; D. base 0.123 m.
Pl. 26
Not examined.
Mended to complete. Surface incrusted.
Pithos with flat base, oval body, rolled everted rim. Single
band 0.025 m. wide, in low relief around lower body. Vertical
loop handles placed on upper body.
Red clay, coarse and gritty.
Compare **498**, with further references.

498 Pithos
P 2787 Burial H 50
H. 1.22; D. 0.69; D. rim 0.52; D. base 0.135; L. handle 0.155 m.
Pl. 26
Not examined.
Mended; large gap in shoulder and rim.
Small flat base, oval body, rolled everted rim. Three bands
in low relief, each 0.03 m. wide, encircling shoulder, belly,
and lower body. Vertical handles set on shoulder at upper-
most band.
Red clay, coarse and gritty. Surfaces plain.
497 and **498**: Hittite Cemetery (*ibid.*, 20, pl. 11i). Compare
other varieties of banded pithoi in the Hittite Cemetery, with
five or three ribs (*Hitt. Cem.*, 19-20, pls. 11g-h, 12a-b, 25b).
Banded type also used for burial at Yanarlar near Afyon
(*Yarnarlar*, fig. 11) and Bağbası, near Karataş-Semayük,
Elmalı (*AJA* 71 [1967] pl. 78, fig. 27).

499 Pithos
P 3000 Burial H 55
H. 0.695; D. 0.545; D. rim 0.358; D. base 0.115 m.
Fig. 24

Almost fully preserved; mended at shoulder.

Small flat base, oval body, hole-mouth form at rim. Two small vertical handles, roughly triangular in section, placed just below mouth.

Coarse gravel-tempered clay, fired dark brown at core; mottled brown and black on exterior. Surfaces plain.

Profile closest to burial pithoi of small cooking pot type, Hittite Cemetery (*Hitt. Cem.*, 21, pls. 12g-i, 25d; all smaller than **499**).

INCISED HANDLE (500)

500   Incised handle
P 4666   Tumulus H, Hittite Cemetery; from fill over Phrygian burnt house, mixed deposit
GPL. 0.068; L. mark 0.028 m.
Fig. 24; Pl. 26

Handle fragment, probably from pitcher. Broken across rear neck attachment; slight gray incrustation on underside of handle.

Incised after firing, at top of handle, with top to neck of vessel: outline of a beaked jug, facing right.

Fine orange (5YR 6/6) clay, with some gritty inclusions. Red (10R 5/8) slip, burnished, on upper surface.

Boğazköy, Unterstadt Level 1 (*Boğazköy* IV, 14-15, pl. 4b and Plan 5, incised jug without beak on necks of pithoi in Temple I magazines; here it surely designates a measure of capacity). Also· Alişar, jug facing left, from deposit of "Post-Hittite" period (*OIP* 29, 410, fig. 47:d 1807; Laroche nos. 345, 354, from Alişar).[111]

NONCERAMIC ARTIFACTS (501-505)

501   Copper or bronze pin
B 1404   Burial H 49
GPL. 0.063; D. shaft 0.0015; D. head 0.006; L. head 0.009 m.
Pl. 26

Broken across shaft; surface worn and pitted.

Straight pin; shaft round in section and tapering slightly to point. Head plain, elliptical in section, with no visible point of attachment to shaft.

502   Copper or bronze pin
B 1405   Burial H 49
PL. 0.052; D. shaft 0.002 m.
Not illus.

Broken at distal end; surface pitted and nicked.

Round in section, tapering to a point now missing. Proximal end hammered flat and curled around one and one-half times to form head.

Similar examples with loop head from burials H 25 (inhumation) and H 36 (pithos) (*Hitt. Cem.*, 31-32, pls. 17n-p, 18a). Also Boğazköy Unterstadt Levels 4 to 1, a long-lived type (*Kleinfunde*, 83, fig. 33; *Kleinfunde Unterstadt*, 12-13).

503   Knuckle bones
BI 406   Burial H 54
Not illus.
Not examined.

Six knuckle bones of various sizes; well preserved.
See below, **504**.

504   Knuckle bones
BI 407   Burial H 50
Not illus.
Not examined.

Twenty-six knuckle bones of various sizes; dried out and covered with black spots.

503 and **504**: Knuckle bones occur commonly in the Hittite Cemetery and in Middle Bronze levels at Alişar and Kültepe (*Hitt. Cem.*, 43-44, with further references).

505   Silver ring fragments
ILS 368   Burial H 55
Est. D. 0.21; GTh. 0.004 m.
Not illus.
Not examined

Two fragments of silver ring, poorly preserved.

Silver wire, round in section; originally bent into oval or circular ring.

Silver rings also found in several other Hittite Cemetery burials (H 4, H 17, H 22) and in Middle Bronze burials at Kültepe and Alişar (*Hitt. Cem.*, 35, pl. 20c-g, with further references).

Miscellaneous Contexts   (506-533)

PITCHERS (506 and 507)

506   Spout
P 3335   Over area NW of Megaron 4, Clay Layer
GPL. 0.07; GPW. 0.023 m.
Fig. 24; Pl. 26

Beak spout of pitcher, fragmentary. Broken across spout; sides of trough partially missing.

Shallow trough; rising beak spout with "beard" on underside.

Fine, clean light red (2.5YR 6/6) clay, fired light brown at core. Red slip on exterior continues just inside edges of trough; polished, with hand-burnish strokes visible.

"Bearded" spout: Boğazköy, Unterstadt Level 4 (*Heth. Keramik*, 119, no. 279; pl. 27); Beycesultan Level III (*AnatSt* 6 [1956] 133, fig. 5:16) and Levels II-I (*AnatSt* 5 [1955] 69, fig.

13:1-4; 85, fig. 19:7); Karahüyük-Konya Levels III, I, with relief medallion "eye": (*Karahüyük-Konya Damga*, pl. 27:67-68; pl. 28:69-70); Konya region, unstratified (*Belleten* 22 [1958] pl. II:14-16).

507   Spout
P 3336   Over area NE of Megaron 5, floor 3, cellar
GPL. 0.08; GPW. 0.05 m.
Pl. 26

Trough spout of pitcher, broken across at both ends.

Approximately hemispherical in section, rim slightly flattened.

Fine, clean orange (5YR 6/6) clay, fired gray at core. Light brown (5YR 6/4) slip on both surfaces, very well smoothed and highly lustrous.

---

111. Also discussed in *Gordion Special Studies* I, 2, 5, fig. 1.

ZOOMORPHIC SPOUTS, VESSELS, AND HANDLES (508-514)

508 Spout
P 1080 "Polychrome House," gravelly fill over floor
GPH. 0.042; L. head 0.028; W. head at ears 0.028 m.
Pl. 27
Fragmentary zoomorphic spout. Damaged around ears, broken across neck.
Head with tubular snout, small holes where something may have been attached as eyes; stubby ears. Perforated from mouth through neck.
Buff (7.5YR 7/4) clay with many gritty inclusions; cleaner "self-slip."

509 Spout
P 1358 Clay Layer over Phrygian paving near "Polychrome House"
GPH. 0.0505; L. head 0.068; W. head at ears 0.029 m.
Pl. 27
Fragmentary zoomorphic spout.
Ears, tip of nose slightly damaged; broken across neck.
Tubular snout, short ears; mouth formed by round hole. Spout continues through neck. Probably horse.
Fine orange clay, slightly gritty; fired grayish on interior. Red (10R 5/6) slip on exterior, burnished over nose and rear of head.

510 Vessel
P 4469 Clay Layer over NE Phrygian Citadel Wall
GPH. 0.05; GPL. 0.048; W. 0.054 m.
Pl. 27
Fragmentary zoomorphic vessel. Preserved is front part of body, and behind shoulders; head and rear parts missing; lower parts of front legs broken away.
Barrel-shaped body, with standing limbs indicated by flat ridges.
Coarse orange (2.5YR 6/8) clay, very gritty; fired light brown at core. Red slip, burnished, on surface.

511 Vessel
P 1373 Clay Layer over N Court of Phrygian Gate
GPH. front 0.052; GPL. 0.09; W. across rear 0.048 m.
Pl. 27
Fragmentary zoomorphic vessel. Lacking head and four legs; chipped at pouring hole.
Barrel-shaped body, four short legs; small applied tail drawn to one side to form part of circle. Hole in center of back, probably used for pouring. Incised mark on back: line with two dashes on either side.
Light red (2.5YR 6/6) clay with buff (7.5YR 7/4) slip.
Boğazköy, Unterstadt Level 4b and unstratified (*Heth. Keramik*, 159, nos. 1332, 1333, pls. 137-138). Also example from Porsuk Level V, with tail forming part of a circle (*Porsuk* I, 38 with n. 154, no. 241, pl. 40). For incised mark, compare example on vessel handle, Boğazköy Unterstadt Level 2 (*Gefässmarken*, 58, fig. 22: B20).

512 Vessel
P 895 Clay Layer over N wall of Phrygian Gate passage
GPH. 0.082; L. 0.099; W. 0.071 m.
Pl. 27
Fragmentary zoomorphic vessel. Lacking neck and mouth; three legs and rear slightly damaged.
Barrel-shaped body on four stubby legs. On top near front end, stump of vertical neck; at rear, round hole. Tail formed by pinched-up ridge.
Orange (5YR 6/6) clay, gritty; surfaces plain.

Boğazköy, debris of Büyükkale Level III (*Heth. Keramik*, 158, no. 1312, pl. 137).

513 Handle
P 5579 Upper Layer (3) over rear of Megaron 3
GPH. 0.060; W. handle 0.02; GTh. 0.013 m.
Pl. 28
Single sherd preserves handle with animal head. Top of head and both ends of handle broken off. Some of surface gone.
Vertical handle, ovoid in section. Animal head with bulging eyes and long snout affixed to handle.
Light brown clay with gray core, highly micaceous. Entire handle and head covered with red slip; good lustrous polish on right side and top, but minimum polish, if any, on left.

514 Ram handle
P 2400 Upper layers, over TB 4/5 anterooms
GPH. 0.061; W. horns 0.033 m.
Pl. 28
Ram's head affixed to vessel handle. Head and neck are preserved; slip somewhat chipped.
Vertical handle forms long arched neck, round in section and hollow. Eyes indicated by circles, mouth by slit; horns, grooved, curve back and then forward to jaws.
Fine orange clay, fired gray at core. Surfaces covered with red (10R 5/6) slip.

PAINTED SHERDS (515 and 516)

515 Painted fragments
P 4570a-f, h, i Clay and rubble bed of Middle Phrygian Building U wall
a GPW. 0.158; Est. D. body 0.15; *b* GPW. 0.072; Th. handle 0.02; *c-f, h, i* GPWs. 0.036; 0.051; 0.051; 0.043; 0.038; 0.030 m.[112]
Fig. 24; Pl. 28
Eight fragments, consisting of: *a* one mended section from bottom and lower body, *b* handle, *c* a rim sherd, *d-f, h, i* five small body sherds.
Bucket-shaped vessel, perhaps jar, with horizontal handle at rim. Painted area in matt red (10R 5/6) on tan (5YR 7/4) slip: two zones of oblique lines forming crosshatched pattern, under rim.
Orange (5YR 7/6) clay, gritty, with some "gold" mica; well fired. Surface below painted area apparently "self-slipped." Interior plain.
Below, **516**.

516 Painted sherds
P 5599 + P4570g Clay Layer over CC 3 Building
P 5599: GPL. 0.038; GPW. 0.0415; GTh. 0.005 m.
P 4570g: GPW. 0.04 m.
Not illus.
Two sherds, nonjoining, broken on all sides from vessel of unknown shape. Some gray-white incrustation on interior; exterior scratched and worn.
On exterior, painted matt red stripes crossing at oblique angles to form a net pattern. On one edge of P 5599, part of a small circular area in relief, *ca.* 0.0014 m. across, painted over in red.
Orange-brown clay, gritty and micaceous, with some crushed limestone temper. Interior plain, with wheelmarks clearly visible. Exterior covered with tan slip, well smoothed and polished.
515 and **516**: Above, **332, 333**, with further references.

---

112. P 4570g belongs to a separate vessel, **516**.

INCISED SHERDS (517-521)

517   Incised base
I 158   Layer 5, Middle Phrygian-Hellenistic fill above area between Megara 1 and 2
GPL 0.096; W. incised line 0.005 m.
Fig. 24; Pl. 28
Fragment of flat base of jar or bowl.
On exterior, incised before firing: triangle with short line inside it, perpendicular to the base; apex of triangle at base of vessel.
Orange (5YR 6/4) clay, gritty and micaceous; surfaces plain. Wheelmarks visible on exterior, smoothed on interior.
Below, **520**.

518   Incised body sherd
I 125   Under Hellenistic floor in area above N wall of N court of Phrygian Gate
GPL. 0.13; GPW. 0.064; W. incised line 0.003-4 m.
Fig. 24; Pl. 28
Body sherd of closed vessel, probably jar.
On exterior, neatly incised before firing: triangle with a short line inside the figure, perpendicular to the base.
Buff (7.5YR 7/4) clay, gritty; interior gray. Surfaces plain.
Below, **520**.

519   Incised body sherd
I 194   Middle Phrygian level in front of Building H
GPL. 0.076; PL. mark 0.035; W. incised line 0.002-5 m.
Fig. 24; Pl. 28
Body sherd from large closed vessel, perhaps jar or pithos. Interior surface worn and pitted.
On exterior, incised before firing: triangle with short line inside it, perpendicular to the base; almost fully preserved.
Tan (7.5YR 6/4) clay, rather coarse and gritty; fired gray at core. Exterior covered with "self-slip," interior plain.
Below, **520**.

520   Incised body sherd
I 144   Hellenistic layer (3) above anteroom of Megaron 10
GPL. 0.116; GPW. 0.07 m.
Fig. 24; Pl. 28
Body sherd from closed vessel, probably jar. Very slightly incrusted.
On exterior, incised before firing: triangle with a short line inside it, perpendicular to base.
Clay gritty; surfaces plain. Fired gray, perhaps from secondary burning.
517-520: Above, **447** with further references; also **493**.

BASE (521)

521   Base
I 245   Field trench between Küçük Hüyük and City Mound
GPL. 0.115; W. incised line 0.0045-0.005 m.
Fig. 24; Pl. 28
Base fragment of vessel with flat base, probably jar. Base fully preserved.
On exterior in center of base, incised before firing: double arrow.
Buff (7.5YR 7/4) clay, gritty and rather coarse. Apparently slipped on interior, now flaking.
Possibly Iron Age.
No exact parallels. Single arrows are common graffiti: Gordion (*Gordion Special Studies* I, 1, 4, fig. 1); Boğazköy, Büyükkale Level IIa, Unterstadt Levels 3-2 (*Gefässmarken*, 60-61, fig. 23); Alaca (*Belleten* 29 [1965] figs. 6-9); Korucutepe Phase I (*Korucutepe* 3, 91, pl. 12D). A similar sign in Linear B appears at Miletus on a pithos of Mycenean IIIC type (*IstMitt* 29 [1979] 102-103, pl. 22:3).

FIGURINES (522-525)

522   Ram
T 111   Clay Layer immediately over TB 8
GPH. 0.033; L. head 0.031; W. across horns 0.027 m.
Pl. 28
Ram. Broken across neck; back of head chipped.
Long cylindrical face, little indication of features. Horns formed by two coils of clay placed on top of head.
Orange (5YR 6/6) clay, gritty; cream (10YR 8/3) slip.
Boğazköy, from Büyükkale, in debris in front of Hittite city gate (*Heth. Keramik*, 158, no. 1304, pl. 137).

523   Horse
T 43   Phrygian Gate area; top of Clay Layer over North Court
GPH. 0.06; L. head 0.052; W. 0.033 m.
Pl. 29
Horse. Head and part of neck preserved; head damaged, broken at neck. Mane originally applied, now mostly missing.
Head with applied forelock, ears, mane, and halter.
Fine tan (5YR 6/4) clay, gritty; cream-buff (10YR 8/3-8/4) slip on surface.
Below, **524**.

524   Horse
P 4388   Clay Layer over CC 3 Building
GPH. 0.066; L. head 0.042; W. 0.032 m.
Pl. 29
Horse. Broken at base of neck; ears, mane and mouth chipped.
Head with applied forelock, mane, and halter.
Fine tan (5YR 7/4) clay, with few gritty inclusions; well fired. Cream-buff (10 YR 8/2-8/3) slip on exterior.
523-524: Boğazköy (*Heth. Keramik*, 159, no. 1328, pl. 137).

525   Horse
T 50   Clay Layer over Phrygian "Polychrome House"
GPH. 0.044; L. head 0.034; W. head 0.0205 m.
Pl. 29
Horse. Broken across base of neck, ear; most of mane, half of bridle missing.
Head with erect ears; muzzle, eyes and nostrils formed by punched holes; bridle and mane from applied strips of clay.
Fine orange-buff (5YR 7/6) clay, with gritty inclusions; fired lighter (7.5YR 7/4) on surfaces. Roughly finished by hand.

LOOMWEIGHTS (526-529)

526   Loomweight
MC 102a   Clay Layer over CC 2-3 Buildings
L. 0.129; GTh. 0.033 m.
Pl. 29
Complete.
Crescent-shaped loomweight, bluntly finished at ends; almost rectangular in section. String-hole pierced at either end.
Fine buff-cream (10YR 7/4) clay, with some gritty inclusions. Hand-formed and smoothed.
Below, **529**.

527   Loomweight
MC 102b   Clay Layer over CC 2-3 Buildings
L. 0.111; GTh. 0.037 m.
Pl. 29
Complete.
Crescent-shaped loomweight, bluntly finished at end; oval in section. String-hole pierced at either end.
Buff (7.5YR 7/4) clay, gritty. Hand-formed; well smoothed.
Below, **529**.

528 Loomweight
MC 130 Clay Layer over area between TB 4 and Megaron 2
GPL. 0.085; GTh. 0.038 m.
Pl. 29
Circa one-half preserved; chipped near break.
Crescent-shaped loomweight. Preserved end, concave in section with slight depression in center of edge. Pierced for suspension.
Buff (7.5YR 7/4) clay, gritty; apparently fired gray at core. Hand-formed; roughly hand-finished.
Below, **529**.

529 Loomweight
MC 200 Clay Layer over area NW of Megaron 9 (NE Bldg).
GPL. 0.123; W. 0.036; GTh. 0.026 m.
Fig. 24; Pl. 29
Almost fully preserved; broken through suspension hole at one end.
Crescent-shaped loomweight. Blunt ends, unevenly flattened; approximately oval in section. Pierced at both ends. Stamped three times at one end of one flat surface: rough double crescent.
Orange clay, gritty; fired gray at core. Hand-formed, smoothed.
526-529: A ceramic category found at most central Anatolian sites in Middle Bronze and Late Bronze levels (*Heth. Keramik*, 76, with discussion and references in n. 483); but it has not been found at Maşat (*Maşat* II, 120). For the stamped double crescent (**529**), Karahüyük-Konya Level I (*Karahüyük-Konya Damga*, 95, pl. 224:687).

SPINDLE WHORL (530)

530 Spindle whorl
MC 184 Clay Layer over area N of North Court of Phrygian Gate
H. 0.022; D. 0.042; D. perforations 0.0075, 0.009 m.
Fig. 24; Pl. 29
Complete, with some prefiring flaws.
Truncated conical in profile. In top, deep depression around hole.
Buff clay, well polished.

DISK (531)

531 Disk
P 4441 Clay Layer with burned mudbricks above CC 3 Building
D. 0.04; Th. 0.008 m.
Pl. 29
Fragmentary disk-shaped object, broken across approximate diameter.
One face flat and unworked; other has circular depressions of varying depth, *ca.* 0.004-0.0045 m. across, arranged in two concentric circles around a central depression.
Pale orange clay, gritty and micaceous; surfaces plain.

SEALS AND SEALINGS (532 and 533)

532 Hieroglyphic seal impression[113]
SS 209 In rubble foundation of Megaron 12 cross-wall
H. 0.0135; D. 0.021 m.
Pl. 29
Complete except for hole in center of impressed surface.
Clay bulla of conical shape. On base, an impression of Hittite hieroglyphic stamp seal: encircling guilloche; signs in center.
Very fine clay, fired gray throughout.

533 Four-sided bead seal
SS 260 Northeast side over Phrygian City Wall, Layer 1
L. 0.014; W. 0.0092; Th. 0.0082; D. string hole 0.003 m.
Pl. 29
Intact; some wear on edge.
Rectangular with two opposite long faces a little wider than the other pair. String hole completely through lengthwise, a bit off-center. The four seal faces are lightly incised to form simple pictures: (1) a figure enthroned before a tree; (2) a four-spiked star over possible small crescent; (3) a cross with long stem over a disjoined short straight base line (ankh?); (4) a plant with two pairs of opposite leaves.
Hard gray-black stone with visible striations.

Supplementary Items from Soundings under Megaron 10 and Megaron 12

(S1-S68)

MEGARON 10 (S1-S63)

LAYER 16

JAR (S1)

S1 Jar
Not inv. Layer 16
GPL. 0.075; GTh. 0.006 m.
Pl. 30
Body sherd from small closed vessel, jar or teapot. On exterior, horizontal ridge at junction of neck and shoulder.

Orange (5YR 6/6) clay, relatively fine and clean. Tan-orange slip on exterior, well smoothed and burnished. Interior plain, with wheelmarks visible.

LAYER 15 (S2)

BASE (S2)

S2 Pedestal base
Not inv. Layer 15
D. base 0.085; GTh. 0.0075 m.
Fig. 28

---

113. Previous publication, H. G. Güterbock in *Young Symposium*, 55, with discussion and further references.

Edge of pedestal base, probably from bowl or pitcher. *Circa* two-thirds of circumference preserved; mended from several joining sherds. Exterior discolored.

Fine light reddish brown clay, slightly gritty; fired gray at core. Exterior and edge covered with red slip, wheel-burnished, and slightly lustrous in places. Interior plain, almost completely smoothed of wheelmarks.

LAYER 14   (S3-S7)

BOWL (S3)

S3   Bowl
Not inv.   Layer 14
Est. D. rim 0.23; GTh. 0.007 m.
Fig. 28
Rim sherd of bowl with inverted rim. Rim worn; a few chips and scratches; traces of incrustation on lower surface.

Orange clay, rather gritty; well fired. Both surfaces very well smoothed, covered with good brown slip, slightly lustrous.

COOKING POT (S4)

S4   Cooking pot
Not inv.   Layer 14
Est. D. rim 0.22; GTh. 0.012 m.
Fig. 28
Rim sherd of hole-mouth cooking pot. Blackened in places on exterior; some incrustation on both surfaces.

Reddish brown clay, very gritty, with "gold" mica flakes; well fired. Surfaces plain.

JAR OR JUG (S5)

S5   Jar or jug
Not. inv.   Layer 14
Est. D. rim 0.11; GTh. 0.006 m.
Fig. 28
Mended from three joining sherds. Rim and neck section of vessel with cylindrical neck, everted rim. Green discoloration on interior; some incrustation on exterior. Perhaps from jar or jug.

Orange clay, clean and well fired. Red slip on exterior and rim, continues inside vessel *ca.* 0.02 m. Slipped surface well smoothed, not lustrous. Interior plain, wheelmarked.

PEDESTAL BASES (S6 and S7)

S6   Pedestal base
Not inv.   Layer 14
Est. D. base 0.12; GTh. 0.013 m.
Fig. 28
Fragment of pedestal base, probably from pitcher. *Circa* one-third of circumference preserved, broken across near upper edge of pedestal. Base worn, slightly discolored; broken edges incrusted.

Fired pale buff on bottom, plain and wheelmarked. Upper surface well smoothed, covered with light reddish brown slip, not lustrous. Slip continues just below upper surface.

S7   Pedestal base
Not inv.   Layer 14
Est. D. base 0.14; GTh. 0.027 m.
Fig. 28

Fragment of pedestal base preserves most of profile of base, probably from pitcher. Slip worn; some incrustation on upper surface; discolored on base, incrusted and discolored on edges.

Fired pale buff on bottom. Cherry red slip on upper surface, now mostly worn away but somewhat lustrous where preserved. Upper surface well smoothed. Bottom plain and wheelmarked.

LAYER 13   (S8-S12)

BOWLS (S8-S10)

S8   Bowl
Not inv.   Layer 13
Est. D. rim. 0.18; GTh. 0.0055 m.
Fig. 28
Rim sherd of bowl with incurved, thickened rim. Rim chipped; both surfaces discolored.

Orange clay with some inclusions but relatively clean and fine; well fired. Surfaces plain. Interior and rim faintly wheelmarked and smoothed; exterior wheelmarked.

S9   Bowl
Not inv.   Layer 13
Est. D. rim 0.30; GTh. 0.008 m.
Fig. 28
Rim sherd of carinated bowl with gradually thickened rim. Rim chipped; some discoloration.

Buff clay, fairly gritty; well fired. Surfaces plain, heavily wheelmarked.

S10   Bowl
Not inv.   Layer 13
Est. D. rim 0.26; GTh. 0.007 m.
Fig. 28
Rim sherd of carinated bowl with broad, thickened rim; rim flattened slightly across top. Surfaces worn, pitted, heavily discolored green; some incrustation on interior.

Buff clay, gritty and coarse, with large flecks of "gold" mica; well fired. Surfaces plain, heavily wheelmarked.

JAR (S11)

S11   Jar
Not inv.   Layer 13
Est. D. rim 0.17; GPL. 0.087; GTh. 0.01 m.
Fig. 28
Body sherd from carinated jar. Interior somewhat incrusted; both surfaces heavily discolored green. Probably from teapot with basket handle.

Pinkish tan clay, with some gritty inclusions but relatively clean, good fabric. Both surfaces plain, wheelmarked.

HANDLE (S12)

S12   Handle
Not inv.   Layer 13
GPL. 0.0829; W. handle 0.0166 m.
Fig. 28; Pl. 30
Handle fragment, broken across handle and at place of attachment at rim. Surfaces considerably discolored.

Handle, round in section, rises above rim. Probably from teapot with basket handle.

Buff clay, somewhat gritty. Surfaces plain, partly smoothed.

LAYER 12 (S13-S24)

BOWLS (S13-S19)

S13 Bowl
Not inv. Layer 12, Pit B
Est. D. rim 0.30; GTh. 0.01 m.
Fig. 28
Rim fragment of large bowl, mended from two joining sherds. Some discoloration on both surfaces; some of broken edges dark gray. Hemispherical form with thickened rim curving slightly inward.
Orange clay, very gritty; mostly well fired. Core shows "laminated" appearance. Exterior possibly coated with very thin clay wash, cracked in several places. Surfaces wheelmarked, with interior slightly more smoothed than exterior.

S14 Bowl
Not inv. Layer 12, Pit B
Est. D. rim 0.22; GTh. 0.007 m.
Fig. 28
Rim section of bowl, mended from several joining sherds. Exterior partly blackened; interior discolored; traces of incrustation on both surfaces. Hemispherical form, with rim curving very slightly inward.
Orange clay, gritty; seems to be fired secondarily, mottled to orange tan, well fired. Surfaces plain. Interior mostly smoothed of wheelmarks; exterior wheelmarked.

S15 Bowl
Not inv. Layer 12, Pit B
Est. D. rim 0.21; GTh. 0.007 m.
Fig. 28
Rim section of bowl, mended from several joining sherds; *ca.* one-third of rim circumference preserved. Rim chipped; both surfaces discolored, with a few traces of incrustation. Bowl with inverted rim overhanging the upper wall; uneven interior.
Orange clay, gritty; fired gray at core. Surfaces plain, wheelmarked; exterior roughly finished.

S16 Bowl
Not inv. Layer 12, Pit B
Est. D. rim 0.20; GTh. 0.0071 m.
Fig. 28
Rim section of bowl, mended from three joining sherds. Some discoloration on both surfaces. Relatively shallow form with thickened rim.
Tan clay, gritty; firing not certain. Some crushed lime temper visible on exterior. Interior smoothed; exterior wheelmarked, roughly finished.

S17 Bowl
Not inv. Layer 12, Pit B
Est. D. rim 0.22; GTh. 0.006 m.
Fig. 29
Rim section of bowl, mended from three joining sherds. Blackened on exterior. Relatively shallow form with broad rim.
Orange clay, gritty; firing unknown. Both surfaces plain, wheelmarked.

S18 Bowl
Not inv. Layer 12, Pit B
Est. D. rim 0.32; GTh. 0.0108 m.
Fig. 29
Rim section of large bowl, mended from two joining sherds. Some discoloration, incrustation on both surfaces. Large bowl with outer profile indented slightly just below broad rim; preserves beginning of rounded base.
Orange clay, very coarse and gritty, with some crushed lime temper; well fired. Interior coarse, but here and on rim mostly smoothed of wheelmarks. Exterior very roughly finished.

S19 Carinated bowl
Not inv. Layer 12, Pit A
Est. D. rim 0.30; GTh. 0.0105 m.
Fig. 29
Rim sherd of carinated bowl with thickened, sloping rim. Some dark discoloration on rim and interior; worn.
Reddish brown clay, gritty. Both surfaces covered with good red slip, smoothed but not lustrous. Slip applied to vessel in visible bands.

JARS (S20 and S21)

S20 Jar
Not inv. Layer 12
Est. D. rim 0.22; GTh. 0.0048 m.
Fig. 29
Rim sherd of jar, probably teapot, with carinated profile, plain rim. Exterior blackened below carination; some thin incrustation on interior.
Orange clay, somewhat gritty but good fabric. Both surfaces well smoothed and slipped; rim and exterior fired brown, interior fired cherry red.

S21 Jar
Not inv. Layer 12
Est. D. rim 0.20; GTh. 0.007 m.
Fig. 29
Rim sherd of jar, probably teapot, with gently carinated profile. Worn; some faint blackening on both surfaces.
Orange-brown clay, somewhat gritty; fired lighter at surfaces. Both surfaces covered with red slip that begins to disappear on interior below carination. Both surfaces well smoothed; exterior retains some luster.

PITHOS (S22)

S22 Pithos
Not inv. Layer 12, Pit B
Est. D. rim 0.48; Th. rim 0.042; GTh. 0.032 m.
Fig. 29
Rim sherd of pithos of hole-mouth shape. Surfaces somewhat incrusted.
Red clay, very coarse and gritty. Surfaces covered with dull reddish brown "self-slip."

PITCHER HANDLE (S23)

S23 Pitcher handle
Not inv. Layer 12, Pit B
GPH. 0.13; W. handle 0.025; GTh. wall 0.011 m.
Fig. 29; Pl. 30
Handle and adjoining rim section, mended from several joining sherds. Surfaces somewhat discolored, especially interior. Vertical handle, oval in section. Probably from pitcher with gentle carination.
Reddish yellow clay, somewhat gritty; firing not certain. Surfaces plain, wheelmarked. Handle smoothed, perhaps from wear.

SHERD WITH PLASTIC DECORATION (S24)

S24 Sherd with plastic decoration
Not inv. Layer 12
GPL. 0.0477; GPW. 0.0435; GTh. 0.007; W. of plastic decoration 0.02 m.

Pl. 30

Body sherd with applied plastic decoration. Slight incrustation on both surfaces. Plastic decoration of pellet form on exterior above carination.

Orange clay, somewhat gritty. Red slip, rather messily applied, on exterior, smoothed and matt. Interior plain, wheelmarked.

Applied pellet on bowl, Boğazköy, Nordwesthang-Büyükkale Level 8b (*Nordwesthang-Büyükkale*, 39, no. 287, pl. 31); also on neck of pitchers, Asarcık Level V (*IstMitt* 16 [1966] 64, fig. 4:3, 4).

LAYER 11 (S25-S35)

BOWLS (S25-S27)

S25   Shallow bowl
Not inv.   Layer 11
Est. D. rim. 0.27; Th. rim 0.0055 m.
Fig. 29

Rim sherd of shallow bowl with slightly incurved rim. Inner side of rim chipped; some incrustation on both surfaces.

Orange clay, gritty; well fired. Surfaces heavily wheelmarked, rather carelessly finished.

S26   Carinated bowl with horizontal handle
Not inv.   Layer 11
D. rim unknown; Th. rim 0.0062 m.
Fig. 29; Pl. 30

Rim sherd of carinated bowl with thickened rim, horizontal handle broken across above rim. Surfaces discolored green; some thin incrustation over most of sherd. Handle, approximately round in section, rises above rim.

Orange clay, gritty; exterior and handle smoothed of wheelmarks but rather coarse ware. Interior wheelmarked.

S27   Carinated bowl with horizontal handles
Not inv.   Layer 11
Est. D. rim 0.24; GPL. 0.043; GPW. 0.074; Th. rim 0.0087 m.
Pl. 30

Rim and handle fragment from carinated bowl with thickened rim, horizontal handle. Worn; some thin incrustation. Handle, round in section, rises above rim.

Orange clay, quite gritty; well fired. Red slip on handle, exterior and inner rim; slip rather dull but surfaces well smoothed. Interior wheelmarked, less well smoothed.

JAR (S28)

S28   Jar
Not inv.   Layer 11
Est. D. rim 0.25; Th. rim 0.0174 m.
Fig. 29; Pl. 30

Rim sherd of jar with broad, angular rim; horizontal ridge on exterior upper wall. Sherd slightly worn, broken edges incrusted.

Orange clay, somewhat gritty. Both surfaces covered with light reddish brown slip, smoothed and polished.

COOKING POTS (S29 and S30)

S29   Cooking pot
Not inv.   Layer 11
Est. D. rim 0.35; GTh. 0.026 m.
Fig. 29

Rim sherd of hole-mouth cooking pot.

Brown clay, coarse and gritty. Surfaces roughly finished.

S30   Cooking pot with vertical handle
Not inv.   Layer 11
Est. D. rim 0.60; Th. rim 0.03; GTh. 0.012 m.
Fig. 29; Pl. 30

Rim sherd of large hole-mouth cooking pot preserves handle in full. Interior blackened; surfaces heavily incrusted; handle abraded. Vertical handle at shoulder, approximately oval in section with convex lower surface.

Reddish brown clay, very coarse and gritty; well fired.

JUGS (S31 and S32)

S31   Jug
Not inv.   Layer 11
Est. D. rim. 0.14; Th. rim 0.0145; GTh. 0.077 m.
Fig. 29; Pl. 30

Rim sherd of jug; thickened rim. Some green discoloration on both surfaces.

Reddish yellow clay, some gritty inclusions but relatively clean; fired paler at surfaces. Plain, wheelmarked.

S32   Jug
Not. inv.;   Layer 11
Est. D. rim 0.09; W. handle 0.0345; Th. rim 0.015; GTh. 0.0058 m.
Fig. 29; Pl. 31

Rim sherd of jug with thickened rim. Surfaces discolored green; slightly incrusted. Scar of vertical handle, oval in section, on neck.

Orange clay with some gritty inclusions but relatively clean. Rim and exterior smoothed and covered with light brown slip, originally somewhat lustrous. Interior fired reddish yellow, plain and wheelmarked.

HANDLE (S33)

S33   Vertical handle
Not inv.   Layer 11
GPL. 0.10; W. handle 0.023; Th. handle 0.012; GTh. 0.0084 m .
Fig. 29; Pl. 31

Vertical handle and place of attachment, broken on all sides from wall of vessel; handle preserved in full. Handle worn, slightly abraded. Probably from jar with two vertical handles set at maximum diameter of vessel. Handle approximately oval in section, with rounded upper surface and flat lower surface.

Orange clay, somewhat gritty but good fabric, well fired. Surfaces plain.

BASES (S34 and S35)

S34   Flat base
Not inv.   Layer 11
Est. D. base 0.06; GTh. 0.0117 m.
Fig. 29

Fragment of flat, wheel-turned base. Some incrustation on interior. From closed vessel, probably jar.

Orange clay, very gritty; well fired. Surfaces covered with very thin clay wash, fired pale orange-buff at surfaces. Interior and bottom very roughly finished.

S35   Ring base
Not inv.   Layer 11
Est. D. base 0.12; GTh. 0.012 m.
Fig. 29

Fragment of ring base, probably from jar.

Orange clay, gritty. Surfaces wheelmarked, plain.

LAYER 7 (S36-S42)

BOWLS (S36 and S37)

S36 Shallow bowl
Not inv.   Layer 7
Est. D. rim. 0.27; GTh. 0.012 m.
Fig. 30
Rim sherd of shallow bowl with thick, inverted rim.
Orange-buff clay, gritty and coarse, well fired.

S37 Bowl with vertical handle
Not inv.   Layer 7
D. rim unknown; GPL. 0.086; W. handle 0.017; GTh. 0.007 m .
Fig. 30
Rim and handle of bowl with vertical handle; handle preserved in full. Some incrustation on handle and both surfaces. Simple rim; handle, oval in section, attached at rim and at greatest diameter of bowl.
Orange clay, somewhat gritty; well fired. Rim, handle, and exterior smoothed and covered with good slip, fired red to reddish brown. Interior plain, wheelmarked.

PLATES (S38 and S39)

S38 Plate
Not inv.   Layer 7
D. rim unknown; GTh. 0.012, 0.028 m.
Fig. 30
Rim sherd of shallow bowl or plate. Horizontal grooves on upper interior surface near edge of vessel.
Orange clay, gritty. Red slip on lower surface; upper surface plain.

S39 Plate
Not inv.   Layer 7
D. rim unknown; GTh. 0.012, 0.028 m.
Fig. 30
Rim sherd of large plate with broad, flat rim.
Orange clay, gritty and coarse. Dark reddish brown matt slip on both surfaces.

SPOUT (S40)

S40 Pitcher spout
Not inv.   Layer 7
GPL. 0.075; Th. spout trough 0.0114 m.
Pl. 31
Spout of beaked type, with curved end, from pitcher. Broken irregularly across spout trough, tip of spout broken. Surfaces slightly incrusted.
Orange clay, somewhat gritty but good fabric; well fired. Surfaces and inner rim of trough covered with reddish brown slip, well smoothed and polished.

SHERDS WITH PAINTED OR GROOVED DECORATION (S41 and S42)

S41 Painted sherd
Not inv.   Layer 7
GPL. 0.068; PW. 0.087; GTh. 0.0114 m.
Pl. 31
Body sherd from vessel with painted decoration. Interior worn; exterior scratched and worn, pitted. From closed vessel of roughly globular form. Exterior preserves area of brown slip, unevenly applied, mottled from reddish brown to light brown to dark brown.
Buff clay, slightly gritty; well fired. Solid buff-slipped sur-

face below brown zone. Exterior well smoothed, matt. Interior plain, wheelmarked.

S42 Grooved sherds
Not inv.   Layer 7
a GPL. 0.0486; GPW. 0.0526; GTh. 0.0079 m.
b GPL. 0.053; GPW. 0.077; GTh. 0.0079 m.
Pl. 31
Two nonjoining body sherds from same vessel. Very worn, heavily discolored. From medium closed vessel. Across face of both sherds are parallel horizontal grooves, shallow and rather neatly formed: four on each sherd.
Dark orange clay, somewhat gritty. Exterior covered with brown slip, smoothed. Interior plain, wheelmarked.

LAYER 6 (S43-S50)

BOWLS (S43-S47)

S43 Bowl
Not inv.   Layer 6
Est. D. rim 0.24; GTh. 0.007 m.
Fig. 30
Rim sherd of bowl with inverted, almost vertical rim. Slip very worn.
Orange clay, relatively fine and clean. Thin red slip on exterior extending to below carination, and on interior rim.

S44 Bowl
Not inv.   Layer 6
Est. D. rim 0.23; GTh. 0.006 m.
Fig. 30
Rim sherd of shallow hemispherical bowl with plain rim. Surfaces discolored.
Orange clay, with some gritty inclusions, but relatively fine and clean. Surfaces plain.

S45 Bowl
Not inv.   Layer 6
Est. D. rim 0.24; GTh. 0.011 m.
Fig. 30
Rim sherd of relatively shallow bowl with inverted, almost vertical rim.
Orange clay, somewhat gritty. Surfaces plain, wheelmarked.

S46 Bowl
Not. inv.   Layer 6
Est. D. rim 0.26; GTh. 0.01 m.
Fig. 30
Rim sherd of shallow bowl with inverted rim, overhanging upper wall.
Orange clay, somewhat gritty. Surfaces plain, wheelmarked.

S47 Shallow bowl
Not inv.   Layer 6
Est. D. rim 0.22; GTh. 0.008 m.
Fig. 30
Rim sherd of shallow bowl with broad, thickened rim.
Orange clay, fine and clean. Surfaces plain.

PLATE (S48)

S48 Plate
Not inv.   Layer 6
Est. D. rim 0.28; GTh. 0.011 m.
Fig. 30
Rim sherd of plate. Some incrustation on exterior.
Orange clay, with some gritty inclusions. Surfaces plain.

JAR (S49)

S49   Jar
Not inv.   Layer 6
Est. D. rim 0.40; GTh. 0.015 m.
Fig. 30
Rim sherd of large jar with sharply everted, flat rim.
Orange clay, somewhat gritty; fired lighter at surfaces. Surfaces plain.

COOKING POT (S50)

S50   Cooking pot
Not inv.   Layer 6
Est. D. rim 0.25; GTh. 0.0105 m.
Fig. 30
Rim sherd of cooking pot with steep shoulder narrowing towards neck, rim thickened on outside. Interior blackened.
Reddish brown clay, very coarse and gritty, with some "gold" mica. Surfaces plain.

LAYER 4   (S51-S63)

BOWLS (S51-S54)

S51   Bowl
Not inv.   Layer 4
Est. D. rim 0.17; GTh. 0.005 m.
Fig. 30
Rim sherd of bowl with tapered rim. Rim chipped at both ends of sherd. Hemispherical form with wall tapering to thin, upright rim.
Fine orange clay, with little grit; well fired. Paler, buff area on interior upper wall suggests that bowl was fired with a similar vessel inside it, thus at different temperatures. Surfaces plain, heavily wheelmarked.

S52   Shallow bowl
Not inv.   Layer 4
Est. D. rim 0.29; GTh. 0.0075 m.
Fig. 30
Rim sherd of very shallow bowl with inverted rim. Some thin incrustation on all surfaces, especially upper.
Dark orange clay, somewhat gritty and containing a few large inclusions, but not coarse; well fired. Surfaces plain, wheelmarked.

S53   Shallow bowl
Not inv.   Layer 4
Est. D. rim 0.24; GTh. 0.0075 m.
Fig. 30
Rim sherd of shallow bowl with broad, slightly thickened rim. Some dark discoloration, blotched, on both surfaces; some thin incrustation.
Tan clay, with some gritty inclusions; well fired. Smeared appearance in places. Surfaces plain, wheelmarked but smooth.

S54   Shallow bowl
Not inv.   Layer 4
Est. D. outer rim 0.38; GTh. 0.0095 m.
Fig. 30
Rim sherd of large shallow bowl with broad, thickened rim. Traces of dark discoloration on lower surfaces and rim, more consistently on interior; thin incrustation on broken edges and sporadically on surfaces.
Orange-tan clay, gritty and rather coarse, with some crushed lime temper; well fired. Buff-tan on slip both surfaces. Wheelmarked; bottom surface and rim partly smoothed, by wear?

JARS (S55 and S56)

S55   Jar
Not inv.   Layer 4
D. rim unknown; GTh. 0.008 m.
Fig. 31
Rim sherd of small jar with gently everted rim. Inner rim chipped; traces of incrustation on both surfaces.
Orange clay, rather gritty but not coarse; fired buff on surfaces. Exterior wheelmarked; interior and rim smoother, from wear?

S56   Jar
Not inv.   Layer 4
D. rim unknown; GTh. 0.01 m.
Fig. 31
Rim sherd of jar with everted rim. Faint blackening on interior; traces of incrustation on both surfaces.
Orange-brown clay, gritty but not especially coarse; well fired, orange-brown at surfaces. Wheelmarked.

JUG (S57)

S57   Jug
Not inv.   Layer 4
Est. D. rim 0.10; GTh. 0.008 m.
Fig. 31
Rim sherd of jug with thickened rim. Worn. Rim abraded on both surfaces; some incrustation on interior.
Orange-brown clay, gritty and rather coarse. Interior wheelmarked; browner area on exterior below rim may represent traces of a thin "self-slip," where surface now cracked.

BASES (S58 and S59)

S58   Base
Not inv.   Layer 4
GPH. 0.052; GTh. 0.007 m.
Fig. 31
Base and adjoining lower body of closed vessel, probably jar. Broken unevenly all around. Some incrustation, greenish discoloration. Interior uneven. Gently rounded base; walls rising rather steeply to globular lower vessel.
Orange clay, with some gritty particles; marks of fired vegetal temper on base, as if vessel rested on and collected temper on moist surface before firing. Interior wheelmarked, somewhat rough; exterior well smoothed, possibly with "self-slip," now mostly gone.

S59   Ring base
Not. inv.   Layer 4
GPH. 0.032; D. base 0.105 m.
Fig. 31
Ring base fragment, probably from large jar. Circa two-thirds of ring circumference preserved; broken unevenly just above point where lower wall of vessel begins. Upper surface roughened for attachment of vessel interior. Gray incrustation over most of exterior.
Orange clay, gritty and rather coarse, with some large inclusions. Exterior wheelmarked, roughly finished.

RIM (S60)

S60   Trefoil rim?
Not inv.   Layer 4

Est. D. vessel 0.18; GTh. 0.009 m.
Fig. 31; Pl. 31

Rim sherd of vessel with thickened rim, globular closed upper body. Rim indicates an uneven circumference, thus probably from a trefoil-necked jug or pitcher. Small area of rim preserved, chipped; some incrustation, faint discoloration on interior. Interior uneven.

Orange clay, slightly gritty but generally clean, good pottery, with "silver" mica; well fired, tan on both surfaces. Rim smooth, interior wheelmarked; exterior burnished with mostly vertical strokes, clearly visible.

VESSEL WITH LUG (S61)

S61   Vessel with lug
Not inv.   Layer 4
GPL. 0.084; W. lug 0.0325; GTh. 0.008 m.
Fig. 31; Pl. 31

Body sherd of coarse vessel with lug, broken from vessel wall on all sides. Exterior fairly thoroughly blackened; some blackening on interior. Worn, especially on exterior. Probably a cooking pot.

Coarse, very gritty clay; now fired dark orange on interior and dark brown on exterior. Interior plain, with some marks that suggest manufacture by slow wheel. Exterior covered with matt slip, partly smoothed. Wheelformed and finished by hand?

HANDLE (S62)

S62   Handle
Not inv.   Layer 4
GPL. 0.13; W. handle 0.026; GTh. 0.0087 m.
Fig. 31; Pl. 31

Rim and vertical handle preserve handle in full, with place of attachment to shoulder and rim. Worn; some incrustation on exterior. Part of interior surface eaten away; discolored green.

Upper end of handle attached directly to rim. Vertical handle, upper surface convex with palpable spine ridge. Probably pitcher.

Buff clay, gritty, with "silver" mica. Exterior and handle well smoothed, covered with red-brown slip, still lustrous on part of handle. Upper part of interior surface preserves some red-brown slip, suggesting that it continued inside vessel.

VESSEL NECK AND HANDLE (S63)

S63   Vessel neck and handle
Not inv.   Layer 4
GPH. 0.086; W. handle 0.029; GTh. 0.017-0.011 m.
Fig. 31

Fragment from neck of vessel preserves part of neck, rim and vertical handle. Worn; some incrustation along broken edges, with traces on handle and surfaces; blackened on lower interior.

Vessel with cylindrical neck; sherd thicker at base and begins to flare, indicating that this is base of neck. Handle joins rim directly. Handle, approximately oval in section, has vertically ribbed upper surface. Probably from jug or pitcher with ribbed handle.

Tan clay, somewhat gritty. Inner rim, handle and exterior wall smoothed and covered with brown slip, probably originally lustrous. Interior smoothed, plain. Vessel handmade.

Early Bronze Age.

MEGARON 12

LEVEL IVB   (S64-S68)

BOWLS (S64-S66)

S64   Bowl
Not inv.   Level IVB
Est. D. rim. 0.30; GTh. 0.0095 m.
Fig. 31

Rim sherd of shallow hemispherical bowl with thick walls and incurved rim. Interior uneven. Blackened over most of interior and partly on rim.

Orange clay, fired tan at surfaces; heavily micaceous, with mostly "black" mica visible on tan surface. Surfaces plain, wheelmarked; smoothed or worn on exterior. Exterior near base preserves impressions of vegetal temper, as if bowl was placed on such material before firing.

S65   Bowl
Not inv.   Level IVB
Est. D. rim 0.32; GTh. 0.011 m.
Fig. 31

Rim section preserves most of bowl profile; mended from three joining sherds. Surfaces chipped, worn; blackened unevenly over most of exterior, rim and interior. Some greenish discoloration on rim and part of interior.

Large hemispherical bowl with outer profile indented below flat rim.

Light brown clay, somewhat gritty and very micaceous, with a "silver" mica concentration on both surfaces. Surfaces well smoothed. Rim and exterior appear to have been "self-slipped" with very thin clay-colored slip, then burnished. Wheelmade? Appears to be wheelformed and finished by hand.

S66   Shallow bowl
Not inv.   Level IVB
Est. D. outer rim. 0.28; GTh. 0.0122 m.
Fig. 31

Rim section of large shallow bowl with broad, slightly overhung rim, mended from two joining sherds. Chipped and worn. Grayed in areas on both surfaces; some greenish discoloration on rim and exterior. Surfaces pitted and cracked.

Dark orange clay, very gritty and coarse; large gritty inclusions visible on surfaces. Surfaces plain; wheelmarked, especially on exterior.

JARS (S67 and S68)

S67   Jar
Not inv.   Level IVB
Est. D. rim 0.20; GTh. 0.0065 m.
Fig. 31

Rim sherd of small hole-mouth jar. Rim worn. Blackened over most of interior and all of exterior, as secondary heating or as deliberate firing?

Clay originally perhaps tan or buff, preserved in small area on edge of sherd; gritty, with many visible inclusions. Surfaces plain; wheelmarked.

S68   Jar
Not inv.   Level IVB
D. rim unknown; GTh. 0.0136 m.
Fig. 31

Rim sherd of jar with strongly everted rim with profiled upper surface. Worn; blackened area on lower rim. Grayed throughout.

Original clay color uncertain. Clay gritty, with some flecks of "gold" mica; contains vegetal temper. Surfaces apparently covered with buff slip originally; strongly wheelmarked.

Bronze Age Pottery From Early Iron Age Levels

Analysis of the Material

In both deep soundings at Gordion, under Megaron 10 and Megaron 12, phases containing Late Bronze Age pottery were succeeded without apparent break by strata containing a majority of Late Bronze Age pottery with steadily increasing percentages of Phrygian (Early Iron Age) gray wares. The Iron Age pottery from these levels (Megaron 10 Layers 3-1 and Megaron 12 Level IVA) is catalogued and analyzed by G. Kenneth Sams in his forthcoming comprehensive study of Early Iron Age ceramic production at Gordion.[1] Bronze Age pottery from these levels is treated in the present volume for two reasons. First, it will not be catalogued or examined closely in the Iron Age volume. Second, it

furnishes the only available information on the duration of Bronze Age ceramic production at the site.

Since the earliest Iron Age levels have been explored in only a few scattered areas of the City Mound which could not be directly linked to each other, their stratigraphic and chronological relationship to the preceding periods of occupation is not well understood.[2] Further excavation of these levels, encompassing also substantial horizontal exposures, should yield additional stratigraphic testimony as well as a larger corpus of pottery with which to reconstruct ceramic developments. A summary of the relationship of the available material to previous ceramic developments at Gordion is given at the end of this chapter.

Description of Sequences

MEGARON 10 ANTEROOM

LAYER 3 (534-544)

A very small number of sherds, about 20 diagnostic examples, is available for Layer 3. The concurrence of ceramic groups closely follows that of Layer 4. Orange and buff gritty wares in shallow bowls with thickened or angular rims (535, 537) and plates (539), augmented by fine bowls (534, 536), form about half of the collection. A ledged jar rim, 541, is fired to an unusually dark orange color but may be of Late Bronze ancestry, descending from rim types attested in Layer 7 (317 and 318). A large jar with everted rim (543) is equipped with handles at the shoulder. It seems to belong to a

long-established vessel type, although its heavy, dense fabric is not characteristic of Bronze Age manufacture. A related example of this unusual fabric occurs in Layer 1 (556). A jar of cooking pot fabric (544) with narrowing shoulder and thickened rim, has a shape rare for this traditional ceramic category. A related example (S50) from Layer 6 may provide a Late Bronze Age prototype.

As in Layers 6 through 4, buff or orange wheelmade samples distinguished by unusual shape, surface treatment, or micaceous concentration are represented in small quantities. A red-slipped carinated bowl (538) is conceivably a survivor or descendant of earlier Bronze Age fashions, but its dull surface finish does not match previous standards and it contains, exceptionally, vege-

---

1. *Gordion* IV.

---

2. G.K. Sams discusses the stratigraphic and ceramic testimony in detail and reviews previous literature in his forthcoming volume, *Gordion* IV.

tal temper. Other specimens likewise resist classification within well-documented categories. A large plate has matt red painted decoration (**540**). A small jar (**542**) is distinguished by its red-slipped surface with micaceous concentration. Another example with a surface concentration of "silver" mica is a tan-slipped neck fragment of a jar or bottle (not catalogued).

Layer 3 also produced 7 examples of the tan- or gray-fired handmade pottery, often with incised decoration, first attested in Layer 4. One brown-slipped bowl (**582**) has a profile resembling wheelmade red- or tan-slipped examples in Early Phrygian Building Level I.[3] A gray wheelmade sherd with grooved decoration completes the known ceramic repertory.

LAYER 2   (545-550)

Only a few diagnostic sherds, about 9, were kept from Layer 2; to what extent they provide a useful sample is therefore unknown. They represent three ceramic groups. First are familiar buff and orange gritty wares, in shapes resembling those of the preceding Layers 4 and 3: bowls with broad rims (**546**, and **547** with partial buff slip), plates (**548**), jars with everted rims (**549**), and jugs (**550**). Second, a bowl rim with a shallow groove below the outer rim (**545**) provides an example of the wheelmade group with "silver" mica concentration, here present both in the fabric and on the surface. A related profile occurs in Megaron 10 Main Room Layer 2 (**569**). Finally, Layer 2 illustrates the Transitional or Iron Age handmade pottery: a tan sherd with incised dashes and horizontal grooves; and a dark-fired sherd, coarse and gritty, with vertical notches.

LAYER 1   (551-568)

Only diagnostic samples were saved from the uppermost layer of the Megaron 10 deep sounding. These form a collection consisting of roughly 70% Late Bronze Age orange and buff pottery in both characteristic and previously unattested shapes, a few examples of wheelmade pottery with noticeable "silver" mica, and a few specimens of the Transitional or Iron Age handmade group. Phrygian pottery is present in both gray monochrome and painted varieties. Some Middle Bronze sherds and one or two Early Bronze fragments seem to be extrusive.

Most of the Late Bronze Age pottery conforms to the types represented in Layers 3 and 2: shallow bowls with broad rims (**557, 558**), plates (**559, 560**), jugs (**565-567**), ring bases probably from jars (**568**), in plain gritty buff

and orange wares (**567** with reddish brown slip). A plate with dull buff slip (**561**) illustrates a large, broad-rimmed variety known at Gordion in a few examples, from Megaron 10 Layers 8-5 (**257, 344, 353, S38, S39**) and Megaron 12 Level IVA (fragment, not catalogued). Other fragments document previously attested shapes or types, such as pitcher handles, jars with everted rims, small jugs (with trefoil rim?), and cooking pots. A buff-slipped flask fragment also occurs.

Remaining samples mostly fall outside the established Late Bronze Age repertory. These include a group with possible ties to the buff and orange tradition but distinguished by their unusual fabric, shape, or surface treatment. A large shallow bowl with broad overhung rim (**556**) has a dense, heavy fabric unlike the normal gritty class. Other previously unknown features are unusually elaborate rims with exterior bulge (**554, 555, 562**). A jar rim with horizontal ridge and vertical handle (**563**) is also new, closely matched by an example from Main Room Layer 2 (**573**). Bowls with indented profile also seem unexpected (**551, 552**). This group displays a marked preference for a thick buff slip, often very carelessly applied. None of these examples is claimed by the Phrygian experts.

Layer 1 also furnished a few examples of pottery with micaceous concentration. A carinated bowl representing this group (**553**) has a close relative in Early Phrygian Building Level I (**582**, red-slipped) and in a handmade, brown-slipped example from Layer 3.[4]

Handmade pottery of Iron Age type occurs in a few examples. Phrygian gray wares and painted specimens form the remainder of the collection.

MEGARON 10 MAIN ROOM

LAYERS 2-1   (569-581)

Small collections of pottery from the accumulation within the Main Room of Megaron 10 are used selectively here, since the exact provenience of component sherds is not known in detail. Moreover, the correlation of these layers with those in the Anteroom sounding remains problematic.[5] From Layer 2 are mostly Late Bronze Age buff and orange gritty wares in shallow bowls and plates (**571**). A buff-slipped rim may belong to a wide-mouthed jug (**576**). Unusual items related to pottery of Anteroom Layer 1 are represented, such as bowls with overhung rim (**570**) and a small jar with exterior ridge (**573**). A jar with flaring shoulder and lid-rest is new (**574**). A coarse, micaceous bowl rim with indented profile (**569**) has already been mentioned in

---

3. G.K. Sams, *Gordion* IV.
4. P 5733.

5. G.K. Sams reviews the stratigraphic evidence for correlating these layers, *Gordion* IV.

relation to a bowl from Layer 3 (**545**). Also present in Layer 2 are gray ware handles with incised decoration and Phrygian gray pottery.

Layer 1 likewise yielded mostly Late Bronze Age pottery: bowls, plates, jars with everted rims, jugs, a vessel with pointed base, cooking pots (one with plastic nipple), all in small fragments. Nontraditional specimens are bowls with indented profile (**577, 578**), a carinated buff-slipped bowl (**579**), a small orange jar (**580**), and a coarse jar rim (**581**). Jars and other shapes occur in Phrygian gray ware. A flat red-slipped handle fragment may be from an Early Bronze Age vessel.

EARLY PHRYGIAN BUILDING
(582-584)

Excavation of the Early Phrygian Building in 1965 revealed an important sequence of Early Iron Age levels, numbered I to V. Pottery from these levels is catalogued and analyzed in the forthcoming volume by G. Kenneth Sams on Iron Age ceramic production.[6]

The assemblage from Level I is described briefly here because of its possible relationship to the pottery recovered from Transitional strata of the deep soundings. A few items are catalogued to help illustrate unusual, non-Phrygian ceramic groups of the Megaron 10 and Megaron 12 sequences.

The earliest level, Level I, yielded ceramic groups very similar to the assemblages of Megaron 10 Layer 4 and Megaron 12 Level IVB. Pottery of Early Phrygian Building Level I, known from approximately 100 sherds, consists almost exclusively of Late Bronze Age varieties, mostly buff and orange gritty wares, in shallow bowls, jars with everted rims, and ring bases. Two or three sherds of handmade red-slipped ware are probably Early Bronze Age survivals. A red-slipped beak spout fragment may be earlier than most of the Bronze Age specimens.

In addition to Late Bronze Age pottery of standard types, Level I produced two other groups represented in Megaron 10 Layers 4-1 and in Megaron 12 Levels IVB and IVA. First is the wheelmade, heavily micaceous fabric with careful surface treatment, exemplified in a carinated bowl (**582**) and a small jar (**583**). The second group is the Transitional or Iron Age handmade category, in simple jars with wide mouths and incised rim ornament very similar to an example in Megaron 12 Level IVB (Pl. 32).

Level V consists of the fill over the Early Phrygian Building, deposited when the structure went out of use. It is a mixed deposit, with examples ranging in date from Early Bronze through Early Iron Age. This level produced a flask fragment, **584**, better preserved than the example retrieved from Megaron 10 Layer 1 noted above.

SOUNDING BENEATH MEGARON 12

LEVEL IVA (585-596)

Level IVA produced about 200 sherds. The major ceramic groups are buff and orange gritty fabrics, plain or with red or brown slip; and Phrygian gray wares, including shapes with counterparts in the latest levels preceding the Kimmerian destruction at Gordion. These groups appear in approximately equal quantities. As in Megaron 12 Level IVB, an unusual class with micaceous concentration, and a handmade group with incised or impressed decoration, form a tiny fraction of the total assemblage.

About one-third of the buff and orange pottery preserves red or brown slip, often partial and dull. These samples occur in shapes represented earlier in the second-millennium repertory at Gordion, with counterparts in Levels VC and IVA, clearly survivals of lower levels. A few sherds are Early Bronze residuals. The remainder is plain buff and orange pottery, dominated by gritty, wheelmarked manufacture, often fired gray at the core. Most of the shapes continue trends of Level IVB and match those of Megaron 10 Layers 5 and 4. Shallow bowls with thickened, broad rims are popular (**588-591**), plates continue (**592**; also large coarse fragment, not catalogued). A jar with everted rim (**594**) resembles examples from Megaron 10 Layers 5 and 4. Other traditional shapes are trefoil pitchers, jugs, cooking pots, pithoi (**596**), and vessels with pointed base.

Two wheelmade specimens are unusual. An everted rim from a bowl or jar (**593**) has a burnished tan surface similar to a bowl fragment in Megaron 10 Layer 4 (**390**). It also preserves a band of dark brown, glazelike slip on the inner rim, perhaps linking it to a jar rim with brown interior band from Megaron 10 Layer 8 (**271**). A coarse shallow bowl (**585**) is distinguished by a heavy concentration of "silver" mica in the biscuit, pointing to close ties with examples isolated in the descriptions of Megaron 10 Layers 6-4 in chapter III.

Handmade pottery, tan or dark-fired with incised or plastic decoration, appears in a very small quantity (Pl. 32). As noted above, a few Level IVA samples of this ware joined vessel fragments of Level IVB, indicating some mixing of the deposits.

---

6. G.K. Sams also discusses the excavation and stratigraphy of the Early Phrygian Building in *Gordion* IV.

Summary

Available quantities of pottery from Early Iron Age levels below Megaron 10 and Megaron 12 are very small and result for the most part from unspecified selection procedures. Moreover, detailed analysis of the assemblage from each level depends on the forthcoming comprehensive publication of Iron Age categories and their relative chronology at Gordion. Consequently, examination of the Bronze Age pottery in relation to ceramic developments traced in preceding levels of the deep soundings is confined to a few observations.

Among the groups described in this chapter, the general impression is one of close continuity with Late Bronze Age and Transitional ceramic developments. The available collections, while small and selective, consist almost exclusively of Late Bronze and Early Iron Age pottery. The absence of Bronze Age sherds reflecting a wide chronological range contrasts with at least some of the Early Iron Age fill deposits, such as Early Phrygian Building Level V, which contained examples from Early Bronze through Early Iron Age. Megaron 10 Layers 3 and 2 produced no such obviously mixed deposits. Whether they represent telescoped deposits of Early Iron Age accumulation will be judged by the Phrygian experts on the basis of the Early Iron Age pottery.

Megaron 10 Layer 3 closely resembles in ceramic groups and individual shapes the material from layers immediately preceding it. The dominant Late Bronze Age buff and orange gritty wares appear in shapes popular in Layer 4, especially shallow bowls and plates. Remaining groups also refer to recent developments within the Megaron 10 sequence. A wheelmade group distinguished by micaceous surface concentration, attested in Layers 6 through 4, continues in very small quantities. Handmade pottery of the type introduced in Layer 4 is again represented, as is Phrygian gray ware. Layer 2 is scarcely known, but the same groups and characteristic shapes are present. With Megaron 10 Layer 1, previously unknown variations are introduced, mostly on buff-slipped jars and bowls. Some of these novel forms also appear in Layers 2 and 1 of the Main Room of Megaron 10. This situation could reflect continued production and development of the Late Bronze Age ceramic tradition. The variety of ceramic groups observed in Early Iron Age levels supports the picture suggested by Late Bronze and Transitional assemblages, that these eras brought to Gordion new pottery styles external to the Hittite tradition and that they continued to be produced in the Early Iron Age.

A few specific shapes or features appear only in the Transitional or Early Iron Age levels and may afford links among ceramic developments in the various soundings. First is a tan-slipped bowl with indented profile, found in Megaron 10 Layer 4 (**390**) and in Main Room Layer 1 (**578**). A relative with shallower proportions occurs in Megaron 10 Layer 2 (**545**), Main Room Layers 2 (**569**) and 1 (**577**) and Megaron 12 Level IVA (**585**). In tan- or red-slipped pottery with micaceous surface concentration—first attested in Layer 6—is a carinated bowl common to Megaron 10 Layer 1 (**553**) and Early Phrygian Building Level I (**582**), which has a close counterpart in an example of handmade, brown-slipped pottery from Layer 3.[7] Such ties between Late Bronze or Transitional levels and those of the Early Iron Age again hint at continuity of ceramic production at Gordion. Some shapes whose Late Bronze origin is known from other sites, such as the flask with central rib, are thus far preserved at Gordion only in the Early Iron Age levels (**584**; fragment in Megaron 10 Layer 1, not catalogued).

As with the other correlations enumerated above, only further exposure of the Iron Age levels can help to settle the question of stratigraphic, cultural, or ceramic continuity between the Late Bronze and Early Iron Age levels at Gordion. Coexistence of Hittites and Phrygians is surely critical to the notion that Early Iron Age pottery of handmade manufacture developed into wheelmade gray wares primarily as a result of close contact with local potters working in Late Bronze Age traditions.[8] Other categories of evidence, such as a sherd incised with both a Bronze Age graffito and a Phrygian graffito, imply an overlap of cultural practices.[9] At the least, the available material encourages optimism that pertinent levels exist at the site, renewed investigation of which might help to illuminate a dark period of Anatolian history.

---

7. P 5733.

8. G.K. Sams will elaborate this hypothesis in *Gordion* IV. The appearance of buff micaceous pottery in the latest Bronze Age, Transitional, and Early Iron Age levels suggests a different interpretation. If the regional home of the group lies in northwestern and western Anatolia, as survey data imply, its presence at Gordion could reflect contact with this area, where wheelmade gray pottery formed a long and dominant tradition throughout the second millennium B.C. Perhaps the primitive handmade pottery belongs to southeastern European cultures without ethnic ties to Phrygians. The characteristic Phrygian gray pottery may prove to be fully understood with reference to western Anatolian gray wares of the second millennium. Publications of known stratified collections of this pottery should provide a basis for comparisons with Early Phrygian ceramic developments.

9. *Gordion Special Studies* I, 53, 73, 1A-4 and 2B-172.

Catalogue of the Bronze Age Pottery from Early Iron Age Levels

City Mound (534-596)

MEGARON 10 ANTEROOM (534-568)

LAYER 3   (534-544)

BOWLS (534-538)

534   Shallow bowl
Not inv.   Layer 3
Est. D. rim 0.23; Th. 0.0067
Fig. 25
Rim sherd of shallow bowl with tapered rim. Faint discoloration on interior.
Pale orange clay, gritty, fired lighter at surfaces. Both surfaces seem to be covered with thin buff slip, matt and almost white. Thin orange streaks on exterior may be traces of painted red bands.

535   Bowl
Not inv.   Layer 3
D. rim 0.27; Th. 0.0065 m.
Fig. 25
Rim sherd of relatively shallow bowl, with thickened incurved rim. Partly grayed on interior.
Pale brown clay, somewhat gritty. Interior smoothed; exterior somewhat roughly finished, wheelmarked.

536   Bowl
Not inv.   Layer 3
Est. D. rim 0.17; GTh. 0.002 m.
Fig. 25
Rim sherd of shallow bowl with plain rim. Traces of gray incrustation on surfaces.
Orange clay, fine and clean; well fired. Surfaces fired tan; smoothed.

537   Bowl
Not inv.   Layer 3
Est. D. rim 0.30 m; GTh. 0.007 m.
Fig. 25
Rim sherd of shallow bowl with angled rim. Rim chipped; unevenly grayed over most of sherd from secondary firing.
Orange at core, buff at surfaces, relatively clean; surfaces wheelmarked.

538   Bowl
Not inv.   Layer 3
Est. D. rim 0.24; GTh. 0.0064 m.
Fig. 25
Rim sherd of small carinated bowl with thickened rim rounded across top. Worn; slip flaking off rim; some thin incrustation. Shallow horizontal groove on exterior just above carination.
Buff clay, grit- and vegetal-tempered; well fired. Reddish brown slip on both surfaces; dull and matt but evenly applied.

PLATES (539 and 540)

539   Plate
Not inv.   Layer 3
Est. D. rim 0.22; GTh. 0.006 m.
Fig. 25

Rim sherd of plate with slightly thickened rim. Some thin incrustation on upper surface.
Dark orange clay, gritty, well fired. Surfaces plain, strongly wheelmarked.

540   Plate
Not inv.   Layer 3
D. rim unknown; GTh. 0.0124 m.
Fig. 25
Rim sherd of large plate with vertical rim. Some incrustation on both surfaces and broken edges.
Orange clay, gritty; seems to be well fired. Rim and wide band on both surfaces covered with matt red slip or paint. Neatly applied on exterior. Interior has additional painted decoration, or carelessly applied area, below band. Rest of vessel plain.

JARS (541-543)

541   Jar
Not inv.   Layer 3
Est. D. rim 0.37; GTh. 0.007 m.
Fig. 25
Rim sherd of jar with wide, ledged rim. Some incrustation on surfaces and broken edges.
Dark orange clay, coarse and gritty. Surfaces plain, heavily wheelmarked.

542   Jar
Not inv.   Layer 3
D. rim unknown; GTh. 0.0057 m.
Fig. 25
Rim sherd of small jar with everted rim. Rim chipped, worn; blackened on rim and exterior from secondary burning. Most of interior missing.
Orange-tan clay, somewhat gritty; micaceous concentration on slipped area. Rim and exterior covered with red slip, smoothed but not lustrous. Slip continues to top of rim; interior apparently left plain.

543   Jar
Not inv.   Layer 3
Est. D. rim 0.44; GTh. 0.0145 m.
Fig. 25
Rim sherd of large jar with everted rim. Rim chipped; some incrustation on all surfaces. Trace of handle scar preserved on body below outer rim, indicating vessel had vertical handles at shoulder.
Dark orange clay, gritty but not coarse; heavy, dense fabric. Fired pale orange at surfaces. Interior plain, wheelmarked; exterior partly smoothed of wheelmarks.

COOKING POT (544)

544   Cooking pot
Not inv.   Layer 3
Est. D. rim 0.20; GTh. 0.0095 m.
Fig. 25
Rim section of cooking pot mended from two joining sherds. Rim chipped; blackened on exterior; surfaces thinly

incrusted with gray. Vessel with steep walls, narrowing gradually towards thickened rim.

Orange-brown clay, coarse and very gritty; seems well fired. Surfaces plain, wheelmarked.

LAYER 2 (545-550)

BOWLS (545-547)

545 Bowl
Not inv. Layer 2
Est. D. rim 0.34; GTh. 0.0095 m.
Fig. 25
Rim sherd of large bowl with shallow groove below exterior rim. Traces of incrustation; blackened on upper interior and most of exterior.

Orange clay, very coarse and gritty; heavily micaceous, so that a concentration of "silver" mica is visible on interior surface. Surfaces plain; exterior seems to be smoothed of wheelmarks.

546 Bowl
Not inv. Layer 2
Est. D. rim 0.22; GTh. 0.0068 m.
Fig. 25
Rim sherd of bowl with broad rim. Some gray incrustation on interior; rim slightly worn. Interior uneven.
Orange clay, gritty. Surfaces plain, heavily wheelmarked.

547 Shallow bowl
Not inv. Layer 2
Est. D. rim 0.28; GTh. 0.0172 m.
Fig. 25
Rim sherd of shallow bowl with broad rim. Rim chipped; some gray incrustation on exterior.
Orange clay, gritty. Exterior apparently plain, wheelmarked. Rim and interior covered with buff slip, matt and dull. Surfaces smoothed.

PLATE (548)

548 Plate
Not inv. Layer 2
Est. D. rim 0.35; GTh. 0.0095 m.
Fig. 25
Rim sherd of plate with slightly overhung rim. Some thin incrustation on surfaces.
Orange clay, gritty; fired pale orange at surfaces. Plain, wheelmarked. Rim and interior partly smoothed, perhaps from wear.

JAR (549)

549 Jar
Not inv. Layer 2
Est. D. rim 0.32; Th. rim 0.0255; GTh. 0.01 m.
Fig. 25
Rim sherd of jar with everted rim. Rim slightly chipped and very worn; some incrustation on exterior. Grayed area on interior, from secondary heating.
Orange clay, coarse and gritty; surfaces pitted from gritty inclusions fired out. Surfaces plain, wheelmarked.

JUG (550)

550 Jug
Not inv. Layer 2

Est. D. rim 0.10; Th. at rim 0.0135; Th. wall 0.009 m.
Fig. 25
Rim sherd of jug. Rim chipped; surfaces and edges slightly incrusted.
Orange clay, gritty, with a few flecks of "gold" mica; well fired. Rim and exterior perhaps covered with thin clay wash. Surfaces heavily wheelmarked; interior somewhat roughly finished.

LAYER 1 (551-568)

BOWLS (551-558)

551 Bowl
Not inv. Layer 1
Est. D. rim 0.22; GTh. 0.0085 m.
Fig. 25
Rim sherd of bowl with thickened rim, shallow but palpable indentation on exterior below rim. Some incrustation on exterior.
Tan-orange clay, relatively clean; well fired. Interior plain, wheelmarked. Exterior covered with "self-slip," partly smoothed; burnish marks visible.

552 Bowl
Not inv. Layer 1
Est. D. rim 0.30; GTh. 0.0095 m.
Fig. 25
Rim sherd of shallow bowl with plain rim, shallow indentation on exterior below rim. All surfaces somewhat incrusted.
Tan-orange clay, with some gritty inclusions. Buff slip, rather hastily and unevenly applied, on both surfaces; mostly smoothed of wheelmarks.

553 Bowl
Not inv. Layer 1
D. rim unknown; GTh. 0.0087 m.
Fig. 26
Rim sherd of carinated bowl with slightly outturned rim. Both surfaces chipped, somewhat pitted; very worn.
Orange clay, gritty; heavily micaceous, with concentration of "silver" mica visible on both surfaces. Interior plain, smoothed of wheelmarks; exterior covered with "self-slip," smoothed.

554 Bowl?
Not inv. Layer 1
Est. D. rim 0.30; GTh. 0.0055 m.
Fig. 26
Rim sherd of relatively shallow vessel, perhaps bowl, with ledged rim; plastic bulge on rim exterior. Rim chipped; thin incrustation on all surfaces.
Orange clay, gritty. Opaque buff slip, heavily wheelmarked, on all surfaces.

555 Shallow bowl
Not inv. Layer 1
D. rim unknown; GTh. 0.008 m.
Fig. 26
Rim sherd of shallow bowl with thickened rim; plastic bulge on rim exterior. Rim worn. Faint blackening and traces of incrustation; interior pitted from firing out of grits.
Dark orange clay, very gritty; with some "gold" mica. Surfaces plain.

556 Shallow bowl
Not inv. Layer 1
Est. D. 0.40; Th. rim 0.0362; GTh. 0.0122 m.
Fig. 26

Rim sherd of large shallow bowl with broad, overhung rim. Surfaces discolored green; area under rim heavily incrusted.

Pinkish tan clay, fairly clean, with much "silver" mica; dense, heavy fabric. Surfaces plain, smooth; interior wheel-marked, exterior and rim mostly smoothed of wheelmarks.

557   Shallow bowl
Not inv.   Layer 1
Est. D. rim 0.28; GTh. 0.0095 m.
Fig. 26
Rim sherd of shallow bowl with broad, slightly overhung rim. Surfaces generally grayed; exterior thinly incrusted.

Buff clay, coarse, with flecks of "gold" mica visible on surfaces. Rim and interior partly smoothed, apparently with "self-slip." Exterior rough and wheelmarked.

558   Shallow bowl
Not inv.   Layer 1
Est. D. rim 0.30; GTh. 0.0077 m.
Fig. 26
Rim sherd of shallow bowl with slightly thickened rim. Blackened on both surfaces.

Orange clay, slightly gritty. Surfaces plain, wheelmarked.

PLATES   (559-561)

559   Plate
Not inv.   Layer 1
Est. D. rim 0.25; GTh. 0.0095 m.
Fig. 26
Rim sherd of plate with thickened rim. Faintly blackened on exterior; traces of incrustation.

Orange clay, gritty; well fired. Surfaces plain; wheelmarked, especially exterior.

560   Plate
Not inv.   Layer 1
Est. D. rim 0.30; GTh. 0.0062 m.
Fig. 26
Rim sherd of plate with barely thickened rim.

Orange clay, gritty; fired tan on rim and interior. Surfaces plain; wheelmarked.

561   Plate
Not inv.   Layer 1
Est. D. rim 0.48; GTh. 0.0065 m.
Fig. 26
Rim sherd of large plate with broad, overhung rim. Rim chipped; surfaces worn and pitted; thinly incrusted.

Orange clay, gritty, with some "gold" mica. Surfaces covered with dull, opaque buff slip. Wheelmarks partly visible.

JARS   (562 and 563)

562   Jar
Not inv.   Layer 1
D. rim unknown; GTh. 0.0145 m.
Fig. 26
Rim sherd of jar with everted rim; plastic bulge on exterior below rim. Interior partly blackened; rim chipped; sherd worn.

Orange clay, partly gritty, with traces of "silver" mica. Surfaces plain.

563   Jar
Not inv.   Layer 1
D. rim unknown; GTh. 0.009 m.
Fig. 26

Rim sherd of small jar with protruding horizontal ridge below outer rim. Handle scar below ridge indicates vertical handle. Ridge mostly chipped.

Orange clay, relatively clean; well fired. Dull buff slip on all surfaces, carelessly wiped on interior. Interior heavily wheelmarked.

Below, **573**.

PITHOS (564)

564   Pithos rim
Not inv.   Layer 1
D. rim unknown; Th. rim 0.024 m.
Fig. 26
Rim sherd of pithos with wide, everted rim slightly raised at upper edge. Rim damaged; broken unevenly from vessel wall. Some thin blackened areas on both surfaces of rim; sherd worn.

Orange clay, gritty and coarse; interior now gray. Surfaces plain. Exterior wheelmarked; upper surface smoothed of wheelmarks, probably through wear.

JUGS (565-567)

565   Jug
Not inv.   Layer 1
D. rim 0.09; GTh. 0.0065 m.
Fig. 26
Rim sherd, perhaps from jug with slightly everted rim flattened across top. Rim chipped; traces of incrustation. Surfaces slightly pitted from firing out of grits.

Orange clay, gritty; well fired. Surfaces possibly coated with thin clay wash; wheelmarked.

566   Jug
Not inv.   Layer 1
Est. D. rim 0.08; GTh. 0.0079 m.
Fig. 26
Rim sherd of narrow-necked jug with thickened rim. Rim chipped; sherd slightly discolored and incrusted.

Orange clay, gritty. Surfaces plain. Rim and exterior worn or smoothed of wheelmarks; interior plain, wheelmarked.

567   Jug
Not inv.   Layer 1
Est. D. rim 0.09; GTh. 0.007 m.
Fig. 26
Rim sherd of jug with thickened rim. *Circa* one-third of rim circumference preserved. Part of handle scar, from vertical handle, preserved on neck just below rim. Interior partly discolored.

Red clay, gritty. Reddish brown slip on rim and exterior, continuing just inside rim; well smoothed and polished, originally lustrous.

BASE (568)

568   Ring base
Not inv.   Layer 1
Est. D. base 0.13; GTh. 0.0107 m.
Fig. 26
Fragment of large ring base, probably from jar. Broken above base and on base interior. Worn; some gray and green discoloration.

Orange clay, somewhat gritty; fired buff at surfaces. Plain, worn on all surfaces.

MEGARON 10 MAIN ROOM (569-581)

LAYER 2   (569-576)

BOWLS (569-572)

569   Bowl
Not inv.   Main Room, Layer 2
Est. D. rim 0.25; GTh. 0.0095 m.
Fig. 26
　　Rim sherd of shallow bowl with horizontal groove creating indented profile below outer rim. Very worn; some blackening on both surfaces.
　　Orange clay, gritty, with much "silver" mica. Surfaces seem to be covered with "self-slip," smoothed more on exterior than interior. Probably wheelmade, but primitive in appearance.

570   Shallow bowl
Not inv.   Main Room, Layer 2
Est. D. rim 0.28; GTh. 0.007 m.
Fig. 26
　　Rim sherd of shallow bowl with broad, overhung rim. Traces of blackening on both surfaces. Worn on rim and interior, rim chipped.
　　Orange clay, gritty and coarse. Surfaces covered with thin buff slip, wheelmarked.

571   Shallow bowl
Not inv.   Main Room, Layer 2
Est. D. rim 0.22; GTh. 0.007 m.
Fig. 26
　　Rim sherd of relatively shallow bowl with thickened rim. Worn; surfaces pitted.
　　Buff clay, gritty. Surfaces plain.

572   Bowl or jar
Not inv.   Main Room, Layer 2
D. rim unknown; GTh. 0.0075 m.
Fig. 26
　　Rim sherd of vessel with thickened rim, probably bowl but possibly jar or teapot. Base of sherd on interior preserves beginning of carination. Worn and scratched; traces of burning at edge of sherd.
　　Tan clay, gritty. Light brown slip on both surfaces, well smoothed. Burnish marks visible but not lustrous.

JARS (573-575)

573   Jar
Not inv.   Main Room, Layer 2
Est. D. rim 0.21; GTh. 0.008 m.
Fig. 26
　　Rim sherd of small jar with horizontal ridge on exterior below rim. Thin film of gray and black incrustation on both surfaces.
　　Pale orange clay, somewhat gritty but relatively clean. Buff slip on both surfaces, wiped in careless fashion and heavily wheelmarked.
　　Above, **563**.

574   Jar
Not inv.   Main Room, Layer 2
Est. D. rim 0.20; GTh. 0.011 m.
Fig. 26
　　Rim sherd of jar with flaring shoulder, wide sloping rim, shallow lid-rest on interior. Burned over most of interior; core blackened.
　　Tan-brown clay, gritty, with much black and "silver" mica. Surfaces plain, wheelmarked.

575   Jar
Not inv.   Main Room, Layer 2
Est. D. rim 0.33; GTh. 0.008 m.
Fig. 26
　　Rim sherd of jar with everted rim.
　　Orange-brown clay, gritty. Surfaces plain.

JUG? (576)

576   Jug
Not inv.   Main Room, Layer 2
Est. D. rim 0.18; GTh. 0.0055 m.
Fig. 26
　　Rim sherd of vessel with everted, thickened rim; perhaps jug with wide mouth. Worn and thinly incrusted. Surfaces slightly pitted.
　　Orange clay, very coarse and gritty. Buff slip on all surfaces, mostly smoothed or worn of wheelmarks.

LAYER 1   (577-581)

BOWLS (577-579)

577   Bowl
Not inv.   Main Room, Layer 1
Est. D. rim 0.32; GTh. 0.011 m.
Fig. 26
　　Rim sherd of large bowl with outer profile indented below flattened rim. Some incrustation on both surfaces; pitted from firing out of gritty inclusions on surfaces.
　　Tan clay, somewhat gritty; well fired. Interior and exterior to below indentation, heavily wheelmarked; rest of exterior smoothed, perhaps with "self-slip."

578   Bowl
Not inv.   Main Room, Layer 1
D. rim unknown; GTh. 0.013 m.
Fig. 27
　　Rim sherd of large bowl with outer profile slightly indented below flattened rim. Some blackening on both surfaces, especially exterior; blackened partly through core. Surfaces scratched, very worn; interior crumbling; some pitting.
　　Brown clay, coarse and very gritty. Orange-tan slip on both surfaces, well smoothed and matt.

579   Carinated bowl
Not inv.   Main Room, Layer 1
D. rim unknown; GTh. 0.0095 m.
Fig. 27
　　Rim sherd of carinated bowl with rim rounded across top. Rim chipped, sherd worn. Some blackening on both surfaces.
　　Pale orange clay, gritty and rather coarse. Thick buff slip on both surfaces, covering wheelmarks.

JARS (580 and 581)

580   Jar
Not inv.   Main Room, Layer 1
Est. D. rim 0.22; GTh. 0.0045 m.
Fig. 27
　　Rim sherd of small jar with narrowing shoulder; thickened, slightly everted rim. Rim worn, partly blackened.
　　Orange clay, gritty. Surfaces plain, wheelmarked.

581   Jar
Not inv.   Main Room, Layer 1
D. rim unknown; GTh. 0.0125 m.
Fig. 27

Rim sherd of jar of hole-mouth shape, plain rim. Surfaces pitted, worn.

Orange clay, gritty and very coarse. Surfaces plain, wheel-marked.

EARLY PHRYGIAN BUILDING (582-584)

LEVEL I   (582-583)

BOWL (582)

582   Carinated bowl
Not inv.   Level I
Est. D. rim 0.23; GTh. 0.008 m.
Fig. 27
Rim section of gently carinated bowl, mended from three joining sherds. Rim chipped; some pitting and incrustation on both surfaces.

Orange-tan clay, somewhat micaceous, with some gritty inclusions but generally clean, good fabric; well fired. Both surfaces are covered with dark red-brown slip, applied somewhat unevenly especially on interior; well smoothed, matt.

JAR (583)

583   Jar
Not inv.   Level I
Est. D. rim. 0.26; GTh. 0.016 m.
Fig. 27
Rim sherd of jar with thickened rim. Faint blackening, some incrustation on interior. Blackened area on exterior below rim may be residue of painted decoration. Steep-sided vessel, narrowing towards neck.

Orange clay, with much "silver" mica visible on surfaces; good, clean fabric. Rim and exterior covered with light brown slip, well smoothed. Interior below rim plain, wheelmarked.

LEVEL V (584)

FLASK (584)

584   Flask
Not inv.   Level V
Max. D. 0.24; GPW. 0.09; Th. 0.0072 m.
Fig. 27
Fragment broken on all sides, irregularly across top. Surfaces slightly incrusted, rib chipped. From lentoid flask with central rib along circumference of body.

Orange clay, gritty; well fired. Exterior covered with good cream-white slip, very well smoothed but not lustrous. Interior plain, wheelmarked.

MEGARON 12 (585-596)

LEVEL IVA   (585-596)

BOWLS (585-591)

585   Shallow bowl
Not inv.   Level IVA
D. rim unknown; GTh. 0.0095 m.
Fig. 27

Rim sherd of shallow bowl or plate, with outer profile indented below broad rim. Worn, some grayish discoloration on exterior.

Dark orange clay, gritty, with noticeable "silver" mica. Both surfaces covered with thin, dull matt slip, probably tan; now mostly worn or flaked off. "Silver" mica concentration on surfaces.

586   Shallow bowl
Not inv.   Level IVA
Est. D. rim 0.24; GTh. 0.0059 m.
Fig. 27
Rim sherd of shallow bowl with plain rim. Rim chipped; some traces of incrustation on interior; sherd worn.

Orange clay, gritty. Interior and outer rim covered with thin red slip applied unevenly in bands; dull, matt finish. Rest of exterior plain.

587   Bowl
Not inv.   Level IVA
Est. D. rim. 0.21; GTh. 0.0062 m.
Fig. 27
Rim sherd of relatively shallow bowl with tapered rim. Surfaces worn, slightly discolored, scratched.

Buff-orange clay, gritty; fired very pale buff at surfaces. Plain; wheelmarks mostly worn or smoothed on both surfaces.

588   Shallow bowl
Not inv.   Level IVA
Est. D. rim 0.24; GTh. 0.0075 m.
Fig. 27
Rim sherd of shallow bowl with slightly thickened rim. Interior partly cracked and pitted.

Orange clay, very gritty. Both surfaces covered with thin "self-slip," fired tan on exterior surface and buff on interior.

589   Shallow bowl
Not inv.   Level IVA
Est. D. rim 0.25; GTh. 0.007 m.
Fig. 27
Rim sherd of shallow bowl with broad, overhung rim. Surfaces pitted and faintly discolored.

Orange clay, gritty. Surfaces plain, wheelmarked.

590   Shallow bowl
Not inv.   Level IVA
Est. D. rim 0.26; GTh. 0.01 m.
Fig. 27
Rim sherd of shallow bowl with broad rim. Interior grayed; some faint blackening on rim.

Dark orange clay, gritty. Both surfaces apparently covered with very thin "self-slip," through which wheelmarks are clearly visible.

591   Shallow bowl
Not inv.   Level IVA
Est. D. rim 0.31; GTh. 0.008 m.
Fig. 27
Rim sherd of large shallow bowl with broad rim. Faintly blackened on part of exterior and broken edges.

Orange clay, very gritty. Surfaces covered with very thin "self-slip," fired orange-buff.

PLATE (592)

592   Plate
Not inv.   Level IVA
Est. D. rim 0.40; GTh. 0.019 m.
Fig. 27

Rim sherd of large plate. Some blackening on interior surfaces, trace on exterior.

Light brown clay, gritty, with a few flecks of "gold" mica. Surfaces plain, heavily wheelmarked.

JARS (593-595)

593 Jar
Not inv. Level IVA
Est. D. rim 0.36; GTh. 0.015 m.
Fig. 27

Rim sherd of jar with everted, slightly thickened rim. Interior slightly pitted and damaged; slip very worn.

Light brown clay, very gritty; fired grayish at core. Surfaces covered with finer tan coating; on exterior, surface slipped, polished and slightly lustrous. Along flat area of interior rim is a band of dark brown slip, of glazelike appearance.

594 Jar
Not inv. Level IVA
Est. D. rim 0.28; GTh. 0.008 m.
Not ill.

Rim sherd of jar with narrowing shoulder, strongly everted rim. Rim chipped; interior much discolored.

Dark orange clay, very gritty and coarse, with some large inclusions. Surfaces covered with very thin "self-slip," heavily wheelmarked; fired orange on interior surface, buff on exterior.

595 Jar
Not inv. Level IVA
D. rim unknown; GTh. 0.0152 m.
Fig. 27

Rim sherd of jar with steep sides, sharply everted rim with shallow depression on inside.

Dark orange clay, very gritty, with a few large inclusions. Surfaces apparently plain, wheelmarked.

PITHOS (596)

596 Pithos
Not inv. Level IVA
Est. D. rim 0.50; GTh. 0.019 m.
Fig. 27

Rim sherd of pithos with everted rim, faintly but palpably uneven on upper surface. Rim chipped.

Orange clay, very gritty. Surfaces covered with thin clay coating; strongly wheelmarked.

V

Conclusions

The preceding chapters have presented the evidence recovered to date for Bronze Age occupation at Gordion, focusing on the ceramic assemblages retrieved from soundings on the City Mound. Since the pre-Phrygian levels have been tested only in limited excavations, the available sample allows for only tentative observations about the character of the settlement and its cultural affiliations. Nevertheless, some general remarks can be set forth, to be expanded and refined as future investigations contribute additional information.

Gordion provides an important, stratified sequence of Bronze Age material from the western region of the central Anatolian plateau. The nearest site with an excavated sequence of similar duration, Boğazköy-Hattuša, lies some 450 km. to the northeast. This site furnishes dated, stratified material with which to compare the Gordion pottery, although the ceramic record at the Hittite capital may be expected to differ from that of west central Anatolia. Similarities and differences may help to define the relation of the capital to sites in its domain as well as to its provincial neighbors. Gordion should serve therefore as a link between the Hittite heartland in north central Anatolia and regions farther to the southwest, an area thus far outside the reach of Near Eastern or Egyptian absolute chronologies supplied by Anatolian or Aegean synchronisms. Pre-Phrygian Gordion thus constitutes a critical source for connecting the Bronze Age archaeology of western Anatolia with historical developments farther east and for gauging chronological as well as cultural relationships.

Gordion and Anatolian Chronology

Investigations into pre-Phrygian occupation at Gordion contribute new information for Anatolian chronology based on ceramic sequences. The earliest prehistoric remains from the site belong to the Early Bronze I period. This evidence is thus far confined to pottery recovered from two burials underneath tumuli of Phrygian date, F and H, for which no corresponding strata on the City Mound have yet been identified. Nevertheless, these burials indicate an Early Bronze I occupation in west central Anatolia, where the earliest settlements known hitherto, at Polatlı and Asarcık Hüyük, date to Early Bronze II.

Defined habitation levels as presently known at Gordion begin with Early Bronze IIIa or the very end of Early Bronze II as documented in Megaron 12 Level VI, PN-3 Levels 10-8 and some material from associated pits. In this period affinities with nearby west central Anatolian sites, especially Polatlı and Asarcık Hüyük, are clear. Contacts with areas farther afield are few; but Gordion is in touch with ceramic developments shared by sites in the southwest, such as Beycesultan and Aphrodisias. During the following Early Bronze IIIb phase, represented by material from part of Megaron 12 Level VI, PN-3 Level 7 and Pits H and I, close ties continue with the Polatlı area. Gordion also shows connections with the Ankara district sites of Ahlatlıbel and Etiyokuşu. Closer relations with the Çorum region begin to develop with objects comparable to Nordwesthang-Büyükkale Level 9 and Alaca material of uncertain stratification. Ceramic links with Beycesultan VIa, independently dated to Early Bronze IIIb via Cilician and Trojan synchronisms, furnish important confirmation of this scheme.

It is difficult to define the end of the Early Bronze and the beginning of the Middle Bronze occupation at Gordion because the stratification in the different soundings at precisely this juncture is unclear. The earliest excavated layers under Megaron 10 (Layers 18-15) are Middle Bronze and must follow closely upon an Early Bronze IIIa-b occupation as revealed by residual sherds in Layers 18-15. The initial Middle Bronze deposit is linked ceramically to Polatlı Phases III and IV, Asarcık Va, and Boğazköy Nordwesthang-Büyükkale 8d-8c. The deposit of this period seems to document a sequence similar to that of the Nordwesthang-Büyükkale area at Boğazköy.

The second-millennium occupation at Gordion consists of a continuous, unbroken sequence, undisturbed by the occasional destructions that plagued the Hittite captial at Boğazköy-Hattuša, and also free of the disturbance to stratified accumulation caused by monumental constructions there. Gordion provides an important ceramic sequence for the area, where the second millennium has been known only in its initial centuries, at Polatlı, or via an incomplete record, at Asarcık. The detailed record preserved under Megaron 10, and by Megaron 12 Levels VC-IVB, now defines the ceramic development in the Sakarya region around Gordion during the second millennium, and furnishes

a source for correlations with developments at Boğazköy which are independently tied to absolute Near Eastern chronologies via Hittite cuneiform records.

Gordion, with its undisturbed accumulation, paradoxically permits a more precise definition of Hittite Empire pottery than has yet been produced from the capital. Now that the parallel development of Hittite pottery over a wide region of Anatolia has been broadly demonstrated, Gordion's detailed sequence should assist in cases of doubtful stratification or other uncertainty in establishing a more refined relative chronology. Examples include the unstratified Late Bronze Age material from Asarcık Hüyük, which can be assigned to the late Old Kingdom or early Empire. Similarly, the sequences at Mersin and Porsuk can very likely be more confidently placed with the combined aid of Gordion and Tarsus.

Gordion and Anatolian History

Gordion's contribution to Anatolian history consists in the documentation it provides for general Bronze Age occupation and ceramic development, furnishing a detailed source for local developments as well as for assessing relations with other geographical regions. In its early history Gordion follows a career similar to that of other Anatolian sites in its vicinity. The Early Bronze remains suggest a modest settlement with sturdy but unpretentious architecture. Associated pottery supports the impression of a well defined, distinctive west central Anatolian ceramic style. The Early Bronze IIIb settlement seems to end in a burned layer, traced over Megaron 12 Level VI and perhaps over PN-3 Level 7. A like catastrophe occurred at nearby Polatlı, manifested in the burned layer ending Level XV, indicating a destruction at both sites.[1] New ceramic practices, including the general use of wheelmade red-slipped pottery, appear to signal the introduction of different cultural elements after this destruction.

By contrast, Gordion's second-millennium history is remarkable for its apparent unbroken record of gradual growth and slow change, undisturbed by the occasional misfortunes that befell neighbors near and far. This sequence, as yet only tentative because of the limited investigations conducted to date, indicates Gordion's potential for elucidating this long period of Anatolian development. The successful elaboration of

this sequence in the future will provide one of Gordion's major contributions to Bronze Age history.

In a section of the 1956 publication of the Hittite Cemetery at Gordion, M.J. Mellink discussed the archaeological application of the term "Hittite" to the second-millennium necropolis at the site, noting that the continuity between Middle and Late Bronze Age cultural remains in central Anatolia justified the use of a common label to classify them. She also cautioned that this designation does not necessarily coincide with linguistic or political applications of the term and that the apparent similarity and continuity could prove misleading.[2] The pottery and artifacts recovered from the City Mound at Gordion are called "Hittite" in recognition of their archaeological kinship with products of central Anatolian sites displaying proper linguistic and political credentials. Gordion's ceramic testimony of continuity throughout the second millennium, together with evidence of Hittite hieroglyphic seal impressions and graffiti, are pertinent to the history of west central Anatolia during the period dominated by the Hittite Old Kingdom and Empire.

By the early centuries of the second millennium B.C., Gordion's ceramic repertory draws increasingly on the Çorum region of central Anatolia. In this period Gordion and neighboring sites adopt the wheelmade, red-slipped and burnished "Hittite" pottery, first repre-

1. J. Mellaart, *CAH* I:2, rev. ed. (Cambridge 1972), ch. XXIV(a), 703, with additional references.

2. *Hitt. Cem.*, 51-55.

sented in Layers 18-15 under Megaron 10. A conservative orientation emerges as Gordion selects only the more sedate fashions: bowls with bead-rim and horizontal handles, beak-spouted pitchers with carinated profile, and other shapes—all with lustrous but simple red or brown surface finish. More exotic or luxurious innovations represented at Boğazköy, such as painted "Cappadocian" ware, and sophisticated shapes and decoration, are absent from Gordion. Syrian exotica acquired farther east produce an echo in certain shapes, but actual imports are barely represented. Further exposure of these levels, known at present only from the highly restricted sample under Megaron 10, might alter this impression. Yet a similar conservatism is manifested in the contemporary settlements tested at Asarcık Hüyük and Polatlı. Here too the ceramic repertory lacks ostentatious or overtly foreign fashions. An explanation might be sought in local conservatism or traditional independence, or may involve precise commercial or political circumstances. The western plateau region seems not to have participated directly in the international commercial network of the Old Assyrian Colony Period linking central and southeastern Anatolia with Assyria and Northern Syria. Without such organized, sustained exchange, only a trickle of central Anatolian sophistication reached the region west of the Kızıl Irmak. Yet since contact with the Çorum district is unmistakable, Gordion perhaps rated occasional or associate status in trading partnerships or political alliances.

The disasters that brought an end to the Old Assyrian Colony Period settlements at Boğazköy and Kültepe find no counterpart at Gordion. Instead, there is an unbroken development in ceramic evidence and in burial customs, as shown by the fact that the Old Assyrian Colony Period burials in the Hittite Cemetery are succeeded by burials of the same type in the Old Hittite period. A like continuity is reflected in the ceramic development from the phases Megaron 10 Layers 18-15 to those of Layers 14 and 13-12. At approximately this time the settlement at Polatlı is abandoned. This event suggests an archaeological dimension to the investigation of Hittite administration, perhaps reflecting the consolidation or agglomeration of nearby settlements. The occupation at Gordion, together with that at Asarcık to the northeast, represents the Old Hittite period in this region.

In the final phase of the Middle Bronze Age, towards the middle of the second millennium, Gordion appears to lie on the western frontier of the Hittite Old Kingdom ruled from the capital at Boğazköy-Hattuša. Hittite records suggest that the plateau west of Ankara may already have been under Hittite control in the time of Hattušili I, since the area known as Zawiya (Arzawa), including the cities Šallapa and Parduwata, was lost to the empire during the reign of the later Old Hittite ruler Ammuna.[3] This information may specifically involve the Gordion region, as other documents place those cities near the river Sehiriya, often identified with the classical Sangarius (modern Sakarya), and situated on the road to Arzawa.[4] At present, Hittite political geography is too uncertain in the areas under consideration to yield any firm basis for historical reconstruction.

Here archaeological sources from Gordion and neighboring sites come to the aid of the historian. Both epigraphical and archaeological finds substantiate a close association between the area of Gordion and Boğazköy in Old Hittite times, supplementing the limited historical evidence now available. Ties with the capital at Boğazköy have already been extended to sites in the Ankara region, notably Inandık and Bitik. A land deed from Inandık, northwest of Ankara, supplies further evidence for such interaction during the reign of Hattušili I. This tablet, written in Akkadian, bears an impression of a "Seal of the Tabarna" dated to the reign of this king.[5] Inandık and Bitik have yielded polychrome relief vases of the style known from Hattuša and other sites in its vicinity.[6] From Bitik are also Old Hittite seals.[7] Finds from Gordion demonstrate close Hittite contacts farther west as well. A clay bulla bearing hieroglyphic signs of Old Hittite form proves direct contact with nearby literate centers, if not with the capital. Pottery and vessel marks from Asarcık Level IV, and pottery from Gordion itself, closely resemble contemporary fashions at Boğazköy.

Yet Gordion also maintained in this period a significant degree of cultural identity with western Anatolia, apparently independent of Hittite encroachment or expansion. This is little reflected in the ceramic domain; Gordion shares a few traits with sites in the Afyon area, such as Kusura and Beycesultan, which are sparsely represented at, or altogether absent from, Boğazköy. More tellingly, the cemetery of pithos burials at Gordion preserves a western Anatolian tradition of considerable antiquity, a conservative spirit manifested also in the contemporary pithos cemetery at Yanarlar near Afyon. A frontier of some kind between the Sakarya and the Hittite heartland might account for the contemporary cemetery of cremation burials at

---

3. *CAH* II:1 (Cambridge 1975), ch. XV, 661-662.

4. Garstang and Gurney, *Geography*, 77-78; G.F. del Monte and J. Tischler, *Die Orts-und Gewässernamen der hethitischen Texte* (Wiesbaden 1978), 333, 544-545; J. Mellaart in *Festschrift Bittel*, 345-348.

5. K. Balkan, *Eine Schenkungsurkunde aus der althethitischen Zeit, gefunden in Inandık 1966* (Ankara 1973) esp. 73-77.

6. K. Bittel, *Die Hethiter* (Munich 1976).

7. H.G. Güterbock in *Young Symposium*, 52, with bibliography.

nearby Ilıca, linking at least part of the region's population to the capital, where cremation begins to be practiced in this period at the Osmankayası cemetery.

For the period of the Hittite Empire Gordion furnishes the only extensive archaeological record for west central Anatolia, since apart from unstratified Late Bronze Age finds from Asarcık Hüyük no habitation sites have been investigated. Gordion has again avoided disaster of the sort that caused the burned layer of Büyükkale IVc. At the end of the Old Kingdom or during the early Empire Asarcık and Inandık were also abandoned. Perhaps some further consolidation of Hittite settlements took place as Hittite interest in the western regions of the empire increased. Farther to the southwest, Beycesultan is abandoned, or diverted from close ties to imperial centers, without having so far yielded signs of Hittite literacy even of glyptic level.

Since the levels of this period at Gordion have only been tested in soundings, the nature of the settlement is still not known. But pottery and other finds, including vessel marks and figurines, are closely paralleled by products from contemporary levels at Boğazköy. The archaeological remains point to a close cultural relationship between these regions, one confirmed by a vessel handle from Gordion stamped with a Hittite hieroglyphic seal. At least part of the Gordion population would appear to have been capable of comprehending, if not composing, messages in this script. Such evidence implies that by this time Gordion and its vicinity were well within direct control of the capital and probably remained so throughout imperial times. The settlement at Gordion and the strongly "Hittite" character of its remains also provide a clearer context for other archaeological evidence of Hittite activity in this vicinity. The rock relief at Gâvur Kalesi near Haymana, to the southeast, and the stele retrieved from Yağri, to the southwest, can now be understood as monuments established in an area under the firm and sustained control of Hatti.[8]

Such archaeological evidence again supplements historical sources hinting at serious Hittite interest in the area. During the empire the major campaign routes from central to western Anatolia seem to have traversed the Sakarya region. Mursili II crossed the Sehiriya river during his march against Arzawa, then was joined by his brother, the king Carchemish, at the city of Šallapa already mentioned in the Old Hittite

sources discussed above. This information, together with toponymic evidence for a preclassical settlement called Spalia or Palaia near modern Sivrihisar, has suggested to some a location for Šallapa in this area.[9] The city was a cult center and apparently also an important junction of principal thoroughfares, since it figures also in the "Tawagalawa Letter," probably from the reign of Hattušili III, as the first stop after Hattuša, enroute to the Lukka Lands.[10] If Šallapa has been correctly located in this region of west central Anatolia, its presence might account in part for the Hittite interest the archaeological remains suggest. No doubt political and economic considerations also contributed to Hittite concern with the area. A more comprehensive assessment of Hittite imperial activity in west central Anatolia obviously requires additional archaeological investigation, both survey and excavation, to document the relationship of this area to well-known Hittite centers as well as to probable vassal states or independent polities. The Gordion probes serve as a start for such investigations, linking the area not only to the east but also to the southwest, as currently known from Beycesultan and Aphrodisias. Such investigations demonstrably hold enormous potential for advances in understanding of Hittite geography as well as of the political and economic history of the second millennium B.C.

Gordion also contributes information to the growing knowledge of sites in Hittite territory gained from investigations of the last twenty years, ranging from the Hittite heartland of north central Anatolia to the border with the Mitanni domains in the southeast. As the ceramic parallels with various sites imply, these investigations document a remarkable ceramic homogeneity throughout the regions under Hittite imperial domination. The nature of these similarities as well as local differences in the ceramic assemblages deserves much further study. They supply important information for defining and analyzing Hittite presence and interaction with local populations and traditions, and would contribute to an understanding of Hittite control or influence, mechanisms of ceramic production and distribution, and perhaps even to Hittite administrative practices. They provide supplemental archaeological sources to a growing number of textual studies of Hittite material culture and cultural practices.[11]

---

8. Bittel, *Die Hethiter*, (Munich 1976) 178-179, figs. 199-200; p. 201, fig. 230.

9. See references cited above, n. 4.

10. Garstang and Gurney, *Geography*, 77-78; S. Heinhold-Kramer, *Arzawa* (Heidelberg 1977), 174-178, suggests a date for the document in the reign of Muwatallis; cf. T.R. Bryce, *BibO* 36 (1979) 60-64, with additional references.

11. Recent studies, with further bibliography, include M. Popko, *Kultobjekte in der hethitischen Religion* (Warsaw 1978), 84-92; Y. Coşkun, *Boğazköy metinlerinde geçen bazı seçilme kap isimler* (Ankara 1979); H. Ertem, *Keban Project 1973 Activities* (Ankara 1979). 39-41. For the general subject of Hittite archaeological and textual studies, R. Lebrun, in *Archéologie et religions de l'Anatolie ancienne: Mélanges en l'honneur du professeur Paul Naster* (Louvain 1983), 135-156.

The Transition to the Iron Age

Gordion's contributions to Bronze Age history include material evidence for the period of transition from Late Bronze to Early Iron Age, as yet a highly enigmatic phase on the Anatolian plateau. The stratigraphic and ceramic testimony has already been summarized in chapters I, III, and IV.[12] In Megaron 10 Layer 4 and Megaron 12 Level IVB a few examples of an alien handmade pottery appear in a stratum otherwise consisting of Late Bronze Age pottery. The succeeding levels, in both soundings, contain a sizable quantity of Late Bronze Age pottery, 50-60% of the total, with the remainder consisting of familiar gray and black Phrygian types.

Interpretation of the human history these ceramic developments represent must be cautiously attempted, given the extremely limited exposure of these levels. Moreover, the relationship of these handmade ceramic intrusions to Early Phrygian pottery requires a thorough independent analysis.[13] From a Bronze Age perspective, two observations merit special recognition. First, the Late Bronze pottery of Megaron 10 Layer 4 and Megaron 12 Level IVB unquestionably represents a continuation of the ceramic trends documented in earlier levels in both trenches, with a gradually larger proportion of buff and orange fabrics in plates and jars of increasingly standardized manufacture. A small quantity of unusual wheelmade pottery with distinctive micaceous content also links these levels. This clear relationship to the assemblage of preceding levels prohibits interpretation as a mixed deposit. Second, neither level attests to a final burning or major destruction. The assignment of this stratum to the twelfth century B.C. with a possible later continuation has already been proposed from parallels elsewhere with the Late Bronze Age pottery and its handmade accompaniment.[14]

This situation contrasts with developments as they are currently known at other sites on the plateau. At Boğazköy the general outline of events is clear, if its details are not. The capital is burned and life very much disrupted *ca.* 1180 B.C., the era of the latest datable records. A period of meager continuing occupation seems to follow. On the citadel, Büyükkale, some four centuries of abandonment appear to precede the Phrygian occupation, although in other areas of

the site there are hints that life continued in a much diminished style.[15] Elsewhere in central Anatolia a burned level followed by a period of abandonment at Karaoğlan, Alaca Hüyük, Maşat, Firaktin, and Porsuk cannot be precisely dated but may well be associated with the Boğazköy catastrophe.[16]

Yet this sequence of events did not extend throughout the Hittite domains. At Tarsus a destruction by burning ended the Late Bronze IIa phase, but no hiatus in occupation seems to have intervened prior to the IIb period. Ceramic continuity between the two phases is clearly documented.[17] To the east, in the Euphrates region, a peaceful transition from Late Bronze to Iron Age apparently took place at Korucutepe in the Keban area. Here Late Bronze II buildings were reoccupied and some pottery of this period continued to be used. The beginning of the Early Iron Age, however, is marked by a radical departure from prior ceramic traditions. Handmade, and wheelformed, hand-finished vessels with previously unknown decorative treatment are introduced.[18]

In this fragmentary, chronologically uncoordinated set of circumstances, meaningful patterns are difficult to detect. This fact may reflect a real historical complexity during these critical centuries of transition, which saw vast and comprehensive changes in the ethnic and political configuration of Anatolia. Current evidence invites speculation but is also frustrating in its limited nature, and additional archaeological documentation of this dark period is plainly needed.

Gordion will play a key role in any such investigations. The pertinent levels are preserved, and the possibilities of dating them closely via ceramic synchronisms, seals, and perhaps even written records, are good. Indeed, the site holds the enormous promise for exploring Hittite and Phrygian relationships that its excavators initially surmised.[19] Bronze Age Gordion, as viewed in Anatolian perspective, is remarkable for its unbroken record of gradual growth. Centuries of life passed without invasion or disruption, a distinction achieved by few other Bronze Age sites, and one which surely earned the admiration of arriving Phrygians in search of a stable and prosperous place to settle.

12. Above, pp. 1-6, 27-96.

13. This is currently being undertaken by G.K. Sams in preparing the Gordion pre-Kimmerian Destruction Level pottery for publication.

14. Above, pp. 47, 95.

15. P. Neve, *Büyükkale: Die Bauwerke* (Berlin 1982), 142.

16. K. Bittel, *Jahresbericht Frankfurt* 1977; *Porsuk* I, 15, 42.

17. *Tarsus* II, 203-205.

18. *Korucutepe* 3, 155-156.

19. R.S. Young, *Archaeology* 3 (1950) 13, "Levels V and VI;" *idem, UMB* 17, no. 4 (Dec. 1953) 39; Mellink, *Hitt. Cem.*, 57.

TABLE 1
EARLY BRONZE AGE ANATOLIA

	Gordion	Polatlı	Boğazköy	Beycesultan	Troy
		Phase III			V
				VI	
EB IIIb	PN-3A I pits	Phase II	NWH-BK 9		IV
	PN-3 7				
	NCT VI late			XII	III
	PN-3A II			XIII	IIg
EB IIIa	PN-3 8	Phase I			
	NCT VI early			XVI	IIa
				XVII	
EB II					I
				XIX	
				XX	
EB I	Tum. F cist				
	grave			XL	

TABLE 2
MIDDLE AND LATE BRONZE AGE ANATOLIA

	Gordion	Boğazköy	Polatlı	Beycesultan	Kültepe	Maşat	Tarsus
Trans.	NCT IVB NB 4						
LB II	NCT VA NB 9-5	Ust 1 BK III				I │ II	LB IIb LB IIa
LB I	NCT VB NB 11-10	Ust 2 BK IVb-a NWH-BK 6		I │ II		III │ │ IV	LB I
MB IV	NCT VC NB 13-12	Ust 3 BK IVc NWH-BK 7		III		V	
MB III	NB 14 NB 15	Ust 4 BK IVd NWH-BK 8a		IV	Karum Ib		
MB II	NB 18	NWH-BK 8b	Phase IV		Karum II		
MB I		NWH-BK 8c NWH-BK 8d	Phase III	V	Karum III │ Karum IV		

Appendix

Comments on Sections of the Bronze Age Mound

The schematic section of the mound is based on the three soundings which reached the Early Bronze Age levels (PN-3/3A, North Central Trench Megaron 12, and Megaron 10) and the two (Megaron 12 and Megaron 10) which encountered Hittite levels overlying the Early Bronze Age deposits.

It became evident that in the center of the northeast part of the mound, in PN-3/3A, under the front part of Megaron 12 and under part of the cella (North Central Trench or NCT), Phrygian levels of the Midas period lay in close proximity to the top of an Early Bronze Age mound which was preserved to an absolute level of *ca.* 4.50 m. The NCT sounding reached Early Bronze strata at an absolute level of -1.10 m. at a distance of some 15 m. to the southeast of the Early Bronze remains in PN-3/3A. In the Megaron 10 sounding, again some 15 m. to the southeast, the Early Bronze stratum barely surfaced in the groundwater level at -4.00 m.

The relevant deep level in NCT (VC) revealed an east-west wall, built of large yellowish limestone blocks and patched with mudbricks of 40 cm. length (Plan 11). This wall had a battered south face. Its preserved height was 1.70 m. Its core could not be examined, but this type of wall usually served as a retaining wall for an embankment with a fortification in the manner of Troy I period walls, e.g., at Troy itself or at Demirci Hüyük. It is suggested here and in the restored schematic section (Plan 12) that the Early Bronze wall in NCT formed the edge of the Early Bronze Age citadel of Gordion, and that the 10 x 3 m. sounding in NCT obliquely cut through the face and outer edge of the defensive embankment, behind which the early levels of the third-millennium citadel should be preserved.

To the outside of this embankment was a floor with much rubble and burnt bricks, evidence of a destruction level the debris of which may have been dumped to the outside of the citadel. The jar **92** with its contents could have contained a burial just outside of the wall,

although no human skeletal remains were preserved and the rim was broken and ashes had found their way in.

The PN-3/3A area preserved some 5-6 m. of additional accumulation of Early Bronze Age stata (-1.10 to +4.50) presumably in the northeast of Gordion's Early Bronze Age citadel. At the preserved top of this mound, the levels belonged to the Early Bronze IIIb period (see pp. 11-12, 14). We can expect a sizeable and durable occupation of Gordion in the third millennium B.C.

The center of the Early Bronze citadel was likely to have been to the west and southwest of PN-3/3A, given the shape of the City Mound and also considering the consistent downward slope of strata to the north of the Early Bronze III buildings excavated in 1961. This slope would possibly have continued to the north edge of the Early Bronze mound, although the structures excavated in 1961 and 1965 may have stood on terraces of their own in a citadel extending to the north.

The Early Bronze walls, just to the north of Megaron 12 (shown in Plans 3, 11; Pl. 3), Wall II and Wall P, belonged to a sizeable building which continued under Megaron 12. The outer wall (II) was built of stone and timber foundations, with running beams along both faces over which the mudbrick of the superstructure had crumbled away. The doorway had a stone threshold block measuring 1.60 x 1.50 x 0.15 m. with a door opening of 0.90 m. width; the pivot was at the inside (south side) of the door opening. The corridor into which one entered was bordered by a mudbrick wall preserved to a 1.05 m. height. This wall's thickness remains to be determined; its plaster coats added 13 cm. to its north face. The mudbrick superstructure stood on longitudinal beams. This building looks well planned and well used; it had several floor levels. A small room (annex) protected the doorway on the outside.

The upper level walls (Wall I, running north-south) belonged to a different building, also large, and maintaining the orientation of its predecessor. It was set on a layer of gray clay which formed a bedding also for its floors. This wall had a beam channel along its east side at foundation level; the inner face of the wall had a straight stone edge. The main part of the building was to the west of this wall.

This upper level had suffered interference by pits, postholes, and working floors belonging to an early Phrygian stage. There was hardly any evidence for the Hittite occupation of the PN-3/3A area; the same was true in the sounding under the pebble pavement along the front porch of Megaron 12. Phrygian activities touched immediately upon Early Bronze remains, pits were dug into pure Early Bronze strata, with no signs of artificial leveling of the area. There was no sign of a violent conflagration to mark the end of the Early Bronze occupation of this presumed citadel; the upper level had burnt matter and burnt patches, but none of the telltale debris that marks catastrophic destruction by burning. On the other hand, the debris in front of the Early Bronze "rampart" in NCT Megaron 12 was of the kind associated with conflagration.

The profile of the Early Bronze citadel mound may have sloped down to the southeast as suggested in the schematic section (Plan 12). A series of second-millennium terraces accumulated against the Early Bronze mound along this and presumably the other sides of the earliest citadel. Their base was the final "lower town" of the Early Bronze period at a level of -1.10 m. under Megaron 12 and -4.00 m. under Megaron 10. Below these now waterlogged levels, further Early Bronze habitation is to be expected. The burnt wall stump in the bottom of the Megaron 10 sounding is a remnant of the "lower town" of Early Bronze Gordion, a signal of a catastrophic end not attested on the citadel. The outer edge of the Early Bronze site has not yet been reached.

We can compare Early Bronze Gordion, with its lower mound surrounding a prominent citadel, to more important larger sites, the best example of which may be Alişar with the separate history and prehistory of its citadel mound and lower terraces.

Second-millennium habitation at Gordion was not a modest squatters' operation. Instead, sizeable and continuous occupation is attested by the well-stratified deposits sampled in the Megaron 12 cella and Megaron 10 soundings, and historical contacts with the developing Hittite Old Kingdom and Empire are suggested by the inventory (see pp. 38-45). If the central citadel is a promising field for future excavation of Early Bronze enterprise at Gordion, the terraces will reveal the Hittite role (and name?) of the town at the Sangarius crossing.

For the form of the Hittite mound, we have fewer clues and more puzzles. The section shows gently sloping levels built up against the stump of the old citadel and extending towards the southeast. If we continue the levels beyond the edge of the sounding in Megaron 10, we approach the area of an Early Phrygian gate and its postern ramp successor, parts of a developing Early Phrygian fortification system at the east edge of the mound. It is probably also the area of the Hittite east gate and east fortifications, which have not yet been identified in deep soundings.[1]

A lower Hittite city may have grown up on the terraces around the earliest citadel, with ample space for residential and administrative activities.

The presence of an Old Hittite bulla (**532**) is the kind of clue that points to the importance of Gordion in the network of Old Hittite expansion, and a status that required protection of the site. The form of the mound in Hittite times, the form of its individual and public buildings, and its fortifications remain to be determined by future excavations. The schematic section may serve as an impetus and challenge to promote the excavation of Bronze Age Gordion and its transition from the Hittite to the Phrygian era.

---

1. In 1963, a cut in the south corner of the porch of Megaron 9 went down into a solid mudbrick structure, conceivably the interior of a Hittite rampart, but the sounding was limited and not recorded in detail.

Concordance

B 1366	82	P 225	88	P 3380	12	P 5287	52
B 1404	501	P 226	89	P 3385	16	P 5288	64
B 1405	502	P 227	90	P 3387	22	P 5289	39
B 1576	346	P 228	87	P 3390	277	P 5290	34
B 1577	335	P 229	94	P 3391	5	P 5291	35
B 1578	280	P 230	96	P 3392	7	P 5292	36
B 1582	279	P 253	1	P 3393	184	P 5293	37
B 1591	128	P 528	2	P 3401	53	P 5294	73
B 1635	336	P 789	92	P 3404	40	P 5295	72
B 1644	210	P 895	512	P 3405	295	P 5296	31
B 1657	281	P 1080	508	P 3406	8	P 5297	66
B 1658	383	P 1358	509	P 3407	6	P 5298	32
BI 406	503	P 1373	511	P 3610	100	P 5299	69
BI 407	504	P 2400	514	P 3703	99	P 5300	77
G 311	347	P 2595	58	P 4388	524	P 5301	76
I 125	518	P 2606	59	P 4441	531	P 5302	50
I 144	520	P 2625	23	P 4469	510	P 5303	48
I 158	517	P 2626	17	P 4570a-f,	515	P 5304	45
I 194	519	P 2627	46	h, i		P 5305	47
I 245	521	P 2762	496	P 4666	500	P 5306	41
I 623	447	P 2763	494	P 5283a-d	56	P 5307	78
I 624	493	P 2765	495	P 5272	91	P 5308	70
ILS 368	505	P 2786	497	P 5273	93	P 5309	44
ILS 461	211	P 2787	498	P 5274	95	P 5310	43
MC 40	492	P 3000	499	P 5275	67	P 5311	30
MC 41	471	P 3301	332	P 5276	54	P 5312	62
MC 102a	526	P 3329	254	P 5277	75	P 5313	33
MC 102b	527	P 3331	177	P 5278	57	P 5314	74
MC 130	528	P 3332	151	P 5279	29	P 5315	61
MC 184	530	P 3333	152	P 5280	55	P 5316	38
MC 185	79	P 3334	60	P 5281	28	P 5317	9
MC 200	529	P 3335	506	P 5282	71	P 5318	375
MC 230	278	P 3336	507	P 5284	65	P 5319	374
MC 245	80	P 3344	270	P 5285	68	P 5320	367
MC 312	334	P 3378	25	P 5286	63	P 5321	370

P 5322	**366**	P 5338	**275**	P 5461	**157**	SS 209	**532**
P 5323	**302**	P 5339	**276**	P 5462	**97**	SS 220	**382**
P 5324	**303**	P 5340	**268**	P 5463	**120**	SS 223	**381**
P 5325	**321**	P 5341	**273**	P 5464	**109**	SS 260	**533**
P 5326	**323**	P 5342	**253**	P 5465	**110**	ST 64a	**4**
P 5327	**319**	P 5343	**252**	P 5466	**414**	ST 64b	**3**
P 5328	**306**	P 5344	**202**	P 5467	**413**	ST 467	**83**
P 5329	**308**	P 5345	**203**	P 5468	**409**	ST 546	**337**
P 5330	**300**	P 5346	**197**	P 5469	**446**	ST 547	**282**
P 5331	**330**	P 5347	**198**	P 5470	**460**	ST 561	**13**
P 5332	**324**	P 5455	**192**	P 5471	**469**	ST 562	**11**
P 5333	**333**	P 5456	**191**	P 5579	**513**	T 43	**523**
P 5334	**331**	P 5457	**175**	P 5599,	**516**	T 50	**525**
P 5335	**322**	P 5458	**176**	P 4570g		T 98	**101**
P 5336	**320**	P 5459	**190**	P 5603	**51**	T 111	**522**
P 5337	**325**	P 5460	**185**	SS 117	**470**	T 125	**81**

Türkçe Özet

Ankaranın 100 kilometre batısında bulunan Gordion, M.Ö. 1,000 yılları başında gelişmiş olan Frig İmparatorluğunun başkenti olarak tesbit edilmiştir. 1950-1973 yılları arasında Pennsylvania Üniversitesi Müzesinin kazılarında Gordion tarihinin bu unutulmaz dönemine ait mimari, tümülüs ve diğer buluntular ortaya çıkarılmıştır. Gordion'un Tunç Çağı daha az biliniyor. 1951-1953 ve 1962 yıllarında Hitit mezarlığında yapılan kazıların yanısıra, 1950, 1961 ve 1965 yıllarında "City Mound" olarak adlandırılan bölümde Frig katlarının altında araştırmalar yapılmıştır. Sonuç, M.Ö. 3,000 sonlarından başlayarak, Frig dönemine kadar asırlar boyu yerleşmelerin varlığı kaydedilmiştir.

Sonuç, Frig döneminden evvel, M.Ö. 3,000 sonlarında başlayan ve asırlar boyu süren yerleşmelerin varlığı stratigrafik olarak kaydedilmiştir. Bu ilk yerleşmelerin daha kapsamlı incelenmesi ileriki yıllara bırakılmakla beraber, şimdiye kadar ortaya çıkarılan bilgi ve malzemenin ayrıntılı olarak yayınlanması Gordion'daki Frig devri öncesine ait, Batı Anadolunun geç 3cü ve 2ci bin yerleşmelerine ışık tutacaktır.

Bu malzemeyi yayına hazırlarken Ankara Anadolu Medeniyetleri Müzesinde ve Gordion'da muhafaza edilen kazı buluntularını araştırdım. Bütün çanak, çömlekler, etiketlenmiş olarak kazı deposunda incelenmeye hazır durumdadır. Tunç Çağına ait envanterli buluntular Gordion müzesinde teşhirde ve depoda bulunmaktadır. Bütün çalışmalar, T.C. Kültür ve Turizm Bakanlığı Eski Eserler ve Müzeler Genel Müdürlüğü izni ile 1979, 1981 ve 1982 yıllarında tamamlanmıştır. Ankara Anadolu Medeniyetleri Müzesi eski Müdürü, Raci Temizer, Ankara ve Gordion müzelerindeki malzemenin incelenmesinde çok kolaylık gösterdi. İstanbul Arkeoloji Müzesi eski müdürü Nuşin Asgarinin izni ve Gülay Tigrel'in yardımları ile Körte kardeşlerin Gordion kazı buluntularını incelemek fırsatını buldum. Profesör Tahsin Özgüç ve Boğaz-

köy kazı başkanı Peter Neve'nin izinleri ile yerleşmelerden çıkarılan seramik örneklerini inceledim. Dr. Machteld Mellink Tunç Çağına ait "City Mound" 'un şematik bir kesiti ile şehrin görünüşü hakkında açıklamalar yaptı.

Gordion'da ilk tarihöncesi kanıtı Eski Tunç Çağına ait Frig Tümülüs F'in altındaki mezar içinde bulunan seramiktir. "City Mound" bölümünde ilk kesin yerleşme katları Eski Tunç IIIa veya Eski Tunç II'nin sonunda başlar, North Central Trench'de Frig yapılarının ve Megaron 12'nin altına kadar devam eder. Eski Tunç IIIa ve IIIb'nin çanak çömlekleri el işi olup, kırmızı veya kahverengi astarlı ve perdahlıdır. En yakın bağlantılar Gordion'a yakın mesafede olan Polatlı I, II ve Asarcık Höyük V iledir. Daha uzak mesafeli bağlantılar, Eski Tunç III döneminde Nordwesthang-Büyükkale 9 ve Beycesultan VIa ile çağdaş olduğunu gösterir. Gordion'da bir yangın katı ile sona eren bu dönem yerleşmesi, Polatlı XV ile çağdaş olabilir.

Gordion'da 2ci bin yerleşmesi Megaron 10 sondajında ve North Central Trench'de bulunmuştur. Megaron 10 altındaki bugüne kadar kazılan en eski katların Orta Tunç Çağına ait olması, çarkta yapılmış, kırmızı astarlı, "Hitit" tipi çömleklerin bulunmasından anlaşılıyor. M.Ö. 2,000 yıllarında kırmızı astar bırakılmış ve çoğunluğu düz, boz renkli ve turuncu çömlekler almıştır. Bu iki sondajda 2,000 yıllarını temsil eden katlar, birkaç el işi çömlek dışında, kesintisiz olarak geç Tunç Çağı çömleklerini kapsayan kata kadar devam eder. Böylece, Gordion'da Demir Çağına geçiş huzurlu olmuş, Boğazköy-Hattuşa'daki tahribat Gordion'da olmamıştır. Gordion kazıları, batı Anadolunun seramik silsilesini, ve İç ve Güneybatı Anadolu arasındaki bağlantıları kurduğu gibi, Tunç Çağı sonu, Demir Çağı başındaki gelişmeleri araştırma imkanlarını sağlamıştır.

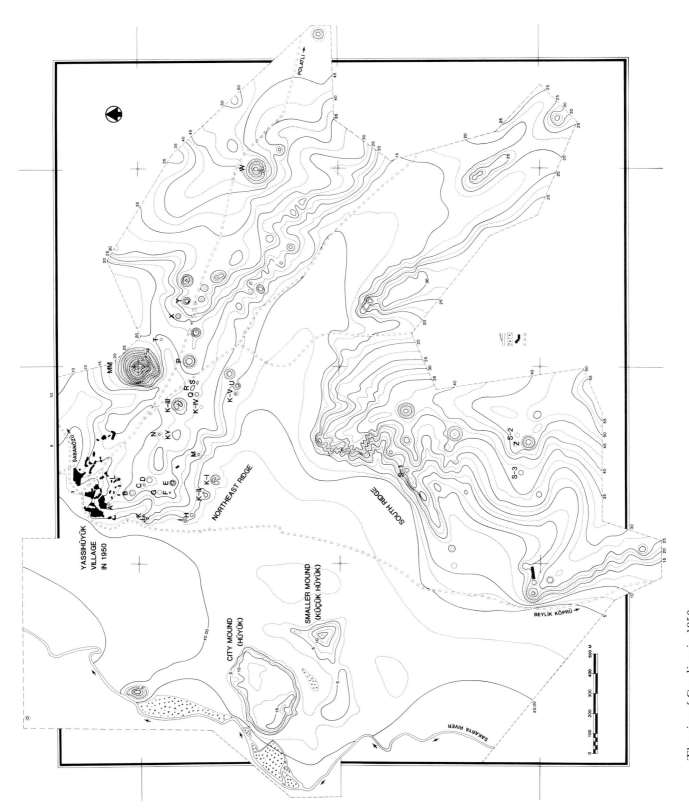

The site of Gordion in 1950.

PLAN 2

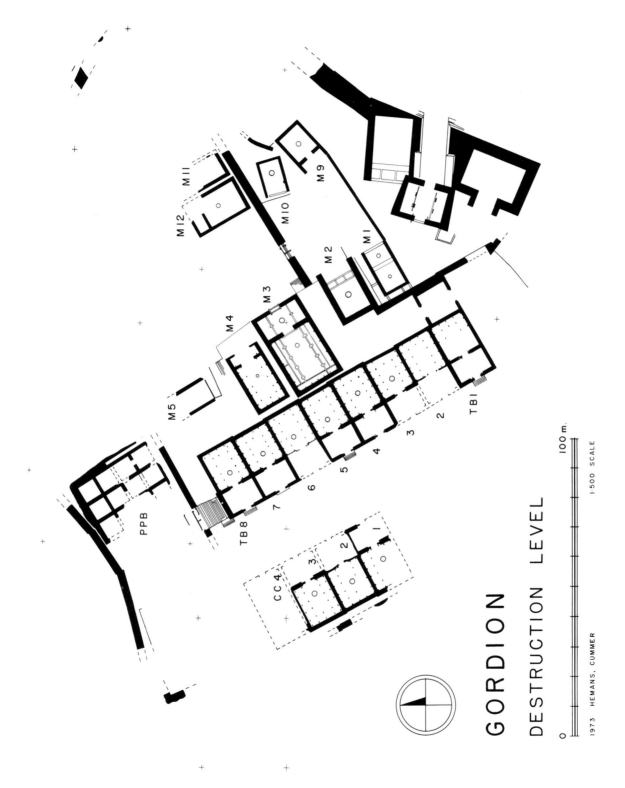

GORDION
DESTRUCTION LEVEL

1973 HEMANS, CUMMER

1500 SCALE

100 m.

Plan of the city at the Kimmerian Destruction Level.

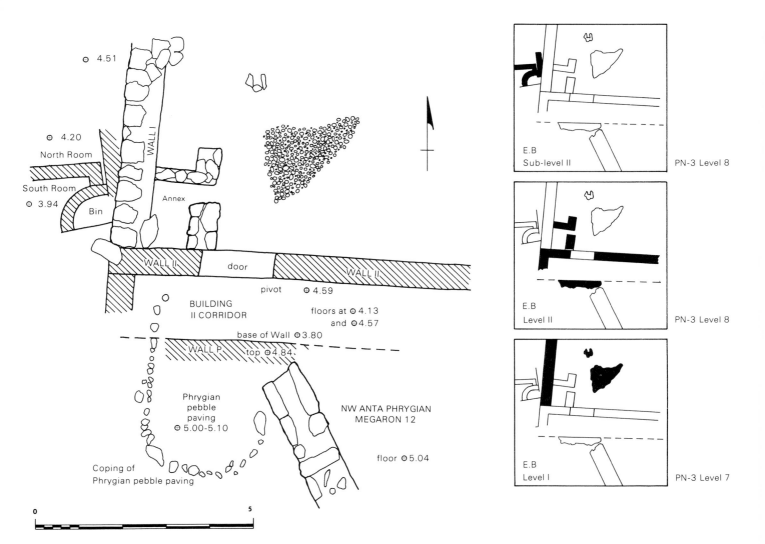

⊙ 4.51

⊙ 4.20

North Room

South Room

⊙ 3.94 Bin

WALL I

Annex

WALL II door

WALL II

pivot ⊙ 4.59

BUILDING
II CORRIDOR

floors at ⊙ 4.13
and ⊙ 4.57

base of Wall ⊙ 3.80

WALL P top ⊙ 4.84.

Phrygian
pebble
paving
⊙ 5.00-5.10

NW ANTA PHRYGIAN
MEGARON 12

floor ⊙ 5.04

Coping of
Phrygian pebble paving

0   5

E.B
Sub-level II   PN-3 Level 8

E.B
Level II   PN-3 Level 8

E.B
Level I   PN-3 Level 7

Trench PN-3/3A. Early Bronze Levels I and II.

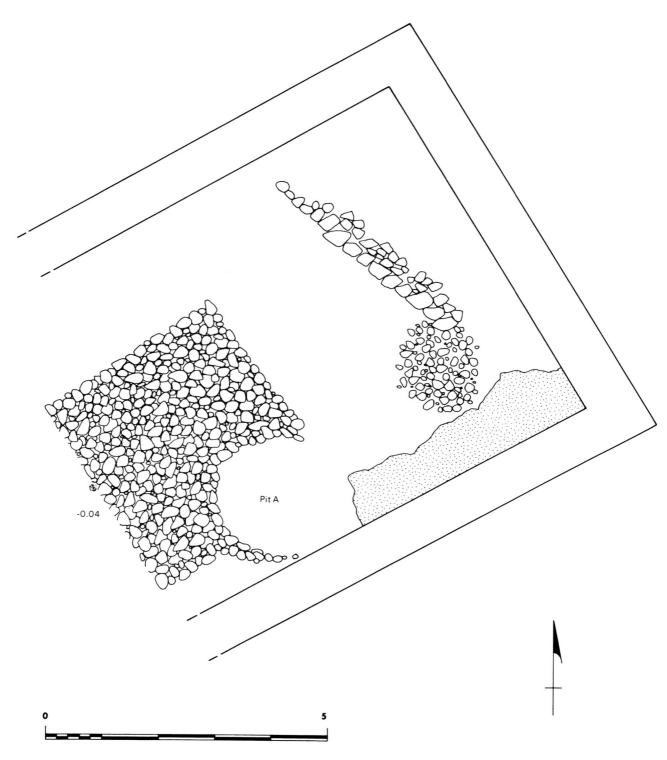

Pit A

-0.04

0   5

Megaron 10, Floor 9.

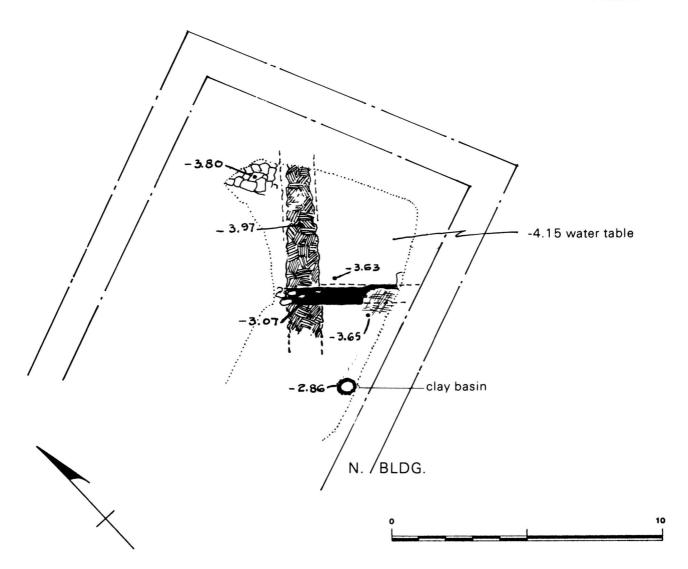

-3.80

-3.97

-4.15 water table

-3.63

-3.07

-3.65

-2.86 ○ —clay basin

N. / BLDG.

0   10

Megaron 10, Floor 14 and below.

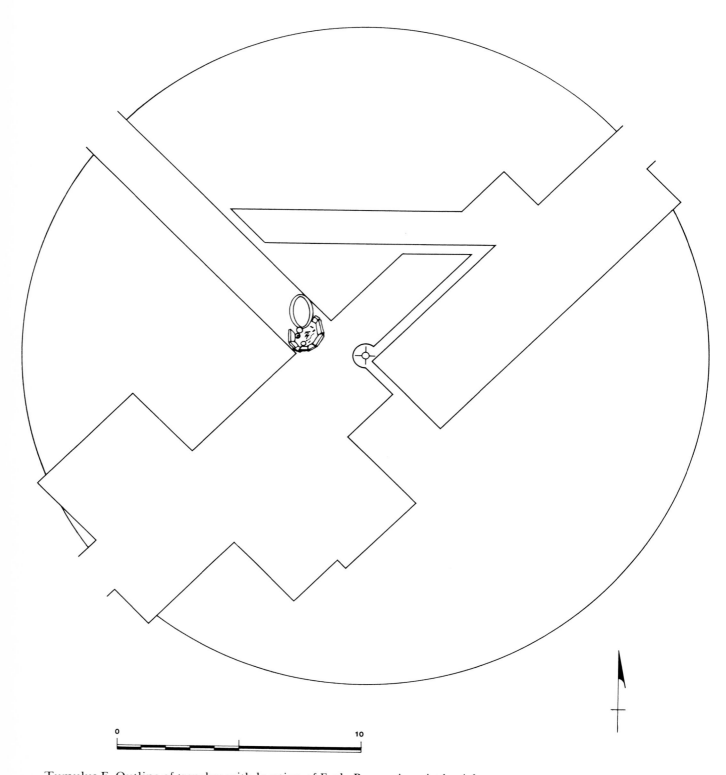

Tumulus F. Outline of trenches with location of Early Bronze Age cist burial.

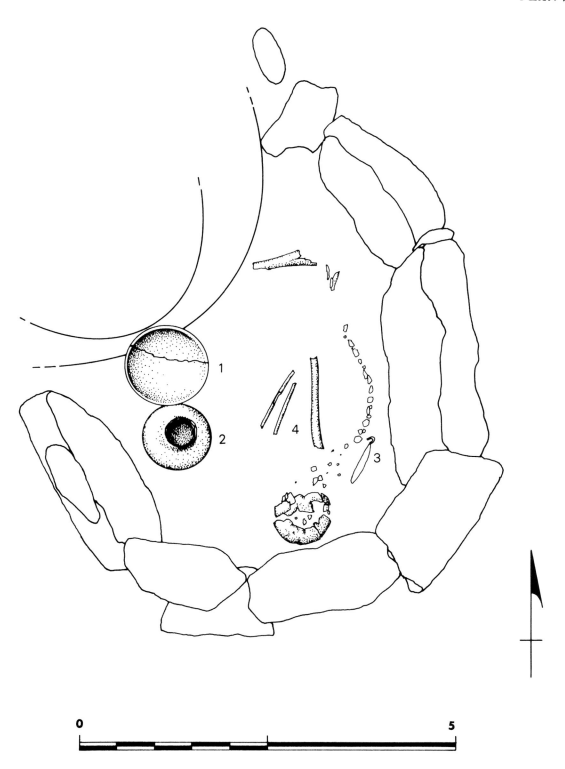

Early Bronze Age cist burial under Tumulus F.

PLAN 8

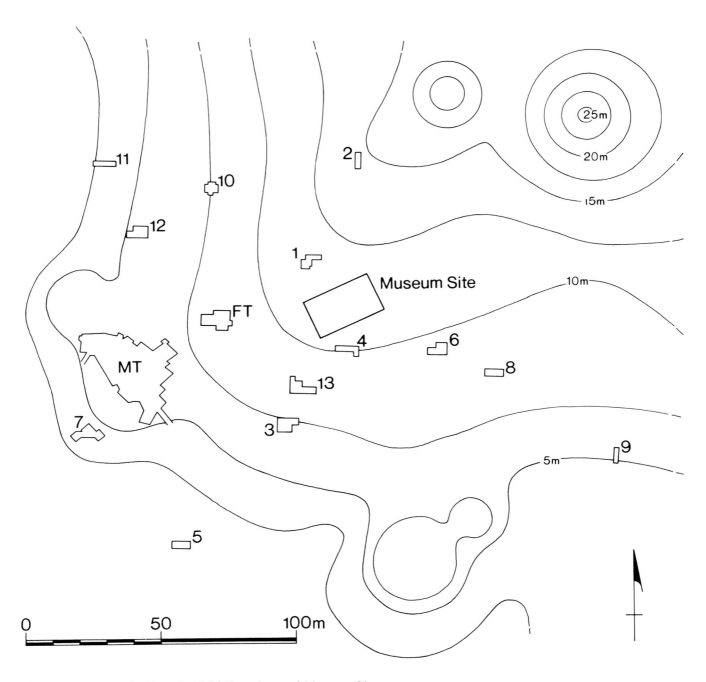

Cemetery area: Main Trench, Field Trenches and Museum Site.

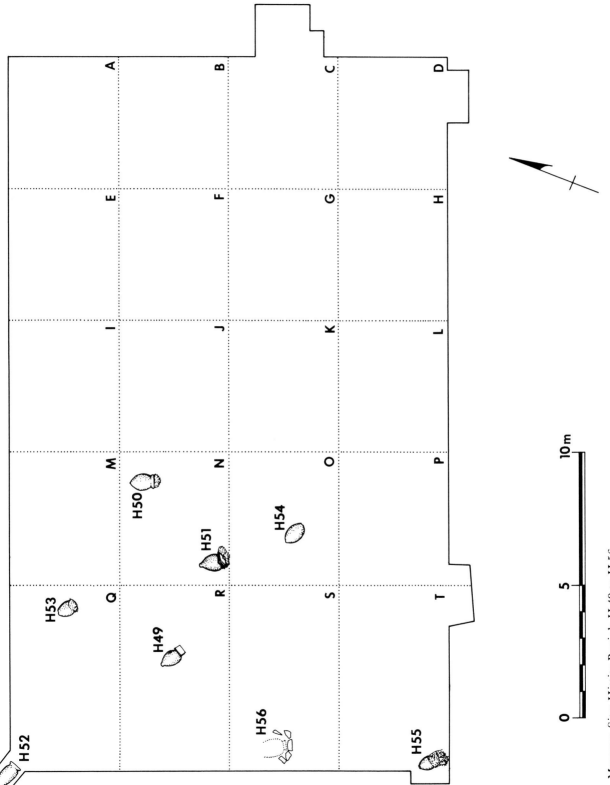

Museum Site: Hittite Burials H 49 to H 56.

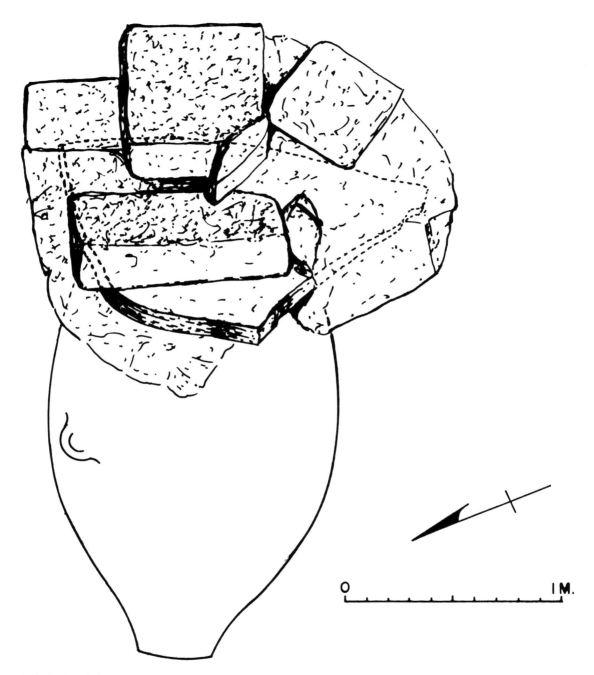

Hittite Burial H 49.

0   1M.

Tumulus F, Cist Grave

1

2

PN-3, Level 10

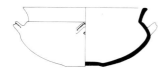

5

PN-3, Level 9

6

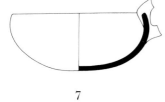

7

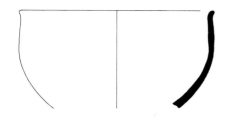

8

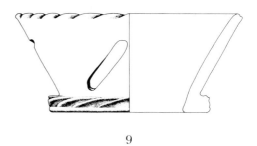

9

PN-3, Level 8

12

PN-3, Level 7

14

15

16

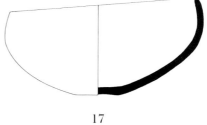

17

18

1, 2 *1:10*; 5-18 *1:4*

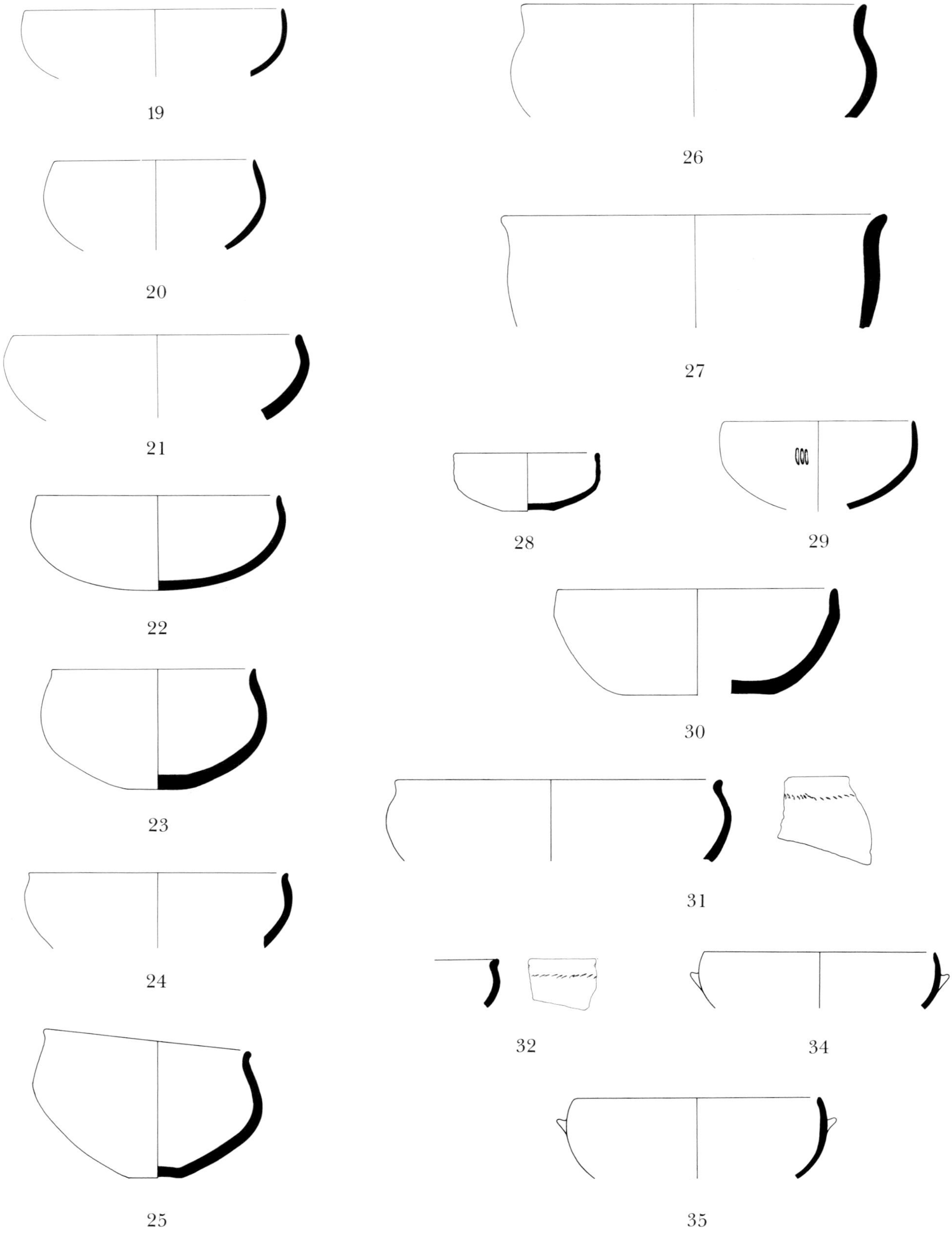

FIGURE 2

19

20

21

22

23

24

25

26

27

28   29

30

31

32   34

35

1:4

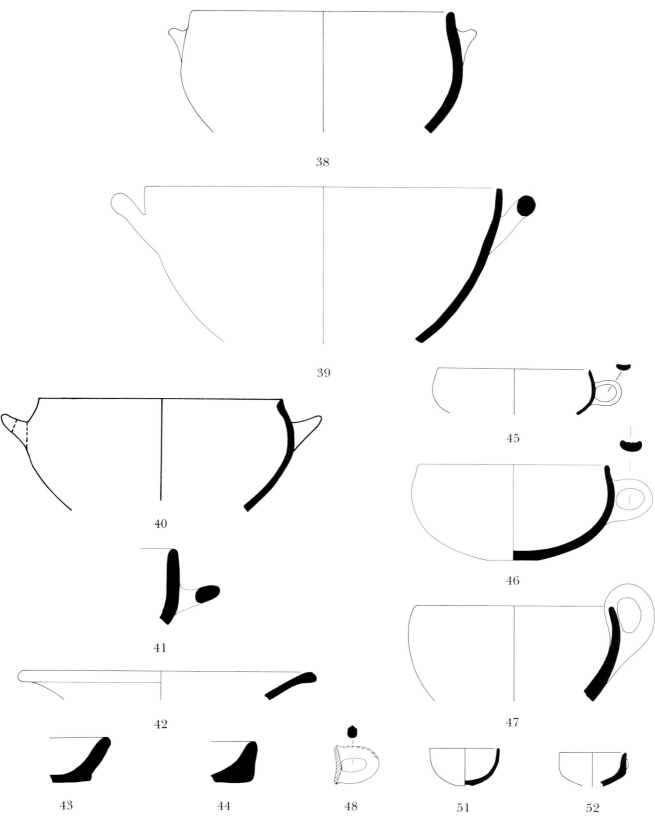

FIGURE 4

53

55

62

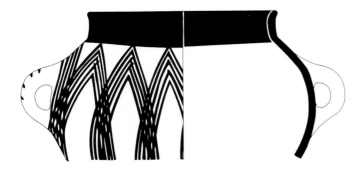

56

64

65

66

57

68

58

70

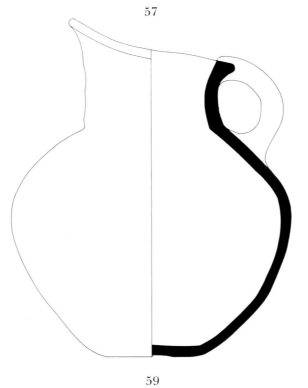

59

72

1:4

Megaron 12, Level VI

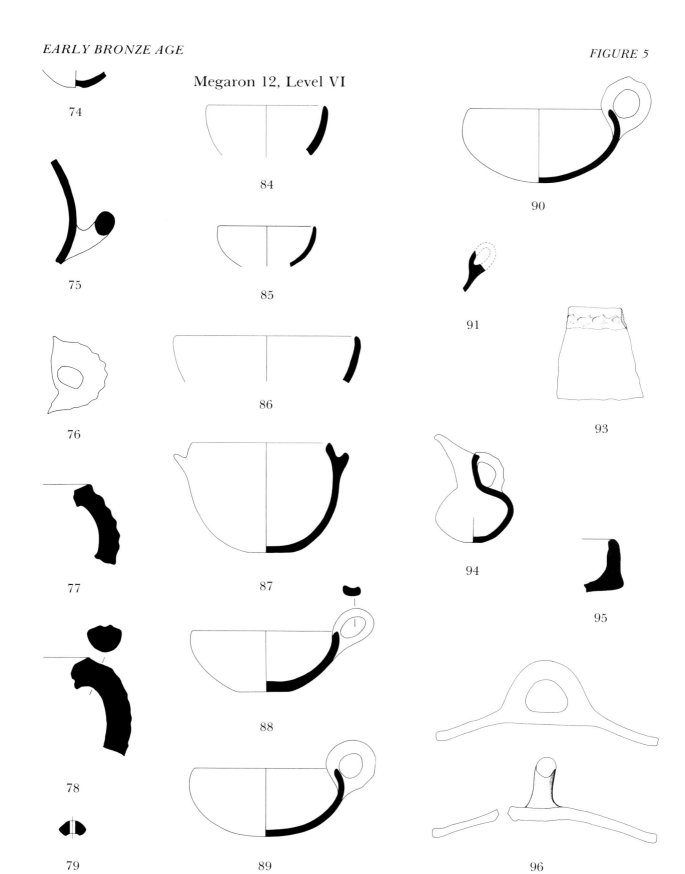

74

75

76

77

78

79

84

85

86

87

88

89

90

91

93

94

95

96

1:4

FIGURE 6

Megaron 10, Layer 15

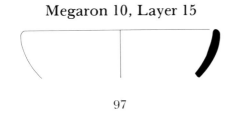

97

Miscellaneous Contexts

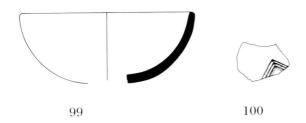

99   100

Megaron 10, Layer 18

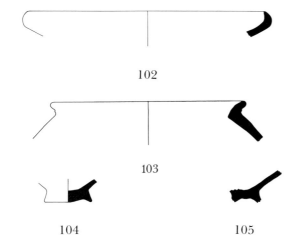

102

103

104   105

Megaron 10, Layer 17

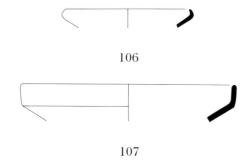

106

107

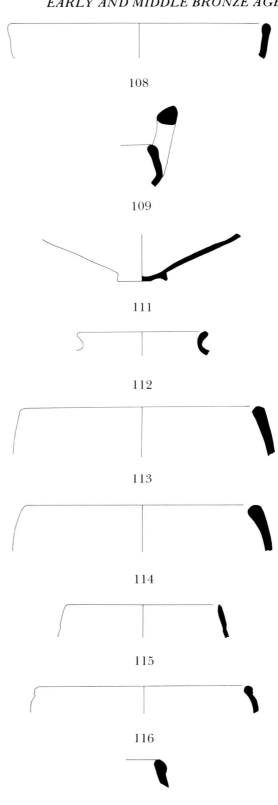

108

109

111

112

113

114

115

116

117

Megaron 10, Layer 16

Megaron 10, Layer 15

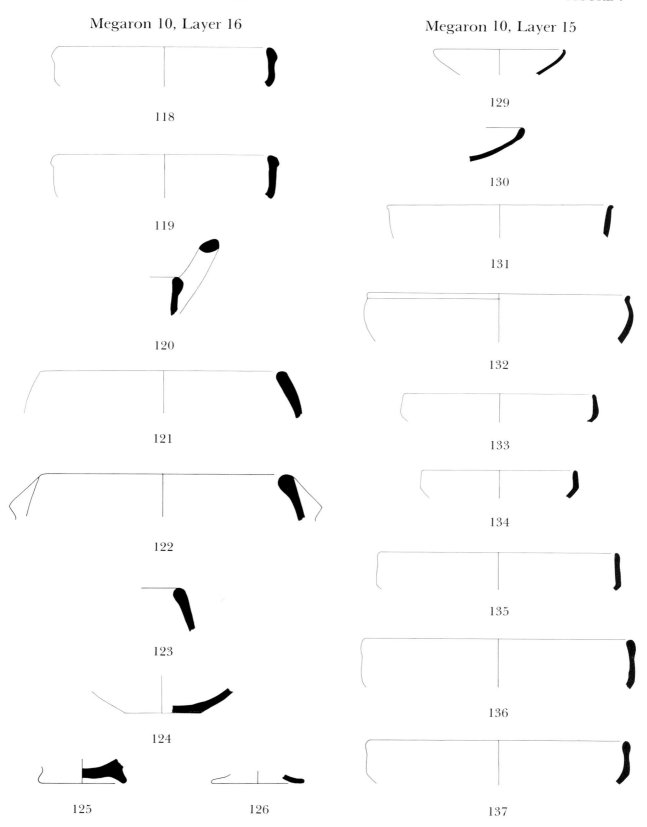

118

119

120

121

122

123

124

125   126

129

130

131

132

133

134

135

136

137

1:4

FIGURE 8

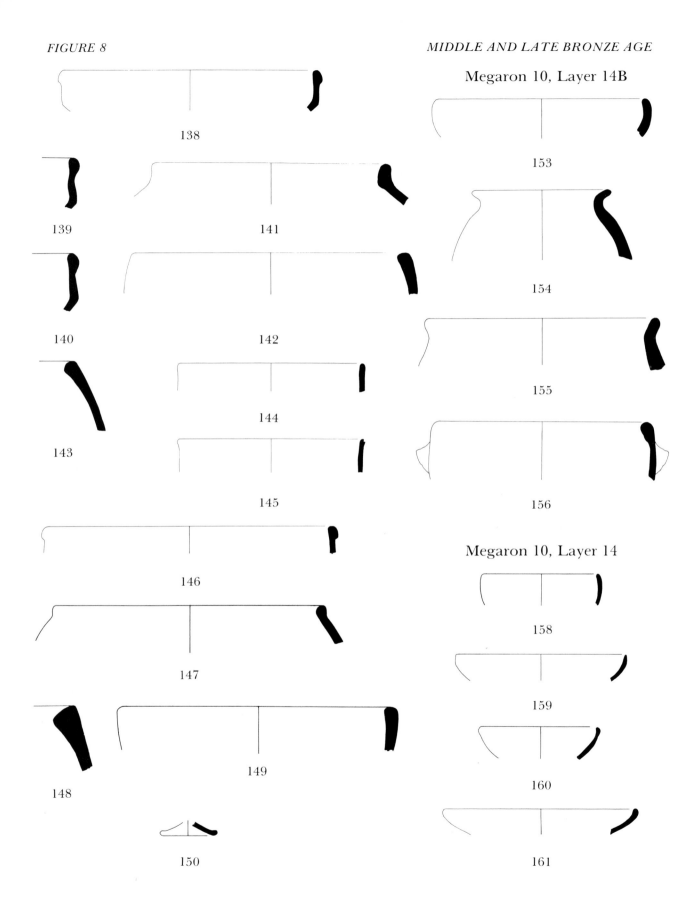

Megaron 10, Layer 14B

138

139

140

141

142

143

144

145

146

147

148

149

150

153

154

155

156

Megaron 10, Layer 14

158

159

160

161

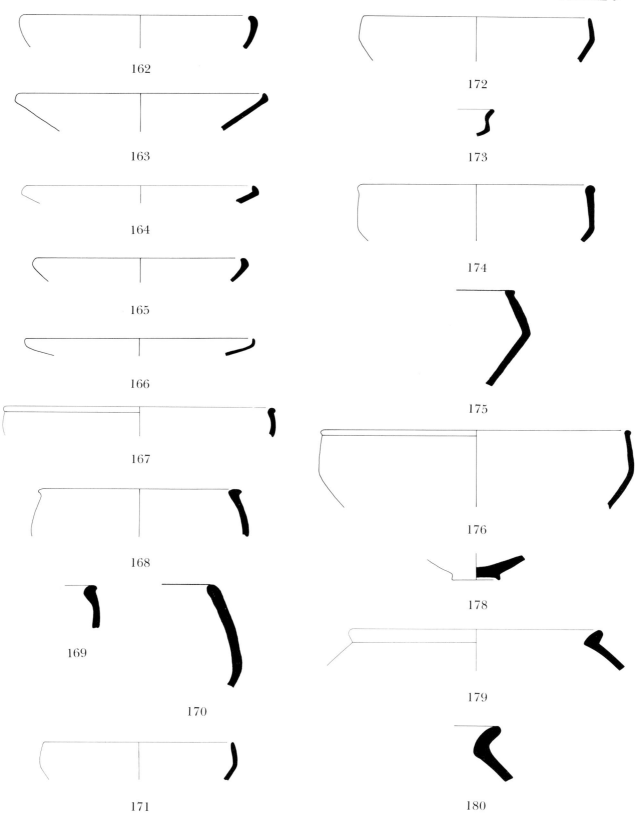

FIGURE 10   *MIDDLE AND LATE BRONZE AGE*

181

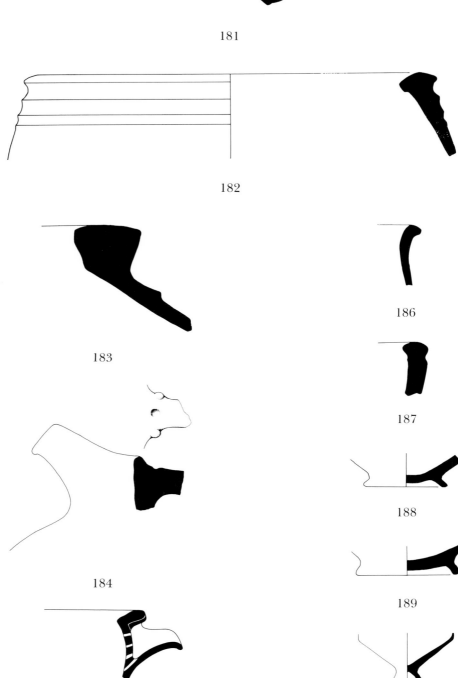

182

183

184

185

186

187

188

189

190

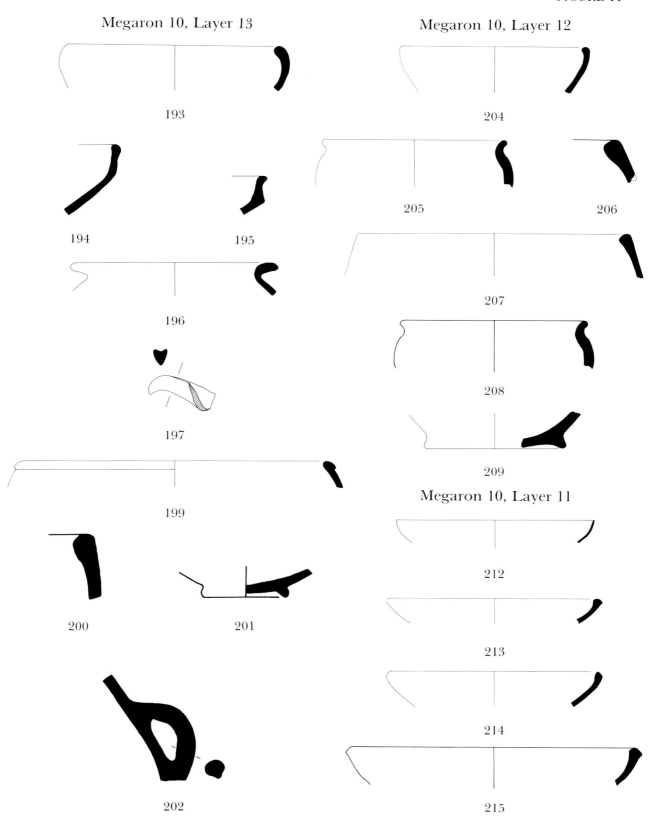

Megaron 10, Layer 13

193

194   195

196

197

199

200   201

202

Megaron 10, Layer 12

204

205   206

207

208

209

Megaron 10, Layer 11

212

213

214

215

1:4

FIGURE 12

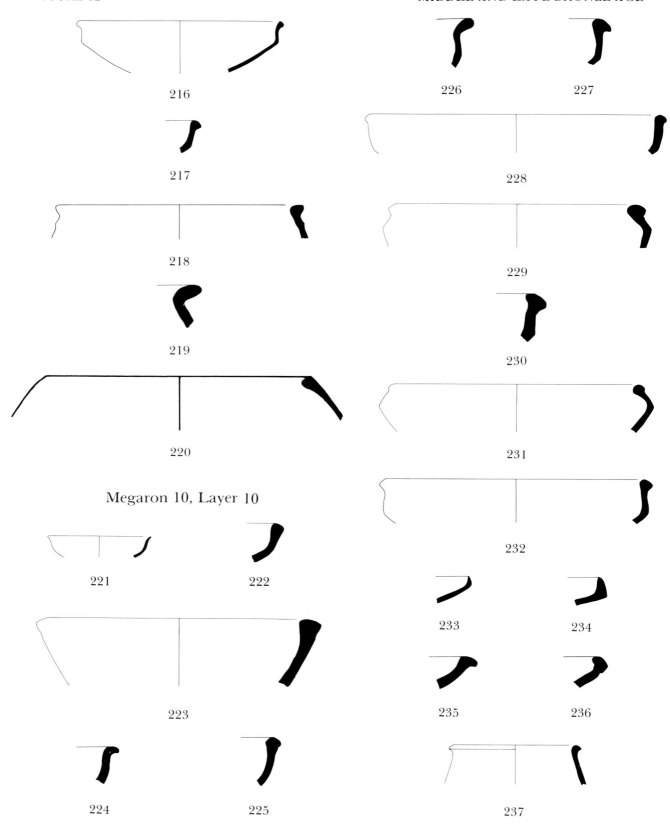

216

226   227

217

228

218

229

219

230

220

231

Megaron 10, Layer 10

221   222

232

223

233   234

235   236

224   225

237

FIGURE 13

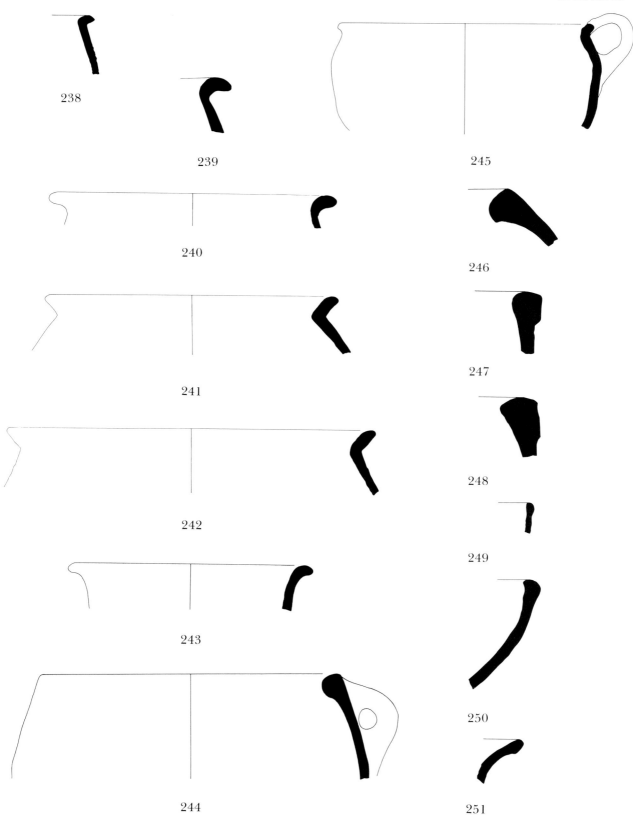

238

239

240

241

242

243

244

245

246

247

248

249

250

251

1:4

FIGURE 14   MIDDLE AND LATE BRONZE AGE

Megaron 10, Layer 8

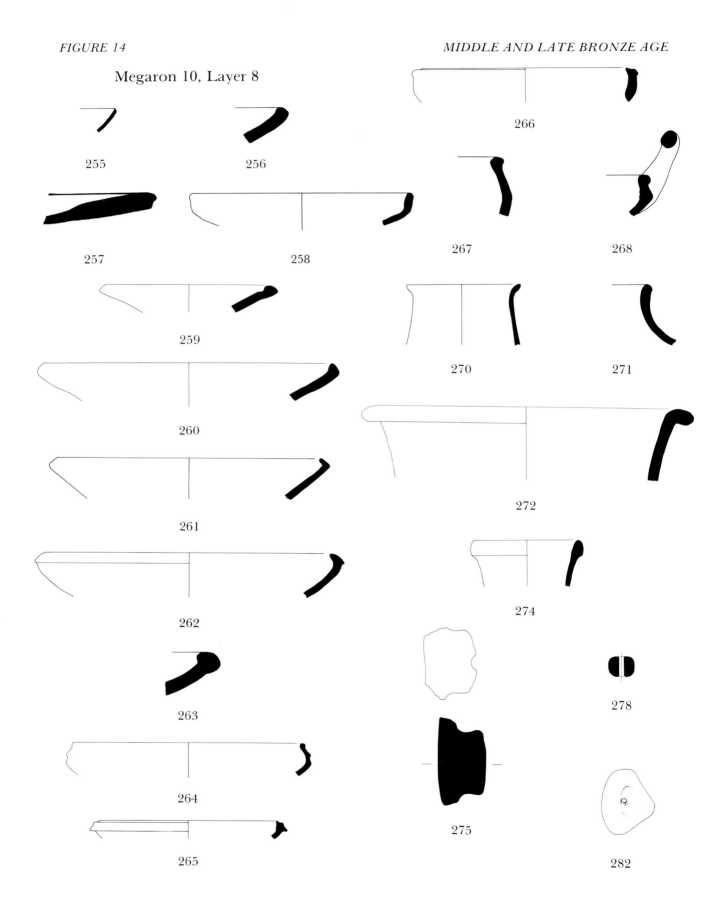

255

256

266

257

258

267

268

259

260

270

271

261

272

262

274

263

275

278

264

265

282

1:4

Megaron 10, Layer 7

283
284 
285 

286
287 
288 

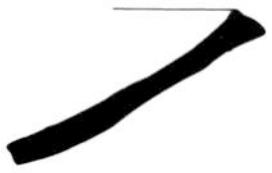

289
290 
291 

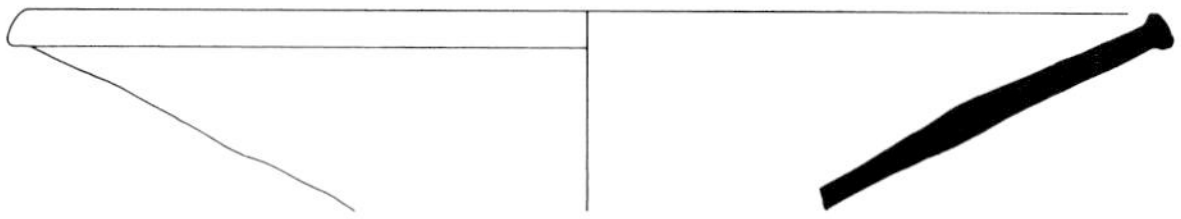

292

293

294

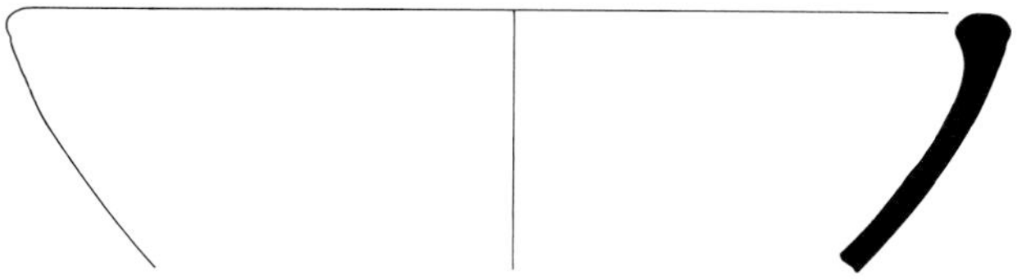

295

296

297
298 

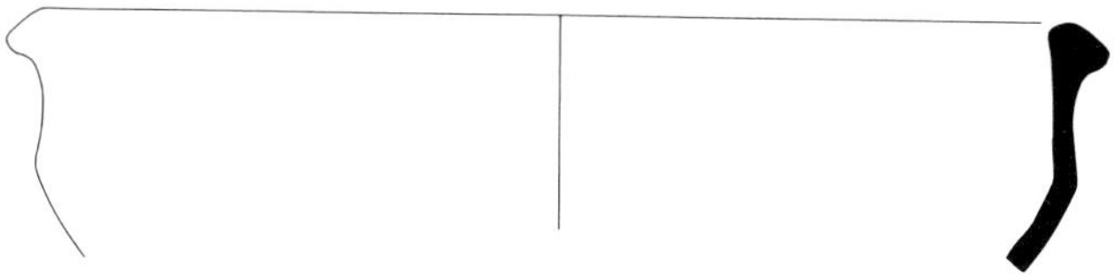

299

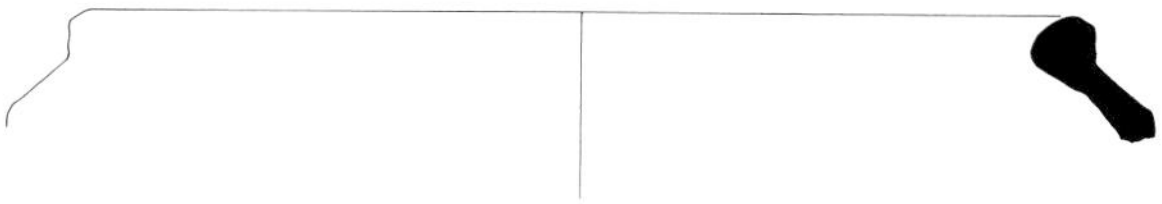

300

301

302

303

304

305

306
307 

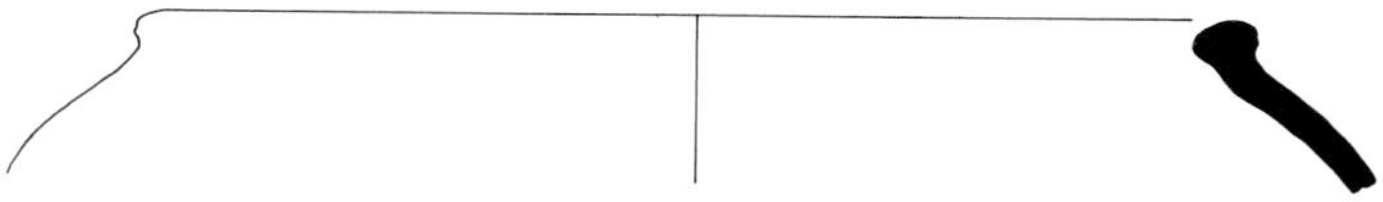

308

1:4

FIGURE 16

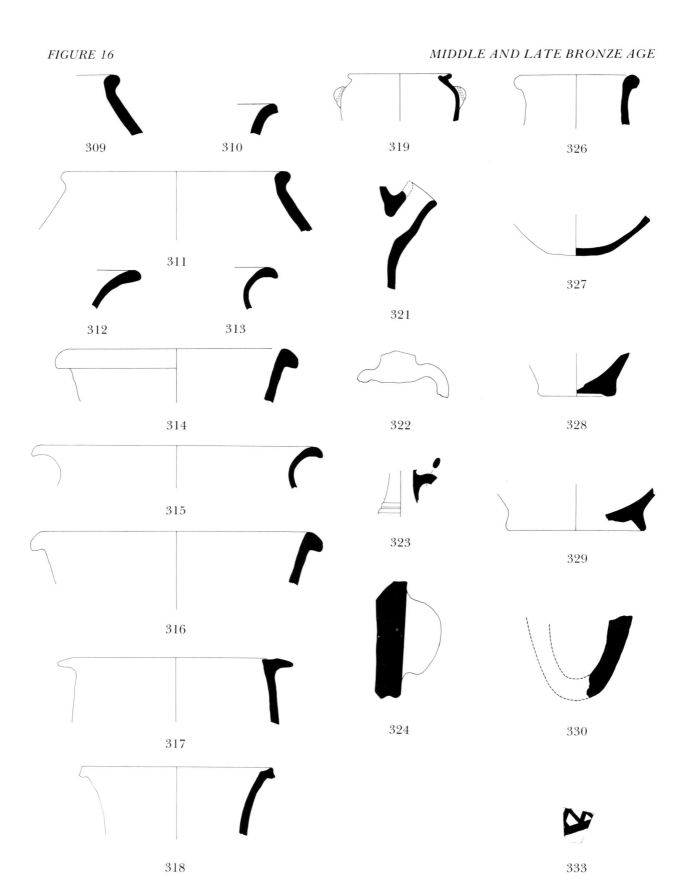

309

310

319

326

311

321

327

312

313

314

322

328

315

323

316

329

317

324

330

318

333

Megaron 10, Layer 6

Megaron 10, Layer 5

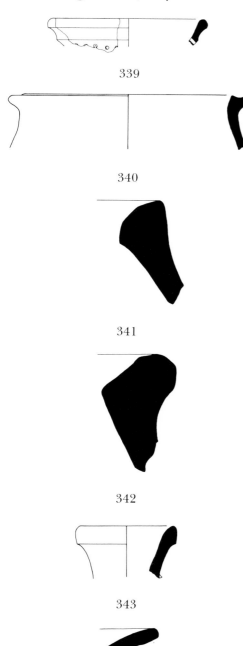

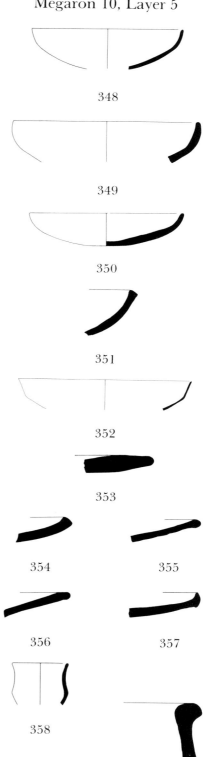

339

340

341

342

343

344

345

348

349

350

351

352

353

354

355

356

357

358

359

1:4

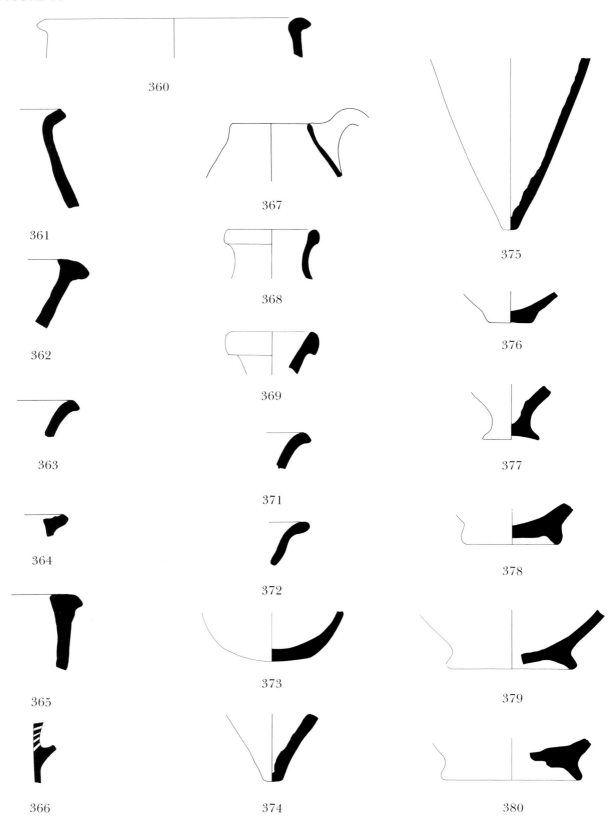

360

361

362

363

364

365

366

367

368

369

371

372

373

374

375

376

377

378

379

380

1:4

Megaron 10, Layer 4

Megaron 12, Level VC

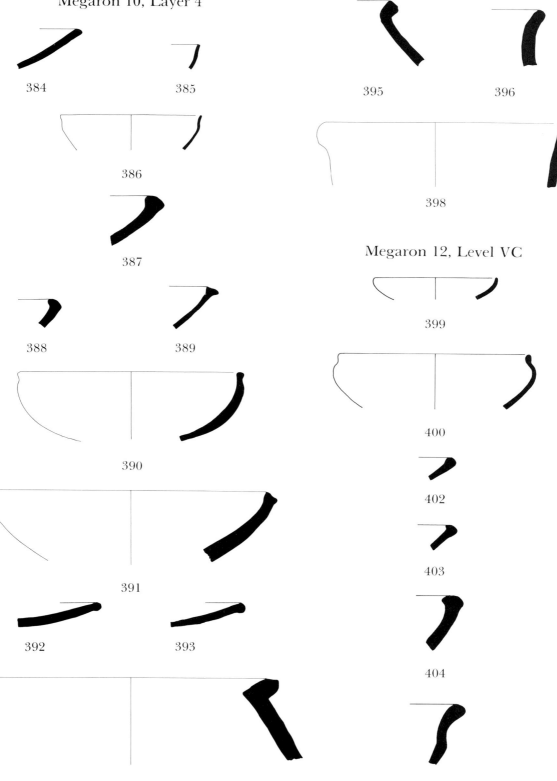

384

385

386

387

388

389

390

391

392

393

394

395

396

398

399

400

402

403

404

405

1:4

FIGURE 20

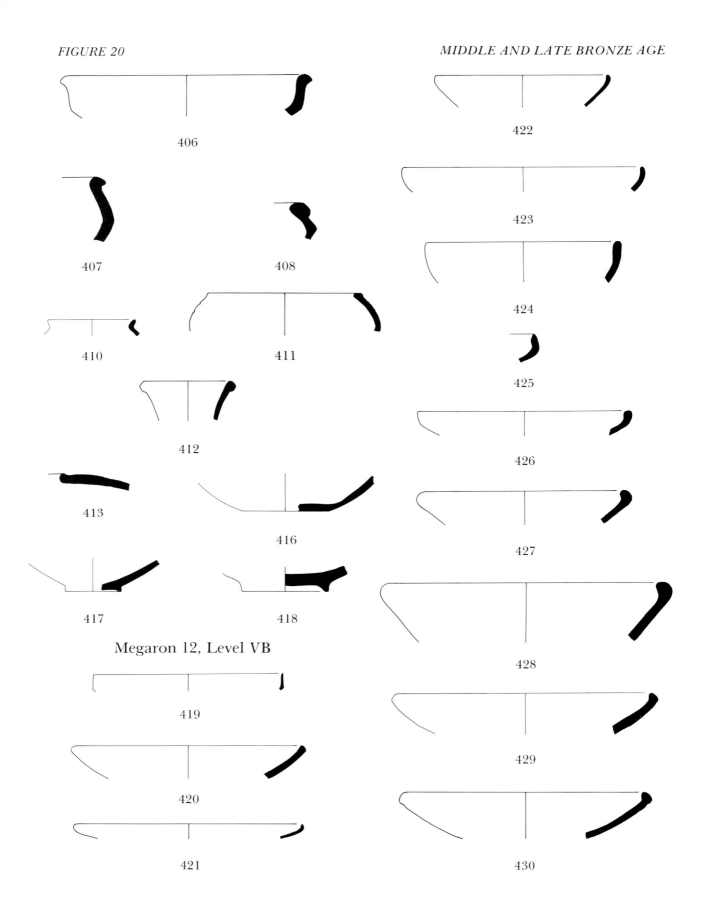

406

422

407

408

423

424

410

411

425

412

426

413

416

427

417

418

428

Megaron 12, Level VB

419

420

429

421

430

FIGURE 21

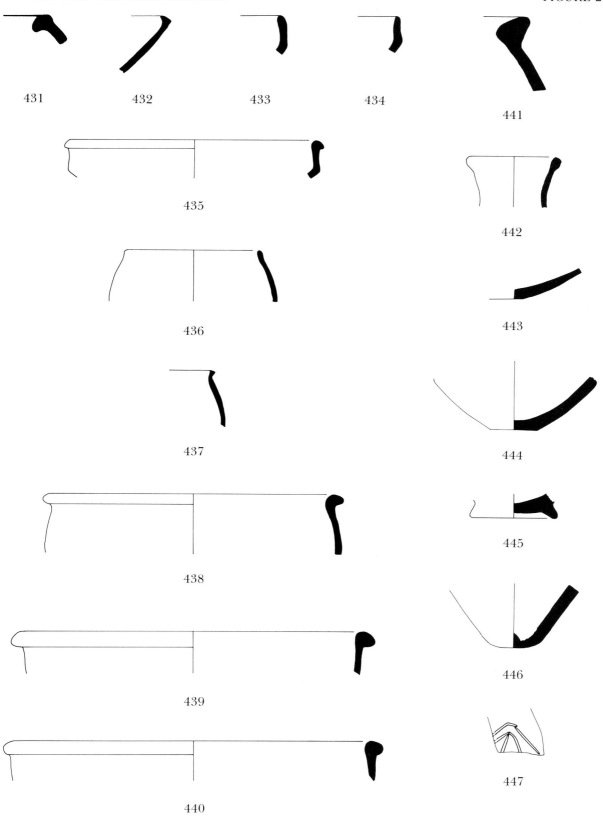

431

432

433

434

441

435

442

436

443

437

444

438

445

439

446

440

447

1:4

FIGURE 22

Megaron 12, Level VA

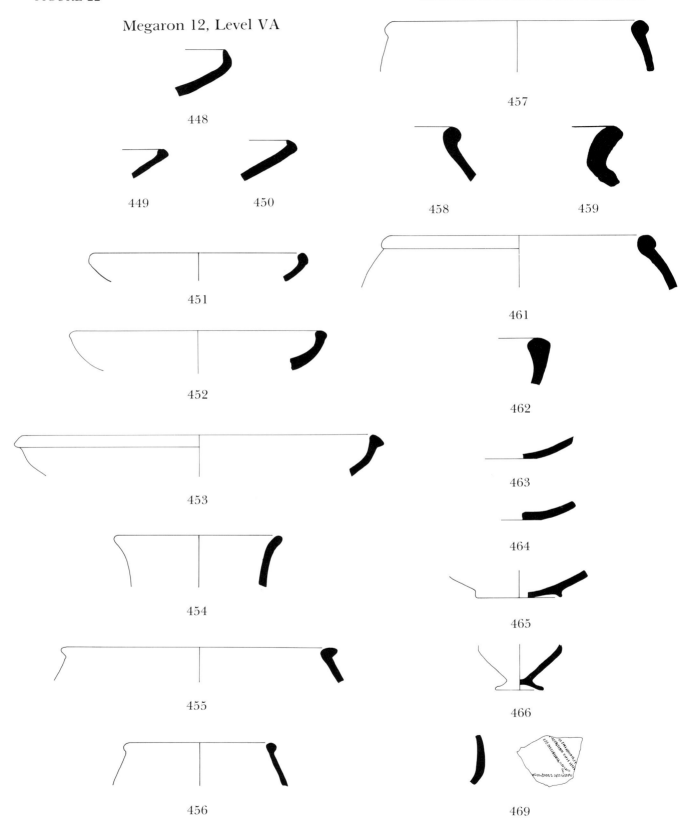

448

449

450

451

452

453

454

455

456

457

458

459

461

462

463

464

465

466

469

Megaron 12, Level IVB

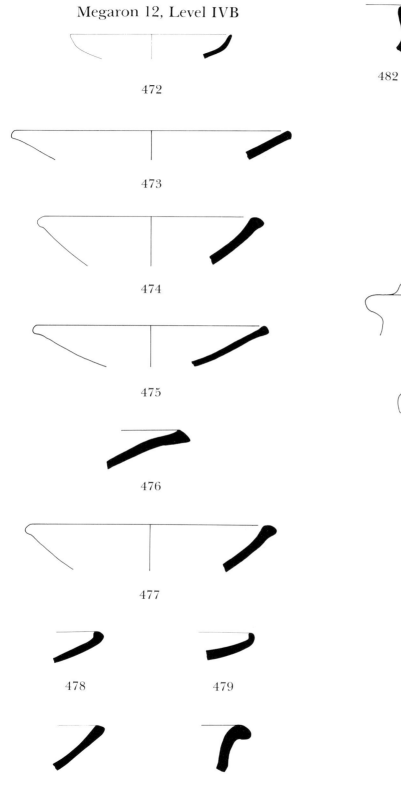
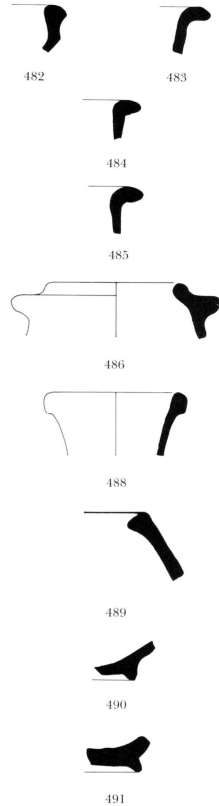

1:4

FIGURE 24   MIDDLE AND LATE BRONZE AGE

North Central Trench
Pre-IC Level

Burials

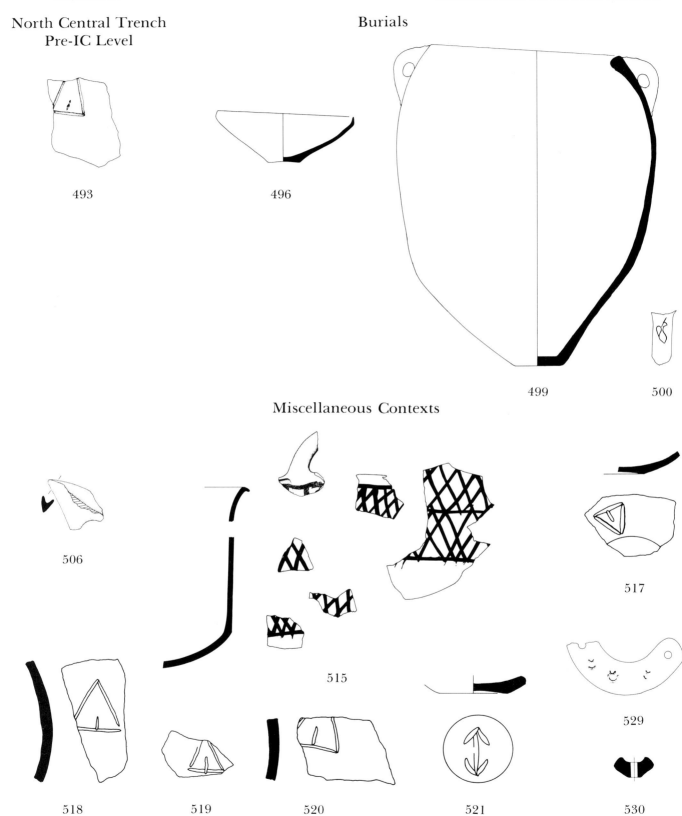

493

496

499   500

Miscellaneous Contexts

506

515

517

518   519   520   521   529

530

1:4

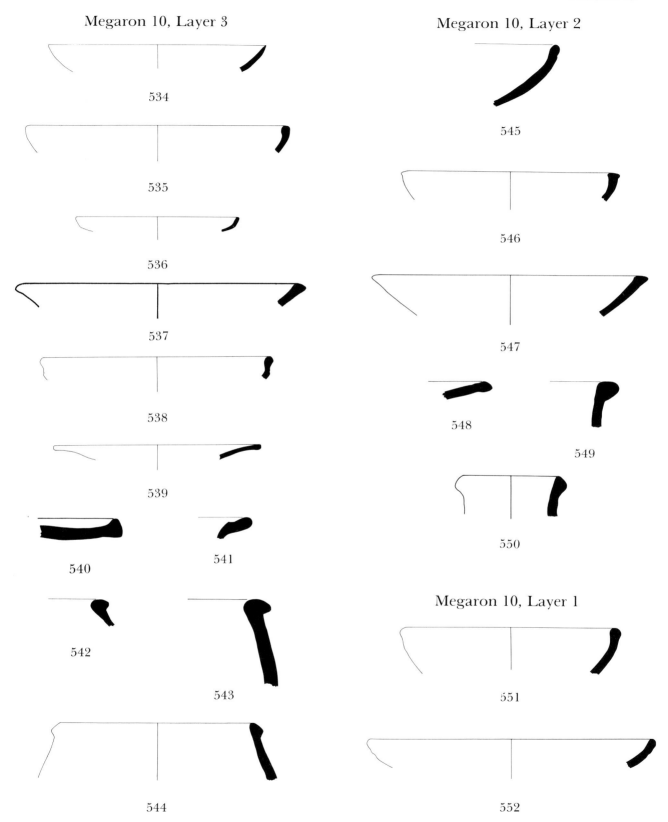

Megaron 10, Layer 3

534

535

536

537

538

539

540

541

542

543

544

Megaron 10, Layer 2

545

546

547

548

549

550

Megaron 10, Layer 1

551

552

1:4

FIGURE 26

EARLY IRON AGE LEVELS

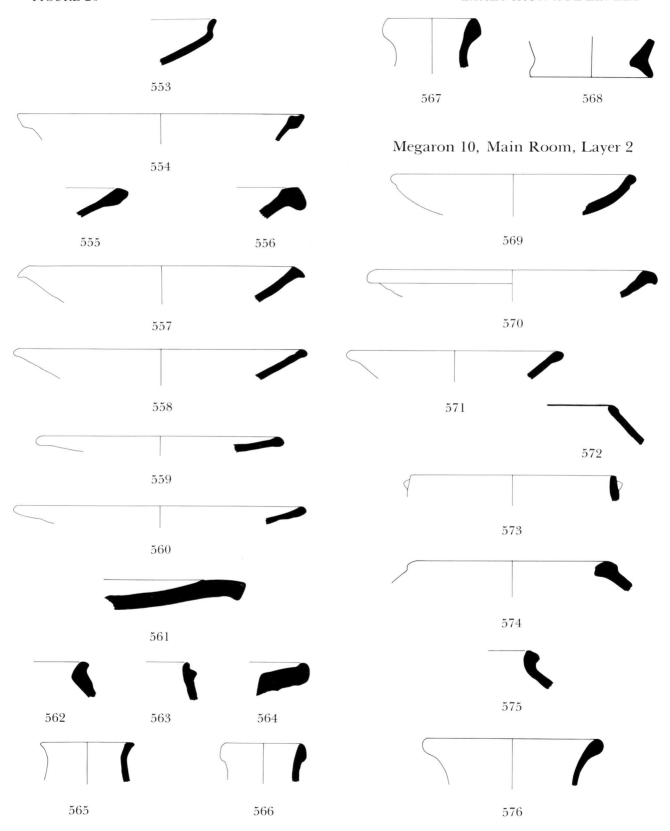

553

554

555 556

557

558

559

560

561

562 563 564

565 566

567 568

Megaron 10, Main Room, Layer 2

569

570

571 572

573

574

575

576

1:4

Megaron 10, Main Room, Layer 1

577   578   579

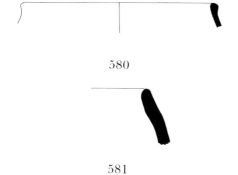

580

581

Early Phrygian Building, Level I

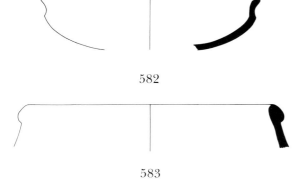

582

583

Early Phrygian Building, Level V

584

Megaron 12, Level IV A

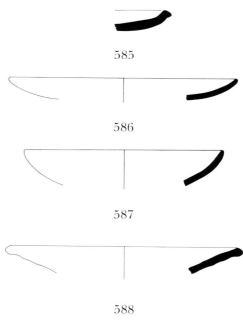

585

586

587

588

589

590

591   592

593

595   596

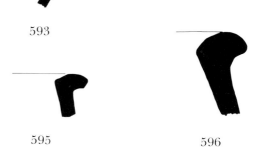

1:4

FIGURE 28

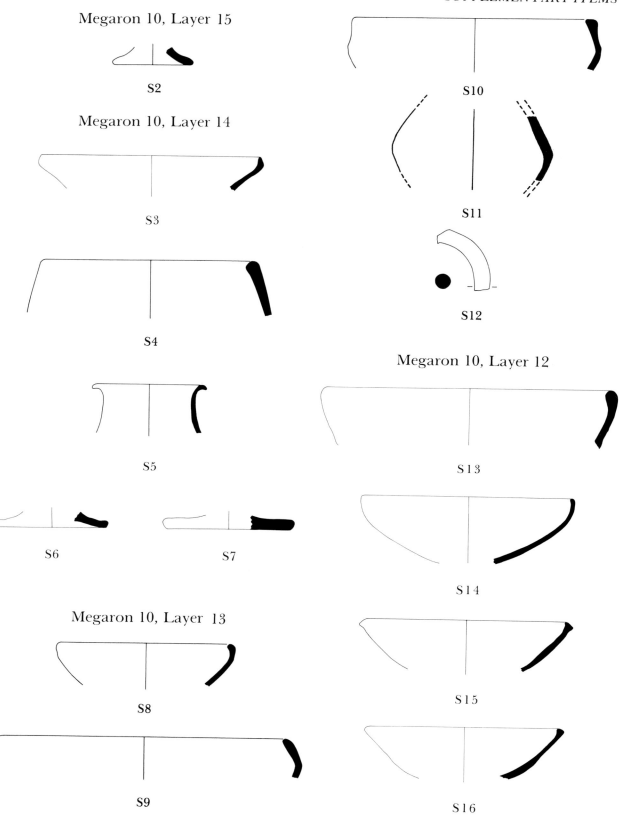

Megaron 10, Layer 15

S2

Megaron 10, Layer 14

S3

S4

S5

S6   S7

Megaron 10, Layer 13

S8

S9

S10

S11

S12

Megaron 10, Layer 12

S13

S14

S15

S16

1:4

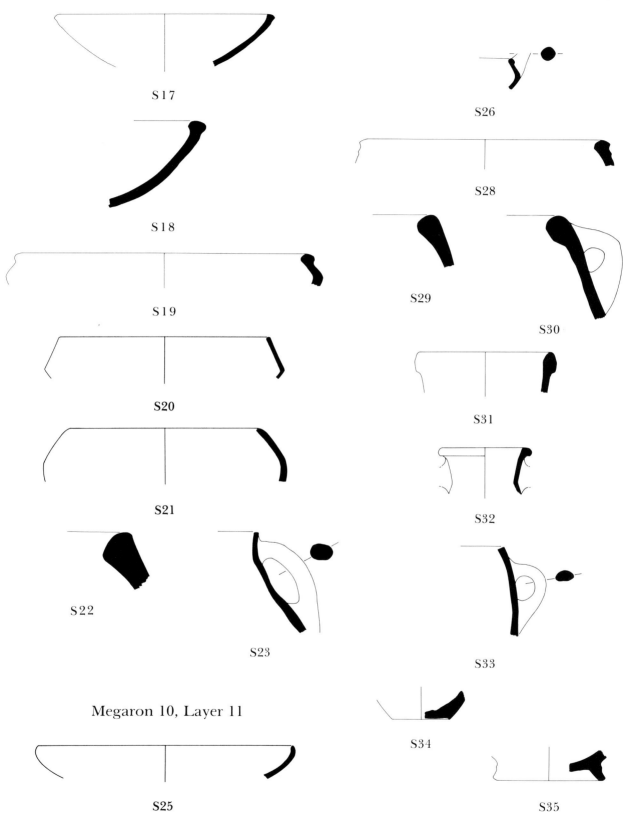

S17

S18

S19

S20

S21

S22

S23

Megaron 10, Layer 11

S25

S26

S28

S29

S30

S31

S32

S33

S34

S35

1:4

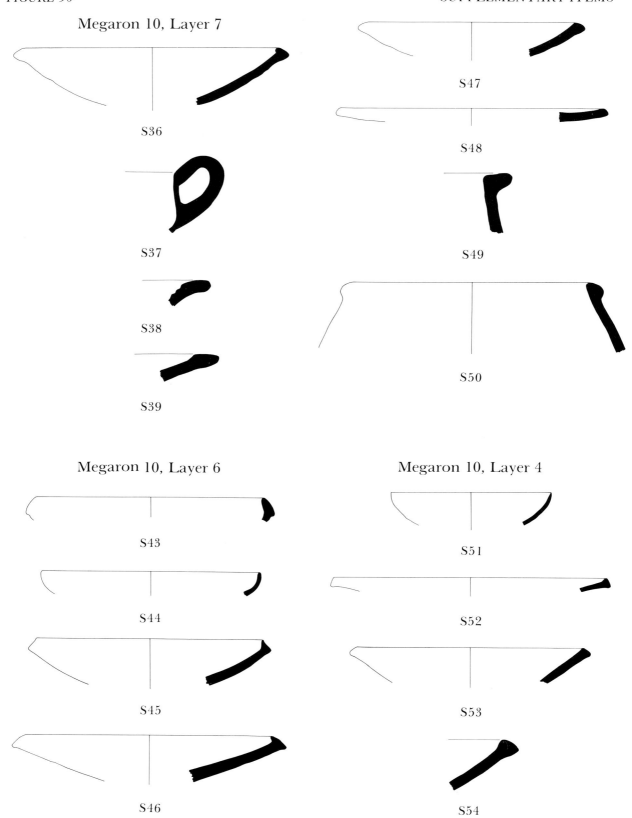

Megaron 10, Layer 7

S36

S37

S38

S39

S47

S48

S49

S50

Megaron 10, Layer 6

S43

S44

S45

S46

Megaron 10, Layer 4

S51

S52

S53

S54

1:4

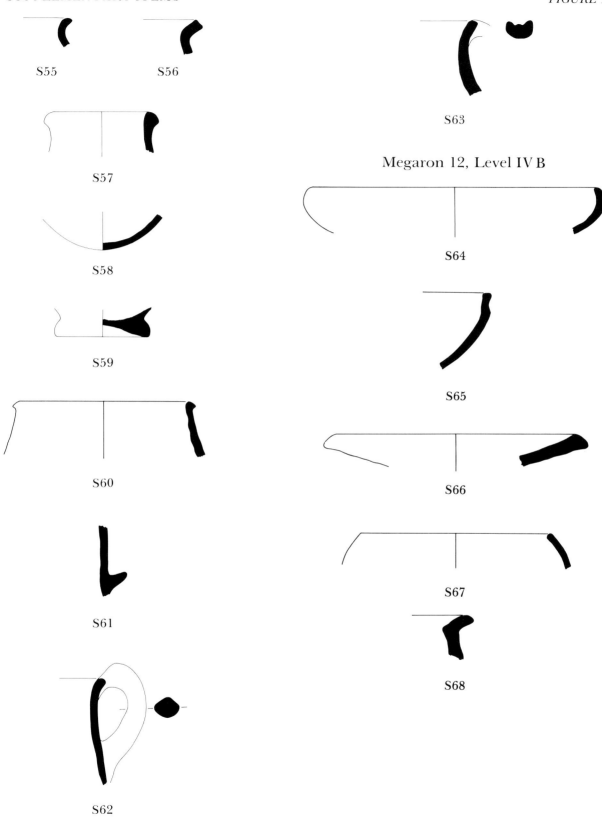

Megaron 12, Level IV B

S55

S56

S63

S57

S64

S58

S65

S59

S66

S60

S67

S61

S68

S62

A.   Air View of the Gordion site. From slightly west of south.

B.   Megaron 12 Deep Cut. Wall at Level V.

PLATE 2

INTRODUCTION

A. Trench PN-3/3A. Wall I. Pits H and I at lower left. From slightly west of north.

B. Trench PN-3/3A. Walls I and II. From north.

Trench PN-3 3A (foreground). Walls I and II and "annex" in Deep Cut. Megaron 12 (background) at Phrygian floor level, except for Deep Cut at rear of cella. From northwest.

PLATE 4

INTRODUCTION

A.   Megaron 10 Deep Cut. Levels as excavated. From east.

B.   Megaron 10 Deep Cut. Floor 9 paving in foreground. From east.

A.   Northeast Ridge, Tumulus F. Cist burial of the Early Bronze Age (at right) cut through by later burial (at left). From slightly north of west.

B.   Northeast Ridge, Museum Site cemetery cut. Tumulus E (background left) and Tumulus MM (right). From southwest.

PLATE 6

INTRODUCTION

A. Northeast Ridge, Museum Site cemetery cut, section R. Burial H 49, closed. From northwest.

B. Northeast Ridge, Museum Site cemetery cut, section R. Burial H 50, open. From north.

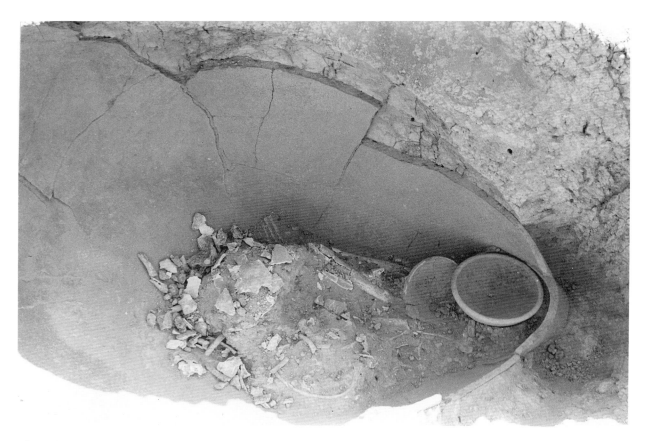

C. Northeast Ridge, Museum Site cemetery cut, section R. Burial H 50, open. From northeast.

A.   Northeast Ridge, Museum Site cemetery cut, section N. Burial H 51, closed. From southeast.

B.   Northeast Ridge, Museum Site cemetery cut, section N. Burial H 512 closed. From north.

PLATE 8   *INTRODUCTION*

A.   Northeast Ridge, Museum Site cemetery cut, section Q. Burial H 52, open. From above, at northwest.

B.   Northeast Ridge, Museum Site cemetery cut, section Q. Burial H 52, closed. From east.

A.   Northeast Ridge, Museum Site cemetery cut, section O. Burial H 54, open. From northeast.

B.   Northeast Ridge, Museum Site cemetery cut, section T. Burial H 55, closed. From north.

PLATE 10

EARLY BRONZE AGE

1   *(1:5)*   2   *(1:5)*

3, 4   *(2:5)*   5   *(3:5)*

6   *(2:5)*   7   *(2:5)*

8   *(3:10)*   9   *(3:10)*

10   *(1:5)*   11   *(1:5)*   12   *(3:5)*

13   *(3:5)*   16   *(3:10)*   17   *(3:10)*

22   *(3:10)*   23   *(3:10)*

25   *(3:10)*   28   *(3:10)*

PLATE 12

29   *(3:10)*   31   *(2:5)*   32   *(3:5)*

33   *(3:5)*   34   *(2:5)*   35   *(2:5)*

36   *(1:2)*   37   *(1:2)*   38   *(1:5)*

40   *(1:5)*

39   *(1:5)*   44   *(2:5)*

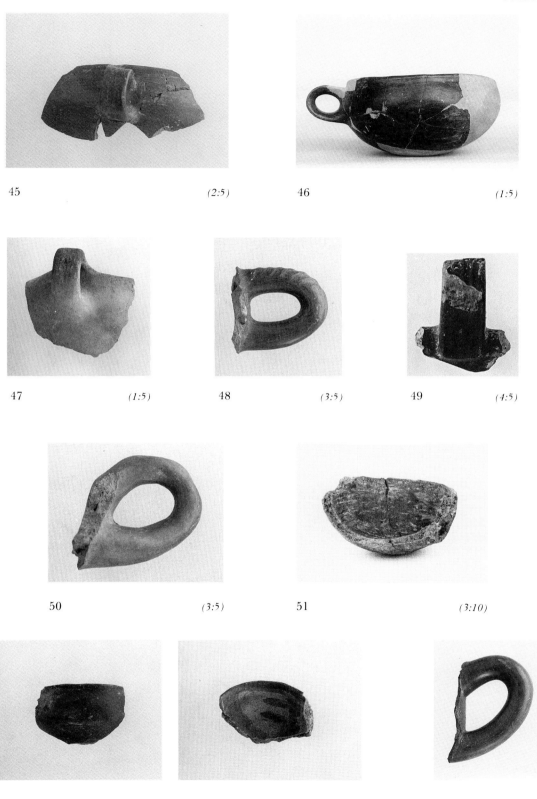

45   *(2:5)*   46   *(1:5)*

47   *(1:5)*   48   *(3:5)*   49   *(4:5)*

50   *(3:5)*   51   *(3:10)*

52   *(2:5)*   54   *(1:5)*

PLATE 14

EARLY BRONZE AGE

53

(4:5)

55

(3:5)

56

(3:10)

57

(1:5)

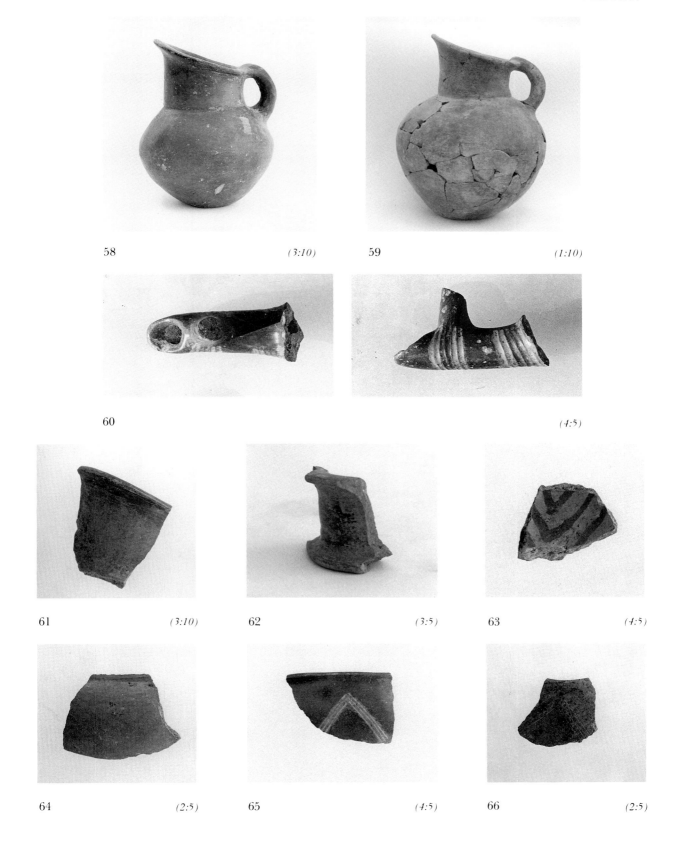

58   *(3:10)*   59   *(1:10)*

60   *(4:5)*

61   *(3:10)*   62   *(3:5)*   63   *(4:5)*

64   *(2:5)*   65   *(4:5)*   66   *(2:5)*

PLATE 16

EARLY BRONZE AGE

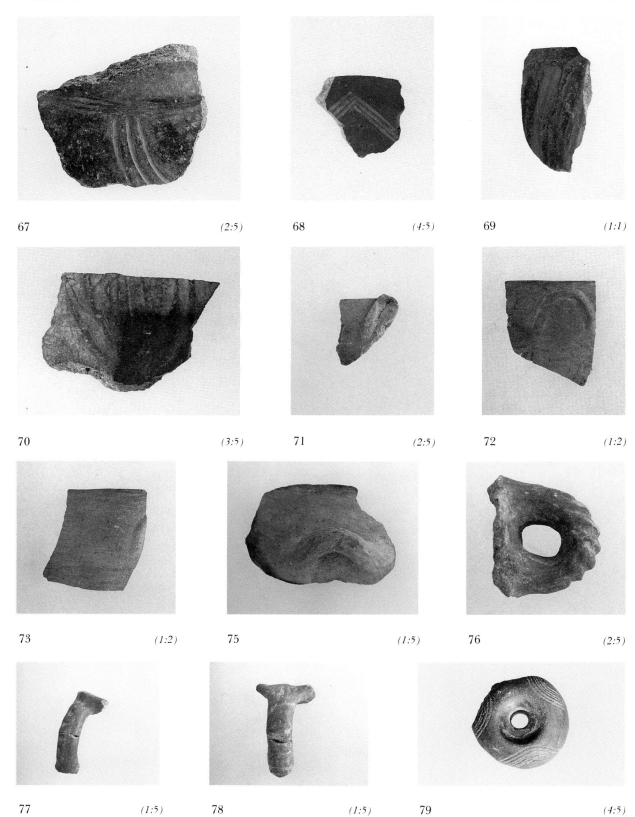

67 (2:5)

68 (4:5)

69 (1:1)

70 (3:5)

71 (2:5)

72 (1:2)

73 (1:2)

75 (1:5)

76 (2:5)

77 (1:5)

78 (1:5)

79 (4:5)

80   *(1:1)*   81   *(1:1)*   82   *(1:1)*

83   *(3:5)*

87   *(2:5)*   88   *(3:10)*

89   *(3:10)*   90   *(3:10)*

PLATE 18

EARLY BRONZE AGE

91 (3:5)

92 (1:10)

93 (2:5)

94 (2:5)

95 (2:5)

96 (1:5)

97 (2:5)

98 (2:5)

99   *(1:5)*   100   *(3:5)*   101   *(4:5)*

109   *(3:10)*   110   *(3:10)*   120   *(3:10)*

127   *(2:5)*   128   *(1:1)*   151   *(2:5)*   152   *(2:5)*

157   *(2:5)*   175   *(1:5)*

PLATE 20   MIDDLE AND LATE BRONZE AGE

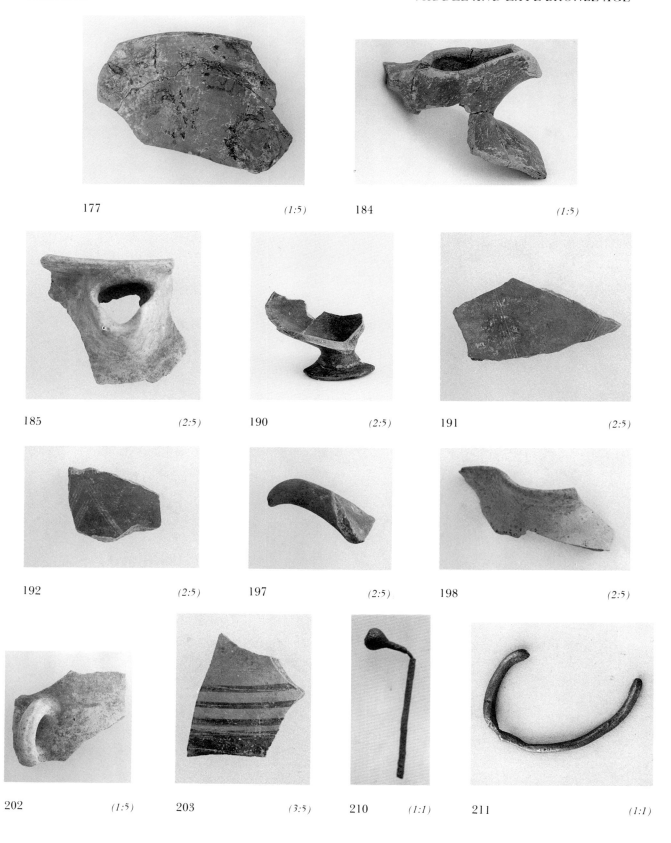

177   (1:5)   184   (1:5)

185   (2:5)   190   (2:5)   191   (2:5)

192   (2:5)   197   (2:5)   198   (2:5)

202   (1:5)   203   (3:5)   210   (1:1)   211   (1:1)

231, 232 (2:5)

238 (2:5)

252 (3:5)

253 (3:5)

254 (2:5)

268 (1:5)

269 (1:5)

270 (2:5)

273 (1:5)

275 (2:5)

276 (2:5)

277 (2:5)

278 (4:5)

PLATE 22

280   (1:5)

295   (1:5)

279   (2:5)   281   (1:1)   300   (2:5)

302   (2:5)   303   (2:5)   306   (2:5)

308   (2:5)   319   (2:5)   320   (2:5)

321   (1:5)

322   (1:5)

323   (2:5)

324   (1:5)

325   (2:5)

330   (1:5)

331   (2:5)

332   (3:5)

333   (3:5)

335   (1:1)

334   (2:5)

336   (3:5)

PLATE 24   *MIDDLE AND LATE BRONZE AGE*

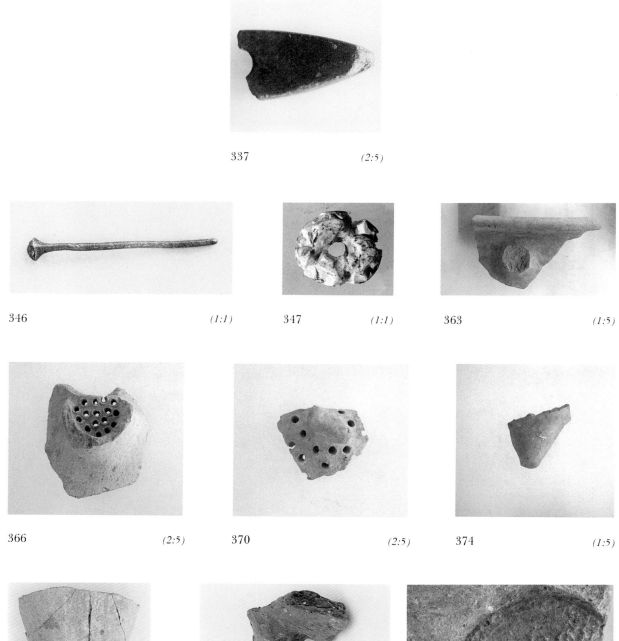

337   (2:5)

346   (1:1)   347   (1:1)   363   (1:5)

366   (2:5)   370   (2:5)   374   (1:5)

375   (1:5)   381   (2:5)

382   *(1:1)*   383   *(3:5)*   397   *(1:5)*   409   *(1:5)*

413   *(2:5)*   414   *(3:5)*   446   *(2:5)*   447   *(2:5)*

460   *(2:5)*   467   *(2:5)*   468   *(2:5)*

469   *(2:5)*   470   *(2:5)*   492   *(3:5)*

PLATE 26   MIDDLE AND LATE BRONZE AGE

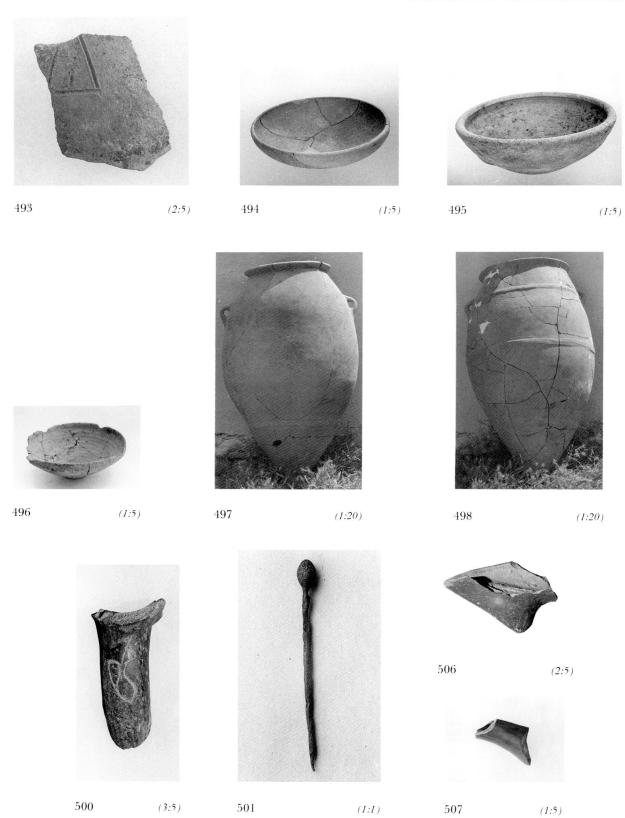

493   (2:5)   494   (1:5)   495   (1:5)

496   (1:5)   497   (1:20)   498   (1:20)

500   (3:5)   501   (1:1)   506   (2:5)

                                                                           507   (1:5)

508   *(3:5)*

509   *(3:5)*   510   *(3:5)*

511   *(2:5)*

512   *(2:5)*

PLATE 28

MIDDLE AND LATE BRONZE AGE

513   *(2:5)*

514   *(2:5)*

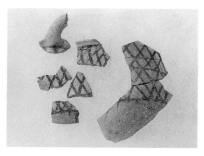

515   *(1:5)*

517   *(2:5)*

518   *(1:2)*

519   *(1:2)*

520   *(2:5)*

521   *(2:5)*

522   *(4:5)*

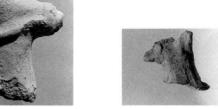

523   *(2:5)*   524   *(2:5)*   525   *(2:5)*

526   *(1:5)*   527   *(1:5)*   528   *(1:5)*   529   *(1:5)*

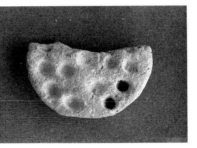

530   *(4:5)*   531   *(4:5)*   532   *(1:1)*

533   *(1:1)*

PLATE 30   *SUPPLEMENTARY ITEMS*

S1   *(3:5)*   S12   *(3:5)*   S23   *(2:5)*

S24   *(3:5)*   S26   *(3:5)*   S27   *(3:5)*

S28   *(3:5)*   S31   *(3:5)*

S30   *(2:5)*

S32　　　　　　　　　*(3:5)*　　　S33　　　　　　　　　*(3:5)*

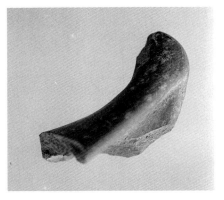

S40　　　　　　　　*(3:5)*　　　S41　　　　　　　　　　　　　　*(3:5)*

S60　　　　　　　*(3:5)*　　　S61　　　　　　　*(3:5)*　　　S62　　　　*(2:5)*

PLATE 32

HANDMADE POTTERY

A. P 5667 handmade closed vessel from Megaron 12, Layer IVb

B. P 5669 Handmade closed vessel from Megaron 12, Layer IVb

C. P 5671 Handmade bowl with incised decoration from Megaron 12, Layer IVa

D. P 5673 Handmade closed vessel with incised decoration from Megaron 12, layer IVa

DAT
Troy
Sakarya
Demirci Hüyük
Asarcık/Ilıc
Porsuk
Yağrı
Beyköy
Akpınar
İzmir
Hermus
Sardis
Karabel
Afyon
Yanarlar
Kusura
Beycesultan
Meander
Miletus
Aphrodisias
Karatas-Semayük
N
Mediterranean Sea
0